A WORLD OF CAKE

A WORLD OF
CAKE

150 Recipes for Sweet Traditions
FROM CULTURES NEAR AND FAR

Krystina Castella

Storey Publishing

The mission of Storey Publishing is to serve our customers by
publishing practical information that encourages
personal independence in harmony with the environment.

Edited by Margaret Sutherland and Nancy W. Ringer
Art direction and book design by Alethea Morrison
Text production by Jennifer Jepson Smith

Photography by © Renee Anjanette Photography, except as noted on page 343
Art direction, cake designs, and photo styling by Krystina Castella
Food styling by Sienna DeGovia
Pastry cheffing by Grace Cho and Larena Farreta
Maps by © Jennifer Daniel
How-to illustrations by Alison Kolesar
Kanji symbols by StockKanji.com

Indexed by Christine Lindemer, Boston Road Communications

Storey Publishing
210 MASS MoCA Way
North Adams, MA 01247
www.storey.com

Printed in China by R.R. Donnelley
10 9 8 7 6 5 4 3 2

LIBRARY OF CONGRESS CATALOGING-IN-PUBLICATION DATA

Castella, Krystina.
   A world of cake / by Krystina Castella.
      p. cm.
   Includes index.
   ISBN 978-1-60342-576-6 (paper w/ flaps : alk. paper)
   1. Cake. 2. Desserts. 3. Cookery, International. I. Title.
TX771.C35 2010
641.8'653—dc22
                              2010020752

CONTENTS

DEDICATION

For my incredible husband, Brian Boyl, who provides tremendous support on all of my baking adventures. Thanks!

ACKNOWLEDGMENTS

This book would not have been possible without the help of the cookbook librarians, pastry chefs, food historians, food enthusiasts, and international community of students at the college where I teach. All contributed ideas, recipe suggestions, and their opinions on the cakes I should taste and bake. I am so grateful for the global community of friends I made and the outpouring of generosity from people with a common goal — the sharing of cake culture and all of the great traditions and feelings it represents.

A special thank-you to the team who brought this book to life: Margaret Sutherland, acquisitions editor; Pam Art, publisher; Alethea Morrison, art director; Nancy Ringer, editor; Jennifer Jepson Smith, production designer; Mars Vilaubi, photo editor; Rebecca Springer, copy editor; Renee Anjanette Kalmar, photographer; Joe Coonan, photo assistant; Sienna DeGovia, food stylist; Larena Faretta, pastry chef; Grace Cho, pastry chef; Emily Sandor, photographer; and Sarah Scheffel, editor.

For the Love of Cake

YUMMMM . . . THE SEDUCTIVE POWER OF CAKE. From East to West, primitive to progressive, most common to most avant-garde, cakes are good for the soul. They draw people together, enliven celebrations, and in one charming and blissful indulgence embody the rituals and histories of cultures around the world. The cakes we create in our own kitchens can transport us anywhere in place or time, from modern-day Tokyo to medieval England, from colonial Indonesia to ancient Egypt. At home we can tinker with recipes to modernize traditions, incorporate local ingredients, or personalize recipes to make them our own.

Cakes are rich with meaning and symbolism, inspired by the celebrations that surround them. As a curious cake lover, I've always been interested in this crossover between cultural and culinary history. Why are fruitcakes traditionally made for Christmas, and why would my friends bring home a box of pineapple cakes from their trip to Taiwan? Why do Japanese street vendors in Brazil sell red bean cakes alongside the local favorites, corn cakes and pineapple pudium? I wanted to know, and I wanted to learn to choose the right (or perfectly inappropriate) cake for the occasion — whatever the occasion. What could be a better way to learn about food history, cultural evolutions, religions, ingredients, and techniques than through baking some cakes? So I launched on my quest to explore the cakes of the world.

Questions aside, *eating* and *celebrating* are (usually) the primary focus when you're talking about cake, and cultures around the world are marvelously inventive in making scrumptious sweet treats that will just about knock your socks off. Learning to make these cakes is an adventure unto itself. If you enjoy learning new baking techniques, you must explore the simplest fried fritters from Africa and the elaborate marzipan rings of the Scandinavian kransekake. If you live for decorating, the artful French croquembouche, the unsettlingly realistic Austrian rehruecken, and the elaborate Canadian Yule log are food art at its best. If novelty is your aim, the signature cakes of cultures far and wide, from Scottish Dundee cake to Indian milk cakes to Australian frog cakes, provide a wondrous palette to choose from. And if you're a foodie looking for an excuse to celebrate with something new, the cake holidays of the world await, with plenty of recipes with which to astound your friends.

Through the course of collecting and reinventing recipes and writing this book, I've found two common themes:

Cake traditions are alive, evolving every day. Mooncakes are traditionally eaten during the Chinese Midautumn Festival, when families climb a mountain for a better view of the moon. The festival is now celebrated in Chinatowns worldwide, with no mountain in sight but more mooncakes than you can feast your eyes on, with fillings ranging from the traditional bean pastes to ice cream and chocolate. The Twelfth Night cake, a traditional Catholic creation for the Epiphany, has evolved into the king cake, now enjoyed by the fun-loving, costumed (or half-naked) celebrants at Mardi Gras carnivals, from Venice to São Paulo to New Orleans.

Cakes are global, and cultures and customs are fusing. Rice cakes, common at tea ceremonies in Japan, can be found at Fourth of July picnics in New England and Bastille Day festivities in Paris. The American cupcake craze has spread to Dubai, along with Las Vegas–style hotels. In India, American strawberry shortcakes and German Black Forest cakes are all the rage at birthdays. The croquembouche is just as much at home at a French wedding as it is at a Chinese-Jewish wedding. And Koreans still prepare saeng, a traditional celebration cake, for birthdays and holidays, but you'll find it now topped with Western-style buttercream and, for Christmas, super-cutesy Santas, elves, and Christmas trees.

In *A World of Cake*, you'll find more than 150 recipes for what I believe are the greatest cakes on earth. In addition to their phenomenal flavors, what makes each of these cakes a standout is its cultural significance, its importance as a branch on a cake family tree, or its spread and evolution from region to region — or all three. As much in the world as can fit in the pages of this book is represented. You won't find all cakes, but you will find the classics and more than a few unknown gems. I hope this book will encourage you to get out there and experience some of them, heading off into the sinfully sweet, mouthwatering, eye-opening world of cake adventures.

CHAPTER 1

Cake Walk

A Sweet Tour of Cake History, Culture, and Language

TEACH AT THE ART CENTER COLLEGE OF DESIGN in Pasadena, California. The spark that ignited *A World of Cake* came from a bake sale we held on campus to raise money for scholarships. The bake sale, an American creation, needed no explanation to our American students, but it was a new concept for the students from abroad. They asked, "What's a bake sale?" I told them, "Bring a cake, we'll sell it, and the money will help pay your tuition." That inspired them.

But this was not your ordinary bake sale. Many students e-mailed home for their favorite recipes. And *home*, for students at our school, ranges far and wide. We have students from all 50 states, so American cakes were well represented: German chocolate cake, Texas sheet cake, mud cake, Lady Baltimore cake, pineapple upside-down cake, and more, each with a regional flair from back home. All were delicious and very traditionally cakelike.

We also have students from all over the world, and I found their cakes truly amazing. Our international students had translated "cake" through the culinary traditions of their homelands with wonderful inventiveness. Their cakes did not always look or taste like what Westerners usually envision when they picture cakes. We had steamed rice cakes, mooncakes, turnspit cakes, fried cakes, and choux pastry cakes. We had green tea cakes, Japanese rare cheesecakes, cornmeal cakes, and cassava cakes. We had baklava, sweet empanadas and tamales, dumplings, Swiss rolls, fritters, tarts, and tortes. The display was simply incredible — and eye-opening.

I soon learned that these cakes were much more to the students than simple sweets to eat. The students were all excited to talk about their cakes, to tell each other the stories behind them: the cultural history of the cakes, the significance of their components or preparation, the role the cakes had in their homelands, and more. Some cakes were rooted in special occasions or holidays; others were everyday street foods. Some were elaborate concoctions designed to celebrate harvest, a time of plenty; others were simple preparations based on survival foods, designed to fill people up to carry them through the day. Some cakes were very traditional, with recipes dating back centuries and using indigenous ingredients; others were modern fusion cakes, reflecting the influences of generations of immigration and global trade.

The bake sale led me to realize that I wanted to redefine and contemporize the word *cake* for today's world. With this book, my goal is to expand the definition of *cake* with a global perspective. If a culture defines a dish as *cake*, then it's cake. Who are we to argue? After all, the more cakes we all know about, the better. Yum!

To begin, we'll delve into the history of cake, from its first manifestation as a flat cake baked on a hot stone through its evolution to the global-fusion style combining ingredients and techniques from around the world. After all, making cake is no longer a matter of simply mixing together some butter, sugar, flour, and eggs and baking it in the oven. Steaming, frying, and grilling — or even smoking in a termite hill, if you can find one — are all cake preparation methods. Rice flour, ghee, ube yam, matcha, and bean pastes are part of the mix. And how these different methods and ingredients came to be a part of cake culture is a discussion full of interesting stories.

While we're at it, we'll talk about how cake has influenced culture and vice versa. How have agricultural developments and global trade influenced indigenous cakes? Which cakes are reserved for particular celebrations, and what significance do they contribute to the events? What can a culture's cakes tell you about its sensibilities and priorities? These questions and more take us on a splendid tour of cake culture.

We'll also discuss the cake family trees, which examine the evolution of specific types of cakes and shows us how they relate to each other. We'll finish with practical cake-making know-how. You'll find here the tools and techniques for creating great cakes, from traditional to modern, from common to exotic, from single sheet layer to architectural marvel, and everything in between.

So kick back and enjoy this new adventure. Whether you make them yourself or find them in your travels, anytime or anywhere, cakes are a delightful treasure to investigate, admire, and, of course, eat.

The Story of Cake: A Good Idea Conquers the World

ANCIENT CIVILIZATIONS, FROM THE CHINESE TO THE EGYPTIANS AND GREEKS, all prepared cakes as offerings for the gods. As religious and cultural rituals were established, cakes developed as the ultimate special food. Up until the eighteenth century culinary record keeping was sparse, and much of what we know about cake in these early times comes from little bites, embedded in writings about something else. But as tomb drawings, Greek plays, tax records from medieval convents, Arabic shipping records, and Mongolian military reports tell us, cakes have come a long way since their first appearance in human culture. Here's the story.

5000 BCE to 500 CE: The First Cakes

The Egyptians are credited with developing the first sweetened bread that we can call a cake. Wheat, first cultivated in the Middle East around 8000 BCE, was a staple in their diet; they ate it as porridge or fermented it into beer. Within a few millennia, sometime between 5000 and 3000 BCE, Egyptians moved on to making cakes. For a sweetener they used honey, which was known to be an excellent preservative and to have medicinal properties. They held these sweetened breads in such high regard that they were left as tomb offerings for the gods. (The leftover crumbs have enabled us to determine that the cakes were made with coarse wheat flour, yeast, honey, eggs, milk, and spices.)

These honey cakes were formed by hand into balls and baked in shallow pans on hot stones, a method that is still used today in rural areas of the Middle East, Africa, and India. As the balls of dough relaxed in the pan, gravity naturally formed each into a round, the most iconic cake shape today. The cakes soon took on ceremonial importance and along with it various shapes of symbolic importance, from birds to rings, fish, crescent moons, and many others.

Along the way the Egyptians figured out that adding fruits such as dates and figs to cakes would further sweeten them. By 1500 BCE such fruitcakes were traditional fare at harvest festivals, and they were sweet, spicy, crunchy, and chewy but still flat. Over time the Egyptians developed ovens, cake molds, and a sourdough type of starter yeast that yielded fluffier cakes.

Flat cakes were just being invented in other parts of the world at this time. Swiss lake villagers were making crude grain cakes, similar to oatcakes, while Aryans in northern India baked cakes underground in clay pots. And the Aryans initiated the tradition of offering sweets to guests as a symbol of hospitality.

THE ANCIENT GREEKS: CAKE INNOVATORS

Within the history of cakes, the ancient Greeks can be seen as prolific innovators. They improved upon Egyptian honey cakes, added nuts (pistachios and pine nuts) to fruitcakes, developed oat cakes, and discovered that beer could be used

HISTORY ACCORDING TO CAKE

8000–1000 BCE

CAKE CREATIONS: flat cakes, fruitcakes, honey cakes

CULTURAL MOVEMENTS: Middle Easterners cultivate wheat and brew beer; Asians cultivate rice

Terraced rice fields in Yunnan Province, China

Cultivated wheat

as a leavener. They came up with the idea of frying fritters in olive oil, and perhaps most important to cake history, they invented cheesecake, using goat's milk. They also created dozens of symbolically rich breads and cakes for holidays and other celebrations, including what is thought to be the world's first wedding cake.

As the art of baking developed in ancient Greece, it came to be a professional undertaking, with trained bakers making breads, cakes, and pastries in large ovens and selling their goods to the public in local markets. A strict bakers' guild system arose and remained in place for hundreds of years.

THE ROMANS: CAKE DISTRIBUTORS

What the Greeks invented, the Romans improved upon and brought to the masses. From the rise of the Roman Republic (509 BCE) through the fall of the Roman Empire (476 CE), Roman militaries and attendant camp followers brought cake baking techniques to the wider Mediterranean, Europe, northern Africa, and beyond — and in true cross-cultural fashion brought back with them new ingredients, processing techniques, and baking tools, facilitating the mingling and meshing of widely disparate culinary traditions.

The Romans created a cake dough with high-gluten white wheat, eggs, and butter that was baked into loaves, yielding a cake with a texture much like that of today's yeast cakes. They expanded upon the Greek cheesecake, using different cheeses and milks, scenting them with bay leaf, sweetening them with fruits and honey, and cooking them in skillets. They also added crusts to cheesecakes; in fact, sometimes they wrapped the whole cheesecake in a pastry shell.

Perhaps modeled on the Greek system, at around 168 BCE the Collegium Pistorum, or Roman bakers' guild, was formed. Guild bakers were required to be members for life; once a baker, always a baker. On the bright side, bakers were the only craftsmen who were also freemen; all other trades were worked by slaves. By the turn of the millennium Rome was home to hundreds of *pistrinae*, or bakeries with on-site flour mills.

The Romans assigned class symbolism to their cakes far more than religious symbolism. The type of cake you ate was determined by your place in society, with upper-class citizens indulging more frequently and with more rare ingredients. Wealthy homes served cakes several times a week.

500 to 1300:
The Era of Trade

Exploration coupled with migration to bring a vast new wealth of agricultural and culinary tools to cultures across the globe. Sugarcane, originating in New Guinea, traveled with migrating tribes to Southeast Asia and India. Indians invented various ways of processing sugar from the cane, and sometime after the year 600, Arab traders brought both the processing know-how and the sugarcane plant itself to the Middle East. By 715 sugarcane had reached Spain. The stage was set for an explosion of innovations with sweets.

THE MIDDLE EAST: CAKE CAPITAL

The Middle East, at the crossroads of Asia, India, and Europe, found itself at the cusp of culinary evolution as fruits, nuts, grains, and sweeteners, and all the myriad ways of preparing them, began to cross their natural borders and sweep across

1000 BCE–100 CE

CAKE CREATIONS: cheesecakes, oat cakes, seed cakes

CULTURAL MOVEMENTS: Egyptians begin shaping cakes to resemble animals; sugarcane cultivation spreads from New Guinea to Southeast Asia; Rome establishes its first baking guild

An engraving in the tomb of Egyptian pharoah Ramses III depicting a bakery with many types of loaves, including ones that are shaped like animals

Cut sugarcane

the continents. Phoenician sailors brought wheat from Lebanon and nutmeg and cinnamon from Malaysia. Turks introduced millet, peaches, apricots, and almonds. Explorers brought back sesame seeds from Africa, cardamom from India, saffron from Kashmir, and lemons and oranges from Asia. All came together in a vibrant burst of cake evolution.

Sometime between the eighth and eleventh centuries, Persians began making phyllo, a thin, layered, flaky pastry, and immediately on its heels — or perhaps as part and parcel — came baklava, which layers phyllo with nuts and honey. Persians further established themselves as players in cake history by infusing cakes with rosewater, cardamom, and pistachios and stuffing sweet pastries with almonds and sugar. Classic recipes in this vein exist even today (such as the Iranian pomegranate cake on page 234 and the pistachio-rosewater cake on page 232). Arabs, for their part, developed marzipan, doughnuts, and various other kinds of flaky pastries, making great use of Indonesian spices and Asian citrus fruits.

IN THE EAST: RICE CAKES GALORE

Though Marco Polo is sometimes named as the first early European trader to visit the Far East, by the time of his journey in 1271 the East–West exchange had already been clearly established. From before the birth of Christ, the famed Silk Road, connecting China, Southeast Asia, India, Persia, Arabia, northern Africa, and southern Europe, carried goods far and wide over many overland and sea routes. It is perhaps the means by which rice cultivation, thought to have originated in Thailand, made its way to India and China and from there to Japan and Korea.

By the eighth century, rice cakes could be found in various forms throughout the Pacific Rim, from the mochi of Japan to the tteok of Korea. Mochi — cakes of glutinous rice with soybeans, adzuki beans, or chestnuts — were originally a special food eaten only by nobility at religious events. Over time, they began to be prepared in countless variations for a wide variety of occasions, including the formal tea ceremony.

Like mochi, Chinese mooncakes were at first reserved for special events, and even today they are most especially associated with the Midautumn Festival, a lunar celebration. Traditionally these cakes, with a pastry crust and sweet filling, were round, like the moon, and stamped with an image of a rabbit, Chang'e (the moon goddess), the symbol for longevity, or some other meaningful design. It's said that mooncakes played an integral role in the Chinese revolt against Mongolian rule in the thirteenth century. The Mongols did not eat mooncakes, and so the leaders of the rebellion distributed mooncakes with a secret message baked inside them, informing people to revolt on the 15th day of the eighth month, the day of the Midautumn Festival. The revolt was successful, and mooncakes secured a spot in Chinese national tradition.

MEDIEVAL EUROPE: ENCHANTED WITH EXOTICS

Traders on the Silk Route, Crusaders returning from the Middle East, and the constant influx of immigrants introduced medieval Europeans to the wondrous spices, fruits, nuts, and other specialties of distant lands. Gingerbread is the iconic cake of the era; Crusaders are thought to have carried it back to their homelands with them, and the spicy-sweet cake spread like wildfire across the continent.

100–1200

CAKE CREATIONS: baklava, gingerbread, king cakes, mochi

CULTURAL MOVEMENTS: Middle Easterners invent phyllo; Crusaders returning from the Middle East bring sugar and spices back to Europe; Mayans begin processing cacao into a beverage; Asians begin preparing rice cakes

Mayan dish showing a metate to grind cocoa

Godefroy de Bouillon, a French knight and leader of the First Crusade

Tea in Japan

In addition to ginger, the European upper classes began to enjoy a wealth of spices imported from Southeast Asia and India in their baked goods, including cinnamon, nutmeg, cloves, and saffron. Sugar became the hottest new culinary commodity. At the time it was considered a healthful and curative food; in fact, sugar-sweetened cakes were prescribed for pregnant women.

For the masses, of course, sugar was a luxury beyond reach, and honey remained the most common sweetener of the age. Honey-sweetened cakes would be augmented with jams, preserves, compotes, and sweet pastes as fillings or toppings.

As sugar became more popular, some religious leaders began to proclaim sweets to be evil, on a par with alcohol, and placed restrictions on their consumption. In this matter Thomas Aquinas was a savior. Although he became a saint for being an influential philosopher and theologian, for me one of his greatest contributions was his declaration that sweets are not food, and therefore they could be eaten on the then abundant religious fasting days. Perhaps as a result, nuns and priests of the time developed many new sweets that were often linked to specific religious holidays, highlighting cakes as a pleasurable way to transform pious occasions into upbeat celebrations. Portuguese nuns, for example, invented barrigas de freira (nuns' bellies; see page 200), while Spanish nuns developed tarta de Santiago (St. James' cake; see page 199) and Italian nuns created cassata (page 196).

In writing of the curative properties of sweets, Nostradamus instructed that they should look as good as they taste, and medieval cake makers rose to the task. Gold leaf, gemstones, and silver could be found as cake toppings, as could more edible concoctions such as candied fruits and flowers and marzipan. Cakes and decorative toppings alike were sometimes dyed for special effect, and they might be sprinkled with sugar that had been specially processed to have a bigger grain, making it more reflective and sparkly.

Medieval courts introduced the idea of serving cakes and other sweets at the end of a meal, a practice that was expanded upon centuries later by the French. Being very expensive, the cakes were served with great pomp and elaborate ceremony, including specially designed serving platters, cutting and serving tools, and plates.

1300 to 1600: The Renaissance

With the advent of the philosophy of humanism, food came to be seen as nourishment for both body and soul, with the goal of eating well to support the body, take pleasure, and advance cultural refinement. Among the upper class and common people alike, the preparation of food was recognized as offering an elevated life experience.

Due to agricultural improvements and increasing overseas commerce, once exotic and rare ingredients became more readily available and less expensive, allowing cake makers to kick into creative high gear. Here we see the first incarnation of the modern home cook, who combines traditional regional resources with ingredients from around the world. A surge of new kinds of cakes ensued, and the consumption of cakes became an everyday affair.

Up until this time yeast had been the main leavener for cakes. In fact, cakes were not cakes in the modern sense but simply sweetened breads, whether flat or raised with yeast. However, a new culinary creation now rocked the baking

1200–1400

CAKE CREATIONS: carrot puddings, kolache, kugelhopf, mooncakes, panforte, simnel cake

CULTURAL MOVEMENTS: sugar becomes abundant for European upper classes; European cakes are introduced to Asia

Alsatian earthenware molds for kugelhopf

1400s

CAKE CREATIONS: panettone, St. James' cake, stollen, trifles

CULTURAL MOVEMENTS: sugarcane is brought to the New World for cultivation; coffee is introduced to Africa and Arabia

Arab women grinding coffee in Palestine

world: sponge cakes. These airy, lightly textured cakes are leavened simply by vigorously beaten eggs; the air bubbles in the eggs expand during the baking, thereby raising the cake. This technique is thought to have originated in Spain, but it quickly spread throughout Europe and beyond, even to the far ports of Asia (see, for example, Japanese kasutera cake on page 280).

Renaissance cakes were refined and sophisticated, designed to have both visual and taste appeal. Through about 1500, chefs often combined sweet, salty, bitter, and sour flavors in one dish, as each corresponded to and supported one of the four bodily humors, according to the popular understanding of physiology at the time. Baked goods with candied meat were not uncommon — they may sound awful to the modern eater, but in the Middle Ages they were said to support both the body and the spirit.

Large and loud banquets were popular, consisting of many courses, including fruitcakes, cheesecakes, and fried cakes. Chefs took great pains to sculpt food — whether meat, bread, or cake — into playful visual dramas, honoring the host or commemorating the event. Over time the sculpting of savory foods fell out of fashion, but the practice of artfully decorating cakes has continued to develop into today.

As the sugar was taken out of the savory courses of the meal, the cakes at the end of the meal became sweeter, and sugar sculpting became a true art form. In England, for example, inspired by the narrative table feasts and sugar sculptures of Egypt and Istanbul, the Tudors used marzipan and sugar to make sculptures of animals, castles, trees, and people. A new table sculpture was brought out for each course. Guests rarely ate these sweets; the ephemeral works were created simply to exhibit the power and wealth of the hosts.

1600 to 1800: Colonialism

By the 1600s almost every neighborhood in Europe had its own bakery. Most of the baking was done in large mills outside of towns, while the shops were outlets for sales. The production volumes that spilled out of these bakeries made baked goods more affordable, and many middle-class people now bought their breads and cakes instead of making them at home.

Though innovative bakers began using wooden or metal molds to shape cakes, in Europe round fruitcakes were still the most common confections of the time. Pound cake, a rich butter cake, was invented in England in the early 1700s and quickly became popular across the continent. Yeast cakes were on the decline, and sponge cakes were gaining in popularity. And in 1742 pearl ash, a precursor to baking soda, was discovered and soon found use as a leavening agent, enabling the creation of quick breads.

Around the world, British, Dutch, French, and Spanish colonists struggled for footholds in North and South America, India, Australia, and Africa. These pioneers must really have missed the cakes and breads of their homelands, because they developed a hardy do-it-yourself attitude toward baking. Whether they paid (dearly!) for the ingredients or grew the wheat, churned the butter, and processed the sugar themselves, they persevered, sharing their baking techniques with indigenous peoples and learning new ones from them. Dutch cakes were baked in Africa, and English cakes in India, Scottish cakes in New Zealand, Portuguese

1500s

CAKE CREATIONS: Black Forest cake, cassata, shortbread, sponge cakes

CULTURAL MOVEMENTS: Spaniards bring cacao beans to Europe, where they are ground and mixed with sugar to make drinking chocolate; Nostradamus writes of the curative properties of sugar

Portrait of Nostradamus

1600s

CAKE CREATIONS: coffee cake, doughnuts, meringue, Parkin, strudel

CULTURAL MOVEMENTS: boiled icings are used to frost cakes; Europeans develop molds and hoops to shape cakes

Tin molds for shaping tea cakes

cakes in Brazil, French cakes in Canada, and Spanish cakes in Mexico. And throughout the world, great new fusion experiments had delightful results.

CENTRAL AMERICA: NEW TROPICAL DELIGHTS

Until Europeans made inroads in the Americas, most Renaissance cakes were simple improvements of medieval cakes. The New World, however, offered up an infusion of new ingredients, most notably chocolate.

We have the Mayans and their explorations of the rain forests to thank for chocolate. They ground cacao beans and steeped them to prepare a bitter beverage, sometimes flavored with chiles. Aztecs did the same, adopting the drink for daily use and religious occasions. Spaniards of the mid-1500s brought cacao back to Europe, where it was mixed with sugar to make the cocoa we are familiar with today. Sweetened chocolate became wildly popular (and in the early twentieth century found its way into cake recipes).

Chocolate was not the only culinary treasure European explorers seized upon in Central America. Coffee beans, vanilla beans, peanuts, and various fruits, including papaya, guava, and pineapple, soon made their way into the European palate. Many were transported to distant colonies in similar climates, where they were cultivated in great plantations, with local indigenous people supplying the (often forced) labor.

THE CARIBBEAN: SUGAR AND SPICES

The New World, too, soon became home to European plantations. The tropical Caribbean islands had a climate remarkably like that of the Spice Islands, and soon they were home to immense plantings of ginger, cinnamon, nutmeg, and other Asian spices.

On his second voyage to the New World, in 1493, Christopher Columbus brought sugarcane to Hispaniola and Cuba. Here and throughout the Caribbean, the transplants thrived, and the sugar trade became a driving force in the colonial era. With sugarcane plantations established in the Americas, refined sugar became more readily available and affordable, and sweets became a mainstay of the middle-class masses. Perhaps as a result, the mid-1600s saw the first icings on cakes, made by boiling sugar, egg whites, and flavorings.

Rum, a by-product of sugar refinement, also became more readily available and affordable, and it quickly found its way into cake recipes. Rum is a good preservative, and rum cakes became a staple of Caribbean pirate fleets, able to withstand the rigors of long sea journeys.

EARLY AMERICA: THE MELTING POT

Like their far-flung cousins, colonies in America depended on the ingenuity of homemakers to prepare traditional cakes in new environments. Whether French, German, Dutch, or English in origin, cake recipes took on new flavors and ingredients in the New World. And the incredible diversity of peoples who found themselves living side by side made America a true melting pot, the epicenter of fusion cuisine. Scottish scones became American shortcakes, served with strawberries. Dutch fried cakes became American doughnuts, the Swiss roll became the American jelly roll, the German streusel became the American buckle — the culinary leaps are too many to name.

1700s

CAKE CREATIONS: carrot cake, croquembouche, madeleines, nuns' bellies, petits fours, pound cake, sticky buns, vacherin

CULTURAL MOVEMENTS: pearl ash is marketed as a leavener; fusion cuisine gets a jump-start from European colonists scattered around the globe

Spices such as cinnamon, nutmeg, and ginger spread to the New World.

As befits thrifty pioneers the world over, American cake makers used whatever ingredients were readily available. Maple syrup, molasses (a by-product of sugar production), rum, and honey (home beekeeping was a prolific operation) were used alongside refined sugar as sweeteners. Native nuts, from the pecan (the only uniquely American nut) to the walnut and chestnut, found their way into recipes, as did native berries, from huckleberries to cranberries, blackberries, and strawberries, and the multitudes of other local foods.

1800 to 2000: Mass Marketing

As the Industrial Revolution began to gain momentum, milling technologies improved, and refined white flour became more like the high-quality stuff we use today. Baking ovens, too, saw major advancements, particularly in regard to temperature control. In the mid-1800s sodium bicarbonate, or baking soda, came on the scene as a reliable leavener, and soon after it was mixed with acid salt and cornstarch to make baking powder. The hand-cranked eggbeater, invented in 1870, vastly shortened the time needed to whip eggs, making sponge cakes a possibility for even the most harried homemaker. As these and other culinary tools were developed and mass-marketed, along with cookbooks, baking came to be part of the necessary repertoire of the housewife. Her reputation might lie in the airiness of her sponge cake or the richness of her chocolate cake. Cake was king.

During this time the world saw its first star chef, Antoine Carême (1784–1833) of France. He is considered to be the most important pastry chef of the modern era, with a supreme talent for creating truly extravagant cakes, such as the croquembouche (page 99). Perhaps thanks to Carême, pastry making took off, with tortes, croissants, strudels, Danishes, and tarts in infinite variety. The next star of the times was Queen Victoria, who popularized high tea and the requisite tea cakes — recipes for which grew in abundance as the custom passed around the world.

The American layer cake now entered the scene, and in the early 1900s buttercream frosting began to supersede boiled icing as the topping of choice. But the invention to truly shake the cake world was the boxed cake mix of the 1920s. By the 1950s they were all the rage, marketed to the teeth as the ultimate in convenience and luxury. Betty Crocker's 1947 campaign for its ginger cake urged, "Just Add Water and Mix!" — and consumers did.

Major manufacturing brands such as Pillsbury, Betty Crocker, Nestlé, and General Mills began producing recipe booklets pushing their own products. They also sponsored bake-off competitions, which became wildly popular. As the years passed, the recipes and cake mixes stretched in the never-ending quest for the best new idea. Mocha cakes, marble cakes, checkerboard cakes, fairy cakes, date cakes, pineapple upside-down cakes, red velvet cakes — regional specialties from all over the world were simplified, packaged, and made into mass-market commodities.

The 1900s also saw the initiation of home cake decorating as an art form. Up until this time elaborate cake decorating was a mostly professional occupation, part of the repertoire of trained pastry chefs. Most cake decorators kept their unique techniques a secret, except for two generous souls, Dewey McKinley Wilton and Joseph Lambeth. During the Great Depression Wilton decorated wedding cakes for

1800s

CAKE CREATIONS: American apple stack, angel food cake, arrollado with dulce de leche, Battenberg cake, Boston cream pie, bûche de Noël, Dobos torte, Indian milk sweets, Lamington, marble cake, muffins and cupcakes, Norwegian omelette, pastéis de nata, prinsesstårta, quatre quarts, quick breads, rehruecken, Rigó Jancsi cake, Runeberg cake, Sachertorte, strawberry shortcake, tea cakes, tres leches cake, Victoria sponge cake

CULTURAL MOVEMENTS: condensed milk and evaporated milk are invented; baking soda and baking powder are marketed as leaveners; hand-cranked beater becomes popular

Hand-cranked eggbeaters become popular.

hotels and clubs. He started a cake decorating school in 1929 (it still exists today), and in the 1940s he began manufacturing and marketing decorating products. The "Wilton Way" of cake decorating was simple enough for anyone to do at home. A few years later, Lambeth published a book giving instructions for a decorating style now named for him, in which layers upon layers of icing create intricate three-dimensional designs. Over the next few decades, cake decorating came to be a respected craft. In 1976 the International Cake Exploration Societé formed in Monroe, Michigan, and each year it holds an annual conference that includes competitions, demonstrations, and classes.

From the mid-1900s onward, Western-style baking slowly but surely gained ground internationally. Whether in Asia, Africa, South America, or beyond, classic butter cakes, foam cakes, and pastries, very sweet and usually frosted or filled, looked to be on their way to becoming the norm, out-competing regional favorites for shelf space in groceries and bakeries.

The Present: Global Fusion

What are the cake trends of this century? Baking is back, with a revival of the do-it-yourself movement and a strong focus on fresh and local foods. Cooks everywhere seem to have turned their attention back to traditional recipes, ingredients, and techniques — but always with an eye toward innovation.

Old-style rustic ingredients such as cornmeal, rice flour, potato flour, and oats are seeing a resurgence in popularity, combined with international flavors such as lemongrass, fennel, ginger, pomegranate, and lychee. And vintage recipes

of the mid-1900s, of late disdained for being overprocessed, underflavored, or simply too "grandma-style," are making a comeback, from southern red velvet cake (page 46) to Caribbean hummingbird cake (page 62).

Modern gourmets strive for unusual flavor combinations, like lavender and pineapple, chocolate and cayenne, Grand Marnier and sage, and coconut and mint. And ethnic fusion is a growing trend. You might see an Indian milk sweet, for example, with strawberry sauce, or a Japanese rice cake with chocolate filling. American angel food cake might be drizzled with a sweet green-tea glaze, and New York–style cheesecake might feature taro and citrus.

Whatever the influences that shape them, modern cakes are culinary marvels, the result of thousands of years of human endeavor and innovation. From snack cakes dished out by street vendors to banquet showpieces labored over by master chefs, cakes play a central role in cultures far and wide. Has any other food elicited such sweet delight for so long in human history?

1900s–TODAY

CAKE CREATIONS: Bundt cake, chiffon cake, devil's food cake, frog cake, German chocolate cake, hummingbird cake, Japanese Swiss rolls, lolly log, Marta Rocha torte, molten chocolate cake, Nanaimo bar, New York cheesecake, opera gateau, Pavlova, pineapple upside-down cake, Queen

Mother cake, red velvet cake, Taipei pineapple cake

CULTURAL MOVEMENTS: refrigerators, electric mixers, and modern ovens are invented; buttercream frosting becomes popular; commercial cake mixes and prepared frostings become prevalent

The birth of modern appliances

THE WORLD TOUR OF
Cake Holidays

WITH THE CALENDAR ON THE FOLLOWING PAGES you can transcend geographical and ideological boundaries to celebrate cake holidays whenever you please. Each month here offers a handful of holidays that are particularly cake-appreciable. For some holidays, iconic cakes give the celebration the ring of authenticity. No Mexican Day of the Dead celebration, for example, is complete without pan de muerto (bread of the dead). For other occasions cross-cultural pairings are appropriate, such as Iranian pistachio-rosewater cake for Valentine's Day, or Scottish Dundee cake (with Guinness) for Super Bowl Sunday. Whatever the cake, this calendar offers justification for gustatory satisfaction the whole year round.

The exact date of many of these holidays is variable; a quick search on the Internet can give you the date for any particular year.

Buddhist monks at Songgwangsa temple in South Korea knead the dough for making rice cakes.

JANUARY

JANUARY 1
New Year's Day
- Greek vasilopita (page 202)

JANUARY 6
Epiphany, a Christian holiday commemorating the coming of the three Magi to Christ or (depending on who you ask) the baptism of Christ
- French galette des Rois (page 51)
- Mexican rosca de reyes (page 51)
- New Orleans king cake (page 50)

- Portuguese bolo rei (page 51)
- Spanish tortell (page 51)

MID-JANUARY
Coming of Age Day, the second Monday in January, a Japanese celebration for those who have turned 20 in the previous year
- Japanese kasutera cake (page 280)

MID-JANUARY
Ati-Atihan, on the third weekend in January, a three-day Filipino festival celebrating religious freedom with around-the-clock dancing and music
- Filipino ube cake (page 289)

LATE JANUARY/EARLY FEBRUARY
Basant Panchami, the first day of spring in the Hindu calendar
- Indian malpuas (page 246)

LATE JANUARY/EARLY FEBRUARY
Lunar New Year, the second new moon after the winter solstice, celebrated in many Asian cultures
- Chinese nian gao (page 258)
- Vietnamese banh bo nuong (page 290)

FEBRUARY

EARLY FEBRUARY
Super Bowl Sunday, the first Sunday in February, the championship game of the U.S. National Football League
- Scottish Dundee Guinness cake (page 146)

FEBRUARY 5
Runeberg Day, celebrating the birthday of the Finnish poet Johan Ludvig Runeberg
- Finnish Runeberg cake (page 164)

FEBRUARY 14
Valentine's Day, a day to honor St. Valentine and celebrate love
- French Queen of Sheba cake (page 101)
- Iranian pistachio-rosewater cake (page 232)

MID-FEBRUARY
Presidents' Day or Washington's Birthday, the third Monday in February, commemorating the first president of the United States
- Washington cherry almond cake (page 282)

FEBRUARY/MARCH
Holi, the Hindu festival of colors
- Indian gulab jamun (page 252)
- Bangladeshi jalebi (page 253)

FEBRUARY/MARCH
Purim, a commemoration of the deliverance of Jews from massacre by Persians
- Israeli seed cake (page 230)
- Russian lemon poppyseed cake (page 177)

FEBRUARY/EARLY MARCH
Bolludagur (Bun Day), the Monday before Lent begins, celebrated in Iceland as a day of indulgence before the fasting of Lent
- Icelandic vatnsdeigsbollur (page 168)

FEBRUARY/EARLY MARCH
Shrove Tuesday, the day before Lent begins, celebrated by many Christians as a final day of indulgence before the fasting of Lent
- Buttermilk doughnuts (page 44)
- New Orleans king cake (page 50)
- Welsh cakes (page 148)

MARCH

MARCH 11
Decoration Day, a Liberian national holiday on which people clean and decorate the graves of their ancestors as a way of mourning and celebrating lost loved ones
- Liberian upside-down pumpkin-plantain cake (page 213)

MID-MARCH
Nowruz, the Persian New Year, on the first day of spring, celebrated in many areas formerly under Persian rule

- Indian milk cakes (page 248)
- Iranian pomegranate cake (page 234)

MARCH 19
St. Joseph's Day, a Christian feast day for the sainted husband of Mary, mother of Jesus
- Bolognese rice cake (page 194)
- Zeppole (page 195)

LATE MARCH/EARLY APRIL
Mothering Sunday, the fourth Sunday of Lent, a primarily European celebration of motherhood
- Irish simnel cake (page 150)

LATE MARCH/APRIL
Easter, a Christian feast to commemorate Christ's resurrection
- Greek lambropsomo (page 204)
- Irish simnel cake (page 150)
- Italian colomba pasquale (page 188)
- Polish mazurek (page 180)
- Russian saffron cake (page 176)
- Slovenian potica (page 182)

APRIL

EARLY APRIL
Sham el Nessim, the first Monday after Coptic Easter, an Egyptian celebration of spring
- Egyptian basbousa (page 208)

APRIL 13
Songkran, the Thai Buddhist New Year
- Thai mango-lychee ice cream cake (page 292)

APRIL 25
Liberation Day, celebrating Italy's liberation by Allied troops in World War II
- Italian cassata (page 196)

APRIL 25
ANZAC Day, an Australian holiday commemorating those who fought at Gallipoli in Turkey during World War I and more broadly all those who have served in the country's armed forces
- New Zealand taro cheesecake (page 308)

APRIL/MAY
Vesak Day, Buddha's birthday, falling in the fourth month of the Chinese lunar calendar
- Malay steamed sponge cake

MAY

MAY 1
May Day, a holiday marking the end of the winter that is rooted in the Celtic Beltane celebrations
- French pain d'épices (page 102)
- Sweet Scottish scones (page 147)
- Swiss vacherin (page 113)

EARLY MAY
Samjinnal, the Korean celebration of the arrival of spring, on the third day of the third lunar month
- Korean sugared-flower hwajeon (page 273)

MAY 5
Cinco de Mayo, celebrating the 1862 Mexican victory over the French at Puebla
- Mexican churros (page 78)

LATE MAY/EARLY JUNE
Corpus Christi, a Christian holiday falling on the Thursday after Trinity Sunday, in honor of the Eucharist
- Spanish galletas de miel

LATE MAY/EARLY JUNE
Lazybones Day, a celebration of youth in the Netherlands, on the Saturday before Whitsunday
- Dutch luilakbollen (page 128)

LATE MAY/EARLY JUNE
Shavuot, a Jewish holiday falling on the sixth day of the month Sivan and commemorating Moses receiving the Ten Commandments at Mount Sinai
- New York cheesecake (page 38)

JUNE

JUNE
The Queen's (or King's) Official Birthday, celebrated on various Mondays in June in many of the member countries of the Commonwealth of Nations
- English Queen Anne's cake (page 137)
- English Queen Mother cake (page 138)
- English Victoria sandwich cake (page 136)

JUNE 1
Madaraka Day, a Kenyan holiday commemorating the country's 1963 assumption of self-rule before independence from England
- Kenyan banana cake (page 221)

JUNE 6
Sweden's National Day, generally considered its independence day
- Swedish prinsesstårta (page 160)

MID- TO LATE JUNE
Summer solstice, a big event in Scandinavia
- Danish brunsviger (page 155)
- Faroe Islands hazelnut oatcakes (page 169)

MID- TO LATE JUNE
Festas Juninas, celebrating SS. Peter, John, and Anthony
- Brazilian corn cake (page 85)

JUNE 24
Festa do São João (Festival of St. John), a Portuguese street festival
- Portuguese nuns' bellies (page 200)

JULY

JULY 1
Canada Day, the national day of Canada
- Canadian maple-walnut tourlouche (page 55)
- Canadian Nanaimo bar (page 61)

JULY 4
Independence Day, United States
- Angel food cake (page 34)
- Strawberry shortcake (page 35)

JULY 14
Bastille Day, a national holiday in France commemorating the fall of the Bastille in 1789
- French apple-lemon charlotte russe (page 112)
- French opera gateau (page 104)

JULY 21
National Lamington Day in Australia
- Australian Lamingtons (page 304)

JULY 29
St. Olaf's Wake, commemorating the death of St. Olaf, once king of Norway, who is credited with bringing Christianity to much of Scandinavia, in battle in 1030
- Faroe Islands hazelnut oatcake (page 169)

AUGUST

EARLY AUGUST
Friendship Day, on the first Sunday in August, an international holiday honoring friendship
- Japanese friendship cherry blossom cake (page 282)

AUGUST 9
Singapore National Day, celebrating the island's independence from Malaysia in 1965
- Singaporean pineapple huat kueh (page 287)

MID-AUGUST TO EARLY SEPTEMBER
Ramadan, the ninth month of the Islamic lunar calendar, observed with fasting from sunup to sundown (note that the Islamic calendar is shorter than the Gregorian calendar, so while Ramadan falls in August at the time of this book's publication, it will migrate through the calendar over the following years)
- Bangladeshi jalebi (page 253)
- Indian kalakand (page 248)
- Iranian baklava (page 235)
- Palestinian qatayef (page 237)

AUGUST 17
Indonesian Independence Day, celebrating the nation's independence from the Netherlands
- Indonesian pandan cake (page 288)
- Indonesian zucchini-mango cake (page 64)

AUGUST 17
Moulay Idriss Moussem, a Muslim religious festival honoring Moulay Idriss I, an eighth-century descendant of Muhammad and founder of the first Islamic kingdom in Morocco, in the town named for him in Morocco, which is now a holy pilgrimage site
- Moroccan snake cake (page 210)

AUGUST 31
Hari Merdeka, Malaysia's Independence Day, celebrating the country's 1957 independence from Britain
- Malaysian tapioca pearl raisin cake (page 286)

SEPTEMBER

EARLY SEPTEMBER
Eid-al-Fitr, a three-day Muslim celebration marking the end of Ramadan (and, like Ramadan, the celebration will migrate through the Gregorian calendar)
- Iraqi date spice cake (page 242)
- Jordanian kanafeh (page 236)

EARLY SEPTEMBER
Labor Day in the United States and Canada, celebrated on the first Monday in September
- German chocolate cake (page 48)

EARLY TO LATE SEPTEMBER
Rosh Hashanah, Jewish New Year, on the first day of the seventh month of the Jewish calendar
- Israeli mit lechig (page 227)

MID-SEPTEMBER
Feast of San Gennaro, an 11-day street fair in New York City's Little Italy (and elsewhere) honoring Januarius, the patron saint of Naples
- Zeppole (page 195)

SEPTEMBER 15
Guatemala's Independence Day, celebrating the nation's independence from Spain in 1821
- Guatemalan tamale corn cakes (page 82)

SEPTEMBER 16
Mexico's Independence Day, celebrating the nation's independence from Spain in 1810
- Mexican almond meringue cake (page 79)

LATE SEPTEMBER/EARLY OCTOBER
Chuseok, a three-day harvest festival in Korea, held on the fifteenth day of the seventh lunar month
- Korean hodo kwaja (page 271)
- Korean chrysanthemum steamed lemon cake (page 272)

LATE SEPTEMBER/EARLY OCTOBER
Midautumn Festival, celebrated on the full moon of the fifteenth day of the eighth lunar month
- Chinese mooncakes (page 260)
- Taiwanese pineapple cakes (page 266)

OCTOBER

OCTOBER 2
Gandhi Jayanti, a holiday commemorating the birthday of Mahatma Gandhi
- Indian malpuas (page 246)
- Indian gulab jamun (page 252)

OCTOBER 12
Our Lady of Aparecida celebration, a feast day to celebrate the Virgin Mary, who is said to have *aparecida* (appeared) to fishermen in 1717
- Brazilian yuca cake (page 84)

MID-OCTOBER
Canadian Thanksgiving, celebrated on the second Monday in October
- Canadian cranberry quatre quarts (page 54)
- Canadian maple-walnut tourlouche (page 55)

OCTOBER 16
Jamaican National Heroes Day, honoring seven national heroes of the nation's history
- Jamaican hummingbird cake (page 62)

OCTOBER 26
Austrian National Day, commemorating Austria's first day as an independent and sovereign nation following occupation after World War II
- Austrian apple strudel (page 123)
- Austrian kugelhopf (page 127)

OCTOBER 28
Ochi Day, a Greek national day commemorating the country's refusal to give Mussolini's forces passage in the early days of World War II
- Greek tiropita (page 205)

LATE OCTOBER TO EARLY NOVEMBER
Diwali, a five-day-long celebration, also known as the Festival of Lights and Hindu New Year
- Indian gulab jamun (page 252)
- Indian kalakand (page 248)

NOVEMBER

NOVEMBER 2

Day of the Dead, a Hispanic celebration honoring one's ancestors

- Mexican pan de muerto (page 74)

NOVEMBER 5

Guy Fawkes Night, also known as Bonfire Night, marking the downfall of Guy Fawkes's 1605 plot to blow up the English houses of parliament

- Parkin (page 132)

NOVEMBER 15

Shichi-Go-San (seven-five-three), a Japanese celebration for boys turning three or five and for girls turning three or seven, ages that are considered important milestones in Japanese culture

- Japanese baked cheesecake (page 278)
- Japanese cream puffs (page 168)

NOVEMBER 16

Estonian Day of Declaration of Sovereignty, a national holiday commemorating the country's 1988 declaration of independence from the Soviet Union

- Estonian sponge fruit cakes (page 181)

LATE NOVEMBER

Thanksgiving Day in the United States, celebrated on the fourth Thursday of the month as a day to give thanks for divine goodness and/or the fall harvest

- Canadian cranberry quatre quarts (page 54)
- Cherokee wild huckleberry cake (page 42)
- Liberian upside-down pumpkin-plantain cake (page 213)

LATE NOVEMBER TO EARLY DECEMBER

Eid al-Adha, the Muslim Festival of Sacrifice, falling on the tenth day of the twelfth month of the Islamic calendar and commemorating the willingness of Abraham to sacrifice his son in obedience to God

- Iranian baklava (page 235)
- Iranian pistachio-rosewater cake (page 232)
- Nigerian chin-chin (page 209)

DECEMBER

DECEMBER 13

St. Lucia's Day, a Christian feast day for the martyred saint Lucia and an important celebration in Sweden

- Swedish Lucia cats (page 158)

MID- TO LATE DECEMBER

Hanukkah, the Jewish Festival of Lights, an eight-day celebration of the rededication of the holy temple in Jerusalem

- Greek loukoumathes (page 195)

DECEMBER 16–24

Misa de Gallo, nine days of dawn masses leading up to Christmas in the Philippines, each of which is followed by the consumption of holiday fare, sold right outside the churches by street vendors

- Filipino pandan puto (page 288)
- Filipino sweet potato puto (page 289)
- Filipino ube puto (page 289)

DECEMBER 24 AND 25

Christmas Eve and Christmas Day, on which Christians celebrate the birth of Jesus Christ and exchange gifts (see page 58 for more discussion of Christmas cakes)

- Armenian nutmeg cake (page 226)
- Australian Pavlova (page 302)
- Canadian bûche de Noël (page 56)
- French pain d'épices (page 102)
- German stollen (page 122)
- Italian panettone (page 188)
- Italian cassata (page 196)
- Italian panforte (page 186)
- Korean saeng cream cake (page 270)

DECEMBER 26

Boxing Day, celebrated in most regions with British influence (British Isles, Canada, South Africa, Australia, Bahamas, Barbados), as a time to give small gifts or tips to service people

- Bahamian johnnycakes (page 71)
- Canadian maple-walnut tourlouche (page 55)
- English Victoria sponge cake (page 136)
- South African souskluitjies (page 219)

DECEMBER 26 THROUGH JANUARY 1

Kwanzaa ("first fruits" in Swahili), a traditionally African-American holiday honoring African heritage and culture

- Kenyan banana cake with crunchy n'dizi (page 221)
- Liberian upside-down pumpkin-plantain cake (page 213)

- Malian fruit and vegetable fritters (page 214)
- Ugandan groundnut (peanut) cake (page 220)

DECEMBER 31

Hogmanay, the Scottish New Year's Eve celebration

- Scottish Dundee cake (page 146)
- Sweet Scottish scones (page 147)

DECEMBER 31

Omisoka, Japan's New Year's Eve, on which people commonly prepare for the new year by cleaning their entire house

- Japanese dorayaki (page 276)
- Japanese mochi (page 274)

Let's Talk Cake: From Fruitcakes to Funnel Cakes

THE WAY I SEE IT, EVERY CAKE HAS A FAMILY TREE. The roots are the cakes that led to the creation of a basic recipe. The master recipe is the trunk. The branches are all the offspring of the master recipe. Branches evolve, seeds drop, and new recipes grow, traveling far from the trunk with new ingredients and preparation methods. In order to make sense of cakes' relationships to each other, we can categorize them by how they are prepared and their essential ingredients. Here are the cake classifications for the adventurous epicurean in you to explore.

BUTTER CAKES

Melt-in-your-mouth butter cakes are also sometimes called raised cakes or shortened cakes. Butter heightens the natural flavor of the cakes, while also yielding a creamy yellow color. They are made by creaming butter and sugar until they yield a fluffy mixture, then adding a leavener such as baking powder. They are often paired with fruit, whether flavored with extracts, juices, or zests or served alongside fresh fruit or fruit sauces. Pound cakes are a type of butter cake.

Battenberg cake

EXAMPLES: *Canadian quatre quarts (page 54), English Battenberg cake (page 142)*

CHEESECAKES

Cheesecakes are creamy and dense. Depending on the locale, they are made with many types of cheese, from cream cheese to cottage cheese, feta, quark, and goat's milk cheese. Crusts (if they have one) range from graham cracker to cookie, phyllo, or shortbread. Some are baked; others are not. Different ingredients may be included, from fruits and nuts to candies and chocolate. They are traditionally made in a springform pan.

New York cheesecake

EXAMPLES: *Catalan cheesecake (page 198), Japanese baked cheesecake (page 278), New York cheesecake (page 38)*

CHIFFON CAKES

Like *foam cakes*, chiffons get their volume from the air beaten into their eggs. The difference is that they contain oil, which makes them very moist.

EXAMPLE: *Venezuelan orange-chocolate chiffon cake (page 89)*

orange-chocolate chiffon cake

DOUGHNUTS

Doughnuts are small cakes usually cooked by being deep-fried or baked. The dough is usually sweet and leavened by yeast or baking powder. Often they are round, and they contain any number of fillings, from jellies to custards.

EXAMPLES: *American buttermilk doughnuts (page 44), Mexican churros (page 78), Peruvian picarones (page 95)*

churros

DUMPLINGS

Dessert dumplings are small balls or strips of sweet dough that are traditionally cooked by being boiled or steamed, though they can also be baked or poached. Dumplings are sometimes filled with fruit or served with a sauce.

EXAMPLES: *Indian gulab jamun (page 252), South African souskluitjie (page 219)*

souskluitjie

FLAT CAKES

Some flat cakes are flat because they don't contain a leavener, while others are simply cooked in thin layers. They range widely in texture, from light crepes to hearty pancakes. Though they can be among the finest of cakes, they can also be among the most primitive, and many are still common in regions of the world where baking ovens are not common.

apple stack

EXAMPLES: *American apple stack (page 40), Caribbean johnnycake (page 71), Indian malpuas (page 246), Korean hwajeon (page 273), Palestinian qatayef (page 237)*

FOAM CAKES

These airy, lightly textured cakes require skill and patience. Although they aren't always easy to make, there is a big reward: they are virtually fat free. These cakes are leavened (raised) by having air bubbles beaten into either whole or separated eggs. The bubbles expand while baking. They include *sponge cakes* and *meringues*.

angel food cake

EXAMPLE: *American angel food cake (page 34)*

FRITTERS

Fritters are pieces of fruits, vegetables, edible flowers, or other ingredients that are dipped in batter and then fried into a cake. The batter is different in different cultures. French beignets are made with choux pastry, Thai mung-bean fritters are made with a rice flour and coconut milk batter, and Malian fruit and vegetable fritters are made with a thick flour-based batter.

fruit and vegetable fritters

EXAMPLES: *Malian fruit and vegetable fritters (page 214), Thai three chums cake (page 294)*

FRUITCAKES

Fruitcakes are *butter cakes* or *yeast cakes* made with dried or candied fruits and nuts. The batter or dough is usually sharply spiced. They range in texture from the dense Italian panforte, which has just enough batter to hold together the heavy ingredients, to the Italian panettone, a light and bready *yeast cake*. They are often soaked in rum, brandy, or sugar syrup and wrapped and left to mellow for several weeks.

panforte (left); panettone (right)

EXAMPLES: *German stollen (page 122), Irish simnel cake (page 150), Italian panforte (page 186) and panettone (page 188), Scottish Dundee cake (page 146), Trinidadian black cake (page 63)*

HONEY CAKES

Honey cakes are sweetened with honey instead of or in addition to sugar. They can be *yeast cakes*, *butter cakes*, or *foam cakes*. Middle Eastern honey cakes are often flavored with just honey; sometimes they are soaked in a honey syrup for additional flavor. European honey cakes are often sharply spiced to create gingerbread-like cakes.

Cherokee wild huckleberry cake

EXAMPLES: *Cherokee wild huckleberry cake (page 42), Iranian baklava (page 235), Israeli honey cake (page 227)*

ICE CREAM CAKES

Ice cream cakes either are made entirely of ice cream or combine cake and ice cream. They often have a crunchy crust or center of crushed cookies.

mango-lychee ice cream cake

EXAMPLES: *French Norwegian omelette (page 109), Italian cassata gelato (page 196), Thai mango-lychee ice cream cake (page 292)*

MERINGUES

A meringue cake is a type of *foam cake* made with egg whites — no yolks or any other kind of fat. Meringue can also be prepared as a topping for another kind of cake, as in the French Norwegian omelette (page 109).

Pavlova

EXAMPLES: *Pavlova (page 302), Swiss vacherin (page 113)*

MILK CAKES

Western milk cakes are simply cakes that rely heavily on milk products, whether condensed or evaporated milk, sour cream, heavy cream, or even coconut milk. Indian milk cakes are made with fresh and dried milk products, especially paneer, a local cheese, and border on candy in texture and flavor. They come in hundreds of varieties.

EXAMPLES: *Indian kalakand (page 248), Nicaraguan tres leches cake (page 80), Sri Lankan hot milk sponge cake (page 255)*

tres leches cake

MOONCAKES

Mooncakes, of Chinese origin, can now be found across Asia, from Korea to Indonesia, as well as in any city with a large Asian population. These baked pastries contain a range of fillings, from pastes of lotus seed, taro, mung bean, and red bean to glutinous rice, jellies, ice cream, chocolate, walnuts, and lychees. The crust is traditionally embossed with symbols, patterns, or characters.

EXAMPLES: *Chinese mooncakes (page 260), Taiwanese pineapple cakes (page 266)*

mooncakes

OATCAKES

These are rustic cakes prepared with oats in addition to or instead of flour. They are common in the cold climates of northern Europe.

EXAMPLE: *Faroe Islands hazelnut oatcake (page 169)*

hazelnut oatcake

PASTRIES

Pastry cakes, also called simply pastries, are made with buttery, light, and flaky pastry dough. The dough is made from flour, fat (butter), and liquid (water or milk), with or without eggs. Phyllo was one of the first pastry doughs. The pastry dough may form

strudel

the crust of a cake, as in the case of a cheesecake, or the entire cake, as in the case of fried dough.

EXAMPLES: *Austrian strudel (page 123), French croquembouche (page 99), Moroccan m'hanncha (page 210)*

QUICK BREADS

Though they are called breads, quick breads can be cakes. They use a fast-acting leavener, such as baking powder or baking soda, that allows them to be baked immediately upon being mixed. They are an alternative to **yeast cakes**. Most cakes, in fact, are quick breads.

EXAMPLES: *Greek vasilopita (page 202), West Indian calabaza pudding cake (page 64)*

calabaza pudding cake

RICE CAKES

Rice cakes are made either of whole-grain rice or of rice flour, instead of or in addition to wheat flour.

EXAMPLES: *Bolognese rice cake (page 194), Chinese nian gao (page 258), Nepali carrot-rice cake (page 254)*

nian gao

SHORTBREADS

The term *shortbread* is short for *shortening bread*. It describes a cake or cookie made with a large amount of shortening.

EXAMPLES: *American strawberry shortcake (page 35), Welsh cakes (page 148)*

Welsh cakes

SPONGE CAKES

This type of **foam cake** is traditionally made with whole eggs but no other fat, although some contemporary recipes contain a little additional fat. It has a spongy texture, hence the name. Roll cakes are made from sponge cakes.

EXAMPLES: *Génoise sponge cake (page 108), Japanese kasutera (page 280), Swiss rolls (page 116)*

roll cakes

TARTS

Tarts are a kind of pie baked in a pastry shell, with or without a pastry top. They may contain jellies, custards, fruits, or any other kind of filling.

EXAMPLE: *Portuguese pastéis de nata (page 201)*

pastéis de nata

TORTES

Torte is the German word for cake, though it is now used to describe a moist cake made with many eggs and, traditionally, ground or grated nuts and bread crumbs.

EXAMPLES: *Hungarian Dobos torte (page 172), Austrian Sachertorte (page 126), Brazilian Marta Rocha torte (page 86)*

Marta Rocha torte

TRIFLES

A trifle is a cake (often a sponge cake) soaked in a syrup or liqueur and filled or topped with custard, cream, or preserves.

EXAMPLE: *English zabaglione cream-berry trifle (page 140)*

zabaglione cream-berry trifle

YEAST CAKES

Yeast cakes, as you might imagine, use yeast as a leavener. These cakes have a breadlike texture.

EXAMPLES: *Austrian kugelhopf (page 127), Italian panettone (page 188), New Orleans king cake (page 50), Swedish Lucia cats (page 158)*

king cake

Cake Artists

Art is the center of my life. I feel lucky to be surrounded and inspired by creatives: people who are constantly envisioning and inventing the future. And I am constantly amazed at how many of these people choose cake as a means of expression.

There are two types of cake artists. First are the creative cake makers, who invent recipes, bake, sculpt, and decorate cakes that are pieces of art. The pastry bag is their paintbrush, and flour, sugar, butter, and other edible ingredients their palette. They find inspiration not only in traditional places, such as crafts stores, supermarkets, and ethnic groceries, but also the world around them. Nature provides new designs for chocolate leaves; the trim of a gown provides details for the next wedding cake; the rise of a new cultural trend offers ideas for a cake that has never before been seen or eaten. A toolbox filled with colorful sugars, candies, star tips, and cookie cutters, along with lots and lots of practice, is all they need to create edible art that makes cake lovers smile — or even swoon.

The second type of cake artists includes fine artists, functional artists, illustrators, and crafters who make art about cake. Fine artists create conceptual pieces that make us think about our relationship to cake and all of the emotions surrounding it. In galleries I've seen life-size plywood sculptures with stacks of layers jutting out like cake layers and gold-studded snack cakes gridded to pattern an entire room, floor to ceiling. On the streets I've seen graffiti artists leave their mark with a quirky stencil illustration and their tag — "cake." Animators post videos on YouTube with titles like *Cakey! The Cake from Outer Space.* Collage artists work with retro images of cakes, placing them in a context where they become giant sand castles. Painters elevate doughnuts and glasses of milk through still-life compositions that reveal a fresh take on these everyday pleasures. Crafters use their skills to blow glass layer cakes, knit cupcakes, felt slices of cakes, and make clay Black Forest cake jewelry. And of course there are those lucky illustrators who have their own greeting card business or who design for a large manufacturer and spend all their time drawing and painting cakes, all day, every day, in as many ways as they can imagine. For these and so many other thinkers and makers, cake is the perfect artistic medium to explore.

A Field Guide to Cakes

Cakes of the British Isles tend to be dense.

American cakes tend to be fluffy.

African cakes are generally crispy.

Asian cakes are generally chewy.

THESE ARE VAST GENERALIZATIONS, OF COURSE, especially since globalization has brought international influences to cuisines around the world. But if you're looking for a particular kind of cake to satisfy a craving — chewy, creamy, dense, or fluffy — these charts offer up candidates from among the recipes in this book to suit your mood perfectly.

DENSE

FRUITCAKES
- black cake
- Dundee cake
- mit lechig
- panforte
- persimmon festival cake
- simnel
- stollen
- tamale corn cake

FLAT CAKES
- apple stack cake
- johnnycake
- malpua
- qatayef
- Welsh cake

SEED AND NUT CAKES
- Brazil nut cake
- groundnut (peanut) cake
- hazelnut oatcake
- hodo kwaja (walnut cake)
- kransekake
- lemon poppyseed cake
- maple-walnut tourlouche
- mazurek
- pistachio-rosewater cake
- potica (nut roll)
- seed cake
- tarta de Santiago (St. James' cake)

PASTRY CAKES
- apple strudel
- baklava
- coconut cake
- croquembouche
- feng li su (pineapple cake)
- kanafeh
- mooncake
- quince empanada
- snake cake
- vatnsdeigsbollur

VEGETABLE CAKES
- calabaza pudding cake
- hummingbird cake
- Queen Anne's cake (carrot cake)
- ube cake
- upside-down pumpkin-plantain cake
- yuca cake
- zucchini-almond cake

SPICE CAKES
- date spice cake
- galleta de miel (honey cake)
- New World spice cake
- pain d'épices (gingerbread)
- pandan cake
- Parkin
- Runeberg cake
- saffron cake

FRESH FRUIT CAKES
- banana cake with crunchy n'dizi
- Cherokee wild huckle-berry cake
- Dorset apple cake
- friendship cherry blossom cake
- kiwifruit–macadamia nut cake
- mango cake
- pineapple-chocolate cream cake
- pomegranate cake
- strawberry shortcake

CREAMY → CHEWY

CUSTARD CAKES
- barrigas de freira (nuns' bellies)
- Nanaimo bar
- pastéis de nata (cream tart)
- prinsesstårta
- tapioca pearl raisin cake
- zabaglione cream–berry trifle

ICE CREAM CAKES
- cassata gelato
- mango-lychee ice cream cake
- Norwegian omelette

CHEESECAKES
- baked cheesecake with coffee jelly
- Catalan cheesecake
- crostata di ricotta (Roman ricotta cheesecake)
- kalakand
- New York cheesecake
- taro cheesecake
- tiropita

CANDY CAKES
- kagemand
- lolly log
- Turkish delight cake

RICE CAKES
- banh bo nuong (cow cake)
- Bolognese rice cake
- carrot-rice cake
- hwajeon
- kanom sam kloe (three chums cake)
- mochi
- nian gao

CREAMY TO CHEWY

DENSE → FLUFFY

CHOCOLATE CAKES
- Black Forest cake
- bûche de Noël
- devil's food cupcake
- German chocolate cake
- orange-chocolate chiffon cake
- Queen of Sheba cake
- red velvet cake
- rehruecken
- Rigó Jancsi cake
- Sachertorte

SWEET BREADS
- Belgian buns
- king cake
- kolache
- kugelhopf
- lambropsomo
- luilakbollen (lazybones cake)
- pan de muerto
- panettone
- pineapple huat kueh
- saffransbullar (Lucia cats)
- sou tao (longevity peach buns)
- sweet Scottish scones

FRIED CAKES
- chin-chin
- churros
- cinnamon buttermilk doughnuts
- fruit and vegetable fritters
- funnel cake
- gulab jamun
- jalebi
- zeppole

MERINGUE CAKES
- Pavlova
- torta del cielo
- vacherin

BUTTER CAKES
- basbousa
- Battenberg cake
- chocolate fondue with orange cake
- corn cake
- cranberry quatre quarts (pound cake)
- dorayaki
- Lamington
- petits fours glacé
- rum cake
- souskluitjie
- tres leches cake

SPONGE CAKES
- angel food cake
- apple-lemon charlotte russe
- arrollado con dulce de leche
- cassata Siciliana
- charlotte royale
- chrysanthemum steamed lemon cake
- Dobos torte
- frog cakes
- génoise petits fours
- génoise sponge cake
- hamburger and fries
- kasutera cake
- lagkage
- Marta Rocha torte
- milk sponge cake
- opera gateau
- pan di Spagna
- saeng cream cake
- Swiss roll
- Victoria sandwich cake

DENSE TO FLUFFY

Mastering Cake: Simple Techniques with Standout Results

KNOWING THE FINER POINTS of a few standard techniques can make all the difference between a good cake and a great one. Once you learn the subtleties of these kitchen essentials, you'll find they have a tremendous impact on the results of your baking endeavors.

Selecting Bakeware

For cakes that will be baked, the choice of cake pan or baking sheet affects not only the cake's crust and texture but also how it cooks. In general, light-colored bakeware is generally better for baking cakes, as it won't brown the cakes as much as dark-colored bakeware will.

Most cake pans and baking sheets are made of metal. Aluminum is most common, as it is an excellent heat conductor. However, aluminum may react with some acidic foods, changing the flavor of the dish. To guard against such a reaction, you might prefer your aluminum pans and sheets to be clad, or covered in a nonreactive coating.

Stainless-steel and carbon-steel baking pans are becoming more popular, as they do not corrode or react with acidic food. They don't conduct heat evenly, though, and so they should have an aluminum or copper core to facilitate heat conduction.

Glass is also an excellent heat conductor, but it absorbs heat rather than reflecting it. For this reason, the oven temperature generally must be set 25 degrees lower if you're using glass bakeware instead of metal bakeware. Ceramic bakeware does not retain heat well, but it is fantastic for cakes that require long, slow cooking.

Silicone bakeware is new to the market, with mixed reviews. It conducts heat evenly, allows easy removal of the baked cakes, and will not corrode or react with acidic foods. And the best part of baking with silicone is the incredible diversity of shapes the pans offer. But because silicone pans are flexible, they can be hard to move when filled with batter. Manufacturers make racks to give the pans stability; you also could simply place them on a rigid baking sheet before filling them. And some cooks complain that they give food an off flavor — to be fair, though, other cooks deny any off flavor and rave about silicone's versatility.

Most baking pans are one-piece molds, but springform pans have an upright detachable rim fastened to the bottom of the pan with a buckle. When the cake has been baked, you unfasten the buckle and the rim springs free from the cake. You could use a springform pan for any cake, but it's most useful for fragile cakes that would be difficult to lever out of a one-piece pan, such as cheesecakes.

Nonstick coatings can be useful, keeping cakes from sticking to pans and baking sheets. Just keep in mind that some recipes (like the upside-down pumpkin-plantain cake on page 213) *want* the burnt caramelization that comes from uncoated bakeware; a nonstick coating would prevent that reaction.

Of course, as a general rule, if a recipe calls for a particular kind of bakeware, use it. If you don't have it, pick the closest alternative.

Specialty Baking Pans

A tube pan is necessary for making an angel food cake.

A Bundt pan is a tube pan with fluted sides.

A springform pan is necessary for cheesecakes.

Cake rings are useful for layered cakes and can be used either for baking or for setting ice cream in the right shape.

Mixing Dry Ingredients

Mix dry ingredients together at the outset, before you mix together anything else. Measure flour using the dip-and-sweep method: dip the measuring cup into the flour and then level it off with a table knife. If you first cream together the butter and sugar or whip up the eggs, and then you take the time to mix together the dry ingredients, your first mixture will deflate, and you will have a tougher cake.

Creaming Butter and Sugar

Before it is creamed, butter should be soft enough to push right through it with your finger. Cut the softened butter into small pieces and combine with the sugar in a clean bowl. Beat at medium-high speed for about 2 minutes, until the mixture is light and fluffy. It should change in color from yellow to cream and have the consistency of whipped cream.

Separating and Beating Eggs

Eggs are easiest to separate when cold. For a good split, crack the egg on a flat surface, not the rim of a bowl. Pull apart the eggshell over a bowl, using one half of the shell to cup the egg. Allow the whites to drop into the bowl, passing the yolk back and forth between the shell halves to encourage the whites to separate from the yolk.

If you're separating more than one egg, pour the egg whites you've just separated into another bowl, and start the next egg over the now-empty bowl. In this way, if you should accidentally drop some yolk into the bowl, it contaminates just that one batch of whites, and not all the whites you've separated so far. Any yolk in the whites will prevent them from foaming properly.

Eggs whip up more fully when they're at room temperature. (So if you need to separate the eggs, do so early enough that they'll have time to warm up before you begin

Know Your Flours

Different flours have different amounts and types of proteins and starches. Gluten is among the most important to know. It's an elastic protein that gives strength and cohesion to baked goods. Gluten is "developed" by being worked, which stretches the gluten fibers and causes it to bind to itself. The more the gluten is developed, the more cohesion it gives the dough. Kneading, for example, works the gluten intensively, while simple spoon mixing works it only slightly.

WHITE FLOUR
Most of the recipes in this book use all-purpose white flour, which has a moderate amount of gluten. Some call for cake flour, which has less gluten and so yields a lighter, airier cake. You can try substituting one for the other, but the resulting cakes are not always what they're meant to be.

WHOLE-WHEAT FLOUR
Unlike white flour, whole-wheat flour contains the germ and bran of the wheat grain. For this reason, though it

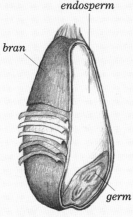

kernel of wheat

has proportionately less gluten than white flour, it can yield a heavier texture. You can substitute whole-wheat flour for *some* of the white flour in a recipe, but the resulting cake may be heavier and have an earthier flavor. If you want to use whole-grain flour instead of white flour, your best bet might be white whole-wheat flour, which is ground from white spring wheat rather than the traditional red wheat. It has a milder flavor and yields a lighter texture than regular whole-wheat flour, and though it's relatively new to the U.S. market, it's been used in Europe for many years.

SEMOLINA
Semolina flour has the highest gluten content of all. It's the coarsely ground endosperm of durum (hard) wheat. Because of its extremely high gluten content, when added to cakes semolina is almost always used in combination with white flour. It has a rich wheaty flavor.

NON-WHEAT FLOURS
Of course, wheat is not the only source of flour. Rice flour is the most popular flour in much of Asia. Long-grain rice is the standard for making flour, but glutinous rice is also common. (The term *glutinous* refers to the stickiness of the rice, not its gluten content. In fact, it has no gluten at all.) Around the world, you can also find flours made from just about any starchy food you can think of, from potatoes to oats, corn, arrowroot, taro, and cassava.

cooking.) The goal when beating eggs is to bring them just to the required stage and not to overbeat them. If you are using an electric mixer, medium-high speed tends to work best.

FOAM STAGE

Beat just until foamy, with plenty of tiny bubbles.

RIBBON STAGE

This stage may be called for when you are mixing eggs or egg yolks with sugar. As the mixture increases in volume and changes in color from bright yellow to light yellow, you are approaching ribbon stage. When the batter is stiff enough that it falls back into the bowl in a ribbonlike line when the beaters are lifted, you're there.

SOFT- OR STIFF-PEAK STAGE

A recipe may ask that you beat egg whites to a soft-peak or stiff-peak stage. At the soft-peak stage, egg whites are opaque but moist, and they should form limp peaks when lifted with the beater. At the stiff-peak stage, which requires an additional minute or two of beating, the whites will be glossy and will hold a firm peak when lifted with the beater.

The Stages of Egg Beating

1. The foam stage is first. You'll see lots of tiny bubbles.

2. You've reached the ribbon stage when the batter is stiff enough to fall in ribbonlike streams.

3. At the soft-peak stage, the whites are opaque and form limp peaks.

4. At the stiff-peak stage, the whites are glossy and hold a firm peak.

Folding

This technique is used to combine two ingredients of different densities (usually batter and beaten egg whites). Add the lighter ingredient to the heavier one just a little at a time, using a rubber spatula to gently lift the heavier mixture around the lighter one. The goal here is to prevent any air trapped in the lighter ingredient from being forced out. Keep folding in this manner until the two ingredients are just combined.

Kneading

As soon as flour is moistened, gluten begins to form. Gluten is necessary to bind the dough and give it strength. Kneading develops the gluten, giving the dough the strength it needs to hold air pockets and rise adequately. If the gluten is not stretched or worked properly, the cake is not able to hold air, and it becomes dense and tough.

Kneading is a simple process of pushing the dough out with the palms of your hands, folding it, turning it 90 degrees, and repeating. It takes 8 to 10 minutes, depending on the recipe, and can be a real workout. Most people don't knead long enough. You'll know you're done when the dough is smooth and almost satiny, and when you poke your finger into it, the indentation remains.

Baking

Pour the batter into the pan from a height, allowing the batter to fold over on itself. This traps air bubbles in the batter, giving the cake volume. Bake cakes in the middle of the oven. If you're baking more than one and have them on upper and lower racks, check the cakes halfway through, and rotate them if one is baking more quickly than the other.

Check your cake for doneness a few minutes *before* the baking time given in a recipe. To check, insert a knife, toothpick, or chopstick into the cake. If it comes out sticky, the cake needs to bake longer. If it comes out clean or with loose crumbs, then the cake is done.

Cooling

When you remove a cake from the oven, set it on a wire rack, which will allow air circulation all around it and encourage even cooling, preventing deflation and sogginess. Dense cakes can be removed from the pan within 5 to 10 minutes of baking; lighter cakes need to settle for 15 to 20 minutes before being removed. To remove the cake from the pan, use a knife to loosen the cake from the pan all around its edges. Turn the pan upside down onto the wire rack, then lift the pan off the cake. If you used parchment paper, peel it off and discard. Invert the cake to right side up and let cool completely.

To prevent their tops from cracking, cheesecakes are best cooled in their pan in the oven, with the oven door slightly ajar, so that they are brought slowly to room temperature.

Deep-Frying

Being fried in oil (or ghee) makes cakes crisp on the outside and moist on the inside. Use a heavy-bottomed pot, which will spread the heat evenly, and keep a lid handy just in case of an unexpected fire. (And if a fire happens, do *not* throw water on it — that will just make it worse. Instead, put the lid on the pot. Depriving the fire of oxygen will cause it to burn out.) You'll also want a deep-fry thermometer, which will tell you how hot the oil is.

To begin, add enough oil to your pot to allow the cakes to move freely. Warm the oil over medium heat until it reaches 365°F on a deep-fry thermometer, or whatever temperature the recipe specifies. Reduce the heat if necessary to maintain this temperature, and do not allow the oil to smoke — that means it is too hot, and the outside of the cakes will brown quicker than the inside will cook. Test the oil by dropping a small bit of bread, dough, or batter into it; it should sizzle and begin to brown immediately.

The three chums cake from Thailand is deep-fried.

Make sure your bread, dough, or batter is at room temperature, which will yield more even results. Drop the bread, dough, or batter into the oil in equal-size amounts, again for even results. As they brown, rotate or flip the cakes with a slotted spoon until they are browned on all sides.

Remove the cakes from the pot with a slotted spoon, allowing any excess oil to drain back into the pot. Place them on a plate or pan lined with paper towels and blot dry. To keep them warm, you can place them in a just-warm oven; place a paper towel between stacked cakes to keep them from becoming soggy.

Use a strainer or slotted spoon to remove any little bits of cake floating in the oil, and then start again.

Steaming

Steaming allows cakes to cook evenly and retain their moisture. Water is usually used for steaming, but liquids such as tea, juice, wine, and beer are also sometimes used and lend unique flavors.

You can use a traditional vegetable steamer for steaming cakes, so long as it has a flat bottom. You can also use a wok or pot fitted with a flat rack to hold the cake pan. You could also use a traditional bamboo steamer, a usually round container with a slotted bottom and a domed lid. You set the bamboo steamer on a rack over a bit of boiling water in a wok or skillet.

Prepare your cake batter or dough before heating the water. (Since you won't use much water, it heats very

Pineapple huat kueh from Singapore is steamed.

quickly.) Fill the wok or pot with water to an inch or two below the rack or steamer bottom. Place the cake in its pan on the rack or in the steamer; if you're cooking more than one, make sure they have some space between them so the steam can circulate. Cover, bring the water to a boil, and steam for the allotted time. Be careful when removing the lid, as the vapor can be scalding.

If you're concerned about the water evaporating before the cake is finished cooking, place a few marbles in the wok or pot. When the water comes to a boil, the bubbles will push the marbles around, making a clattering noise. When the noise stops, that's your cue to refill the wok or pot.

Using a Water Bath

A water bath protects delicate cakes (most commonly cheesecakes) from the direct heat of the oven and also provides humidity for a mild steaming effect. Choose a pan that is at least 2 inches longer and wider than the cake pan. Place the cake pan in the larger pan, and fill the larger pan half to two-thirds full of water. Set the larger pan with the water in the oven to preheat. Fill your cake pan with batter, and set it in the oven in the warm water bath to bake.

If you're using a springform cake pan, you'll want to guard against water from the water bath leaking into the cake pan. Before filling the springform pan with batter, wrap the exterior of the pan with aluminum foil.

You can have most of the benefit of the water bath without actually setting the cake pan in it. Just arrange two racks in the oven to accommodate the water bath pan below and the cake pan above.

Using a Double Boiler

A double boiler allows you to heat items very slowly over low heat without risk of burning them. Chocolate is often melted in a double boiler. When filling the bottom of a double boiler with water, be sure the water doesn't reach up to touch the bottom of the upper saucepan. And once the water in the bottom saucepan has come to a boil, you can reduce the heat to low and still maintain the boiling temperature. If you don't have a double boiler, place a metal or heat-proof glass bowl inside a larger saucepan. Fill the saucepan with water to just slightly below the lip of the bowl. Bring to a boil on a stove top.

Cake Architecture: How to Build Cakes

EVERYTHING I KNOW ABOUT CONSTRUCTING and decorating cakes I learned through practice, although I did get some good tips in art school. Envisioning the relationships between forms, using precision in crafting, and playing with color are all key to a successful design no matter what the medium — including cake.

Constructing Layer Cakes

I used to wonder how bakeries made their layer cakes with perfectly equal layers, while mine were always coming out in different thicknesses. Then I learned their secret: they premeasure the batter into equal portions before pouring it into pans for baking. I tried it, and it works!

If you need to cut a cake into layers, rather than baking the layers separately, set it on a sheet of waxed paper on top of a cutting board or lazy Susan. Measure the cake's height, and divide that number by the number of layers you want to determine the width of each layer. Mark the bottom of each layer with toothpicks inserted into the cake's sides. Then use a long serrated knife to cut horizontally through the cake. Don't try to cut through the cake in one long sweep; instead, cut all around the edges first, turning the cake as you go, and then make a final cut through the cake's center. This will help keep your cut level.

When you have all the cake layers ready, look at them to choose the order for assembly. Save the most even ones for the top and bottom, and any others for middle layers. Make sure the bottom and the top are flat, so that the cake doesn't wobble on its base or look uneven when served.

To construct the cake, mound the filling on the first layer, then use a spatula to spread it out evenly to the edges. Top with the next cake layer, aligning its edges with those of the first layer. Continue filling and layering until all of the layers are stacked.

Frosting a cake can be frustrating if crumbs keep breaking loose and lumping up the frosting. This is particularly an issue if you've trimmed the top layer to make it flat, exposing the cake interior. To solve the problem, first spread a very thin layer of frosting over the top and sides of the cake, and smooth the surface with a spatula. Pick out any larger crumbs, and clean your spatula. Then mound the remaining frosting on the cake in the center, and spread it out over the top and sides evenly. Crumbing should now be minimal.

Working with Phyllo Layers

Phyllo must be kept moist or it will dry out and crack. For this reason it's usually brushed with butter or some other type of oil, and any sheets you're not working with should be covered with a damp towel.

Use scissors or a sharp knife to cut the phyllo sheets to the size specified in the recipe. Generally you'll need four pieces of phyllo for each layer of cake.

Lay one phyllo piece in the bottom of a prepared baking dish. Using a pastry brush, generously brush it with melted butter. Set the next phyllo piece on top, and brush with butter. Repeat for the remaining two phyllo pieces.

Place the filling on top of the first four-piece phyllo layer, then top with another phyllo layer, brushing each piece with butter. Continue layering, following the recipe instructions, until the cake is constructed.

Phyllo is a staple in Middle Eastern, central Asian, and other regional cakes, such as the Greek tiropita shown below.

Constructing Rolled Cakes

Rolled cakes start off as flat rectangular cakes. Bake them in a jelly roll pan, or whatever pan the recipe calls for, lined with parchment paper. When it's baked, transfer the cake, using the paper as a lift, to a work surface while it's still warm. (If you didn't use parchment paper in the cake pan, transfer the cake *carefully* — it will be crumbly while warm — to a piece of waxed paper slightly longer than the cake.)

Position the cake so one of its long edges is closest to you. Test-roll the warm cake — it's easiest to roll it away from you — and trim away the edges if they obstruct the rolling. If necessary to give the cake flexibility, you can score a few slits halfway through the cake.

Top the cake with the filling, spreading it in an even thickness, 1 inch in from the edges. Prepare a serving platter by placing a long piece of plastic wrap on it. Then roll the cake, gently, so that the filling isn't squished out and the cake doesn't crack. Set it on the serving platter, seam side down. Wrap the roll in the plastic wrap and refrigerate for 2 hours to set the filling. Serve at room temperature, cut into slices.

This rolled cake from Argentina has a dulce de leche filling.

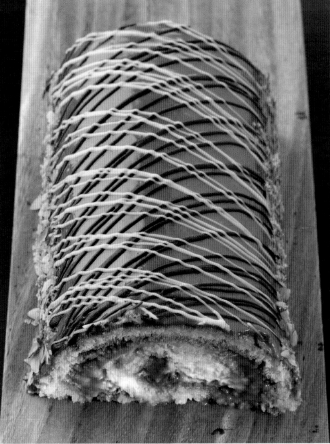

Cake Artifice: How to Decorate Cakes

BEAUTIFUL CAKES TEMPT US THROUGH OUR EYES. We love to look at them, hate to cut into them, and adore eating them. Around the globe, home cooks focus on cakes as an outlet for their creativity. Some simply find cake decorating fun and relaxing, while others are very serious about the art of edible sculpture. To most decorators, the process of creating is just as important as the final cake. But no matter how good or bad our efforts are from a visual point of view, they will always be appreciated for their edible form.

Working with Icing

The simplest decoration is frosting itself, which can be worked into glossy smoothness or swoops, swirls, peaks, or patterns. An icing spatula is helpful here; you can use the side of the tool to smooth frosting or the tip to swirl or lift. Whatever your goal, the first step is to frost the cake completely. Then you can begin patterning the frosting.

Cake edgers and decorating combs are specialized plastic or metal tools with shaped edges or tines that you draw across the frosting to create unique textures or patterns. Of course, you could also simply use the tines of a fork or the edge of a serrated knife to give frosting an interesting effect.

Using a Cake Board

Frosting a cake can be a messy business. Sometimes it's easiest to decorate the cake on a cake board, a sturdy piece of cardboard that you trim to the dimensions of the cake. Once the cake is decorated, you can transfer it, on its cake board, to the serving platter.

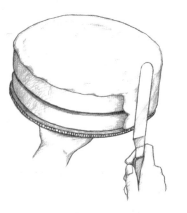

Stenciling

Stenciling is a simple technique with really beautiful results. You can buy premade stencils at most arts and crafts supply shops, or you can make your own by cutting a pattern into a sheet of card stock or waxed paper.

If the cake is frosted, freeze it for 15 minutes so that the frosting hardens and the stencil won't stick to it. Then place the stencil on top of the cake. If the stencil edges are narrow, you might drape waxed paper over the rest of the cake, to keep it clean when you dust the stencil.

Confectioners' sugar, cocoa powder, and cinnamon sugar all work well for stenciling. Which you choose will be determined by the color of the cake; in most cases you want the stencil to be in a contrasting color so that it stands out. Place the sugar or powder in a fine-mesh sifter. Hold the sifter over the stencil and just tap it a few times, giving the stencil an even coating. Then carefully lift the stencil straight up, to keep the sugar or powder from sliding off onto the cake. If necessary, you can clean up the edges with a wet paintbrush or pastry brush.

The beautiful design on this Armenian nutmeg cake is achieved with a stencil and confectioners' sugar.

Stamping and Cutting Marzipan and Fondant

Marzipan (made from almonds; see page 324) and fondant (made from sugar; see page 324) are easily shaped into sculptural decorative forms. You can find many specialized tools for sculpting them, but you can also use toothpicks, bamboo skewers, knives, and cookie cutters. Just think of them as edible clays, and have fun.

The first step is to knead the paste to a workable consistency. Fondant dries quickly, so keep any bit of it that you're not working with covered with a damp towel or plastic. Then roll out the paste to the desired thickness. Any sort of rolling pin will do, but because the pastes are sticky, the work surface should be coated — use confectioners' sugar for marzipan, and cornstarch for fondant.

Cut out the shapes you want, and use a spatula to lift them from your work surface. Press into the surface of the cake, and voilà! Three-dimensional cake art.

The skirt on this doll cake illustrates the sculptural possibilities of marzipan. See page 312 for more about character cakes.

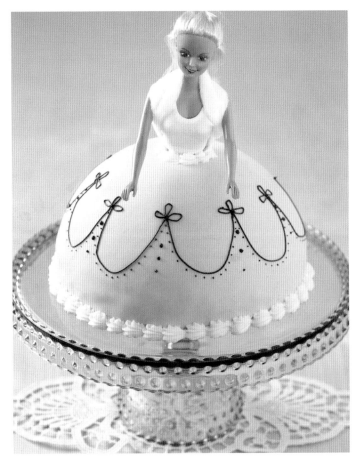

Piping

Piping is a classic technique for decorating cakes, allowing you to shape icing into lines, loops, stars, flowers, and just about any other shape you can think of. Ready-to-use icing pipers are available at most grocery stores. These are icing-filled tubes with built-in piping tips. You simply trim the tip at the spot where it will give you the desired line thickness and squeeze the tube to pipe out the icing. It's a very simple solution for writing messages and creating small decorations if you're in a hurry or you don't have authentic piping equipment on hand.

What is authentic piping equipment? The traditional tool is the pastry bag, a cone-shaped bag used to extrude (pipe) icing, frosting, whipped cream, meringue, or pastry dough through a shaped tip. A coupler secures the tip to the bag. Some pastry bags are disposable, while others are made out of reusable materials such as canvas, parchment, or nylon. Bigger is better here, to minimize the time you spend refilling; 10- and 12-inch bags are the most common, but as you learn to control them you may want to use larger bags. It's helpful to have several pastry bags so you can work with several colors at once.

The tips come in hundreds of shapes, but to get started all you really need are round tips and star tips in an assortment of sizes. The larger tips are for piping thicker mixtures like meringue and pastry dough, while the smaller tips are for delicate writing and the medium-size tips are best for creating borders.

Piping Alternatives

Some people prefer to pipe with a mechanical pastry bag, a stainless-steel or silicone barrel with interchangeable tips. You place the icing in the barrel and crank the handle to press the mixture from the tip. It can be easier to control than a conventional pastry bag.

Recycled squeeze bottles and airtight plastic bags with a corner cut off can also be used to pipe. In fact, plastic bags with a corner cut off are excellent for drizzling melted chocolate.

Piping is not as hard as it seems, but it does take a little skill and practice. Follow the basic tips on the following page and you will soon be a pro — or at least you'll be able to create a legible message on the top of a birthday cake.

How to Apply Piping to Cakes

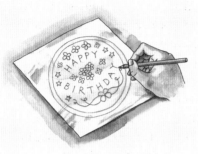   

1. *Sketch out your concept on tracing paper. Lay out the design at the actual size to make sure it will fit on the cake, then use it as a reference.*

2. *When you're satisfied with the design, use a toothpick to trace it on the cake. (If you are going to be doing tons of decorating, you might consider investing in a projector that will shine the image on the cake for you to trace.)*

3. *Mix icing to the proper piping consistency. Thicker icing works well with shaped tips to create borders and flowers, while thinner icing is good for inscriptions, thin lines, and drizzles. Add corn syrup to the icing to give it elasticity.*

4. *Start with the smallest size of tip you think will work. Smaller tips are easier to control than larger ones, and if you make a mistake, you can always pipe over it using a larger tip.*

5. *Do not fill the piping bag any more than halfway full, so that you can better control the extrusion. Twist the top of the pastry bag to close it.*

6. *To pipe, hold the pastry bag between your thumb and the side of your index finger. Squeeze the pastry bag firmly and evenly from the top, and move the tip at uniform speed. Stop squeezing and pull away quickly to end.*

7. *Practice piping on an empty plate before moving on to the cake. If you don't want to waste the frosting, you can always scoop it back into the pastry bag.*

8. *If you're using royal icing, which hardens, you can pipe designs on waxed paper, freeze them, and then use a spatula to lift them onto the cake.*

Inscriptions

Edible inscriptions on cakes became popularized in the mid-1800s, a time when bakers' guilds were growing and cake decorating was becoming ever more elaborate. But the traditional "Happy Birthday" didn't become a common inscription until 1910, when the song was developed. In the midtwentieth century, just as home cake decorating was getting under way, premanufactured letters and numbers became available, making it easy for even the most clumsy cook to write a beautiful message on a cake. Since then, inscriptions have become a classic cake decoration.

When you're getting ready to set your inscription on the cake, you'll want to make sure you don't run out of cake to write on. So place the center letter in the center of your inscription space, and then place the last letter on the far right and the first letter on the far left. Rough in the other letters with a toothpick before setting them in place.

The most popular method of inscribing is piping icing to make letters, but don't let that stop you from exploring other creative avenues of expression.

- Use alphabet cereal — you'll have hundreds of letters to work with.

- Write with candy: candy buttons can be arranged into a mosaic pattern, and lace licorice can be cut and arranged into scripted letters.

- Prepare a batch of marzipan (page 324), roll it out, and cut it into letters with cookie cutters or a knife.

- Create a stencil and sift confectioners' sugar or cocoa powder through it.

- Forget about writing on the cake and write the message on the plate in a sauce instead.

Whatever your chosen method, check your spelling before you start writing — you'd be hugely embarrassed to serve your guests a beautiful cake with an ugly typo.

Top Ten Cake Inscriptions

The same ten cake inscriptions have stolen pride of place for more than a hundred years, not just in English, but in the top five languages of the world. You say they aren't creative? That might be the case, but perhaps we're more interested in being reassuring and are nostalgic when it comes to the messages written on the tops of our cakes.

Happy Birthday!
Congratulations!
It's a [girl/boy]!
Merry Christmas
Celebrate!
Best Wishes
Thank You
Love and Happiness
Happy Anniversary
Class of [XXXX]

Cake Wrap: Storage

The shelf life of a cake and the best place to store it really depend on the cake's ingredients. In general, cakes should be eaten within three days or so. Fried cakes are the exception; they'll lose their crispness and texture within a few hours of being made, and so they should be eaten fresh, not stored.

Dry cakes without dairy layers can be stored at room temperature. They may last longer, but they'll dry out. Phyllo cakes like baklava can also be stored at room temperature. (But if you prefer a chewy texture, store your phyllo cake in the refrigerator, where it will keep for up to a week.)

Cheesecakes and other dairy cakes, as well as any cakes with moist ingredients or fresh fruits, will develop mold if left out and should be stored in the refrigerator. Asian rice cakes should be stored in a sealed container in a dry, cool location, such as the refrigerator.

For a longer shelf life most cakes can be frozen. If a cake is frosted, set it in the refrigerator for a few hours first, to allow the frosting to harden so it won't stick to the wrapping. Then seal the cake in an airtight container or an inner layer of waxed paper and an outer layer of aluminum foil. If you choose the latter method, when it comes time to defrost the cake, remove the wrappings after a couple of hours so that the cake won't stick to them.

CHAPTER 2

North America
Sugar and Spice and Doughnuts Are Nice

FOR A CONTINENT THAT REMAINED MOSTLY ISOLATED from the rest of the world until the fifteenth century, when cheesecakes, fruitcakes, and sponge cakes were already well established, North America has made some impressive contributions to global cake culture. A melting pot of native peoples, African slaves, and French, English, Spanish, Dutch, and German colonizers initiated a firestorm of new baking traditions, which led to an inspirational environment for the development of uniquely American cakes. The continuing immigration of people to this continent from lands near and far has kept the oven hot, making North American cake culture changeable, adaptable, and globally influenced.

The United States has always had a reputation for independence and a hunger for novelty and experimentation — and these qualities are evident in the country's cakes. But often these cakes weren't built from scratch; instead they evolved from the comforting recipes of immigrants' ancestral homelands, incorporating the flavors of local ingredients. An Austrian-American developed the simple Bundt cake as an homage to kugelhopf. Plantation culture of the American South adopted the English tradition of afternoon tea, in the process creating the Lane cake, the Lady Baltimore cake, and more distinctly American cakes than I can list here. And the innovations only continued as the territory spread westward. Today in the western United States, for example, Tex-Mex versions of empanadas are eaten for breakfast, and Japanese-inspired mochi ice cream cakes are common after-dinner treats.

As American cake culture took shape, fast, convenient, and modern became its hallmarks. From the outset, Americans' quest for originality and knack for marketing led us to bring new flavors to the world: think Coca-Cola cakes made from a homespun drink and African fried street cakes transformed into franchised 24-hour doughnut shops. A hunger for ease in home baking led to enthusiastic innovations in baking tools and ingredients, including store-bought cake mix. Television cooking shows, and the celebrity chefs and bakers who host them, have spread our cake innovations to an international audience. And although we did not invent beloved cakes like the carrot cake, trifle, or jelly roll, we sure knew how to popularize them and in the process claim them as our own.

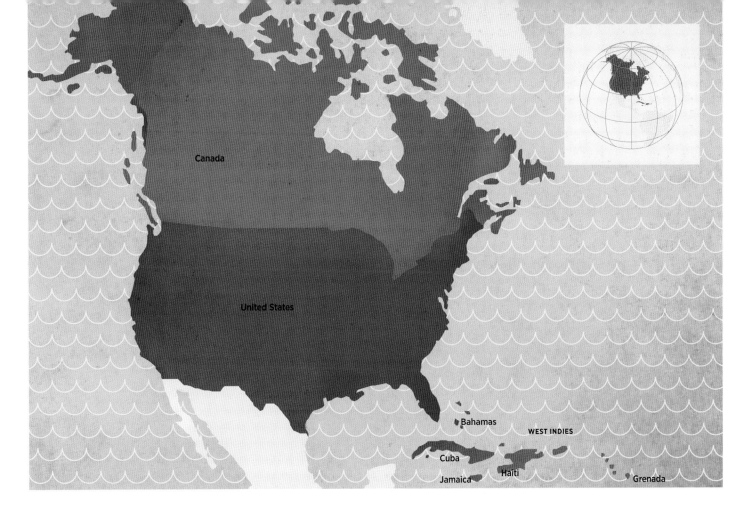

As is the case in most countries, Canada's cakes vary from one end of the country to another. Though I cannot tell you what prototypical Canadian cakes look like, Canadians typically use *homemade*, *warming*, and *wholesome* to describe them. Hands down, the Canadians make the best pound cake in the world (page 54). Many bakeries still make it the old-fashioned way, with a pound each of sugar, butter, eggs, and flour. But the most universally recognized national cake is the Nanaimo bar (page 61), a snack cake that manages to be crunchy and creamy and chocolaty all at the same time.

New World ingredients contribute authentically Canadian flavors to the country's cakes. In fact, baked goods flavored with fresh seasonal ingredients are served at almost every meal. Maple syrup is used as both a sweetener and a flavoring, as in Canadian tourlouche (page 55). Traditional cakes also take full advantage of the abundance of wild berries, including bearberries, blackberries, blueberries, cranberries, gooseberries, salmonberries, saskatoons, and strawberries.

The Caribbean Islands bring the flavors of the tropics to the cakes of North America, enriching them with sugarcane, molasses, coffee, coconut, and rum. The Caribbean is the birthplace of black cake (page 63), a rich, rum-soaked fruitcake based on the English Christmas cake. Today black cakes are left for Santa and his donkey (said to be his transport instead of reindeer and a sled) on Christmas Eve. Sweet potatoes, cassavas, bananas, mangos, and other tropical fruits often end up in the cake batter too. Corn is also an important crop for these islands, and johnnycakes (page 71), cornmeal-based cakes popular in the American East, are a staple here as well.

Early European traders were delighted to stumble upon the tropical islands of the Caribbean. Already home to allspice, annatto, bay rum, and other spices, the islands were soon sown with valuable spices from other tropical regions, such as ginger, cinnamon, and nutmeg, and these imports quickly worked their way into the native cuisine. Because the islands were a key stop on the sugar and spice trade routes, this region was influenced by a wide range of culinary traditions, from those of France, Great Britain, Holland, and Portugal to those of the Middle East, South Asia, Africa, and more. The early settlers of the Caribbean and the American South also exchanged cake recipes. To this day they are tied together by a sweet common heritage of sweet potato cakes, plantain cakes, planter's cakes, and hummingbird cakes (page 62).

Angel Food Cake

Angel food cake is a light and airy sponge cake that relies entirely on the beaten egg whites to rise. Traditionally it is almost white in color (due to the elimination of the yolks) and ring shaped, because it is baked in a tube pan. It can be eaten plain or dressed into an ice cream cake, alongside fresh fruit or rich sauces.

Sponge Cake

- 1 cup cake flour
- 1½ cups superfine sugar
- 2 tablespoons cornstarch
- 10 egg whites
- 1¼ teaspoons cream of tartar
- ¼ teaspoon salt
- 1 teaspoon vanilla extract
- ¼ teaspoon almond extract

Topping

- 2 tablespoons confectioners' sugar

Makes 1 cake (serves 6 to 8)

TO PREPARE

Preheat the oven to 325°F. Butter and flour a 10-inch angel food cake pan (a tube pan with feet, and preferably with a removable bottom).

TO MAKE THE CAKE

Combine the flour, ½ cup of the superfine sugar, and the cornstarch in large bowl; set aside. In a separate large bowl, use a mixer to beat the egg whites, cream of tartar, and salt until frothy. Gradually add the remaining 1 cup superfine sugar, beating until stiff peaks form. Stir in the vanilla and almond extracts. Gradually fold in the flour mixture with a spatula.

TO BAKE

Spoon the batter into the prepared pan. Bake for 50 to 60 minutes, until golden and springy and a knife inserted in the center of the cake comes out clean. Turn the cake upside down to cool in its pan for at least 20 minutes. Then remove the cake from the pan, using a long, sharp knife around the edges to ease it out if necessary. Sprinkle with confectioners' sugar.

VARIATIONS

Chocolate Angel Food Cake

Replace the superfine sugar with confectioners' sugar. Reduce the flour to ¾ cup and add ½ cup unsweetened cocoa powder. Top with 1½ cups chocolate sauce (page 320).

Lemon Angel Food Cake

Add 2 tablespoons lemon juice and the grated zest of one lemon to the cake batter.

Orange-Almond Angel Food Cake

Add 2 tablespoons orange juice and the grated zest of one orange to the cake batter. After pouring the batter into the pan, top with ¼ cup sliced almonds.

History of Angel Food

Also known as snowdrift cake, silver cake, and cornstarch cake, angel food cake was first found in cookbooks in the late 1800s, shortly after the invention of the manual rotary beater and the tube pan. Before the rotary beater, beating egg whites by hand took a lot of strength and time, but with the beater it was a breeze — although today we would probably find even the rotary beater tough, accustomed as we are to electric mixers.

The cake's name is most popularly said to derive from the idea that it is so light that angels could eat it and still fly without being weighted down. But there are other traditions. Angel food cake has been a popular African-American funeral cake for over a century; it's eaten in celebration of the deceased person who has been sent to the angels. The Pennsylvania Dutch have a different take; they enjoy this as a wedding cake and celebrate the couple's being blessed by angels.

Strawberry Shortcake

Traditional shortcakes are made from flaky and tender scone or biscuit dough and topped with whipped cream and strawberries. They are incredibly easy to make for kids and adults alike. Although the scone shortcake is the original, many variations are made with sponge and butter cakes.

Shortcakes
- 2 cups all-purpose flour
- ¼ cup light brown sugar
- 2½ teaspoons baking powder
- ⅛ teaspoon salt
- 6 tablespoons unsalted butter, chilled and cut into cubes
- 1 cup heavy cream

Toppings
- 4 pints strawberries, washed and hulled
- 3 tablespoons granulated sugar
- 2 cups whipped cream (page 323)

Makes 8 individual-serving cakes

TO PREPARE
Preheat the oven to 400°F. Butter two baking sheets.

TO MAKE THE SHORTCAKES
Combine the flour, sugar, baking powder, and salt in a food processor or blender and pulse to blend. Add the butter to the mixture and blend for about 30 seconds, until crumbly. Pour in the heavy cream and process until moist, about 30 seconds.

Roll out the dough to ¾-inch thickness on a floured work surface. Cut out 3-inch circles with a cookie cutter or drinking glass.

TO BAKE
Transfer the shortcakes to the baking sheets and bake for 12 to 15 minutes, until golden. Transfer the shortcakes to a rack to cool.

TO PREPARE THE STRAWBERRIES
Reserve one whole strawberry for each serving. Slice the rest of the strawberries and mix with the sugar.

TO ASSEMBLE
Once the shortcakes are cool, use a serrated knife to slice each one in half. Arrange on serving plates, with the cut sides facing up. Top with sliced strawberries, whipped cream, and one whole strawberry for each serving.

VARIATIONS
Hawaiian Shortcakes
Replace the strawberries with a tropical fruit mixture: Cut 1 small pineapple, 1 small papaya, and 2 mangos into chunks, and combine the fruit chunks with ½ cup chopped macadamia nuts and 1 tablespoon lime juice. Top the shortcakes with the fruit mixture, whipped cream, and flaked coconut.

Sour Cherry Shortcakes
Replace the strawberries with 3 cups pitted sour cherries mixed with ¼ cup brandy and ½ cup sugar. Top the shortcakes with the sour cherry mixture, whipped cream, and whole cherries.

Sponge Strawberry Shortcake
Prepare the Victoria sponge cake batter (page 136). Bake in individual serving molds for 20 to 25 minutes, until golden. Assemble with fresh strawberries and cream.

Strawberry Lemon Cake
Prepare the lemon poppyseed loaves (page 177). Slice the loaves into individual servings and top with strawberries and whipped cream.

Shortcake Parties

Colonial Americans refined the dough for Scottish scones to make the classic shortcake, which they topped with fresh strawberries and whipped cream. The cake was intended to be a celebration of the arrival of summer, as strawberries are among the earliest plants to bear fruit. Shortcake parties became a popular trend in the 1840s and 1850s, and the completion of the transcontinental railroad in 1869 made it possible to transport the berries on ice, so that people across the country could host these events, regardless of the temperature outside. Though shortcake parties have lost steam, I think they're a tradition worth reviving. Try overindulging your own guests at a summer party with these simple cakes we all know and love.

Funnel Cakes

Just thinking about funnel cakes makes me happy. Funnel cakes have evolved from traditional Amish cakes to the ultimate American festival food. Carnivals, street fairs, seaside boardwalks, Renaissance festivals — all sell funnel cakes. These iconic flat cakes are easy to prepare at home. Top them with confectioners' sugar, cinnamon sugar, fruit, chocolate syrup, jam, or nuts.

Fried Cakes

- 2½ cups all-purpose flour
- ¼ cup sugar
- 2 teaspoons baking powder
- ½ teaspoon salt
- 2 eggs
- 1½ cups milk
- 1 teaspoon vanilla extract
- 3 cups vegetable oil

Toppings

- 2 cups sliced strawberries
- 2 cups whipped cream (page 323)

Makes 6 individual-serving cakes

TO MAKE THE BATTER

Combine the flour, sugar, baking powder, and salt; set aside. In a separate bowl, beat the eggs, milk, and vanilla until frothy. Gradually add the flour mixture to the egg mixture until blended.

TO COOK

Pour the oil into a heavy-bottomed pot, and warm over medium heat. Line plates with paper towels for draining the fried cakes. Place a small piece of bread in the oil to test its temperature. When the bread browns, the oil is ready.

Make one cake at a time. Use a funnel with a ⅝-inch opening to pour the batter into the oil, pouring from the center outward, creating a 6-inch round, lacy web. When the cake bottom is lightly browned, use tongs to flip the cake and brown the other side. When it is browned on both sides, use tongs to remove the cake from the pot and place it on paper towels to drain.

TO SERVE

Transfer each cake to a serving plate and top with strawberries and whipped cream.

Amish Cakes

The Amish have no use for art that serves no function; instead they have made their "useful" cakes into masterpieces. Originally German settlers, they brought their prolific baking skills with them to the New World. Baking continues to be an important part of daily rituals and the Amish plain-life philosophy. We owe many of our great American cakes to the Amish, including funnel cakes, angel food cake (page 34), whoopee pies, and shoo-fly pie.

VARIATIONS

Austrian Strauben

When pouring batter into the oil, shape it into a spiral. Top with chocolate hazelnut spread (like Nutella) or plum jam.

Finnish Tippaleipä

Replace the all-purpose flour with whole-wheat flour. Use a small saucepan and layer the dough in ribbons on top of each other to form a brainlike structure. Top the fried cake with confectioners' sugar.

Mexican Funnel Cakes (Apple Fries)

Add 1 cup finely chopped apples to the batter. Top the fried cake with cinnamon sugar.

International "Funnel" Cakes

Variations of funnel cakes can be found all the world round. As an example, the Finnish tippaleipä, traditionally prepared for May Day, is a mound of strings of dough, looking not unlike a bird's nest, sprinkled with sugar. The Indian jalebi (page 253) is also made of dough strings, though it's flat and traditionally soaked in saffron syrup. Mexican funnel cakes, also called apple fries, are layered in stacks and topped with cinnamon sugar. And the Austrian strauben is shaped like a spiral and topped with chocolate hazelnut spread or plum jam.

New York Cheesecake

No cheesecake is as famous as the smooth, cream cheese–based New York cheesecake. This style of cheesecake is also made in Europe, Asia, and South America, with native flavorings and crusts. In fact, you can make your own variation by substituting your favorite flavorings for the ones called for here.

Crust
- 1½ cups graham cracker crumbs
- 3 tablespoons granulated sugar
- 5 tablespoons unsalted butter, melted
- 1 teaspoon honey

Filling
- 5 (8-ounce) bars cream cheese, softened
- 2 tablespoons all-purpose flour
- 1½ cups granulated sugar
- 1 tablespoon confectioners' sugar
- ½ teaspoon cornstarch
- 2 egg yolks, at room temperature
- 1½ teaspoons vanilla extract
- 5 eggs, at room temperature
- Zest of ½ lemon, grated

Toppings
- 2 cups whipped cream (page 323)
- 1 whole strawberry

Makes 1 cake (serves 6 to 8)

TO PREPARE

Preheat the oven to 400°F. Butter and flour a 10-inch round springform pan, and line its outer seam with aluminum foil to prevent leaks. Prepare a water bath: Set the springform pan in another pan that is at least 2 inches larger all around. Pour water into the larger pan until it is half full. Then remove the springform pan and set the larger pan in the oven to preheat.

TO MAKE THE CRUST

Combine the graham cracker crumbs and sugar in a medium bowl. Stir in the butter and honey to moisten the mixture. Press the mixture into the bottom of the prepared pan; set aside.

TO MAKE THE CAKE

Combine the cream cheese, flour, granulated sugar, confectioners' sugar, and cornstarch in a large bowl and beat with a mixer until blended. Beat in the egg yolks and vanilla. Add the whole eggs, one at a time, beating well after each addition. When the mixture is blended, stir in the lemon zest. Pour the batter on top of the crust.

TO BAKE

Place the cake pan in the preheated water bath. Bake for 10 minutes, then lower the oven temperature to 200°F and bake for 40 to 50 minutes longer, or until the top is lightly browned. You will know the cake is ready when it feels bouncy to the touch, or a knife inserted in the center comes out clean.

TO SERVE

Remove from the pan. Spread a thin layer of whipped cream over the top of the cheesecake. Pipe more whipped cream around the edge and place a strawberry in the center. Serve at room temperature. If you need to store the cake or leftovers, cover and refrigerate, and bring back to room temperature before serving.

VARIATIONS

Canadian Blueberry Cheesecake
Pour 1½ cups chopped blueberries into the batter before baking. After the cake is baked, top with 1½ cups blueberry sauce (page 320).

Caribbean Coconut-Rum Cheesecake
Add ½ cup shredded sweetened coconut to the crust. Replace the vanilla with 3 tablespoons dark rum.

Florida Keys Lime Cheesecake
Replace the lemon zest with lime zest. Replace the vanilla with 1 tablespoon lime juice.

Ginger Cheesecake
Replace the graham crackers with gingersnaps. Add ½ teaspoon fresh ginger to the batter.

Swiss Chocolate Cheesecake
Replace the graham crackers with chocolate cookies. Add ¼ cup unsweetened cocoa powder and 1½ cups chopped Swiss chocolate to the batter.

Ugandan Peanut Butter Cheesecake
Replace the graham crackers with peanut butter cookies. Before pouring in the batter, spread ¼ cup peanut butter on the crust and swirl ¼ cup peanut butter into the batter.

The Jewish Deli Connection

When Jews from central and eastern Europe emigrated to America, many settled in New York City, and they brought with them Old World cheesecake recipes. Here they encountered cream cheese, invented in 1872 in Chester, New York. Arthur Reuben Jr., the owner of Reuben's Deli, was the first of several Jewish deli owners in New York City to replace Old World cheeses such as quark, Neufchâtel, and cottage cheeses with cream cheese in his cheesecakes. The cream cheese made the cake creamier and somewhat crumblier when cut. In 1939 Reuben's cake, simple and unadorned, with just a tinge of lemon, won the gold medal at the New York World's Fair. Shortly after, Leo Linderman, owner of Lindy's Deli, started creating decadent cream-cheese cheesecakes with fruit toppings. Soon, Jewish delis across the city joined the competition for the best cheesecake recipe. Since then, New York cheesecake has made its way across the country and around the globe.

Apple Stack Cake

In a traditional apple stack the cakes are shortbread flat cakes cooked in a cast-iron skillet, but I like to prepare the cakes with butter and bake them in the oven. Any type of apple spread — apple filling, applesauce, apple jelly, apple glaze, or apple butter — can be used as the filling between the layers.

Cake

- 3½ cups all-purpose flour, sifted
- ½ teaspoon baking powder
- ¼ teaspoon salt
- 1 teaspoon ground ginger
- 1 teaspoon ground cinnamon
- ¼ teaspoon ground allspice
- ¾ cup (1½ sticks) unsalted butter, softened
- 1 cup dark brown sugar
- 2 eggs, beaten
- ¾ cup buttermilk
- ⅓ cup molasses
- 1 teaspoon vanilla extract

Apple Filling

- 1 tablespoon unsalted butter
- 6 apples, thinly sliced (an assortment works well)
- ½ cup apple juice
- 3 tablespoons sugar
- ½ teaspoon cornstarch

Toppings

- Apple glaze (page 318)
- 1 teaspoon confectioners' sugar

Makes 1 cake (serves 6 to 8)

TO PREPARE

Preheat the oven to 350°F. Generously butter and flour three 7-inch round cake pans.

TO MAKE THE CAKE

Mix together the flour, baking powder, salt, ginger, cinnamon, and allspice in a large bowl; set aside. In a separate medium bowl, use a mixer to cream the butter and sugar. Add the eggs, buttermilk, molasses, and vanilla, and blend until combined. Gradually add the dry ingredients and stir well until blended.

TO BAKE

Roll out the dough with a rolling pin to ¼-inch thickness. Use a knife to cut the dough to fit the prepared pans. Transfer the dough to the pans and bake for 10 to 12 minutes, until lightly browned. Let cool in the pans for 5 minutes, then remove the cakes from the pans and set on a rack to finish cooling. Repeat until all the dough is used up; you should be able to make six cakes in all.

TO PREPARE THE APPLE FILLING

Melt the butter in a large skillet over medium heat. Add the apples and sauté for 2 minutes, stirring occasionally. Add the apple juice, sugar, and cornstarch, and stir. Cover and cook for 4 to 5 minutes, until the apples are softened. Drain off the liquid.

TO ASSEMBLE

Place one cake on a serving dish as the bottom layer. Spread 3 tablespoons apple glaze and ¼ cup sautéed apples on it. Add the next cake layer and repeat. Top the stack with one final cake layer, and dust with confectioners' sugar.

VARIATIONS

Apricot Stack Cake
Use apricot glaze (page 318) and sautéed apricots instead of apple glaze and sautéed apples.

Date Stack Cake
Use date filling (page 321) instead of apple glaze and sautéed apples.

Raspberry Stack Cake
Use raspberry filling (page 322) and fresh raspberries instead of apple glaze and sautéed apples.

Stacked Spice Cake
Use spice cake for the layers; Grenada spice cake (page 67) would work well for this variation.

Appalachian Wedding Cake

In the past in Appalachia, a traditionally poor region of the United States, weddings were casual gatherings often celebrated with potluck food. A bakery wedding cake would be an extravagance, even for this most special occasion. Instead, the apple stack tradition evolved, and it is still practiced today as a form of entertainment to bring guests together.

All of the wedding guests share in the effort of creating the cake by baking one of its layers. The number of layers in the wedding cake stack gauges the couple's popularity. The family of the bride cooks, sweetens, and spices the apples to spread between the layers. At the wedding the guests join in the fun of assembling the cake, trying not to topple it over. Making a stack cake can be so much fun that today it is also prepared and served at family reunions, church suppers, and other large gatherings.

Cherokee Wild Huckleberry Cake

Thanksgiving, the biggest harvest festival celebrated in North America, is usually thought of as a pie holiday — pumpkin, pecan, sweet potato, apple, and so on. It's about time for it to have its own cake, and what could be better than a cake that pays homage to Native Americans, the original colonizers of this continent? This huckleberry cake marries traditional Cherokee foods (native huckleberries, walnuts, honey, and corn flour) with an English honey-butter cake. Huckleberries are similar to blueberries, although they are a bit more tart.

Cake

- 1½ cups all-purpose flour
- ¾ cup corn flour or masa harina
- 2½ teaspoons baking powder
- ⅛ teaspoon salt
- ¾ cup (1½ sticks) unsalted butter, softened
- ¾ cup sugar
- 4 eggs, beaten
- ¾ cup milk
- ¾ cup honey (flavored honey, such as orange, sage, or lavender, works well)
- 1½ cups fresh huckleberries
- ¾ cup walnuts

Glazed Nuts and Berries

- 2 tablespoons honey
- 2 tablespoons water
- ⅓ cup huckleberries
- ¼ cup chopped walnuts

Makes 1 cake (serves 6 to 8)

TO PREPARE
Preheat the oven to 350°F. Butter and flour an 8-inch dome cake pan (or a 9-inch square cake pan).

TO MAKE THE CAKE
Combine the flours, baking powder, and salt; set aside. In a separate large bowl, use a mixer to cream the butter and the sugar until light and fluffy. Add the eggs, milk, and honey and beat well. Slowly blend the flour mixture into the butter mixture. Gently stir in the huckleberries and walnuts.

TO BAKE
Pour the batter into the prepared pan. Bake for 35 to 45 minutes, until a knife inserted in the center comes out clean. Let cool in its pan.

TO GLAZE THE NUTS AND BERRIES
Thin the honey with the water in a skillet over medium heat. Add the huckleberries and walnuts and cook for 1 minute, stirring to coat.

TO SERVE
Flip the cake onto a serving plate, domed side up. Top with the glazed nuts and berries.

VARIATIONS

Blueberry Honey Cake
Replace the huckleberries with blueberries.

Cranberry Honey Cake
Replace the huckleberries with cranberries and omit the nuts.

Cherokee Baking

The early Cherokee were farmers and wildcrafters, growing corn and squashes, collecting nuts and berries, and hunting fish and game. Before Europeans had made inroads into the New World, the Cherokee, like most Native Americans, made flat cakes from grain, in their case corn. As happens everywhere when cultures meet, the European colonization of the Americas led to fusion cuisine. The Cherokee got the buzz for baking, making European-style cakes with corn flour, berries, and nuts, and honey as the sweetener. Such cakes remain popular today, the true progeny of native New World cakes.

Cinnamon Buttermilk Doughnuts

This is a good basic buttermilk doughnut recipe. The potatoes in the batter give the doughnuts durability, so they'll last longer than a day. If you don't have a doughnut cutter, use two round cookie cutters or drinking glasses of different sizes to make the rings.

Doughnuts

1½	cups peeled, diced potatoes
2¾	cups all-purpose flour
2½	cups cake flour
½	cup powdered milk
1	tablespoon baking powder
2	teaspoons baking soda
1½	teaspoons cinnamon
⅔	teaspoon salt
¾	cup sugar
¾	cup buttermilk
½	cup sour cream
3	eggs
3	egg yolks
2	tablespoons unsalted butter, melted
2	tablespoons honey
1½	teaspoons vanilla extract
	Vegetable oil for frying

Toppings

1½ cups any icing or glaze (see Appendix, page 314)

Any topping (such as confectioners' sugar, shredded coconut, chopped nuts, candied citrus peel, chopped dried berries, or seeds)

Makes 18 doughnuts

TO MAKE THE BATTER

Place the potatoes in a saucepan and add water to cover by a couple of inches. Bring to a boil, reduce heat, and simmer for 10 to 12 minutes, until the potatoes are soft. Drain, mash, and let cool.

Combine the all-purpose flour, cake flour, powdered milk, baking powder, baking soda, cinnamon, and salt in a large bowl; set aside. In a separate bowl, cream the potatoes and sugar until smooth. Stir in the buttermilk, sour cream, whole eggs, egg yolks, melted butter, honey, and vanilla until blended. Add the flour mixture and stir to combine. Cover the batter and chill in the refrigerator for 30 minutes.

TO SHAPE

When the dough is chilled, roll it out to ⅝-inch thickness on a floured work surface. Cut rings with a doughnut cutter or two cookie cutters or glasses, with each ring about 3 inches in diameter and the hole about 1 inch in diameter.

TO COOK

Fill a heavy-bottomed pot with a couple of inches of oil, and heat the oil to 365°F. Line a plate with paper towels for draining.

Drop a few of the rings into the hot oil, leaving enough space between them that they can move freely. Fry for 3 to 4 minutes on each side, until brown. Use a slotted spoon to transfer the fried doughnuts to the prepared plate to drain. After the first batch, test one doughnut for doneness by cutting into it to see if the center is cooked. Adjust the cooking time if needed. Continue frying rings until the batter is used up.

TO SERVE

If you like, dip the doughnuts into a glaze or ice them, and add toppings. Let set for 15 minutes. Serve with a nice cup of joe.

History of the Doughnut Shop

Deep-fried cakes have been around for centuries. But the true American doughnut — the ring-shaped cake that is fried and then glazed or sugared — did not become wildly popular until the invention of the doughnut cutter in the late nineteenth century. In the 1920s, the first doughnut machine, which automatically cuts and fries doughnuts, was created. The machine's low cost and ease of operation allowed anyone — not just professional bakers — to make doughnuts well and efficiently, and in the decades that followed doughnut shops became a fixture of the American landscape.

While there is nothing quite like fresh doughnuts in the morning, doughnuts were originally considered snack cakes, not breakfast cakes. But when chains like Krispy Creme and Dunkin' Donuts began serving coffee alongside their doughnuts, the cakes soon became a morning favorite. By the midtwentieth century, doughnuts were quintessential American food. In fact, during World War II, to boost morale the American Red Cross brought doughnuts and coffee to U.S. soldiers stationed in Europe and the Pacific — 1.6 billion doughnuts total!

Red Velvet Cake

This red-dyed chocolate cake is a specialty of the American South. It has a wide-ranging flavor appeal: a bit of sweet from the sugar, a bit of sour from the vinegar and buttermilk, and some bitter from the chocolate. White boiled icing with a hint of cream cheese glazes all three layers, adorned with red cake crumbs. For a wedding cake pull (see page 47), ribbons and a rose-petal topping make a beautiful presentation.

Cake

3	cups all-purpose flour
⅔	cup unsweetened cocoa powder
2½	teaspoons baking powder
1	teaspoon baking soda
1	teaspoon salt
¾	cup (1½ sticks) unsalted butter, softened
2	cups granulated sugar
3	eggs, at room temperature
2	teaspoons vanilla extract
1½	cups buttermilk
⅔	cup canola oil
1	tablespoon vinegar
	Red food coloring
¼	cup bitter dark chocolate, melted and cooled

Cream Cheese Boiled Icing

1¼	cups milk
1¼	cups granulated sugar
¼	cup all-purpose flour
⅛	teaspoon salt
2	teaspoons vanilla extract
¾	cup (1½ sticks) unsalted butter, softened
6	ounces cream cheese, softened

For Cake Pull

3	red roses
½	teaspoon confectioners' sugar
½	teaspoon granulated sugar
	Charms tied to ribbons (one per guest)

Makes 1 cake (serves 6 to 8)

TO PREPARE
Preheat the oven to 350°F. Butter and flour three 8-inch round cake pans.

TO MAKE THE CAKE
Combine the flour, cocoa powder, baking powder, baking soda, and salt in a medium bowl; set aside. In a separate medium bowl, use a mixer to cream the butter and sugar. Beat in the eggs and vanilla until well blended. In another small mixing bowl, stir together the buttermilk, oil, and vinegar, and tint the mixture with red food coloring (about 6 drops). Gradually beat the flour mixture into the butter mixture, alternating with the buttermilk mixture, until well combined. Stir in the melted chocolate.

TO BAKE
Pour the batter into the prepared cake pans. Bake for 35 to 40 minutes, until a knife inserted in the center comes out clean. Let cool in the pans.

TO MAKE THE CRUMBS
Remove the cakes from the pans. Preheat the oven to 200°F. Trim the tops of the cakes so that they are each the same height and have a flat top. Place the cake tops you cut away on a baking tray, and bake for 20 to 25 minutes, until dry. Pulse in a food processor to create crumbs.

TO MAKE THE CREAM CHEESE ICING
Combine the milk and sugar in a medium saucepan, and cook over low heat until the sugar has dissolved. Whisk in the flour and salt and boil for 1 to 2 minutes, until thickened. Remove the pan from the heat and stir in the vanilla. Chill the mixture in the refrigerator for 30 minutes.

Beat the butter and cream cheese until creamy. Beat in the chilled milk mixture until fluffy, 2 to 3 minutes.

TO SERVE
Stack the three cake layers, using the cream cheese icing as a filling between them. Spread more icing over the top and sides of the cake. Spread the cake crumbs over the sides and top, in a pattern or free-form. Refrigerate for 1 hour to let set.

TO PREPARE FOR A CAKE PULL
Top the cake with rose petals and sprinkle with the sugars. Carefully push the charms into the sides of the cake, leaving the ribbons dangling free.

VARIATION
Beet Red Velvet Cake
Increase the flour to 3½ cups. Add 1 cup puréed roasted beets or beet baby food.

A Touch of Red

The color of red velvet cake ranges from a dark red to bright red to brown-red. The first appearance of the color is unknown, though (unsubstantiated) theories abound. Some say the color was intended simply to make the cake distinctive. Others say a chemical reaction between the early types of cocoa powder and buttermilk may have yielded a reddish hue. Still others claim that the use of beets as a sweetener, from a time when sugar was scarce, resulted in a reddish cake. Perhaps we'll never know the reason for the red. But theoretics aside, these days the redder the cake, the better.

The Cake Pull

The cake pull is a quaint bridesmaids' ritual dating back to the Victorian era in the South. Back then it took place at the wedding reception; today it is usually part of the bridal shower or bridesmaids' luncheon. Tiny silver charms attached to ribbons are hidden inside a small tiered cake. Women and girls gather around the cake, each taking a ribbon, and all simultaneously pull their ribbon to reveal the charms. Each charm is said to foretell the recipient's future, whether marriage, children, travel, or wealth. The dreaded thimble is said to predict that the unlucky woman who pulled it will be a spinster. Today, to lighten things up a bit, you will also find charms that represent hobbies and careers, such as tennis rackets and cell phones. Variations of the cake pull are also common at girls' coming-of-age events, including debutante balls, sweet 16 parties, and quinceañeras (see page 81).

German Chocolate Cake

The classic recipe for German chocolate cake features sweet baking chocolate, coconut, and pecans. I add coconut milk and chocolate chunks to boost the coconut-chocolate flavor. To offer a visual cue of the flavor, I use coconut frosting and garnish it with large coconut curls, chocolate shavings, and pecan brittle.

Chocolate Cake

- ½ cup water
- 6 ounces German's Sweet Chocolate (or any sweet chocolate), chopped
- 2 teaspoons vanilla extract
- 2 cups all-purpose flour
- 1 teaspoon baking soda
- ¼ teaspoon salt
- 1 cup (2 sticks) unsalted butter, softened
- 2 cups granulated sugar
- 4 eggs, separated
- ½ cup milk
- ½ cup coconut milk

Pecan Brittle

- 1 cup pecan halves
- 1 cup granulated sugar
- ½ cup light corn syrup
- 1 tablespoon unsalted butter, softened
- 1 teaspoon vanilla extract

Coconut-Pecan Filling

- ¾ cup coconut milk
- ¾ cup evaporated milk
- 4 egg yolks
- 2 ounces German's Sweet Chocolate (or any sweet chocolate), chopped
- 1 teaspoon vanilla extract
- 1 teaspoon light rum
- 1½ cups granulated sugar
- ¾ cup (1½ sticks) unsalted butter
- 2⅔ cups flaked unsweetened coconut
- 1½ cups chopped pecans

Coconut-Cream Cheese Frosting

- 8 ounces cream cheese, softened
- 4 tablespoons unsalted butter, softened
- ½ teaspoon coconut extract
- 1½ cups confectioners' sugar
- ¼ cup coconut milk

Other Toppings

- 2 ounces German's Sweet Chocolate (or any sweet chocolate), shaved into curls
- ½ coconut, shaved into curls

Makes 1 cake (serves 6 to 8)

TO PREPARE

Preheat the oven to 350°F. Butter and flour three 9-inch round cake pans.

TO MAKE THE CAKE

Bring the water to a boil. Pour the boiling water over 4 ounces of the chopped chocolate. Stir in the vanilla and let sit until the chocolate is melted; set aside. Combine the flour, baking soda, and salt in a medium bowl; set aside.

Cream the butter and sugar until light and fluffy. Add the egg yolks, one at a time, beating well after each addition. Stir in the melted chocolate. Add the flour mixture, alternating with the milk and coconut milk, mixing until blended. Stir in the remaining 2 ounces chopped chocolate. Separately, beat the egg whites until stiff peaks form; fold into the batter.

TO BAKE

Divide the batter among the prepared pans and bake for 30 to 35 minutes, until a knife inserted in the center comes out clean. Let cool in the pans for 10 minutes, then remove from the pans and set on a rack to finish cooling.

TO MAKE THE PECAN BRITTLE

Generously butter a large baking sheet. Heat the pecans, sugar, and corn syrup in a saucepan. Cook over medium heat, stirring, until the syrup is golden. Remove from the heat and add the butter and vanilla, stirring until the butter's melted. Quickly pour the mixture onto the prepared baking sheet, spreading it thin. Let the brittle cool and harden, then break into small pieces.

TO MAKE THE FILLING

Heat the coconut milk, evaporated milk, egg yolks, chocolate, and vanilla in a large saucepan, beating with a whisk until blended. Add the rum, sugar, and butter, and cook, stirring, for 10 to 12 minutes, until thickened. Remove from heat. Stir in the coconut and pecans and mix well. Let cool.

TO MAKE THE FROSTING

Beat the cream cheese, butter, and coconut extract until smooth. Beat in the confectioners' sugar and coconut milk a bit at a time, until the frosting reaches the desired spreading consistency.

TO MAKE TOASTED COCONUT CURLS

Preheat the oven to 350°F. Scatter the coconut shavings on a baking tray, and put the tray in the oven. After 2 minutes, use a spatula to toss the curls on the tray, and toast for an additional 1 to 2 minutes, until lightly browned.

TO ASSEMBLE

Stack the cake layers, spreading the coconut-pecan filling between them. Frost the cake with the coconut–cream cheese frosting. Decorate with coconut curls, pecan brittle, and chocolate shavings.

VARIATION

Banana Cake with Coconut-Pecan Filling

Prepare Kenyan banana cake (page 221) instead of German chocolate cake. Follow the instructions above for the filling, frosting, and brittle.

German Chocolate Cupcakes

Divide the batter among buttered and floured large muffin pans. Bake for 18 to 22 minutes. Top with coconut-pecan filling. Pipe coconut–cream cheese frosting onto the middle of each cupcake. Top with pecan brittle.

German's Sweet Chocolate

German chocolate cake is not a German creation. Instead, it's named for the chocolate that was first used to make it. In the midnineteenth century, Englishman Samuel German wanted a baking chocolate that was sweeter than the Dutch-processed cocoa powder that was being used for baking. He added sugar, chocolate liqueur, and other flavorings to his chocolate, and in 1852 Baker's Chocolate Company began selling this new sweet baking chocolate, which it called German's Sweet Chocolate.

Though cakes with German's Sweet Chocolate were common across the American South, the first recognized recipe for what we now consider classic German chocolate cake, layered with coconut-pecan filling, came from a homemaker in Dallas, Texas, who submitted the recipe to a newspaper in 1957 as "German's Chocolate Cake." The recipe was widely reprinted, and as the cake gained popularity, the possessive "s" was lost from its name, making it simply German chocolate cake, which is what we still call it today.

King Cake

Christians around the world boast their own version of king cake, which is named for the three Magi, or kings, who came to honor the baby Jesus. The Magi arrived on the twelfth night after Jesus' birth, the day known as Epiphany (January 6), and thus the cake is also known as Twelfth Night cake or Epiphany cake. The New Orleans king cake is a round or oval coffee cake–like pastry, rolled or braided into a ring. It is traditionally topped with icing and sugars in Mardi Gras colors, with purple representing justice, gold representing power, and green representing faith. The cake may be filled with a variety of fillings, from apple or cherry preserves to cream cheese or almond paste.

Dough

- 1 tablespoon active dry yeast
- 1 cup warm water
- ½ cup sugar
- ½ cup milk, warmed
- 4¾ cups all-purpose flour
- 2 teaspoons salt
- 1 teaspoon grated nutmeg
- 1 teaspoon ground cinnamon
- 1 teaspoon grated lemon zest
- ½ cup (1 stick) unsalted butter, softened
- 5 egg yolks

Assembly

- 1½ cups cream cheese filling (page 321)
- 1 tiny (1-inch) plastic baby or hard candy
- 1 egg white
- 1 tablespoon milk
- 1 cup lemon icing (page 316)
- 1 tablespoon each red, green, and gold colored sugars
- ¼ cup candied cherries, halved (optional)

Makes 1 cake (serves 6 to 8)

TO PREPARE

Dissolve the yeast in the water. Add 1 tablespoon of sugar and the milk. Let sit for 10 minutes.

TO MAKE THE DOUGH

Combine the flour, salt, nutmeg, cinnamon, and lemon zest in a food processor or blender. Pulse three to five times to combine.

In a separate bowl, cream the butter and the remaining sugar until fluffy. Beat in the egg yolks. Gradually add the butter mixture to the flour mixture and process until coarse. Then add the yeast mixture. Pulse eight to ten times, until the dough forms a ball. If it is too sticky, add more flour, 1 tablespoon at a time. If it is too dry, add more water, 1 tablespoon at a time. Place the dough in an oiled bowl and cover. Let sit in a warm, dry place for at least 2 hours, until the dough doubles in volume.

TO ASSEMBLE

Butter a large baking sheet. When the dough is ready, punch it down a couple of times to flatten it a bit. Divide the dough into three equal pieces. Roll out one piece on a floured work surface to about 12 inches by 4 inches with a thickness of about ⅜ inch. Spread one-third of the cream cheese filling over the dough, leaving a bare 1 inch on all sides. Then roll up the long side of the dough, forming a long cylinder, and pinch the edges to seal. Repeat with the other two pieces of dough.

Braid the three cylinders together, then wrap the braid into a circle. Where the ends come together, insert the plastic baby, and pinch the ends together to seal, smoothing the dough to hide the seam. Transfer the ring to the prepared baking sheet and cover with plastic wrap. Let sit for 45 minutes, or until the dough doubles in volume.

TO BAKE

Preheat the oven to 350°F. Beat the egg white with the milk. When the dough is risen, brush it with the egg white mixture. Place the cake in the oven and bake for 35 to 40 minutes, until golden, or a thermometer reads 200 to 210°F. Let cool.

TO SERVE

Pour or pipe lemon icing over the cake. Sprinkle immediately with colored sugars and candied cherries, if desired. Let the topping set before serving.

VARIATIONS

Apple King Cake
Replace the cream cheese filling with 1½ cups apple-raisin filling (page 112).

Cherry–Cream Cheese King Cake
Roll 1½ cups cherry filling (page 321) into the dough along with the cream cheese filling.

Chocolate–Cream Cheese King Cake
Add 1½ cups chocolate chips to the cream cheese filling.

Date King Cake
Replace the cream cheese filling with 2 cups date filling (page 321).

French Galette des Rois
Omit the colored sugar. Top the cake with a golden paper crown.

Mexican Rosca de Reyes
Replace the cream cheese filling with a mixture of ½ cup chopped dried figs, 1 chopped fresh quince, and ¾ cup chopped candied cherries. Top with lemon icing, figs, and cherries.

Portuguese Bolo Rei
Add ½ cup raisins, ½ cup chopped walnuts, and ¼ cup chopped citrus peel to the dough. Top with raisins, nuts, and citrus peel. Traditionally bolo rei is eaten in the days between Christmas and Epiphany.

Spanish Tortell
Add 3 cups marzipan (page 324) and ¼ cup chopped candied red cherries, ¼ cup chopped candied green cherries, and ¼ cup chopped citrus peel to the center before rolling. Top with candied cherries and citrus peel.

King Cake Traditions

The French brought king cake to New Orleans in the eighteenth century, and for a hundred years this cake was associated with the Feast of Epiphany on January 6. A bean, a pea, or a small trinket would be baked into the cake, and the person who found the hidden item was named king of the feast, said to have good luck for the next year.

Over time, the king cake became the official cake of Mardi Gras, the New Orleans carnival that kicks off on Epiphany and ends on Shrove Tuesday. No Mardi Gras party is complete without its king cake. Instead of a bean or trinket, Mardi Gras king cakes have a small ceramic or plastic baby baked into them, said to represent the baby Jesus. The person who finds the baby is charged with, among other duties onerous or joyous, bringing the king cake to the next Mardi Gras party.

Devil's Food Cupcakes

I'm often asked, "If you had to choose just one, what would be your favorite cake?" This is it. I live for chocolate. And I love other chocolate cakes, but devil's food is a classic, a simple, rich cake that is marvelous on its own and can also serve as the base for many other cakes. I often prepare devil's food as cupcakes (this recipe makes 18) and top them with chocolate buttercream. The subtly different chocolate flavors of the cake and frosting really make an outstanding combination.

Cupcakes

- 1 cup water
- 4 ounces semisweet chocolate, cut into chunks
- 2¼ cups cake flour
- 1½ teaspoons baking powder
- 1 teaspoon baking soda
- ¼ teaspoon salt
- 1 cup (2 sticks) unsalted butter, softened
- 1½ cups dark brown sugar
- 1 cup granulated sugar
- 3 eggs
- 2 teaspoons vanilla extract
- ½ cup buttermilk

Topping

- 4½ cups semisweet chocolate buttercream (page 317)

Makes 18 cupcakes

TO PREPARE

Preheat the oven to 350°F. Prepare two cupcake pans with liners.

TO MAKE THE CUPCAKES

Bring the water to a boil. Drop the chocolate into the boiling water and stir until melted. Set aside to cool.

Combine the flour, baking powder, baking soda, and salt in a medium bowl; set aside. In a separate large bowl, cream the butter, brown sugar, and granulated sugar until fluffy. Add the eggs one at a time, beating well after each addition. Stir in the vanilla and the melted chocolate. Gradually add the flour mixture, alternating with the buttermilk; mix until well blended.

TO BAKE

Divide the batter between the prepared pans and bake for 18 to 22 minutes, until a knife inserted in the center comes out clean. Let the cakes cool in the pans for 5 minutes, then remove them from the pans and set on a rack to finish cooling.

TO FROST

Frost the cupcakes with the chocolate buttercream. For flair, use a pastry bag with a large star tip to pipe the frosting in a towering spiral.

VARIATIONS

Australian Butterfly Cakes

Cut the rounded top off each cupcake, and cut the top into two V-shaped wedges to look like wings. Frost the cupcakes with cream cheese frosting (page 316) and place the wings on top. Add sprinkles and sparkly sugar.

Devil's Food Cake with Chocolate Ganache

Pour the batter into two 8-inch round cake pans, and bake for 30 to 35 minutes, until a knife inserted in the center comes out clean. When the cakes are cooled, stack them, using 1½ cups chocolate ganache (page 315) to fill and top the cakes.

Devil's Food and Angel's Food

Though they bear similar names, devil's food cake is not a chocolate version of angel food cake (page 34). Angel food cake is a sponge cake made without any fat. Devil's food cake is a rich butter cake, with a double dose of chocolate. The name addresses its darkness and richness.

The History of the Cupcake

Cupcakes came into being in nineteenth-century America and England. They are said to have been called "cup" cakes because their ingredients were measured out in cups, rather than being weighed. This practice, though common now, was revolutionary then, and it saved cooks considerable time. The name is also sometimes attributed to the then-novel practice of baking cakes in small cups. These small cakes baked quickly, relieving the baker of the stress of trying to bake a large cake in a hearth oven, which not infrequently resulted in a burned cake.

Throughout the twentieth century, cupcakes gained popularity as kids' treats. Since the advent of the twenty-first century, people of all ages have become crazy about these small cakes. Cupcakes are gourmet, playful, hip, and glamorous. You can find cupcake bakeries around the world, wedding cakes composed entirely of cupcakes, cookbooks and magazines devoted to cupcakes, and much more. This craze is here to stay.

Cranberry Quatre Quarts
(Pound Cake)

The pound cake's name derives from its traditional ingredients: 1 pound each of flour, butter, eggs, and sugar. The French *quatre quarts* translates as "four fourths," meaning all four ingredients are used in equal amounts. (If you want to try baking this cake the old-fashioned way, weigh the eggs first, then weigh the other ingredients to the same weight.) French-Canadians have a particular affinity for the quatre quarts for harvest celebrations and have developed many variations with local cranberries, apples, maple syrup, and walnuts. This version uses cranberries in the cake and as a topping; they can, of course, be omitted for a plainer version.

Cake

- ¾ cup (1½ sticks) unsalted butter
- ¾ cup sugar
- 3 eggs, separated
- 1¼ cups flour
- 1 teaspoon vanilla extract
- ¼ teaspoon salt
- 1 cup fresh cranberries

Toppings

- 1 cup cranberry icing (page 315)
- 2 tablespoons chopped dried cranberries

Makes 1 cake (serves 6 to 8)

TO PREPARE

Preheat the oven to 350°F. Butter and flour an 8-inch loaf pan.

TO MAKE THE CAKE

Cream the butter and sugar with a mixer until light and fluffy. Add the egg yolks, one at a time, beating well after each addition. Gradually add the flour and blend well. Stir in the vanilla, and set aside.

Add the salt to the egg whites and beat until stiff. Delicately fold first the egg whites and then the cranberries into the batter, until blended.

TO BAKE

Pour the batter into the prepared pan and bake for 45 to 55 minutes, until a knife inserted in the center comes out clean. Leave in the pan to cool.

TO DECORATE

Drizzle the cake with the icing, or use a pastry bag with a small tip to pipe it on. Top with chopped dried cranberries. Let the icing set before serving.

VARIATION

Apple Pound Cake

Omit the cranberries. Add ¾ cup chopped apples and ½ teaspoon ground cinnamon to the batter. Top the baked cake with 1 cup vanilla icing (page 317).

Maple-Walnut Tourlouche

Maple syrup and walnuts are staples of the Great White North, and they're found in many traditional cake recipes. In this tourlouche, a kind of upside-down cake, maple syrup soaks into a walnut spice cake. It is best served warm, on its own or with a scoop of vanilla ice cream.

Spice Cake

- 1⅓ cups all-purpose flour
- 2½ teaspoons baking powder
- 1 teaspoon ground cinnamon
- ½ teaspoon grated nutmeg
- ¼ teaspoon ground cloves
- ¼ teaspoon salt
- 2 tablespoons unsalted butter, softened
- ½ cup sugar
- 2 eggs
- ⅔ cup plain yogurt

Topping

- 1 cup maple syrup
- 1¼ cups walnuts

Makes 1 cake (serves 6 to 8)

TO PREPARE

Preheat the oven to 350°F. Butter a 9-inch round ovenproof skillet.

TO MAKE THE CAKE

Combine the flour, baking powder, cinnamon, nutmeg, cloves, and salt in a medium bowl; set aside. In a separate large bowl, use a mixer to beat the butter and sugar until creamy. Add the eggs one at a time, beating well after each addition. Add the flour mixture to the butter mixture, alternating with the yogurt, until just blended.

TO MAKE THE TOPPING

Bring the maple syrup to a boil in a small saucepan. Stir in the nuts, then remove from the heat.

TO BAKE

Pour the maple mixture into the prepared pan, covering the bottom of the pan. Spoon the batter on top. Bake for 35 to 45 minutes, until a knife inserted in the center comes out clean. Remove the cake from the oven and let sit for 15 minutes. Turn the cake over onto a serving plate, replacing any nuts that fall loose.

VARIATIONS

Cranberry Tourlouche

Replace the maple-walnut topping with a cranberry sauce: Combine ⅔ cup sugar and 4 tablespoons butter in a saucepan over medium heat, stirring until the sugar is dissolved. Add 1¾ cups cranberries and cook, stirring, for 3 minutes.

Maple-Peach Tourlouche

Reduce the nuts to ½ cup. After placing the maple-nut mixture into the prepared pan, arrange 1½ cups sliced peaches on top. Add the cake batter and bake as directed.

Railway Dining

In the twentieth century the Canadian transcontinental railroads made a big push to promote their gourmet foods and all-day coffee service. Their excellent reputation brought tourists from around the world to explore the beauty of Canada through the windows of dining cars. The menus were designed to allow passengers to taste the ingredients of the regions they passed through. In this way, a single railroad recipe might vary throughout the journey. The maple-walnut tourlouche would be served in eastern Canada, the cranberry tourlouche in central Canada, and the maple-peach tourlouche in western Canada.

Bûche de Noël (Yule Log)

French-Canadians in Quebec have adopted the bûche de Noël as their favorite Christmas cake, serving it at the réveillon (family feast) held after the midnight mass on Christmas Eve. There is no single recipe for bûche de Noël; any rolled cake prepared to look like a Yule log will do. As its defining features, the log has one or two stumps and some sort of mushroom on top. This kitsch version is prepared with a chocolate génoise sponge cake, chestnut cream filling, and dark chocolate buttercream "bark." It is topped with meringue mushrooms, fondant holly leaves, fresh chestnuts, and fresh red currants. For a simpler alternative to frosting the cake, simply dust it with confectioners' sugar.

Chocolate Génoise Cake

- ⅓ cup cake flour
- ⅓ cup cornstarch
- ¼ cup Dutch-processed cocoa powder
- ¾ cup granulated sugar
- 3 eggs
- 3 egg yolks
- ⅛ teaspoon salt

Chestnut Cream

- 30 chestnuts
- 2⅓ cups confectioners' sugar
- 2 tablespoons unsalted butter, melted
- 6 tablespoons heavy cream
- ½ cup superfine sugar
- ½ cup (1 stick) unsalted butter, softened
- 1 egg yolk
- 1 teaspoon vanilla extract
- ⅛ teaspoon salt

Meringue Mushrooms

- 2 egg whites
- ½ cup superfine sugar
- ½ teaspoon vanilla extract
- 2 ounces semisweet chocolate
  Unsweetened cocoa powder

Other Toppings

- 4 cups dark chocolate buttercream (page 315)
- 2 cups fondant (page 324)
- 12 whole chestnuts
- 1½ cups fresh red currants

Makes 1 cake (serves 6 to 8)

TO PREPARE

Preheat the oven to 400°F. Line a 10- by 15-inch jelly roll pan with parchment paper, and butter the paper. Prepare a double boiler with water.

TO MAKE THE CAKE

Mix together the flour, cornstarch, and cocoa in a small bowl. In a separate bowl, use a mixer to beat together the sugar, whole eggs, egg yolks, and salt. Transfer the egg mixture to the top of a double boiler and heat, stirring gently, until the mixture is warm to the touch. Remove from the heat, and beat the egg mixture with a mixer until it has cooled and nearly tripled in volume. Gradually and gently fold the flour mixture into the egg mixture, taking care not to deflate the egg mixture's volume.

TO BAKE

Transfer the batter to the prepared pan, smooth the top, and bake for 10 to 12 minutes, or until just firm to the touch. Let cool in the pan for 5 minutes, then transfer the cake on its paper to a rack to cool further. Remove the paper when the cake is cool.

TO MAKE THE CHESTNUT CREAM

Preheat the oven to 425°F. Prepare each chestnut for roasting by cutting an X into its side and pricking it a few times with a fork. Arrange the chestnuts on a baking sheet and roast in the oven for 20 to 25 minutes, until tender and easy to peel. Remove from the oven, let cool, then peel. Grind the chestnuts, then mix with ⅓ cup of the confectioners' sugar, the melted butter, and ¼ cup of the heavy cream. Set aside.

Cream the superfine sugar with 4 tablespoons butter until light and fluffy. In a separate bowl, beat together the remaining 2 cups confectioners' sugar, the egg yolk, the remaining 2 tablespoons cream, the vanilla, and the salt for 8 to 10 minutes, until thick. Gradually stir the egg yolk mixture into the butter mixture. Stir in the chestnut mixture. Add more heavy cream if necessary to reach the desired consistency for spreading.

TO MAKE THE MERINGUE MUSHROOMS

Preheat the oven to 275°F. Line two baking sheets with parchment paper. Fit a piping bag with a ½-inch plain tip.

Beat the egg whites in a medium bowl until stiff. Add ½ tablespoon of the sugar and beat until stiff and shiny. Gradually beat in the remaining sugar and the vanilla. Spoon the mixture into the piping bag. Pipe 36 1-inch rounded caps and 36 cylindrical stems onto the baking sheets. Bake for 50 minutes to 1 hour, until dry. Let cool on the baking sheets.

Melt the chocolate in a microwave or double boiler. Make a small hole in the center of the flat side of each mushroom cap and fill with melted chocolate. Insert a stem into each cap. Let set. When the chocolate has solidified and the mushrooms are stable, sprinkle them lightly with cocoa powder.

TO MAKE THE FONDANT LEAVES

Roll out the fondant to ⅛-inch thickness. Use a cookie cutter or knife to cut out holly-leaf shapes. Press a real holly leaf against each fondant leaf to emboss it with the pattern of the veins, or use a blunt tool to mark the veins. Gently mold each leaf into an arched shape and drape over a curved surface to dry.

TO ASSEMBLE THE CAKE

Invert the cake onto a sheet of plastic wrap. Spread the chestnut cream over the cake, leaving a 1-inch border. Roll the cake tightly into a log, leaving the plastic on the work surface. Cut a 2- to 4-inch section off one end at a 45-degree angle. Lift the cake, using the plastic wrap as a stretcher, and transfer it to a platter, with the seam side down.

Arrange the cut-off piece to resemble a stump on the branch. Spread the dark chocolate buttercream over the cake with an icing spatula, giving it ridges like bark. Garnish the cake with meringue mushrooms, chestnuts, holly leaves, and bunches of currants.

VARIATION

Vanilla-Mocha Bûche de Noël

Prepare plain génoise sponge cake (page 108) and fill with mocha pastry cream (page 323). Top with vanilla buttercream (page 317), chocolate chunks, and chocolate-covered espresso beans.

The Edible Yule Log

In the Middle Ages, on the night of the winter solstice, the longest night of the year, peasants would burn a large log on their fire to help keep evil spirits at bay while they waited for the sun to rise. The burning of the log through the night was said to represent the victory of light over darkness. As Christianity developed, this pagan tradition came to be associated with Christmastime, and the log was called the Yule log, as part of the celebration of the birth of Jesus. During his reign, Napoléon Bonaparte issued a proclamation for homes to close their chimneys during winter to prevent colds. Without a chimney, the Yule log could not be burned, and so French bakers invented an edible Yule log — the bûche de Noël cake — to keep the festive tradition going.

THE WORLD TOUR OF
Christmas Cakes

FOR THOSE OF US WHO LOVE CAKE, Christmastime is heaven on earth. No other holiday delivers so many different varieties: every region, country, and town seems to have its own specialty for us to look forward to each year. Though it's a Christian holiday, Christmas seems to have become an integral part of cultures across all religions, a global year-end festivity.

Although Christmas is celebrated on December 25, in the United States the baking season starts on Black Friday, the last Friday in November, immediately after we've finished baking (and consuming) our Thanksgiving pies. It's good that the season lasts up to six weeks (until Epiphany on January 6), because we need the time to bake the many specialties that are usually enjoyed only during the Christmas season.

Fruitcakes are the most talked about cake of the season. Some people love them and some people love to hate them — or hate to admit that they love them. The Italian panettone, German stollen, Scottish Dundee, and English Christmas cake and figgy puddings all evolved from the traditional Egyptian fruitcake. The process of making them is a yearly ritual, starting in England as early as summer but in most places five to six weeks ahead of time to allow the flavors to develop.

For me, being a lover of both cake decorating and kitsch, the best cake of the holiday season is the bûche de Noël (page 56). This funny roll cake looks like a chopped log ready to burn in the fireplace. Chocolate frosting mimics bark, and mushrooms are made of meringue. No other Christmas cake blends traditions of Christmas past with those of Christmas today with such realistic endeavor.

Other Christmas cakes — plain or fancy, sweet or spicy, laden with symbolism or the icons of holiday carols — can be found the world round. The cakes below are just a sampling. Merry Christmas!

ARMENIA
Armenians enjoy cakes that are topped with a thick layer of gelatin (usually red) and fruits set into a detailed holiday pattern. Nutmeg cake (page 226) and Christmas pudding made with bulgur wheat are also Armenian specialties.

AUSTRALIA AND NEW ZEALAND
Pavlova (page 302) is a meringue fruit-compote cake that's traditional for Christmas in both Australia and New Zealand. Ice cream cakes are popular Christmas fare in these countries as well, where a chilly dessert is a welcome relief from the heat of the Southern Hemisphere summer.

BRITAIN
We all know the chorus "So bring me some figgy pudding . . . ," and in fact figgy pudding, a steamed, baked, or boiled fig-filled pudding cake, is a British holiday favorite. Christmas cake (page 151), another type of fruitcake baked and iced or steamed as pudding, is also traditional Yuletide fare. These cakes are traditionally prepared as early as September.

CANADA
The Canadian bûche de Noël (page 56) makes a dramatic centerpiece on holiday tables in both Quebec and France.

CHILE
Pan de pascua is a Chilean version of stollen, but without the fruit. It was reinvented by German immigrants to Chile.

CUBA
Buñuelos are traditional Cuban fried Christmas treats twisted into a figure-eight shape. They are popular throughout Latin America. In Mexico the dough is flavored with anise seed and caramel and drenched in cinnamon or guava syrup. In Nicaragua the dough is prepared with cassava, while in Colombia buñuelos are not as sweet as in other countries and they are served alongside custardy natillas.

DENMARK
Spherical aebleskiver are traditional Danish Christmas doughnuts.

FRANCE
The French claim a healthy share of Noël cakes, starting with Alsatian favorites berauweka, a fruitcake, and bredala, a gingerbread. Pain d'épices (page 102) is another Yuletide gingerbread, flavored with anise seed, white pepper, and molasses or honey.

GERMANY
Germans celebrate Yuletide with St. Nicolas cake, a nut cake, and stollen (page 122), a fruitcake.

(continued on page 60)

OPPOSITE PAGE: TOP LEFT, TOP TO BOTTOM: *Japanese Christmas cake, Korean Saeng cream cake (page 270), Chinese Christmas cake;* BOTTOM LEFT: *Pavlova (page 302);* BOTTOM RIGHT: *pain d'épices (page 102)*

GREECE

Christopsomo, a sweet bread prepared every Christmas, is said to ensure well-being in the coming year. The yeast dough is hand formed into representations of the family's favorites pursuits, from cars or boats to soccer balls, favorite animals, and other hobbies.

ITALY

Italians seem to have a Christmas cake for every region, if not every town. In Sicily, cassata (page 196), a sponge cake with dried fruit and ricotta cream, is favored. Panforte (page 186), a candylike ginger fruitcake, brings in the Yuletide in Siena, while panettone (page 188), a Christmas fruitcake often served with mascarpone cream, is enjoyed in cosmopolitan Milan, and castagnaccio, a chestnut-flour cake with pine nuts and raisins, is the cake of choice in the rolling hills of Tuscany.

KOREA

In most countries of the Far East, Christmastime cake is a variation of the Korean saeng cream cake (page 270), a sponge cake topped with whipped cream, chocolates, or other seasonal fruit. The decorations tend to be extensive and over the top, with holly leaves, reindeer, Santa Clauses, puppies wearing Christmas hats, and more. They are so popular that they must be ordered from bakeries months in advance.

NICARAGUA

Pio Quinto is a Nicaraguan Christmas cake that's drenched in rum and topped with custard and cinnamon. Sometimes raisins are added. It's named after Pope Pius V, who served from 1566 to 1572, though why the cake is named after him is unknown.

NORWAY

Tykklefse, a usually thin flat cake, is turned into a thick griddle cake for Christmas, while julekake is the all-around-good potato fruitcake.

PHILIPPINES

Eight out of every ten Filipinos are Catholic, and this is very evident during the Christmas season. From December 16 to December 24 congregations gather every day for a predawn mass. Vendors set up carts beforehand with steamed rice cakes known as puto (see pages 288 and 289), as well as bibingka, rice cakes made with salted eggs, cassava, sesame seeds, and cheese.

POLAND

Christmastime in Poland means babka, a yeasted cake containing raisins, almonds, candied fruits, and nuts. Variations of this cake are served in neighboring countries: bábovka in the Czech Republic and kuglof in Croatia, Slovenia, Hungary, Bosnia-Herzegovina, and Serbia. Poppyseed cake (page 177) is another Polish specialty enjoyed at the holiday table.

PORTUGAL

Bolo rei (page 51), the Portuguese version of king cake, is eaten on Epiphany, or Three Kings' Day.

ROMANIA

Turte is a Romanian delight featuring many layers of thin dough with melted sugar, honey, and walnuts. The layers represent the swaddling cloth that the baby Jesus was wrapped in.

SCOTLAND

Sweetened oatmeal scones with cherries or currants (page 147) are enjoyed during Scottish Christmas celebrations.

SPAIN

Tortell (page 51), the Spanish version of king cake, is filled with marzipan and candied and dried fruits and is also served on Epiphany.

SWEDEN

Swedes open the Christmas season on St. Lucia Day with big trays of Lucia cats (page 158) and gingersnaps at Christmastime.

TURKEY

Turkish delight (a candy) is common Christmas fare, including cakes made with it (page 224).

UKRAINE

Pampushky, Christmas doughnuts made with poppyseeds, prunes, cherries, or apricot jam, are an annual treat.

UNITED STATES

President's cake is a rich yeast cake, like a brioche, made with rose petals, almonds, saffron, and brandy. It's eaten at midnight in the White House for Christmas each year. It has been prepared since the presidency of Abraham Lincoln.

Nanaimo Bar

The Nanaimo bar is a classic snack cake. It comes in a multitude of variations, with its defining features being a crumb base, a custard filling, and a chocolate topping. Traditionally it is not baked but chilled until firm enough to serve.

Crumb Crust
- ½ cup (1 stick) unsalted butter
- 1 cup dessicated unsweetened coconut
- ½ cup granulated sugar
- 1 egg, beaten
- 1¾ cups graham cracker crumbs
- ½ cup chopped almonds
- 6 tablespoons Dutch-processed cocoa powder
- 1 teaspoon vanilla extract

Vanilla Custard
- 2 cups confectioners' sugar
- ½ cup (1 stick) unsalted butter, softened
- 3 tablespoons heavy cream
- 2 tablespoons vanilla custard powder

Chocolate Glaze
- 6 ounces semisweet chocolate
- 4 tablespoons unsalted butter

Makes 1 cake (serves 6 to 8)

TO PREPARE
Butter and flour a 9-inch square cake pan.

TO MAKE THE CRUMB LAYER
Melt the butter in a medium saucepan over low heat. Stir in the coconut, sugar, and egg and cook for 3 to 5 minutes, until thickened. Remove from the heat and stir in the graham cracker crumbs, almonds, cocoa, and vanilla. Press the mixture into the prepared pan and refrigerate for at least 45 minutes.

TO MAKE THE CUSTARD LAYER
Combine the confectioners' sugar, butter, cream, and custard powder. Beat with a mixer until thick. When the crumb layer has chilled, spread the custard over it.

TO MAKE THE CHOCOLATE LAYER
Melt the chocolate and the butter in a double boiler, stirring to blend. Let cool for 5 minutes, then pour it over the custard layer.

TO SERVE
Chill the cake in the refrigerator for at least 1 hour. Cut into 2- by 3-inch rectangular bars to serve.

VARIATIONS
Cherry Nanaimo Bar
Add 2 tablespoons cherry juice and ¾ cup chopped cherries to the custard.

Dark Chocolate Nanaimo Bar
Add 3 tablespoons unsweetened cocoa powder and 2 tablespoons sugar to the custard. Replace the semisweet chocolate in the top layer with dark chocolate.

Irish Cream Nanaimo Bar
Replace the heavy cream in the custard with Irish cream liqueur.

Mint Nanaimo Bar
Add 1½ teaspoons mint extract and 2 drops green food coloring to the custard.

Mocha Nanaimo Bar
Heat the heavy cream for the custard to a boil. Dissolve 1 teaspoon instant coffee in the cream.

Peanut Butter Nanaimo Bar
Replace the almonds in the crumb layer with peanuts. Spread 3 tablepoons peanut butter over the crumbs before adding the custard layer.

Spiked Orange Nanaimo Bar
Add 1 tablespoon grated orange zest to the crumb mixture. Brush 2 tablespoons triple sec over the crumb layer before adding the custard. Add 2 tablespoons orange juice to the custard.

Origins of the Nanaimo Bar

Legend has it that this cake dates back to the 1950s, when a homemaker from Nanaimo, British Columbia, submitted a recipe for it to a magazine contest and won. The publicity led to variations that were printed by many homespun cookbooks published by women's associations and churches.

New Yorkers, however, do not credit the Canadians. They say they invented this cake in the 1930s and continue today to refer to it as New York slices. The Canadians of Nanaimo don't seem to mind. This cake is such a part of the local culture that the city has a mascot named Nanaimo Barney, who is shaped like a giant Nanaimo bar.

Hummingbird Cake

The hummingbird cake is a sharply spiced layer cake made with tropical fruits and filled and topped with cream cheese frosting. It is similar to a carrot cake, without the carrots. Bananas, pineapples, and nuts are always included, but the rest of the ingredients are open to interpretation. Here I have added mango to the traditional recipe and prepared it five layers high. It will compete with any southern granny's cake any day.

Spice Cake

- 3 cups all-purpose flour
- 1 cup light brown sugar
- 1 cup granulated sugar
- 1 teaspoon baking soda
- 1 teaspoon ground cinnamon
- ½ teaspoon ground coriander
- ½ teaspoon salt
- 3 eggs, beaten
- ¾ cup sunflower oil
- 2 teaspoons vanilla extract
- 1 (8-ounce) can crushed pineapple, drained
- 2 medium bananas, mashed
- 1½ cups cubed mango
- 1 cup flaked unsweetened coconut
- 1 cup chopped pecans

Toppings

- 4 cups cream cheese frosting (page 316)
- ¼ cup ground pecans
  Food colorings of choice
- ¼ cup chopped pecans
- ½ teaspoon grated orange zest

Makes 1 cake (serves 6 to 8)

TO PREPARE

Preheat the oven to 350°F. Butter and flour two 8-inch round cake pans and one 8-inch dome cake pan (or another 8-inch round cake pan).

TO MAKE THE CAKE

Combine the flour, brown sugar, granulated sugar, baking soda, cinnamon, coriander, and salt in a large bowl. Stir in the eggs, oil, and vanilla just until the dry ingredients are moistened. Do not beat. Stir in the pineapple, bananas, mango, coconut, and pecans.

TO BAKE

Divide the batter among the prepared pans, giving the dome pan just a bit more than the flat-bottomed pans. Bake for 25 to 35 minutes, until a knife inserted in the center comes out clean. Let cool in the pans for 15 minutes, then remove the cakes from the pans and set on a rack to finish cooling.

TO SERVE

Set aside one-quarter of the frosting for piping. Mix the ground pecans into the remaining frosting. Cut the two flat cakes in half crosswise, so that each becomes two layers. Stack the layers with the domed layer on top, using the cream cheese frosting as a filling between the layers. Then frost the exterior of the cake, and set in the refrigerator to chill for at least 1 hour.

Color the reserved frosting in a variety of springtime colors, and pipe a decorative border around the cake. Top with the chopped nuts and orange peel.

Doctor Bird Cake

In Jamaica, hummingbirds are called doctor birds, and this cake is named for these nectar-loving creatures. For a few generations this cake was known in the southern United States as granny cake, supposedly because every southern granny made it. In the 1970s the cake was featured in *Southern Living* magazine with a more fashionable name, the hummingbird cake. As a symbol of homey southern life, it spread in popularity in America and Australia. A slice of this cake is said to make you hum with happiness. Today it is a popular tea party cake.

Black Cake

The Christmas fruitcake has been making its way around the globe for centuries, and black cake is the Caribbean version. It's a descendant of English plum pudding, though instead of big fruit chunks it contains pulverized fruit, which gives it a smoother texture. Its color and name come from the browning sauce that's added to the batter. You can buy browning sauce in any Caribbean market, though you can also make your own by caramelizing sugar at home (see the sidebar). Black cake is also a well-loved wedding cake. In the Caribbean gifting a homemade black cake is a sign of great affection and intimacy.

Fruitcake

- ½ cup chopped dried pineapple
- ½ cup chopped dried papaya
- ½ cup chopped dried mango
- ¼ cup chopped raisins
- ¼ cup dried currants
- ½ cup red wine
- 1¼ cups dark rum
- 1 cup all-purpose flour
- 1 teaspoon baking powder
- ½ teaspoon grated nutmeg
- ¼ teaspoon ground allspice
- ¼ teaspoon ground coriander
- ¼ teaspoon ground mace
- 1 cup (2 sticks) unsalted butter, softened
- ½ cup dark brown sugar
- ¼ cup granulated sugar
- 3 eggs
- 1 teaspoon vanilla extract
- 2 tablespoons browning sauce

Topping

- ½ cup chopped dried fruit (pineapple, papaya, mango, raisins)

Makes 6 individual-serving cakes

TO PREPARE

Place the dried fruits in a bowl and pour the red wine and 1 cup of the rum over them; let sit for 2 hours. Then pour the mixture into a food processor or blender, chop to a pulp, and set aside.

Preheat the oven to 350°F. Butter and flour six 3½-inch Bundt pans.

TO MAKE THE CAKE

Combine the flour, baking powder, nutmeg, allspice, coriander, and mace in a medium bowl. In a separate bowl, cream the butter with the brown sugar and granulated sugar. Add the eggs one at a time, beating well after each addition. Stir in the vanilla and browning sauce. Add the flour mixture to the creamed butter, alternating with the fruit pulp and mixing well after each addition.

TO BAKE

Pour the batter into the prepared pans and bake for 40 to 50 minutes, until a knife inserted in the center comes out clean. Let cool in the pans. When the cakes are cool, remove them from the pans and brush with the remaining ¼ cup rum and top with dried fruit. Let sit for 30 minutes before serving.

VARIATIONS

Beer Black Cake

Reduce the rum to ¾ cup. Substitute ¾ cup dark beer for the wine.

British Black Cake

Substitute mixed candied fruit for the pineapple, mango, and papaya. Substitute brandy for the wine.

Homemade Browning Sauce

- ¼ cup dark brown sugar
- ¼ cup boiling water

Set the brown sugar in a saucepan over low heat and cook, stirring, for about 5 minutes, until dark brown and caramelized. Add the boiling water and continue to cook, stirring, until thickened to a syrupy texture, about 5 minutes. Remove from heat and let cool.

Calabaza Pudding Cake

The calabaza is a West Indian winter squash that looks something like a cross between a butternut squash and a pumpkin. It can be used in baking just like a pumpkin; in fact, if you can't find a calabaza, you can use pumpkin in this recipe. The moistness of this cake gives it the texture of pudding. To coax out the hearty flavors of the cake, serve it with mango chutney. Pickled ginger (found in Asian groceries) is another good accompaniment.

Calabaza Pudding Cake

- 3 cups all-purpose flour
- 1 tablespoon baking powder
- 1 teaspoon salt
- 1 teaspoon ground cinnamon
- ½ teaspoon ground allspice
- ½ teaspoon grated nutmeg
- ¼ teaspoon ground ginger
- ½ teaspoon baking soda
- ¾ cup (1½ sticks) unsalted butter, softened
- ¾ cup light brown sugar
- ½ cup granulated sugar
- 3 eggs
- 1 cup calabaza, cooked until tender, puréed, and cooled
- ¾ cup buttermilk
- ½ cup puréed mango
- 2 tablespoons grated lime zest
- 1 tablespoon lime juice
- ½ cup diced calabaza, cooked until tender and cooled
- ½ cup papaya, diced

Mango Chutney

- 3 ripe mangos, diced
- ½ cup light brown sugar
- 3 tablespoons lime juice
- 1 tablespoon freshly grated ginger
- ½ teaspoon whole cloves
- ½ teaspoon ground cumin

Makes 1 cake (serves 8 to 10)

TO PREPARE

Preheat the oven to 375°F. Butter and flour a pyramid-shaped cake mold (or a 9- by 13-inch cake pan).

TO MAKE THE CAKE

Combine the flour, baking powder, salt, cinnamon, allspice, nutmeg, ginger, and baking soda in a large bowl; set aside. In a separate bowl, cream the butter, brown sugar, and granulated sugar until fluffy. Add the eggs one at a time and stir until blended. Stir in the squash purée, buttermilk, mango purée, lime zest, and lime juice. Gently fold the flour mixture into the butter mixture, followed by the diced calabaza and papaya, stirring just until blended.

TO BAKE

Pour the batter into the prepared pan. Bake for 25 to 30 minutes, until a knife inserted in the center comes out clean. Let cool in the pans.

TO MAKE THE MANGO CHUTNEY

Stir together all the ingredients in a medium bowl. Serve alongside the cake.

VARIATIONS

African Pumpkin-Mango Cake
Replace the calabaza with pumpkin purée. Prepare in a 9- by 13-inch baking pan, and bake for 25 to 35 minutes. Top with cream cheese frosting (page 316).

Indonesian Zucchini-Mango Cake
Replace the calabaza with shredded zucchini. Prepare in a 9- by 13-inch baking pan, and bake for 25 to 35 minutes. Top with cream cheese frosting (page 316).

Rum Cakes

Filled with flavors of the Caribbean, this recipe proves that great pound cake gets better when soaked in booze. If you travel to the islands, you shouldn't miss it. Rum cake is the most popular tourist cake of the region, and you'll find it nicely packed in a traditional six-sided box at almost every souvenir shop, ready for you to bring home.

Rum Cake
- 1⅓ cups all-purpose flour
- ¾ teaspoon baking powder
- ½ teaspoon salt
- 1 cup (2 sticks) unsalted butter, softened
- ½ cup sugar
- ¾ cup sweetened condensed milk
- 1 tablespoon dark rum
- 3 eggs

Topping
- 1¼ cups rum syrup (page 319)

Makes 5 individual-serving cakes

TO PREPARE
Preheat the oven to 325°F. Butter and flour five 4½-inch Bundt pans (or an 8-inch tube pan).

TO MAKE THE CAKES
Combine the flour, baking powder, and salt; set aside. In a separate large bowl, beat the butter and sugar until fluffy. Add the condensed milk and the rum. Stir in the flour mixture until blended. Beat in the eggs one at a time until combined.

TO BAKE
Transfer the batter to the prepared pans and bake for 35 to 45 minutes, until a knife inserted in the center comes out clean. Leave the cakes in the pans to cool.

TO SERVE
Remove the cakes from the pans. Pour rum syrup over the cakes, cover, and let sit at least 6 hours before serving.

VARIATIONS

Blue Mountain Coffee–Coconut Rum Cake

Stir ¾ cup shredded unsweetened coconut into the batter. Replace the water in the rum syrup with ½ cup double-strength espresso. Bake in an 8-inch tube pan for 50 minutes to 1 hour.

Puerto Rican Chocolate Rum Cake

Reduce the flour to 1¼ cups. Add ⅓ cup unsweetened cocoa powder and 1 cup chocolate chunks to the batter. Bake in an 8-inch tube pan for 50 minutes to 1 hour.

Miami Lime Rum Cake

Add 3 tablespoons lime juice and 1 teaspoon lime zest to the batter.

Tortugan Pirates

In the 1600s French and English pirates colonized Tortuga Island, off the northern coast of Haiti. The two groups did not always get along, and the island was known as a chaotic center of excessive eating, drinking, and fighting. Pirates, rum, and rum cake go hand in hand; the cakes sustained the pirates on seafaring voyages. Many Tortugan rum cakes are packaged to promote their swashbuckling history, with illustrations of great pirate ships on their boxes.

New World Spice Cake

With the subtle, fresh taste of its spices, this cake needs no frosting. It features cinnamon, nutmeg, cloves, mace, and allspice, the spices for which the New World "Spice Islands" are now well known. Wait until the whole cake is cut and pick the biggest piece.

Spice Cake

- 1½ cups all-purpose flour
- 1 teaspoon baking soda
- 1¼ teaspoons ground cinnamon
- ½ teaspoon grated nutmeg
- ¼ teaspoon ground cloves
- ¼ teaspoon ground mace
- ¼ teaspoon ground allspice
- ½ teaspoon salt
- ⅓ cup molasses
- ⅓ cup boiling water
- 4 tablespoons unsalted butter, softened
- ¼ cup granulated sugar
- 2 eggs

Topping

- 2 tablespoons confectioners' sugar

Makes 1 cake (serves 6 to 8)

TO PREPARE

Preheat the oven to 350°F. Butter and flour an 8-inch square cake pan.

TO MAKE THE CAKE

Combine the flour, baking soda, cinnamon, nutmeg, cloves, mace, allspice, and salt; set aside. Stir the molasses into the boiling water until dissolved; set aside to cool. In a large bowl, cream the butter and sugar until fluffy. Add the eggs to the creamed mixture and beat well. Add the flour mixture to the creamed mixture, alternating with the molasses.

TO BAKE

Transfer the batter to the prepared pan and bake for 30 to 35 minutes, until a knife inserted in the center comes out clean. Let cool in the pan for 5 minutes, then transfer the cake to a wire rack to cool completely. Top with confectioners' sugar.

VARIATION

Chocolate Spice Cake

Reduce the flour to 1¼ cups. Add ½ cup unsweetened cocoa powder and ¾ cup chocolate chunks to the batter. Top with 1½ cups chocolate ganache (page 315).

The New World Spices

The West Indies are sometimes known as the New World Spice Islands, being as renowned for their spices as are the Spice Islands of Indonesia. Allspice is perhaps the best-known native spice, but a great number of imports, including nutmeg, cinnamon, cloves, vanilla, ginger, and pepper, are all heavily cultivated here. In St. George's, the capital city of Grenada, the Saturday morning farmers' market is filled with rickety tables and barrels of fresh goods. Vendors offer handfuls of spices, calling out their wares by repeating their names: "nutmeg nutmeg," "clove clove."

Coconut Cakes

Haitians are big fans of the Day of the Dead, and they pack up special coconut cakes to share at picnics with the spirits in cemeteries. Think of these as the Haitian version of empanadas.

Dough

- ¼ cup water
- 1¾ cups all-purpose flour
- ¼ cup corn flour or masa harina
- 3 tablespoons confectioners' sugar
- ½ teaspoon salt
- ¾ cup (1½ sticks) unsalted butter, cubed

Coconut Filling

- 2½ cups shredded fresh or dried sweetened coconut
- 1 cup evaporated milk
- ¼ cup granulated sugar
- ¼ cup light brown sugar
- 1 teaspoon vanilla extract
- ½ teaspoon ground cinnamon
- ⅛ teaspoon salt

Topping

- ¼ cup flaked unsweetened coconut, toasted

Makes 12 individual-serving cakes

TO MAKE THE DOUGH

Mix the water and ¼ cup of the flour into a paste in a small bowl; set aside. Combine the remaining 1½ cups flour, corn flour, confectioners' sugar, and salt in a food processor or blender. Add the butter and pulse until it resembles a coarse meal. Add the flour paste and process until the dough gathers into a ball. Cover the dough and refrigerate for 30 minutes.

TO MAKE THE FILLING

Mix the coconut, evaporated milk, granulated sugar, brown sugar, vanilla, cinnamon, and salt in a saucepan and cook, stirring, over medium heat until the mixture has thickened.

TO BAKE

Preheat the oven to 350°F. Line two baking sheets with buttered parchment paper. Roll out the dough to ¼-inch thickness on a floured work surface. Use a cookie cutter or knife to cut out 3½-inch flowers or fluted circles. Place 2 to 3 tablespooons of filling on half of each circle, and fold the other half over the filling to form a semi-circle. Pinch around the edges to seal.

Transfer the cakes to the prepared baking sheets. Bake for 25 to 30 minutes, until slightly golden. Transfer the cakes to a rack. Top with flaked coconut, and let cool.

VARIATION

Haitian Fruit-Filled Cakes

Combine 4 cups chopped tropical fruit (guava, pineapple, mango, breadfruit) and ½ cup sugar, 1 teaspoon lemon juice, and ½ teaspoon cornstarch in a saucepan. Heat until the sugar has dissolved and the mixture has thickened. Add to the cakes in place of the coconut filling.

Haitian Pineapple Cakes

Add pineapple filling (page 322) to the cakes in place of the coconut filling.

Dulce de Leche Cakes

Add dulce de leche (page 321) to the cakes in place of the coconut filling.

OPPOSITE PAGE: BOTTOM RIGHT: *mango cakes (page 70);* TOP RIGHT: *johnnycakes (page 71);* AT LEFT: *coconut cakes*

Mango Cakes

Cuban cuisine has strong Spanish, African, and American South influences, with butter cakes, buttercreams, and fresh fruits and nuts featuring prominently in its desserts. Mango is one of the most popular fruits on the island, and these small cakes put it to good use, with fresh mango chunks in the cakes, mango buttercream topping, and a garnish of sliced mango. (For a photo of the cakes, see page 69.)

Mango Cake

3	cups cake flour
1	teaspoon baking powder
½	teaspoon baking soda
½	teaspoon salt
1½	cups (3 sticks) unsalted butter, softened
2¼	cups superfine sugar
7	eggs
½	cup sour cream
2	teaspoons vanilla extract
2	medium mangos, chopped

Toppings

4	cups mango buttercream (page 316)
2	mangos, sliced into thin strips

Makes 12 individual-serving cakes

TO PREPARE

Preheat the oven to 325°F. Line the cups of two six-cup muffin pans with liners.

TO MAKE THE CAKES

Combine the flour, baking powder, baking soda, and salt in a medium bowl; set aside. In a separate large bowl, use a mixer to beat the butter and sugar until fluffy. Add the eggs one at a time, beating after each addition. Stir in the sour cream, vanilla, and mango. Gradually add the dry ingredients and blend.

TO BAKE

Divide the batter among the muffin cups and bake for 25 to 30 minutes, until a knife inserted in the center comes out clean. Remove the cakes from the pans and set on a rack to cool.

TO SERVE

Frost the cakes with the mango buttercream. On top of each cake, arrange mango slices in concentric circles to form a flower.

VARIATIONS

Mango-Coconut Cake

Prepare the cake in two 9-inch round cake pans. Use 1 cup coconut icing (page 315) as a filling between the layers and to frost the cake. Coat with shredded unsweetened coconut. Top with fresh mangos.

Mango-Lemon Cake

Prepare the cake in two 9-inch round cake pans. Use 1½ cups lemon curd (page 321) as a filling between the layers. Frost with mango buttercream (page 316).

Mango-Pineapple Cake

Prepare the cake in two 9-inch round cake pans. Use 1½ cups pineapple filling (page 322) between the layers. Frost with mango buttercream (page 316), and top with fresh mango and pineapple wedges.

Johnnycakes

Simple and rustic, sweet johnnycakes are everyday snack cakes in the Bahamas. Though we use a griddle and white sugar, these cakes are not much different from the earliest cornmeal cakes of the region, cooked over an open fire and sweetened only with honey. (For a photo of the cakes, see page 69.)

1½ cups cornmeal

¾ cup all-purpose flour

1 tablespoon sugar

1 teaspoon salt

2 eggs, beaten

1½ cups milk, heated

2 tablespoons unsalted butter, melted

Makes 14 johnnycakes

TO PREPARE
Generously butter a griddle.

TO MAKE THE BATTER
Combine the cornmeal, flour, sugar, and salt in a medium bowl. Mix in the eggs, milk, and melted butter.

TO COOK
Preheat the griddle over medium heat. Pour the batter onto the griddle in 4-inch rounds. Cook on both sides until cooked through and golden.

TO SERVE
Serve plain or with confectioners' sugar, honey, butter, and/or syrup.

VARIATIONS

Coconut Johnnycake
Add ¾ cup sweetened flaked coconut to the batter. Reduce the milk to ¾ cup and add ¾ cup coconut milk.

New England Johnnycake
Prepare the batter as directed. Bake in an 8-inch square cake pan at 375°F for 20 to 30 minutes. Once cooled, top with sugar.

Peanut Johnnycake
Add ¾ cup chopped peanuts to the batter.

Corn Cakes of the Caribbean

Masa harina and cornmeal are popular cake ingredients in the Caribbean islands, perhaps because corn is a staple crop. In addition to the johnnycake, you can find corn fritters in Jamaica and the Bahamas at Boxing Day festivals. English afternoon tea is commonly served in the region, with tropically spiced hot cross buns with a touch of corn flour. Dominicans prepare a corn cake topped with cinnamon, nutmeg, and cloves and soaked in coconut milk, while on Barbados a creamy corn pudding cake made with coconut milk is traditional.

CHAPTER 3

Latin America
Street Sweets and Festive Quinceañera Cakes

Pᴇᴏᴘʟᴇ ʟᴏᴠᴇ ᴛᴏ sʜᴀʀᴇ ᴛʜᴇ ғᴏᴏᴅs ᴛʜᴇʏ ɢʀᴇᴡ ᴜᴘ ᴡɪᴛʜ, including cakes. Here in Los Angeles many of my friends grew up in Latin America, and some of my best memories of cakes come from celebrations with them. Today this city's neighborhoods are filled with a plethora of Central and South American bakeries that show off the cake cultures of Mexico, Guatemala, Brazil, Peru, and then some.

Maize, thought to have been first cultivated in Mexico, is the foundation of many Latin American cakes, from corn cakes to tamales. Ancient Mayan legend holds that humans were born from corn, and corn is still considered a sacred gift from the gods throughout the region. Other native foods of the region include Brazil nuts, walnuts, cashews, peanuts, sweet potatoes, pumpkins, vanilla bean, and various chiles,

and all can be found in various incarnations in Latin American cakes.

But when it comes to cakes the ingredient that matters the most in this region is chocolate, which is derived from the native cacao bean. Both Mayans and Aztecs drank chocolate as part of their religious practices, and modern-day Latin American bakers make a wide range of chocolate cakes. They often infuse chocolate with unusual flavors, such as cinnamon or even red-hot chiles, or combine it with fruits, as in Venezuelan orange-chocolate cake (page 89) and Peruvian pineapple-chocolate cream cake (page 94), a surprising yet delicious pairing.

Latin American cakes reflect more than Native American ingredients and traditions. They are influenced by the

Portuguese, Spanish, Italian, French, Caribbean, and other colonizers and immigrants who've settled in this region since the sixteenth century. The Spanish brought the sponge cake, which the locals adapted to be prepared with meringue or flavored with cacao beans. The French inspired the sweetened breads now enjoyed for breakfast and dessert. Tropical influences from the Caribbean have led to the incorporation of coconut, bananas, coffee, and various spices in local cakes.

Festivals are a seamless part of everyday life in Latin America. Every town has its own patron saint feast day, with parades, dancing, and lots and lots of food. Harvest time, springtime, religious holidays, independence days, weddings — you name it, there's a festival for it. And all festivals are celebrated with cakes. In Peru you'll find picarones (page 95), made with pumpkins and sweet potatoes, at harvest festivals. In Mexico churros (page 78) are made to celebrate Cinco de Mayo. And Brazilian corn cakes (page 85) celebrate Festas Juninas, a series of festivals giving thanks to SS. John, Peter, and Anthony.

Pan de muerto (bread of the dead) sweet rolls (page 74) are made in many shapes, such as a skull and crossbones. These cakes are very cool but also quite surprising, since generally we think of cakes as upbeat affairs. In Latin America pan de muerto is carried to cemeteries or displayed on altars as offerings to the ancestors as part of the annual Mexican Day of the Dead observances.

No quinceañera, or celebration of a Hispanic girl's 15th birthday, is complete without a proper cake. Typically a quinceañera cake is an almond meringue cake (page 79) or a tres leches cake (page 80), a spongy cake made with three kinds of milk. Choosing this celebration cake is as important as choosing a wedding cake, only the teenage princess is the center of attention instead of a bride. Imagine a multitiered confection in over-the-top girly style bedecked with pink ruffles, glitter, and candied flowers. In Central America family members labor over these cakes for weeks in preparation for the big event.

Latin American birthday cakes almost always include dulce de leche, a sugary, reduced-milk preparation with a sweet, burnt-milk flavor. The Argentinean arrollado with dulce de leche filling (page 321) is a good example of European-influenced technique rolled up with Latin flavor.

Tamales are also a popular Latin American cake. You may think of tamales more as dinner than dessert, but in fact they can be both, depending on how they are prepared. The corn-cake tamales (page 82) of Guatemala, for example, are made with dried fruits and chocolate, much like a traditional fruitcake. Tamale technique varies from culture to culture. Mexicans, for example, insist that tamales should be steamed rather than simmered, while tamales in Honduras, Panama, and Colombia are wrapped in banana leaves rather than corn husks. As is the case around the world, cake culture transforms as it travels from country to country, person to person, each giving the recipes and techniques a particular local flavor. Let's celebrate that!

Pan de Muerto

This yeast sweet bread, traditionally prepared for the Mexican Day of the Dead, is usually designed to look like crossbones and skulls. It's given as an offering to a family's ancestors, but it's labor-intensive to make, and it's delicious, so I would recommend that you make two batches: one for your ancestors to enjoy, and one for your family to eat.

Starter

- 4 cups all-purpose flour
- ⅓ cup granulated sugar
- 1 tablespoon active dry yeast
- 1¼ teaspoons sea salt
- ½ cup water
- 3 eggs

Dough

- 1 cup granulated sugar
- 1 cup (2 sticks) unsalted butter, softened
- Zest of 1 orange, grated
- 4 cups all-purpose flour
- 8 egg yolks
- ¼ cup water
- 4 egg yolks, beaten

Toppings

- 4 tablespoons unsalted butter, melted
- ⅓ cup granulated or colored sugar

Makes 6 to 8 individual-serving cakes

TO MAKE THE STARTER

Combine the flour, sugar, yeast, and salt in a large bowl. Add the water and eggs and beat for about 5 minutes. Place the dough in a buttered bowl and allow it to rise in a warm place until it has doubled in size, about 2 hours.

TO MAKE THE DOUGH

When the starter has risen, give it a light blow to deflate it, and then break it into pieces and place in a mixing bowl. Mix in the sugar, butter, and orange zest. Beat in the flour and the eight egg yolks. Slowly mix in the water until the dough is slightly sticky but smooth. Add additional water or flour if needed.

Lightly knead the dough on a floured work surface, then form it into a round dome. Butter and flour a mixing bowl and place the dough in it, cover, and let sit in a warm place until it has doubled in size, about 2 hours.

TO SHAPE

When the dough has risen, punch it down. Set aside one-quarter of the dough. Mound the remaining dough on a floured work surface. Press fist-size balls of dough into 6-inch rounds. Cover and let rise for 1 hour.

Count the number of dough rounds you have prepared, and divide the reserved dough into that number of parts. Shape each part into two bone-shaped logs, each roughly 7 inches long, pinching in the center so that the ends are wider than the middles. Set on a baking sheet and let rise until the cakes are done rising.

When the dough has risen, set two bones on top of each round, intersecting in the middle to form a crossbones. Brush the cakes with the beaten egg yolks.

TO BAKE

Preheat the oven to 325°F. Butter two baking sheets. Transfer the cakes to the sheets and bake for 15 to 20 minutes, until the cakes are golden and springy. Open the oven door and let sit for 5 minutes.

TO SERVE

Remove the cakes from the oven. Brush the surface of each one with melted butter, and sprinkle with sugar. Let cool before serving.

VARIATION

Rosca de Reyes (for Day of the Dead)

Prepare the dough and shape into a ring, reserving some dough to make bones. Shape 5 bones, as described in the recipe, and top the ring with the bones, candied figs, and candied fruit strips.

The Day of the Dead

On November 2, Mexican families honor their ancestors in a lively and colorful celebration. They set up whimsical altars in their homes, decorated with items and icons that commemorate their loved ones' lives, and they prepare picnics to enjoy at their grave sites, with special foods to be left there as offerings. Though Mexican at heart, Day of the Dead is widely celebrated wherever there is a large Hispanic population, including the American Southwest.

THE WORLD TOUR OF
Cakes for the Dead

FROM CRADLE TO GRAVE, cakes are a major part of every milestone in life. But in many traditions cakes honor the dead just as much as they do the living. They may be brought to grave sites as tokens of remembrance and respect for ancestors. They may be prepared as offerings to propitiate the dead, bringing luck to the living. Or they may be an integral part of burial rituals, mourning the passing of a loved one. Here are some unique mourning traditions and cakes that are part of our lives after we have passed on.

BELGIUM: SOUL CAKES

In Belgium on All Souls' Day people stroll around the neighborhood begging for soul cakes, small buns that resemble hot cross buns, but without the cross on top. It's said that the more soul cakes one eats, the more souls are saved from Purgatory. In the Middle Ages it was customary for poor Christians to offer prayers for the dead in return for soul cakes from wealthy villagers. During the nineteenth and twentieth centuries children would go "souling," which involved singing a soul cake song while riding on, or carrying, the hobby horse known as the hooden horse. Today soul cakes are still given to the poor; often you'll see them stacked in piles at churches on All Souls' Day.

CAMBODIA: NUM ONSAM AND NUM KORM

Bonn Pchum Ben is a 15-day festival held to commemorate the spirits of the dead. Over the first 14 days, people bring to the monks of their local pagodas offerings of food and cakes. Num onsam, a cylindrical cake of glutinous rice with a pork filling, and num korm, a pyramidal cake of rice flour filled with a paste of coconut and palm sugar, are traditional offerings. On the 15th day of the festival, people come dressed in finery to celebrate the dedication of the mass collection of offerings to the spirits.

CHINA: PINK GHOST CAKES

In China the Hungry Ghost Festival is celebrated on the seventh lunar month, known as Ghost Month, when it is believed the dead return for a visit. The hungry ghosts need to be satisfied with foods, including pink steamed cakes, in order for the living relatives to have good fortune. The Chinese believe that during this time tables should remain empty; otherwise the ghosts, who are starving, will devour everything. Foods and cakes are placed in temples and at roadsides to appease the spirits before they cause too much of a disturbance. Similar pink steamed buns are assembled in a towerlike structure at funerals and are offered to the newly initiated hungry ghosts. After that ritual some cakes are scattered around the property and the rest are distributed to guests to eat.

HAITI: COCONUT CAKES

In Haiti Christian practices are combined with voodoo practices. On the Day of the Dead, Haitians visit Baron Samedi, the spirit of the graveyard. They carry coconut cakes (page 68) in a picnic basket to the graveyard and hang out for the day to celebrate their ancestors. They share the cakes with Baron Samedi and the spirits of their relatives.

INDIA: PURAKA CAKES

Puraka is an important ten-day Hindu funeral rite in which cakes feature prominently. Each day a cake made with boiled rice, sesame, honey, milk, sugar, and dried fruits, called a puraka cake, is offered to the dead. There are many lengthy rules that prescribe who is allowed to perform this ritual. After returning from the cremation of the deceased, the nearest relatives create a small altar where each day a cake is offered. The deceased is believed to obtain different parts of the body needed in the afterlife from these cakes. Afterward, the puraka cakes are thrown into sacred waters. The ceremony ends with leaving some food for the birds. If the mourning period can last only one day, then all ten funeral cakes must be offered on that day.

ITALY: FAVE DEI MORTI

The fava bean is associated with death in many Mediterranean cultures. Throughout Italy, fave dei morti (beans of the dead), little bean-shaped cakes made with almonds and cinnamon, are eaten on All Souls' Day, as part of celebrations in honor of loved ones who have passed away. The cakes are said to represent souls united. But the cakes are not simply for remembrances. In Rome, All Souls' Day is the customary time for a man to send an engagement ring to his sweetheart. He packs the ring, in a traditional square white box, inside a larger oval box filled with fave dei morti.

MEXICO: PAN DE MUERTO

One of Mexico's most important holidays, the Day of the Dead is celebrated from October 31 to November 2. Families honor the spirits of their loved ones, who are said to return to their homes to visit during this time period. In preparation for the holiday, families spend weeks preparing cakes, creating altars in their homes, and decorating grave sites. Pan de muerto (page 74) is the traditional offering to the ancestors.

TOP: *In India, a puraka cake is offered to aid the reincarnation of a loved one.*
BOTTOM LEFT: *Offerings of pink ghost cakes for a Hungry Ghost Festival in Singapore.*
BOTTOM RIGHT: *Bread loaves for a Day of the Dead celebration, known in Bolivia as Todos Santos.*

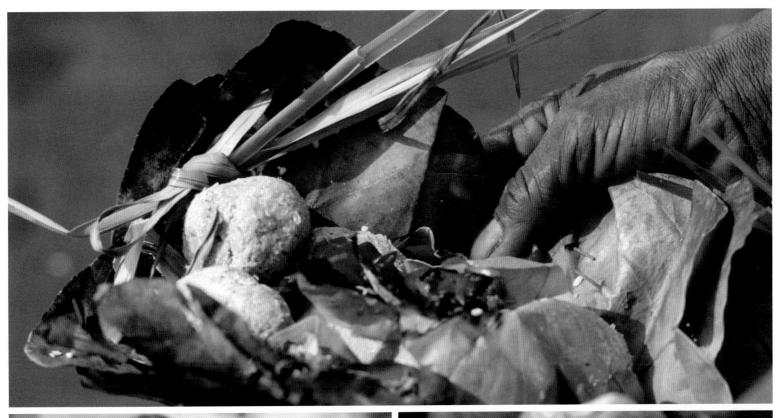

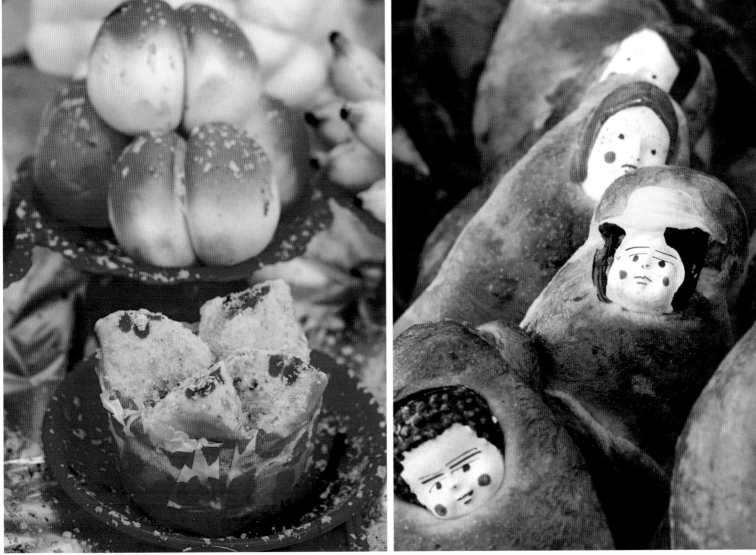

Churros

Whether you're at a Cinco de Mayo festival in Mexico or a Fiesta de San Fermín in Spain, the hypnotic sweet and spicy smell comes from the same sugary creation: churros. These fried pastry cakes are long, narrow doughnuts doused in cinnamon sugar and eaten warm and fresh. To make them at home I use a pastry bag with a large star tip, but if you're going to make them a habit, invest in a churro maker.

Cakes

2	cups water
3	tablespoons unsalted butter
3	tablespoons granulated sugar
2½	cups all-purpose flour
¼	teaspoon salt
2	eggs
	Canola oil for frying

Toppings

½	cup light brown sugar
2	tablespoons ground cinnamon

Makes 8 to 10 churros

TO MAKE THE BATTER

Combine the water, butter, and sugar in a medium saucepan, and warm over medium heat until the butter has melted and the sugar has dissolved. Remove from the heat and add the flour and salt, stirring until smooth. Beat in the eggs one at a time. Spoon the batter into a pastry bag fitted with a ½-inch star tip.

TO FRY THE CHURROS

Fill a large, heavy saucepan with 2 to 3 inches of oil, and warm the oil over medium heat. Line plates with paper towels for draining the fried cakes. Get the topping ready by mixing together the sugar and cinnamon on a plate.

Test the oil by squeezing in a short length of the batter. If it browns quickly, the oil is ready. Squeeze 4-inch lengths of the dough into the hot oil. When the cakes become golden, remove them from the oil and set them on paper towels to blot away excess oil. Roll the churros in the sugar mixture and serve hot. Continue frying cakes until you've used up all the batter.

VARIATIONS

Chocolate Churros

Reduce the flour to 2¼ cups and add ¼ cup Dutch-processed cocoa powder to the batter. Instead of cinnamon sugar, dip the cakes in a topping made from ½ cup granulated sugar and ¼ cup unsweetened cocoa powder. Sprinkle the cakes with more cocoa powder. (And if you're up for some spicy cakes, sprinkle them with chile powder as well.)

Dulce de Leche Churros

Drizzle the cakes with 1 cup dulce de leche (page 321).

About Churros

Churros are Spanish in origin, but they've found a real home in Mexico. Here, churros are very long, at least a foot, giving you the impression that the end is never near. Churrerías, or churros stores, are open all night long, offering these sweet cakes for a late-night snack or early breakfast. Typically churros are dipped in a cup of coffee or syrupy-thick Mexican hot chocolate before they are eaten.

Mexican Hot Chocolate

⅓	cup unsweetened cocoa powder
⅓	cup granulated sugar
1	teaspoon ground cinnamon
⅛	teaspoon salt
4	cups milk
½	cup half-and-half
¾	teaspoon vanilla extract

Makes 4 cups

Combine the cocoa powder, sugar, cinnamon, and salt in a bowl, and mix well. Heat 1½ cups of milk in a saucepan to a low boil. Stir in the cocoa mixture and whisk until smooth. Add the remaining milk and return to a low boil. Whisk in the half-and-half and vanilla and heat to serving temperature.

Torta del Cielo
(Almond Meringue Cake)

This light almond sponge cake is commonly requested by 15-year-old girls for their quinceañera. The heavenly taste comes from the rich almond cream filling and the decorative meringue topping. (For a photo of the cake, see page 81.)

Sponge Cake
- 10 eggs, separated
- Pinch of salt
- 1¼ cups granulated sugar
- 1 teaspoon vanilla extract
- 1 cup ground almonds
- ½ cup cake flour
- 1 teaspoon baking powder
- 1 teaspoon almond extract
- ¼ teaspoon grated nutmeg

Meringue Rosettes
- 4 egg whites
- ¼ teaspoon cream of tartar
- ½ cup superfine sugar
- ½ teaspoon almond extract

Almond Cream
- 1½ cups whole milk
- ⅓ cup granulated sugar
- 1 teaspoon ground cinnamon
- 1½ tablespoons cornstarch
- ½ cup ground almonds
- 1 egg yolk, well beaten
- ¼ cup amaretto

Toppings
- 6 whole almonds
- Thin edible gold leaf
- ¼ cup confectioners' sugar

Makes 1 cake (serves 6 to 8)

TO PREPARE
Preheat the oven to 375°F. Butter and flour two 8-inch round springform pans.

TO MAKE THE CAKE
Beat the egg whites and salt in a medium bowl until stiff peaks form; set aside. In a separate medium bowl, beat the egg yolks, sugar, and vanilla until thickened. Add the ground almonds, flour, baking powder, almond extract, and nutmeg to the yolk mixture and stir to combine. Fold the egg whites into the yolk mixture; do not overmix.

TO BAKE
Pour the batter into the prepared pans and bake for 30 to 35 minutes, until a knife inserted in the center of the cake comes out clean. Let the cakes cool in the pans for 15 minutes, then remove from the pans and set on a rack to finish cooling.

TO MAKE THE MERINGUE ROSETTES
Preheat the oven to 200°F. Line a baking sheet with parchment paper.

Beat the egg whites until foamy. Add the cream of tartar and beat until soft peaks form. Gradually mix in the sugar and almond extract, beating until stiff peaks form.

Transfer the meringue to a pastry bag fitted with a star tip. Pipe the meringue into 1-inch rosettes on the prepared baking sheet. Bake for 60 to 80 minutes, until a hard shell forms on the outer surface. Transfer the rosettes to a rack to cool.

TO MAKE THE ALMOND CREAM
Bring the milk to a boil in a medium saucepan. Lower to a simmer and add the sugar and cinnamon. In a separate small bowl, stir 3 tablespoons from the pan of warm milk into the cornstarch to create a smooth paste. Add the paste to the milk mixture along with the ground almonds. Cook until the mixture thickens, 15 to 20 minutes.

When the mixture has thickened, remove ¼ cup of the hot milk mixture and beat it with the egg yolk to combine. Add the yolk mixture to the saucepan and continue to cook for 2 to 3 minutes, until thickened. Remove from the heat and stir in the amaretto.

TO ASSEMBLE
Stack the two cake layers, using half of the almond cream as a filling between them. Pipe the remaining almond cream around the edges of the cake, in as many mounds as you have meringue rosettes. Top each mound with a meringue rosette.

Wrap each almond in a thin layer of gold leaf. Arrange the almonds in the shape of a flower in the center of the cake. Dust with confectioners' sugar.

VARIATIONS

Chocolate-Almond Cake
Add ½ cup grated Mexican chocolate to the cake batter and ¼ cup grated Mexican chocolate to the almond cream.

Orange-Almond Cake
Add 2 tablepoons grated orange zest and 3 tablespoons orange juice concentrate to the batter. Replace the amaretto in the cream with triple sec and add 1 tablespoon orange juice concentrate.

Tres Leches (Three Milks) Cake

Tres leches cake has as its base a butter cake with a spongy texture. A sweet milky syrup is poured over it, made of whole milk, condensed milk, and evaporated milk — hence the name *tres leches*, "three milks." The recipe was originally created by manufacturers of canned milk in the late 1800s to promote their products; the recipe was on the back of every can. I add sour cream to this cake to make it a bit tart, so this version really has four milks. The variation with rum whipped cream has five. Although Nicaraguans traditionally serve this cake plain, I top it with toasted meringue (the Mexican way) and fresh berries.

Tres Leches Cake

- 2¼ cups all-purpose flour
- 1½ teaspoons baking powder
- ¼ teaspoon salt
- ¾ cup (1½ sticks) unsalted butter, softened
- 1½ cups sugar
- 7 eggs, at room temperature
- 1½ teaspoons vanilla extract
- ½ cup sour cream

Tres Leches Topping

- 1 cup milk
- ½ cup sweetened condensed milk
- ½ cup evaporated milk

Meringue

- 4 egg whites
- ¼ cup sugar
- ⅓ teaspoon cream of tartar
- ¼ teaspoon salt

Topping

- ¼ cup fresh berries (blueberries, raspberries, or strawberries)

Makes 1 cake (serves 6 to 8)

TO PREPARE

Preheat the oven to 350°F. Butter and flour a 12-inch round cake pan.

TO MAKE THE CAKE

Combine the flour, baking powder, and salt in a medium bowl; set aside. In a separate large bowl, cream the butter and sugar with a mixer until fluffy. Add the eggs one at a time, beating after each addition. Stir in the vanilla. Add the flour mixture to the butter mixture, alternating with the sour cream, and mix until blended.

TO BAKE

Pour the batter into the prepared pan and bake for 25 to 30 minutes, until a knife inserted in the center comes out clean. Let cool in the pan.

TO MAKE THE TRES LECHES TOPPING

Stir together the milk, condensed milk, and evaporated milk. When the cake is cool, remove it from the pan and transfer to an ovenproof serving tray. Pierce the cake all over with a fork. Spoon the milk mixture over the cake and let soak for 5 minutes.

TO MAKE THE MERINGUE

Preheat the oven broiler. Whip the egg whites, sugar, cream of tartar, and salt with a mixer until stiff. Spread the mixture over the top of the cake. (For decoration, pipe a pattern in the center that will hold berries, and create patterns in the meringue with a fork or comb decoration tool.) Place the cake back in the oven to broil for 1 to 2 minutes, until the meringue is toasted. (You could also toast it with a torch.)

TO SERVE

Refrigerate the cake for at least 3 hours. Top with berries before serving.

VARIATIONS

Tres leches cake has widespread popularity, and it's a little bit different depending on where it's prepared. In Nicaragua the cake is prepared plain, with no topping, while in Mexico it's often given a meringue topping. In Cuba and Puerto Rico you will find coconut milk replacing the condensed and evaporated milks, and flaked coconut on top. In Argentina and other South American countries, dulce de leche is used as a filling.

Cinco Leches Cake

Top the cake with 2 cups rum whipped cream (page 323) and ¼ teaspoon ground cinnamon.

Cuban Tres Leches Cake

Replace the evaporated and condensed milks with coconut milk.

Peruvian Dulce de Leche Cake

Prepare this cake in two 9-inch round cake pans. Spread 1½ cups dulce de leche (page 321) between the layers.

CAKES ON OPPOSITE PAGE: TOP: *torta del cielo (page 79)*; BOTTOM: *tres leches cake*

The Quinceañera

The Latin American quinceañera is a girl's coming-of-age ritual celebrated on her 15th birthday. In decades past many girls married shortly after the quinceañera, and though today such a rush to full adulthood is rare, it's still a great excuse to have a party. A mass is given in the birthday girl's name and a big celebration, sometimes as big as a wedding, follows. In addition to the music, dancing, and flirting, the cake is a center of the celebration. Cake pulls (see page 47) are common at quinceañeras in the United States. Torta del cielo (page 79) and tres leches cake are the two cakes most often requested for quinceañeras.

Soaking Cake

Soaking a cake with syrup not only gives the cake moisture but also coaxes out its flavor. The technique is used worldwide. The basbousa from Egypt, for example, is soaked in lemon syrup (page 208), the butter cake of Tortuga is soaked in rum (page 66), the Irish simnel cake is soaked in rum and brandy (page 150), and the Latin American tres leches cake is soaked in milk syrup.

Tamale Corn Cakes

I was surprised to see a Guatemalan student bring tamales to a bake sale we had at the college where I teach. I love tamales, but I'd never really thought of them as cakes. However, these sweet, steamed tamales made with dried fruit, chocolate, and corn flour pass the fruitcake bar for me. Tamales are made with the same corn flour as tortillas, but instead of being roasted they are steamed in corn husks, similar to the steamed sponge cakes and rice cakes of Asia. There are many variations of sweet and savory tamales served as desserts in Guatemala, Mexico, and the American Southwest. Making tamales is a great experience, so gather a crowd and include the making as part of the event.

Wrappers

24 corn husks

Pinch of corn flour or masa harina

Filling

⅓ cup chopped dried apricots

⅓ cup chopped dried pineapple

⅓ cup chopped golden raisins

⅓ cup chopped dark or Mexican chocolate

½ cup chopped pecans

1 teaspoon light rum

Corn Cakes

⅓ cup unsalted butter, softened

½ cup sugar

2 cups corn flour or masa harina

1 teaspoon baking powder

1 teaspoon ground cinnamon

¼ teaspoon grated nutmeg

½ teaspoon salt

1 cup water

Makes 18 tamales

TO PREPARE

Prepare two large pots for steaming by filling them with 3 inches of water and fitting them with a steamer. Soak the corn husks in warm water for 1 hour to soften.

TO MAKE THE FILLING

Combine the apricots, pineapple, raisins, chocolate, pecans, and rum in a small bowl; set aside.

TO MAKE THE BATTER

Use a mixer to cream the butter and sugar in a large bowl until fluffy; set aside. In a separate medium bowl, stir together the corn flour, baking powder, cinnamon, nutmeg, and salt. Add the corn flour mixture to the butter mixture and stir until it resembles a coarse meal. Slowly add the water, stopping when the mixture holds together.

TO PREPARE THE TAMALES

Dust some corn flour on the inside of a corn husk. Add about 2 tablespoons of the corn flour mixture, spreading it into a rectangle. Set about 2 teaspoons of filling in the center of the rectangle, and wrap the corn flour mixture around the filling. Fold the corn husk over the filling, and tie the tamale cake together with the ends of the husks. Repeat until you have prepared 18 tamales.

TO STEAM

Stand the cakes up in the steamer. Do not pack them in too tightly, as they will expand while cooking. Cover with the remaining six husks. Cover the pot, bring the water to a boil, and then reduce to a simmer and steam for 1 hour. Test for doneness by opening one husk; if the cake pulls away from the wrapper, it's done.

VARIATION

Maple-Pecan Tamale

Replace the filling with a mixture of 2 cups chopped pecans, ¼ cup dark brown sugar, and ¼ cup maple syrup.

The History of Tamales

Tamales can be traced back to at least 5000 BCE, when they served as a travel food for Aztec, Mayan, and Incan warriors. They worked well — then and now — for travel because they can be prepared ahead of time and warmed when it is time to eat. They are generally thought of as fall and winter food since they make use of the dried corn husks harvested in summer. Since they are a bit labor-intensive, tamales are usually prepared for the holidays and dozens are made at a time.

Yuca Cake

The nations of the tropics share a balmy climate and fertile terrain perfect for growing yuca, also known as cassava or manioc. The plant's tuberous root is a popular starch base for baking throughout the Americas, Asia, and Africa. It can be grated, dried, or made into cassava flour. This recipe calls for grating fresh yuca root, which will cook while baking in the cake.

Yuca Cake

- 1 cup all-purpose flour
- 1 tablespoon baking powder
- ¼ teaspoon salt
- 1½ cups sugar
- 3 tablespoons unsalted butter, softened
- 3 eggs
- 1 cup coconut milk
- 2 cups (1¾ pounds) peeled, shredded yuca root
- ¼ cup shredded, unsweetened coconut

Sweet Milk Sauce

- 7 ounces sweetened condensed milk
- 2 tablespoons whole milk
- ½ teaspoon vanilla extract

Makes 18 individual-serving cakes

TO PREPARE

Preheat the oven to 350°F. Butter and flour eighteen 3-inch Bundt pans (or one 9-inch Bundt pan).

TO MAKE THE CAKES

Mix together the flour, baking powder, and salt in a small bowl; set aside. In a separate medium bowl, beat together the sugar, butter, and eggs. Gradually stir the flour mixture into the butter mixture, alternating with the coconut milk. Stir in the yuca and the coconut.

TO BAKE

Pour the batter into the prepared pans and bake for 20 to 25 minutes, until golden brown and a knife inserted in the center comes out clean. (If you're using the 9-inch pan, bake for 40 to 45 minutes.)

TO MAKE THE SWEET MILK SAUCE

In a small bowl combine the condensed milk, whole milk, and vanilla. Pour the sauce over the warm cakes.

VARIATIONS

Brazilian Yuca Cake
Replace the coconut milk with whole milk.

Honduran Yuca Spice Cake
Add 1 teaspoon ground cinnamon, ½ teaspoon ground allspice, and ¼ teaspoon grated nutmeg to the flour mixture.

Indonesian Pandan Yuca Cake
Replace the coconut milk with whole milk. Add 2 teaspoons pandan extract.

How to Peel Yuca

Yuca root has two peels, a tough outer brown peel and an inner pink one. To peel, slit through both peels lengthwise with a paring knife. Slip the knife under the pink inner layer, and pull off both layers of peel. Once the peel is removed, cut the yuca in half, and remove and discard the fibrous inner core. Shred the white root with a grater.

About Yuca

For thousands of years yuca was an important plant for the indigenous peoples of the Americas. All parts of the plants were used. The leaves were used to create clothing and baskets, and their sharp tips were made into sewing needles. Almost all parts of the plant were eaten — and the same holds true today. The large white blossoms can be eaten fresh or dried, and the rootstock is an ingredient in many dishes and desserts. In particular, tapioca, the starch used to thicken puddings, is derived from cassava root.

Corn Cake

A truly great festival cake, this cornmeal cake is devoured at the many Festas Juninas in southern Brazil. Its simplicity allows it to be easily prepared at home, with many flavor variations. It is a common tea and café cake.

Corn Cake

- 1 cup sugar
- 2 tablespoons unsalted butter
- 2 cups cornmeal
- ¾ cup all-purpose flour
- 2 tablespoons baking powder
- ½ cup corn oil
- 3 eggs
- 1 cup milk

Toppings

- 2 cups whipped cream (page 323)
- Maraschino cherries

Makes 1 cake (serves 6 to 8)

TO PREPARE

Preheat the oven to 375°F. Butter and flour an 8-inch Bundt pan.

TO MAKE THE CAKE

Combine the sugar and butter in a food processor or blender, and pulse three to five times, until blended. Add the cornmeal, flour, and baking powder. Blend for about 30 seconds, until the mixture resembles coarse meal. Add the corn oil, eggs, and milk. Blend to a thick batter.

TO BAKE

Pour the batter into the prepared pan. Bake for 35 to 45 minutes, until a knife inserted in the center comes out clean. Let cool in its pan.

TO SERVE

Remove the cake from the pan. Serve topped with whipped cream and maraschino cherries.

VARIATIONS

Orange Corn Cake

Replace the milk with 1 cup orange juice. Add 1 tablespoon grated orange zest to the batter.

Peruvian Corn Cake (Pastel de Choclo)

Add 1¾ cups golden raisins, ½ teaspoon anise seed, and ¼ cup shredded sweetened coconut to the batter.

Festas Juninas

Festas Juninas is a series of June festivals honoring three saints. St. Anthony's Day is June 13, St. John's Day is June 24, and St. Peter's Day is June 29. These Christian celebrations have blended with local culture over time and are celebrated by most Brazilians regardless of their religious beliefs. At the festivals, everyone from the youngest to the oldest generations joins together to dance the quadrilha around a bonfire. The quadrilha is a theatrical square dance that found its way from the royal courts of Europe to Brazil in the eighteenth century. Traditionally there's a pause in the dance for a short dramatic scene, usually acting out the story of a wedding gone wrong. It's a unique mix of courtly manners, carnival energy, and pantomime.

Marta Rocha Torte

Named after the midtwentieth-century Brazilian beauty who almost won the Miss Universe contest, this cake is very rich and sweet, with alternating layers of white and chocolate cake spread with baba de moça (young lady drooling) custard, meringue, and crocante (caramelized nuts). The cake gets its iconic bright yellow color from being topped with fios de ovos (egg threads), which are made from sugar and egg yolks and resemble angel hair pasta. Most people purchase fios de ovos at groceries or confectioneries, since they are difficult to make at home.

White Cake

- 8 eggs
- ½ cup granulated sugar
- ½ cup all-purpose flour
- 1 teaspoon vanilla extract

Chocolate Cake

- ½ cup all-purpose flour
- ¼ cup unsweetened cocoa powder
- 8 eggs
- ½ cup granulated sugar
- 1 teaspoon vanilla extract

Baba de Moça Filling

- 1½ cups water
- 1½ cups granulated sugar
- 1 teaspoon unsalted butter
- 1 teaspoon vanilla extract
- 8 egg yolks, passed through a sieve
- 7 ounces unsweetened coconut milk

Crocante Filling

- 2¼ cups confectioners' sugar
- ¼ cup water
- 2 cups walnuts

Toppings

- 5 cups meringue frosting (page 316)
- ½ cup fios de ovos

Makes 1 cake (serves 6 to 8)

TO PREPARE

Preheat the oven to 350°F. Butter and flour two 9-inch round cake pans.

TO MAKE THE WHITE CAKE

Beat the eggs and sugar with a mixer for 7 to 10 minutes, until they have doubled in volume. Gently fold in the flour and vanilla until well blended. Pour the batter into a prepared cake pan; set aside.

TO MAKE THE CHOCOLATE CAKE

Combine the flour and cocoa powder; set aside. In a separate medium bowl, beat the eggs and sugar with a mixer for 7 to 10 minutes, until they have doubled in volume. Gently fold in the flour mixture and vanilla until well blended. Pour the batter into the second prepared pan.

TO BAKE

Bake the cakes for 30 to 35 minutes, until a knife inserted in the center comes out clean. Let cool in the pans.

TO MAKE THE BABA DE MOÇA FILLING

Combine the water and sugar in a medium saucepan and heat to 230°F. Remove from the heat. Stir in the butter and vanilla and let cool. Transfer the mixture to a double boiler. Add the egg yolks and coconut milk. Cook in the double boiler over medium heat, stirring, until thickened.

TO MAKE THE CROCANTE FILLING

Preheat the oven to 350°F and butter a baking sheet. Dissolve the confectioners' sugar in the water. Stir in the nuts until coated. Transfer the mixture to the prepared baking sheet and cook in the oven for 5 minutes, until toasted. Remove from the oven.

TO ASSEMBLE

Cut the two cakes in half crosswise to make four layers. Place a chocolate cake layer on a serving platter. Top with baba de moça filling, crocante filling, and a thin layer of meringue. Place a white layer on top, followed by baba de moça filling, crocante filling, and another thin layer of meringue. Place the remaining chocolate layer on top, followed by baba de moça filling, crocante filling, and another thin layer of meringue. Top with the final layer of white cake. Spread the remaining meringue over the cake and top with fios de ovos.

VARIATIONS

Mocha Marta Rocha Torte

Replace the meringue with 5 cups mocha buttercream (page 316).

Pecan-Peach Marta Rocha

Replace the walnuts with pecans. Replace the crocante filling with 1 cup peach preserves.

Marta Rocha

The 1954 Miss Universe contest came down to a tie between Marta Rocha (Miss Brazil) and Miriam Jacqueline Stevenson (Miss America). In the end, the judges based their final decision on the hips, and Stevenson won because hers were smaller. Much fame came to Marta Rocha for losing for such a ridiculous reason. The Marta Rocha torte was created in the 1950s by women bakers from Rio Grande do Sul, Brazil, in her honor.

Brazil Nut Cake

Did you know that not all Brazil nuts are from Brazil? In fact, Bolivia provides more than half the world's harvest. Brazil nut cakes with orange flavoring are popular in the Amazon regions of Bolivia, Peru, and Brazil. They're usually eaten plain or topped with a simple orange or chocolate glaze.

Cake

1½	cups Brazil nuts
1½	cups sugar
2	cups all-purpose flour
1	tablespoon baking powder
½	teaspoon salt
⅔	cup unsalted butter, softened
3	eggs
¼	cup orange juice
	Zest of 1 orange, grated
⅓	cup milk

Topping

1¼ cups orange glaze (page 319)

Makes 1 cake (serves 6 to 8)

TO PREPARE

Preheat the oven to 350°F. Butter and flour an 8-inch tube pan.

TO MAKE THE CAKE

Grind 1 cup of the Brazil nuts with 2 tablespoons of the sugar in a food processor or blender. Transfer to a medium bowl. Stir in the flour, baking powder, and salt, and set aside. In a separate medium bowl, beat the butter and the remaining sugar in a medium bowl until light and fluffy. Add the eggs one at a time, beating well after each addition. Stir in the orange juice and orange zest. Gradually add the flour mixture to the butter mixture, alternating with the milk.

TO BAKE

Pour the batter into the prepared pan. Bake for 35 to 40 minutes, until a knife inserted in the center comes out clean.

TO SERVE

Pour the orange glaze over the warm cake. Top with the remaining ½ cup Brazil nuts.

VARIATIONS

Bolivian Chocolate–Brazil Nut Cake

Add 3 tablespoons Dutch-processed cocoa powder to the batter. Top the cake with 1 cup chocolate glaze (page 318).

Orange Cake

Omit the nuts entirely; increase the flour to 2¾ cups and the orange juice to ½ cup. This version of the cake is popular throughout Brazil.

Brazil Nuts and the Rain Forest

Brazil nuts have been eaten by the indigenous people of the Amazon for thousands of years. Portuguese and Spanish explorers introduced them to Europe as the "almonds of the Andes." The Brazil nut tree takes up to 30 years to bear seeds and can live for up to eight hundred years. In fact, eating Brazil nuts can help protect the rain forests from deforestation. The pods that carry the nuts are collected in the wild by locals, who sell them roadside to large distributors. Harvesting these nuts from the rain forest is one of the few alternatives to jobs that require clear-cutting the trees.

Orange-Chocolate Chiffon Cake

Very simple and very tasty, this marble sponge cake is, like all chiffons, made with oil instead of butter and gets its volume from the air beaten into its eggs. The high oil and egg content makes for a very moist cake. When buying cocoa, bear in mind that Venezuela grows some of the best cacao beans in the world. If you can find Venezuelan cocoa, use it for an authentic flavor.

Chiffon Cake

- 2 cups all-purpose flour
- 1½ cups sugar
- 2 teaspoons baking powder
- 1 teaspoon salt
- ¾ cup orange juice
- 6 eggs, separated
- 6 tablespoons vegetable oil
- 4 teaspoons grated orange zest
- 1 teaspoon vanilla extract
- 1 teaspoon cream of tartar
- ¼ cup unsweetened cocoa powder
- 2 drops orange food coloring

Cocoa Topping

- ¼ cup sugar
- 2 tablespoons unsweetened cocoa powder

Makes 1 cake (serves 6 to 8)

TO PREPARE

Preheat the oven to 350°F. Butter and flour a 10-inch tube pan or angel food pan.

TO MAKE THE CAKE

Combine the flour, 1 cup of the sugar, the baking powder, and the salt; set aside. In a separate large bowl, beat together the orange juice, egg yolks, oil, orange zest, and vanilla. Gradually stir in the flour mixture until just combined; set aside. In a separate small bowl, beat the egg whites and cream of tartar to soft peaks. Add the remaining ½ cup sugar and beat until stiff, glossy peaks form. Gradually fold the egg white mixture into the batter.

Divide the batter in half, then divide one batch in half again, so that you have one larger batch and two smaller batches. Add the cocoa powder to the large batch and the food coloring to one small batch; leave the second small batch plain.

TO BAKE

Pour the chocolate batter into the prepared pan, followed by the plain batter. Gently swirl through the batters with a knife, then top with the orange batter. Bake for 50 to 60 minutes, until a knife inserted in the center comes out clean. Let the cake cool in its pan for 5 minutes. Then turn the cake pan upside down to finish cooling. The cake may drop out as it cools; if it doesn't, use a long, sharp knife around the edges to ease it out once it's completely cooled.

TO MAKE THE TOPPING

Combine the sugar and cocoa powder in a small bowl. Sprinkle the topping over the cake.

VARIATION

Orange Cake with Orange Curaçao Curd

Prepare the cake in two 9-inch round cake pans. Increase the flour to 2¼ cups and omit the cocoa powder. Replace the vanilla in the cake with orange curaçao. Spread 1½ cups orange curd (page 321) between the layers.

History of Chiffon

The vegetable oil cake was invented in California in 1927 by Harry Baker, an insurance salesman and caterer who kept the recipe to himself and his clients for 20 years. He sold it to General Mills in 1947, and the company marketed it under the name chiffon cake. It released a Betty Crocker booklet with 14 chiffon recipes and variations in 1948.

Quince Empanadas

Stuffed empanadas are classics of Latin American cuisine, prepared in different sizes and shapes, depending on where they are made. They can be made with either a savory or a sweet filling. Quince-paste empanadas are Venezuelan baking at its finest.

Quince Paste

- 3 pounds quince, peeled and chopped
- Peels from 2 lemons, cut in long spirals
- 1 tablespoon vanilla extract
- 3 cups granulated sugar
- 2 tablespoons lemon juice

Empanada Dough

- ¾ cup all-purpose flour
- ½ teaspoon baking powder
- ⅛ teaspoon salt
- ½ cup (1 stick) unsalted butter, cold
- 2½ tablespoons cold water

Topping

- 2 tablespoons confectioners' sugar (optional)

Makes 12 empanadas

TO PREPARE

Butter an 8-inch square glass baking dish.

TO MAKE THE QUINCE PASTE

Place the quince and lemon peel in a large saucepan and fill with enough water to just cover the quince. Bring to a boil, then reduce the heat and let simmer for 35 to 40 minutes, until the quince is tender. Remove from the heat and drain. Remove the lemon zest. Purée the quince in a food processor or blender, then add the vanilla.

Return the quince purée to the saucepan. Add the sugar and lemon juice and stir until dissolved. Cook, stirring occasionally, for 1 to 1½ hours, until the quince paste is very thick.

Preheat the oven to 125°F. Spread the paste evenly in the baking pan and bake for 1½ hours, until firm. Let cool.

TO MAKE THE EMPANADA DOUGH

Preheat the oven 350°F. Butter two baking sheets.

Combine the flour, baking powder, and salt in a food processor or blender. Add the butter and pulse for 10 to 15 seconds, until the mixture resembles fine breadcrumbs. Add the water, a few teaspoonfuls at a time, and pulse until the dough can be gathered into a ball.

TO SHAPE

Roll out the dough to ¼-inch thickness on a floured work surface. Cut the dough into 4-inch rounds with a cookie cutter. Spoon 1 tablespoon of quince paste in the center of each round. Moisten the edges with water, fold the dough into a crescent, and press the edges closed. Seal by pressing the edges with the prongs of a fork.

TO BAKE

Place the empanadas on the prepared pans and bake for 15 to 20 minutes, until they are golden brown. Transfer the empanadas to a rack to cool. If desired, dust with confectioners' sugar before serving.

VARIATIONS

Cheese-Quince Empanada

Fill the empanadas with a thin slice of Manchego cheese in addition to the quince paste.

Guava Empanada

Replace the quince filling with guava paste, made simply by using guava instead of quince.

Mango-Pineapple Empanada

Cut a medium pineapple into 1-inch chunks and mix with 2 diced mangos. Add ½ cup sugar and 1 tablespoon cornstarch. Cook in a saucepan over medium-high heat for 7 to 10 minutes, until slightly thickened. Replace the quince paste with the pineapple mixture.

Arrollado con Dulce de Leche

Dulce de leche is a spreadable milk-based sauce with a sweet, burnt-sugar flavor that's common in South and Central American cakes, pastries, and sweets. Its flavor comes from simmering milk with sugar for a long time, until it forms a thick caramel cream. I've added vanilla to the sauce in this recipe to give it an even richer flavor. Of course, you can also simply buy canned dulce de leche in any Latin American market.

Vanilla Dulce de Leche

2 vanilla beans
8 cups milk
2¼ cups sugar
1 teaspoon sea salt

Roll Cake

6 eggs, separated
1 cup sugar
¼ cup milk, warmed
1 teaspoon vanilla extract
1 teaspoon rum
1 teaspoon honey
2 cups cake flour

Assembly

Rum
Confectioners' sugar
2 cups whipped cream (page 323)
3 ounces dark chocolate (optional)
3 ounces white chocolate (optional)
¼ cup sliced almonds, toasted (optional)

Makes 1 cake (serves 6 to 8)

TO PREPARE

Preheat the oven to 350°F. Line an 11- by 15- by 1-inch jelly roll pan with parchment paper cut slightly bigger than the tray. Butter the parchment paper or spray it with baking spray.

TO MAKE THE VANILLA DULCE DE LECHE

Slice the vanilla beans and scrape the seeds into a large saucepan. Add the milk, sugar, and salt to the saucepan. Whisk the mixture over medium heat until it comes to a full boil. Reduce the heat to a low simmer and cook, stirring occasionally, for 3 to 3½ hours, until reduced to 2 to 3 cups, with a caramel thickness. Remove from the heat and let cool.

TO MAKE THE CAKE

Beat the egg whites in a large bowl with a mixer until foamy. Add the sugar and beat until stiff, glossy peaks form. Beat in the egg yolks one at a time. Continue beating 7 to 10 minutes, until the batter is thick and creamy; set aside. Combine the milk, vanilla, rum, and honey in a small bowl. Fold the milk mixture into the egg mixture, alternating with the flour.

TO BAKE

Pour the batter into the prepared pan. Bake for 15 to 20 minutes, or until the cake springs back when touched or a knife inserted in the center comes out clean. Let cool in its pan for 5 minutes.

TO ASSEMBLE

While it's still warm, transfer the cake, still on the parchment, to a work surface. Brush rum evenly over the cake and sprinkle with confectioners' sugar. Holding the long end of the paper, start rolling the cake toward you, peeling the paper away as you roll. When you've rolled up the entire cake, roll the paper around it to secure, and let cool. When the cake is cool, remove the paper and unroll the cake. Spread half of the dulce de leche evenly over the cake, followed by the whipped cream. Reroll the cake as above.

TO SERVE

Place the roll on a serving platter, seam side down. Pour the remaining dulce de leche over the cake to coat. If you're using them, melt the dark and white chocolates separately, then use them to decorate the cake, along with the toasted almonds.

VARIATION

Mexican Almond Roll with Cajeta
Add ¾ cup ground almonds and 1 teaspoon almond extract to the batter. Prepare the dulce de leche with 4 cups cow's milk and 4 cups goat's milk.

Banana Roll with Chocolate
Replace the whipped cream with banana whipped cream (page 323) and the dulce de leche with chocolate glaze (page 318).

French or Argentinean?

Argentineans have a fantastic story about the origins of dulce de leche. They claim that in a war in their country in the early nineteenth century, on a winter afternoon, a general's maid was preparing lechada, a sugared milk drink. Unbeknownst to her, the general of the opposing force was visiting with her general, in the hope of working out a peace treaty. She went to speak with her general in his tent but found the enemy general there instead. Frightened, she ran to find her general's soldiers and forgot about the lechada on the stove. Just as the troops prepared to attack the enemy general, their own general arrived and cleared up the confusion. By then the lechada had burned, but the hungry soldiers ate it and loved it. And the story goes that she had invented dulce de leche.

It's a great story, but in reality dulce de leche most likely originated with the French confiture de lait, a confection very similar to dulce de leche that was created — coincidentally? — in the fourteenth century in a similar military culinary accident.

Pineapple-Chocolate Cream Cake

Throughout my research for this chapter, I came across many different Peruvian cakes made with pineapple, some of them topped with chocolate, an interesting if unexpected combination. This cake tastes great plain, but it's outstanding when glamorized with toasted meringue, chocolate whipped cream, chocolate chunks, and grilled pineapple. The simple addition of cherries transforms it into a Pakistani favorite.

Pineapple Cake

3½	cups all-purpose flour
2½	teaspoons baking powder
½	teaspoon baking soda
¼	teaspoon salt
5	eggs
2	cups sugar
½	cup whole milk
¾	cup vegetable oil
2	teaspoons vanilla
1	teaspoon lemon juice
1¼	cups pineapple juice

Assembly

2½	cups meringue frosting (page 316)
3½	cups pineapple filling (page 322)
2	cups chocolate whipped cream (page 323; optional)
1	cup chocolate chunks (optional)
6	pineapple rings, grilled (optional)

Makes 1 cake (serves 6 to 8)

TO PREPARE

Preheat the oven to 350°F. Butter and flour three 9-inch square baking pans.

TO MAKE THE CAKE

Combine the flour, baking powder, baking soda, and salt in a medium bowl; set aside. In a separate medium bowl, beat together the eggs, sugar, milk, oil, vanilla, and lemon juice. Blend the flour mixture into the egg mixture. Stir in the pineapple juice.

TO BAKE

Pour the batter into the prepared pans and bake for 35 to 40 minutes, until a knife inserted in the center comes out clean. Let cool in their pans.

TO ASSEMBLE

Preheat the oven broiler. Remove the cakes from their pans. Set one cake on a serving platter. Spread the meringue on top of it. Set the second layer on top of it, and top with the pineapple filling. Set the final layer on top, and spread the remaining meringue over the top and sides of the cake. Use a knife or decorating tool to create patterns in the meringue. Broil for 3 to 5 minutes, watching carefully, until browned.

If desired, scoop the whipped cream into a pastry bag fitted with a large star tip, and pipe ridged mounds of whipped cream around the edges of the cake. Arrange chocolate chunks and segments of grilled pineapple on the mounds.

VARIATIONS

Orange-Pecan Pineapple Cake

Replace the milk with orange juice. Add 2 teaspoons grated orange zest and ½ cup ground pecans to the cake batter. Top with 1¼ cups orange glaze (page 319).

Pakistani Pineapple Cake

Add 1 cup fresh cherries to the batter. Top the cake with fresh pineapple and cherries.

south-central provinces like Provence and Laguedoc wheat and chestnut flours are common.

Austria also has a rich tradition of truly irresistible cakes and pastries. Austrian cakes are complex; they are usually made in bakeries by talented pastry chefs and sold by the slice in cafés. The most famous of these cakes is the Sachertorte (page 126).

The Viennese, in particular, are the original creators of the "Danish," the pastry that inspired the Danes to create their own variation.

While in France and Austria cake making is left to the experts, home baking is common in Germany. The Germans treat cakes casually, preparing them for cozy gatherings with family and friends. They make great use of spiced apples and nuts, lemon icing, chocolate, sweetmeats, ginger, and hazelnuts. The German language is filled with terms to describe feelings associated with food. Gemuetlichkeit (comfort and coziness), for example, aptly describes cheesecake, while waldeinsamkeit (forest loneliness) is used to characterize Black Forest cake (page 120), the most popular cake in the world. Germans are also famous for their seasonal specialties; at Christmastime, for example, they bake vast quantities of stollen (page 122) and gingerbread.

The cake culture of Switzerland combines influences from Germany, France, and Italy with unique Swiss elements. Cheese and chocolate are icons of Swiss cuisine, of course. In fact, the country boasts the highest per capita consumption of chocolate of any country in the world, a fact readily evidenced by traditional Swiss cakes such as the schokoladentorte, a chocolate cake with chocolate frosting. Witness also the communal bubbling pot of chocolate fondue (page 114), a unique Swiss experience. Swiss rolls (page 116) and vacherin meringues (page 113) have been adopted into cuisines around the world.

Between Germany and France lies the Netherlands, another powerhouse in baking traditions. The Dutch have a long-standing fascination with food — just look at the abundance of still lifes featuring food from Dutch masters in the sixteenth and seventeenth centuries. Their pastries have Scandinavian influences, and their cakes are seasoned with spices from their former colonies in Southeast Asia and the Caribbean. Oliebollen, the fried dough of the region, was the inspiration for American doughnuts. Luilakbollen (page 128), flavored with orange zest and dotted with cranberries and currants, are traditionally given to children on Lazybones Day; any who fail to rise up out of bed to celebrate the day risk being taunted the rest of the year.

Croquembouche

In keeping with the French sense of over-the-top display, the croquembouche is the ultimate cake sculpture. It was originally created by superstar pastry chef Antoine Carême (1784–1833), who in his time amazed Europe with his sculptural sugar creations. This tower, one of his simpler creations, is made by stacking profiteroles (cream puffs) high in a cone shape. The profiteroles are filled with flavored cream and are traditionally held together with caramel, giving the cake a crunchy texture ("croque en bouche" translates as "crunch in the mouth"). Croquembouches are often decorated with spun sugar, candied almonds, chocolate flowers, or ribbons. They are often made as wedding cakes and for Christmas feasts (when they can be decorated to look like Christmas trees).

If you are new to the croquembouche, I recommend building a cardboard cone as a support for your sculpture and using royal icing to stick the profiteroles to one another. This technique forms the basis of the instructions below. With some experience you will be able to use caramel as the glue and to rely on the profiteroles to support each other; see the sidebar on page 100 for more information about that. (And if making this dessert is going to be your new hobby, purchase a pyramid-shaped croquembouche mold, which will help with the stacking process.)

Profiteroles

- 2 cups all-purpose flour
- 4 teaspoons sugar
- ⅛ teaspoon salt
- 2 cups water
- 1 cup (2 sticks) unsalted butter, softened
- 8 eggs
  Chocolate pastry cream (page 323), chilled

Assembly

- 2½ cups royal icing (page 317)
  Simple sugar candies of choice

Spun Sugar

- 2 cups sugar
- ½ cup light corn syrup
- ½ cup water

Makes 1 cake (serves 6 to 8)

TO PREPARE

Preheat the oven to 375°F. Line two baking sheets with parchment paper.

TO MAKE THE PASTRY DOUGH

Sift the flour, sugar, and salt together in a small bowl; set aside. Bring the water to a boil in a saucepan, then reduce the heat to low, add the butter, and stir until it is melted. Remove the mixture from the heat and immediately stir in the flour mixture with a wooden spoon. Stir vigorously, until the mixture pulls away from the sides of the pan. Transfer the dough to a bowl and add the eggs one at a time, beating well after each addition, until the mixture is shiny and falls from the spoon.

TO BAKE THE PUFFS

Spoon one-third of the dough into a pastry bag with a round tip. Pipe the dough onto the prepared baking sheets in small mounds of about 1½ inches, spacing them 1½ inches apart. Dip a finger in water and use it to gently press down the top of each mound. Then spritz the dough mounds (a spray bottle is helpful here) with water — the moisture will help them rise.

Place the baking sheets in the oven and bake for 15 to 20 minutes for the smallest puffs, until the puffs are golden brown and puffy. Turn off the oven, open the oven door a bit, and let cool for a few minutes before removing. Transfer the puffs to a rack to finish cooling.

Repeat the procedure to make medium-size puffs of about 2¼ inches, baking them for 18 to 23 minutes, and then large puffs of about 3¼ inches, baking them for 20 to 25 minutes.

TO FILL AND DECORATE THE PUFFS

When the puffs have cooled, scoop the chocolate pastry cream into a pastry bag fitted with a medium round tip. Use a sharp, thin knife to poke a hole the size of the pastry bag tip into the center of each puff, insert the tip, and pipe the cream into the puffs.

Scoop royal icing into a pastry bag fitted with a small round tip. Use it to pipe crosshatched lines on the puffs, and let dry.

(continued on next page)

TO ASSEMBLE

Place the cardboard cone on a serving plate. Arrange a ring of large puffs around the bottom of the cone, using royal icing to glue them to each other. Set layers of large puffs above, using the cone as a support and royal icing as glue. When you've used all the large puffs, attach the medium puffs, and then the small puffs, until the puffs form a complete tower and entirely cover the cardboard support. Fill in any remaining spaces with royal icing, and let dry and harden for at least 3 hours. When the construction has set, use royal icing to attach the candies.

TO DECORATE WITH SPUN SUGAR

Spun sugar doesn't last long, so wait until just before you are ready to serve the cake to decorate it. Secure a dozen or so bamboo skewers with a rubber band, and set aside. Combine the sugar, corn syrup, and water in a saucepan over low heat, and cook, stirring, until the sugar dissolves. Cover, raise the heat to medium to bring the mixture to a boil, and then let boil for 2 to 3 minutes, removing the lid to stir occasionally, until the mixture

reaches 310°F. Let the mixture cool for 1 to 2 minutes, until thickened.

Dip the bamboo tool into the saucepan, coating it with liquid sugar. Flick the tool toward the croquembouche, casting the sugar onto it. The sugar should form thin strands upon hitting the puffs. If it doesn't form strands, let the sugar mixture cool another minute or so; if the strands are too lumpy, reheat the sugar mixture. Work your way around the croquembouche, covering it with sugar strands. Serve immediately.

VARIATIONS

Chocolate Croquembouche
In the choux pastry replace ½ cup flour with ½ cup unsweetened cocoa powder.

Christmas Croquembouche
Add 4 drops green food coloring to the choux pastry dough. Fill the puffs with strawberry pastry cream (page 323). Decorate with holiday candies.

Speedy Croquembouche
Use premade cream puffs instead of preparing them at home.

Planning the Tower

This recipe makes two to three dozen profiteroles. Before you begin baking, determine how many batches of the recipe you will need to make, using the following guidelines:

20–24 guests: three batches
25–48 guests: six batches
49–72 guests: nine batches
73–94 guests: twelve batches

When preparing a large croquembouche, make the dough in batches; with an overlarge batch, it's hard to achieve the correct choux pastry texture. Then bake and fill as directed.

Consider making two or three smaller croquembouches using different flavors of choux pastry or fillings, or mix up different flavors within one croquembouche.

The Caramel Croquembouche

The traditional caramel croquembouche does not use a cardboard cone for support — it's all about how you stack the profiteroles. When preparing this caramel version, make the caramel in small batches, as directed below; it will keep sticky longer and you will have more assembly time.

Caramel
6 cups sugar
2 cups water
1½ cups light corn syrup

Makes 3½ cups

TO PREPARE
Follow the instructions on page 99 to prepare the profiteroles. When you are ready to begin assembling the croquembouche, prepare the caramel.

TO MAKE THE CARAMEL
Combine the sugar and water in a large saucepan over medium heat. Bring to a boil, stirring continually, and brushing down the inside of the pan to prevent crystals from forming. Add the corn syrup and continue cooking, stirring continually, until the temperature reaches 320°F. The caramel should be a light golden brown. Remove the pan from the heat immediately.

TO ASSEMBLE
Lightly butter a cake plate. To set a puff, you'll use tongs to pick it up, dip it in the caramel, and set it on the plate. First arrange a series of large puffs in a circle approximately 10 inches in diameter. Fill the circle with more large puffs. Construct subsequent layers similarly, always setting the outside puffs just inside the puffs below them, so that the tower gradually rises to a point. As in the instruction above, use first the large puffs and then medium puffs, finishing with small puffs.

Decorate as specified in the instructions above.

Queen of Sheba Cake

This melt-in-your-mouth chocolate almond cake is slightly undercooked, so the center remains fudgy and chewy. Though it's great on its own, you can also top it with chocolate glaze (page 318) or dust it with unsweetened cocoa powder.

Chocolate Cake

- ¾ cup plus 5 tablespoons sugar
- 1 cup blanched almonds
- ½ teaspoon almond extract
- 6 ounces semisweet chocolate, melted
- ¼ cup double-strength espresso
- 3 tablespoons rum
- ¾ cup (1½ sticks) unsalted butter, softened
- 8 eggs, separated
- ½ teaspoon salt
- ½ cup cake flour

Topping

- 2 cups chocolate glaze (page 318) or confectioners' sugar

Makes 1 cake (serves 6 to 8)

TO PREPARE

Preheat the oven to 350°F. Butter and flour an 8-inch round cake pan.

TO PULVERIZE THE ALMONDS

Add 3 tablespoons of sugar and the almonds to a food processor or blender. Pulse until ground. Stir in the almond extract and set aside.

TO MAKE THE BATTER

Combine the chocolate and espresso in a double boiler and cook over medium heat, stirring continually, until the chocolate is melted. Remove from the heat, stir in the rum, and set aside to cool. In a large bowl, cream the butter and ¾ cup of the sugar until fluffy. Blend the chocolate into the butter and sugar mixture, then stir in the pulverized almonds. Beat in the egg yolks two at a time until well blended. In a separate medium bowl, beat the egg whites and salt until soft peaks form. Add the remaining 2 tablespoons sugar and beat until stiff peaks form. Fold the egg whites into the batter, alternating with the flour, just until blended.

TO BAKE THE CAKE

Pour the batter into the prepared pan and bake for 25 to 30 minutes, until a knife inserted in the center comes out a bit oily but not goopy. Let cool in the pan.

TO SERVE

Cut the cake into wedges, and top with chocolate glaze or confectioners' sugar.

VARIATION

Cherry-Chocolate Queen of Sheba Cake

Add 1½ cups chopped, pitted fresh cherries to the batter. Top with cherry icing (page 315), sliced almonds, and whole cherries.

The Queen of Sheba

Julia Child claimed this chocolate cake as her favorite, and she included a recipe for it in both of her classic cookbooks, *Mastering the Art of French Cooking* and *The Way to Cook*. It is named after the legendary African Queen of Sheba and is meant to be as enticing as the queen herself. She was a guest of King Solomon of Israel in the tenth century BCE. Jews, Christians, Muslims, and Arabs each have a different interpretation of exactly what happened between the two rulers and the level of intimacy of their relationship. Some say it was an affair of state, while others say it was an affair of the heart. All that everyone agrees on is that she brought him spices and gold as gifts, and they had a nice dinner together.

Pain d'Épices (Gingerbread)

In France gingerbread is eaten for Christmas, with whipped cream or lemon crème anglaise, a custard sauce that can be poured on top of the cake or served on the side. In this recipe I toned down the spice a bit for a more subtle taste; if you prefer your gingerbread spicier, simply add more spice. This recipe makes 14 mini gingerbreads.

Gingerbread

- 2 cups all-purpose flour
- 1½ teaspoons baking powder
- 1½ teaspoons ground ginger
- ½ teaspoon ground anise seed
- ½ teaspoon ground cinnamon
- ¼ teaspoon ground white pepper
- ¼ teaspoon grated nutmeg
- ¼ teaspoon salt
- 1 cup light brown sugar, packed
- 4 eggs
- 1½ cups (3 sticks) unsalted butter, softened
- ½ cup milk
- ¼ cup unsulfured molasses
- 1 tablespoon freshly grated ginger
- 2 teaspoons vanilla extract
- 1 teaspoon lemon juice

Lemon Crème Anglaise

- 4 egg yolks
- ⅓ cup granulated sugar
- 1 cup heavy cream
- 2 teaspoons vanilla extract
- Juice of 1 lemon

Topping

- 2 teaspoons slivered lemon zest

Makes 14 individual-serving cakes

TO PREPARE

Preheat the oven to 350°F. Butter and flour fourteen 3½-inch tart pans.

TO MAKE THE GINGERBREAD

Mix together the flour, baking powder, ground ginger, anise seed, cinnamon, pepper, nutmeg, and salt in a medium bowl. In a separate medium bowl, beat the brown sugar and eggs until light and fluffy. Combine the butter and milk in a saucepan over low heat, and stir until the butter is melted. Stir in the molasses, fresh ginger, vanilla, and lemon juice. Stir the dry ingredients into the egg mixture, alternating with the butter mixture, until well blended.

TO BAKE THE GINGERBREAD

Pour the batter into the prepared pans and bake for 20 to 25 minutes, until a knife inserted in the center comes out clean. Let cool in the pans.

TO MAKE THE LEMON CRÈME ANGLAISE

Whisk the egg yolks and sugar in a medium bowl until smooth. Combine the cream and vanilla in a small saucepan over medium heat and cook, whisking continually, for 3 to 5 minutes, until bubbles begin to form around the edges. Scoop out ½ cup of the cream mixture, and slowly pour it into the egg yolks, whisking constantly. Gradually add the egg yolk mixture back to the cream mixture, whisking constantly. Heat for about 2 minutes, stirring constantly, until the mixture thickens. Remove from the heat and stir in the lemon juice.

TO SERVE

Remove the gingerbread from the pans. Serve with the lemon crème anglaise, on top of or on the side of the gingerbread, and garnished with lemon zest.

VARIATIONS

Chocolate-Honey Gingerbread
Replace the molasses with honey. Coat the gingerbread with chocolate ganache (page 315).

Lime–Sorghum Molasses Gingerbread
Replace the lemon juice in the cake and sauce with lime juice. Use sorghum molasses in place of the unsulfured molasses.

Maple-Nut Gingerbread
Add 1 cup chopped walnuts to the gingerbread batter. Replace the molasses with maple syrup.

Orange Gingerbread
Replace the lemon juice in the cake and sauce with orange juice. Add 2 tablespoons grated orange zest to the cake and 1 teaspoon grated orange zest to the sauce.

Gingerbread Squares
Prepare the batter as directed, and bake in an 8-inch square pan for 45 to 55 minutes. Cut into 2-inch squares. Dust with confectioner's sugar.

Gingerbread History

Dark or light, sweet or spicy, ginger-bread is found in many tastes, textures, and forms around the world. Ginger, native to Asia, made its way to the Middle East along the spice trade routes and was introduced to Europe in the eleventh century by returning Crusaders. Ginger quickly caught on, and in medieval times it was one of the most traded spices between Asia and Europe due to its value as a preservative.

The traveling knights may have brought back gingerbread recipes as well, because they brought back everything else needed to make this spicy treat, including sugar and citrus fruits. Monks developed the first European gingerbreads and traditionally ate them for holiday celebrations, including Christmas, a tradition that's persisted through the ages. Carnivals called "gingerbread fairs" took place throughout Europe, each celebrating its own regional variety. Many of these carnivals recurred for centuries, though by the nineteenth century they had all died out.

Even today, regional preferences determine the sweetener of choice. In England gingerbread is sweetened with treacle, the French use brown sugar, and the Germans use honey. In New England maple syrup is preferred, while in the American South gingerbread is made with sorghum molasses.

Opera Gateau

Opera gateaus are the easiest cakes to recognize: they are clearly identified by the word *opera* piped in icing on their top. Individual servings of opera cakes usually have a musical clef on their top. The almond sponge cake layers are soaked in coffee syrup, filled with a coffee buttercream, and topped with chocolate icing. The cake is traditionally square or rectangular in shape, and the sides are left bare to show off the layers.

Almond Cake

2⅔	cups ground almonds
1	cup all-purpose flour
½	teaspoon baking powder
4	eggs
1¼	cups sugar
½	teaspoon grated lemon zest
½	cup (1 stick) unsalted butter, softened
¼	cup apple juice
¼	cup double-strength espresso, at room temperature

Coffee Syrup

½	cup double-strength espresso
⅓	cup sugar

Assembly

3	cups coffee buttercream (page 316)
2¼	cups chocolate ganache (page 315)
¼	cup lemon icing (page 316)
2	tablespoons sliced almonds

Makes 1 cake (serves 6 to 8)

TO PREPARE

Preheat the oven to 350°F. Butter and flour three 10-inch square cake pans.

TO MAKE THE ALMOND CAKE

Combine the ground almonds, flour, and baking powder in a bowl. In a separate medium bowl, beat the eggs, sugar, and lemon zest until blended. Add the butter, apple juice, and espresso and beat until combined. Add the almond mixture to the butter mixture and mix until combined.

TO BAKE

Divide the batter equally among the prepared pans, and bake for 20 to 25 minutes, until a knife inserted in the center comes out clean. Let the cakes cool in their pans for 10 minutes, then remove them from the pans and set on a rack to finish cooling.

TO MAKE THE COFFEE SYRUP

Bring the espresso and sugar to a boil in a small saucepan. When the sugar has dissolved, remove from the heat and set aside to cool.

TO ASSEMBLE

Brush the coffee syrup over the three cake layers. Spread a thick layer of coffee buttercream over one layer. Spread a layer of chocolate ganache over the other two layers. Place one of the ganache-covered layers on a serving plate, and top with the buttercream-covered layer, followed by the remaining ganache-covered layer. Gently press the layers together, and wipe away any excess buttercream that oozes out. (For very clean edges, use a sharp knife to cut off ½ inch of the cake on all sides.)

Spoon the lemon icing into a pastry bag fitted with a small writing tip, and use it to write the word *opera* on top of the cake. Sprinkle with sliced almonds.

VARIATIONS

Cuban Opera Cake

Replace the buttercream with guava sauce. To make the guava sauce combine 3 cups guava pulp, 2 cups sugar, and ¼ cup lime juice in a saucepan and boil for 3 minutes, until thickened.

Norwegian Hazelnut Opera Cake

Replace the almonds with hazelnuts. Fill with vanilla buttercream (page 317) and top with confectioners' sugar and fresh cloudberries (golden raspberries).

Names on Cakes

The opera gateau is said to have been created in the 1930s for a French-American reception at the Paris Grand Opera. It is one of the few cakes that historically has been identified by being inscribed with its name. Another cake that traditionally has its name written on its top is the Sachertorte, which in its original form bore the logo of the Hotel Sacher, molded in chocolate. Although never widespread, the practice may be on the upswing; writing a cake's name on its top to encourage tourists to give it a try is a big trend in Italy these days.

Petits Fours Glacés

Intriguing little bites of cake, petits fours can be made in so many delicious ways. Some have a base so dense that it is almost as far as you can go on the cake spectrum before it turns into a cookie. Others have multiple thin layers of cake with a fruit glaze in the middle. My iced version walks a line in between, with a cakelike base supporting a baked almond filling. I like to cut them into different shapes: squares, diamonds, rectangles, and circles. When they are presented all together, it is hard to know which one to pick.

Dough
- 2 cups all-purpose flour
- 1 teaspoon baking powder
- ¼ teaspoon salt
- 1½ cups (3 sticks) unsalted butter
- ¼ cup sugar
- 2 egg yolks
- 2 tablespoons milk

Almond Paste
- 1¼ cups blanched almonds
- 1⅓ cups sugar
- ½ teaspoon salt
- 2 eggs
- 2 egg whites
- 1 teaspoon vanilla extract
- ½ teaspoon almond extract

Other Toppings
- 2 cups raspberry filling (page 322)
- 2 cups chocolate glaze (page 318)

Makes 18 petits fours

TO PREPARE
Preheat the oven to 350°F. Butter and flour two 8-inch square cake pans.

TO MAKE THE DOUGH
Combine the flour, baking powder, and salt in a medium bowl; set aside. In a separate large bowl, cream the butter and sugar until fluffy. Beat in the egg yolks and milk. Gradually add the flour mixture, stirring just until the dough holds together.

TO BAKE
Divide the dough in half and press into the prepared pans. Bake for 12 minutes, until lightly golden and just firm. Let the cakes cool in their pans.

TO MAKE THE ALMOND PASTE
Grind the almonds with ½ cup of the sugar in a food processor or blender. Transfer to a medium bowl. Add the remaining ½ cup plus ⅓ cup sugar and the salt, and blend. Then add the eggs, egg whites, vanilla, and almond extract, mixing well.

TO ASSEMBLE
Preheat the oven to 300°F. Spread the raspberry filling over the cakes, then spread the almond filling on top. Bake for 20 to 25 minutes, until the almond paste is springy. Let cool in the pans for 10 minutes, then remove the cakes from the pans and set on a rack to finish cooling.

Transfer the cakes to a cutting board, and cut them into 1- by 2-inch pieces. Dip the cakes in chocolate glaze. Decorate as desired.

VARIATIONS
Génoise Sponge Petits Fours
Prepare the génoise sponge cake (page 108) in a buttered and floured 11- by 15-inch jelly roll pan, baking it at 325°F for 10 to 15 minutes, until springy. Let the cake cool, then cut it crosswise into four 5-inch strips. Stack the strips, using 2 cups apricot glaze (page 318) or 2 cups raspberry glaze (page 319) as a filling between them. Top with chocolate glaze (page 318), cut into shapes, and decorate.

Vanilla-Iced Petits Fours
Prepare the cakes with almond and raspberry topping as directed, cutting them into 1- by 2-inch pieces. Prepare 2 cups vanilla icing (page 317) to a pouring consistency. Color with food coloring, if desired. Set the cut-out cakes on a rack and pour the vanilla icing over them. Let the icing harden, then repeat if needed. When the final coat of icing has hardened, decorate as desired.

Petits Fours

Petits fours are fanciful cakes traditionally eaten at teatime but just as hard to resist for dessert. They were developed in the eighteenth century, just as teatime was taking off as a social ritual and fancy cakes were being introduced to common society. Their small size allowed them to bake quickly, which was a clever way to utilize the energy that would otherwise be wasted in a brick oven cooling down after the day's baking was done. In fact, the name *petit four* translates as "small oven."

Petits fours can be made of any type of cake, but generally they break down into two genres: Petits fours glacés (iced) are decorated with fondant, ganache, frosting, or some other topping. Small éclairs and tartlets are included in this genre. Petits fours secs (dry) are more cookielike and generally undecorated. They include cookies, baked meringues, macaroons, and puff pastries. In central Europe petits fours are commonly prepared with a crust base, while Americans seem to prefer the layered sponge cake type with icing.

DESIGN SUGGESTIONS

Petits fours have signature designs and toppings. Here are some common items for decorating your petits fours:

- Candied citrus peel or ginger
- Chocolate-covered fruits, nuts, or coffee beans
- Crystallized flowers
- Delicate designs with fresh fruits and mint leaves
- Ground nuts
- Marzipan roses, fruits, or other cutouts
- Patterns in dark, milk, or white chocolate

Génoise Sponge Cake

This light and airy sponge cake is named after its place of origin, Genoa, Italy. Though Italian in its roots, it was adopted by the French in the fifteenth century and became the basis for much of French patisserie. This cake is leavened solely by the whipped whole eggs. The addition of melted butter makes it more tender than other sponge cakes.

1⅓ cups cake flour

1 cup cornstarch

12 eggs

1½ cups superfine sugar

⅔ cup unsalted butter, melted and cooled

2 teaspoons vanilla extract

Makes 2 cakes (serves 12)

TO PREPARE
Preheat the oven to 375°F. Butter and flour two 8-inch square cake pans.

TO MAKE THE BATTER
Combine the flour and cornstarch in a medium bowl; set aside. Beat the eggs and sugar in a double boiler over medium heat until the sugar has dissolved. When the mixture reaches 110 to 120°F on an instant-read thermometer, remove from the heat. Continue to beat with an electric mixer until the eggs have tripled in volume and become thick. Gradually fold the flour mixture into the batter. Fold in the butter and vanilla.

TO BAKE
Spread the batter into the prepared pans. Bake for 30 to 40 minutes, or until golden brown and the cake shrinks away from the sides. Let the cakes cool in the pans for 5 minutes, then remove from the pans and set on a rack to finish cooling.

VARIATION

Cheddar Cheese Cake

Add ½ cup shredded cheddar cheese to the batter. After 20 to 25 minutes of baking, sprinkle an additional ¾ cup shredded cheddar on top of the cake. Continue baking until the cheese is melted and a knife inserted in the center of the cake comes out clean, about 5 minutes.

Norwegian Omelette

The meringue covering this baked iced cream cake gives it an Arctic appearance, which is what inspired the French to name it the Norwegian omelette. Americans followed suit by naming their version baked Alaska, after the northernmost territory. Why doesn't the ice cream melt in the oven? The meringue insulates the ice cream for the duration of the short baking time. Start this cake early in the morning (you will need freezing time), and serve it hot straight from the oven at a summertime barbecue.

Chocolate Génoise Sponge Cake
- 1⅓ cups cake flour
- ⅓ cup cornstarch
- ¼ cup Dutch-processed cocoa
- 3 eggs
- 3 egg yolks
- ⅛ teaspoon salt
- ¾ cup granulated sugar

Fillings
- 1 quart vanilla ice cream, softened
- 2 cups fresh cherries, pitted and halved

Meringue
- 6 egg whites
- 1½ teaspoons vanilla extract
- ½ teaspoon cream of tartar
- ½ cup superfine sugar

Makes 6 individual-serving cakes

TO PREPARE
Preheat the oven to 375°F. Butter and flour a six-cup muffin pan.

TO MAKE THE CAKES
Combine the flour, cornstarch, and cocoa in a medium bowl; set aside. In a separate medium bowl, beat together the eggs, egg yolks, salt, and sugar with a mixer. Transfer to the top of a double boiler over medium heat and cook, stirring gently, until the mixture is warmed. Remove from the heat and beat with a mixer until the mixture has tripled in volume. Gradually fold the flour mixture into the batter.

TO BAKE THE CAKES
Divide the batter among the cups in the prepared pan. Bake for 25 to 30 minutes, or until just firm to the touch. Let the cakes cool in their pans.

TO ASSEMBLE
Once the cakes have cooled, remove them from the pans. Line the cups of the same muffin pans with plastic wrap, leaving a 2-inch overhang on all sides. Cut each cake into two thin layers. Place one piece of cake in a muffin cup. Spread on a ½-inch-thick layer of ice cream. Top with a few cherries. Set the second piece of cake on the cherries, followed by an additional layer of ice cream. Cover with plastic and freeze for at least 4 hours.

TO MAKE THE MERINGUE
Beat the egg whites with a mixer until foamy. Add the vanilla and the cream of tartar. Beat until soft peaks form. Gradually add the sugar, 1 tablespoon at a time, beating until stiff peaks form.

TO BAKE THE OMELETTES
Preheat the oven to 500°F, and position a rack in the center of the oven. Invert the frozen cakes onto an oven-safe platter, and remove the plastic wrap. Spoon the meringue into a pastry bag fitted with a large star tip, and pipe it over the entirety of the cakes.

Bake in the center of the oven for 2½ to 3 minutes, watching constantly, until the meringue is lightly browned. Serve immediately. (Alternatively, you could use a kitchen torch to brown the meringue.)

History of Baked Ice Cream

Baked ice cream cakes with velvety pastry crusts have been prepared for hundreds of years by the Chinese. Thomas Jefferson often had a version of this Chinese pastry-encrusted cake served to White House guests in the early 1800s. The French claim to have innovated on the Chinese tradition by using meringue as an insulator.

THE WORLD TOUR OF
Meringue Cakes

MERINGUE HAS STOOD THE TEST OF TIME. It was a favorite of Queen Elizabeth I more than four hundred years ago, and it is still a top choice for the wedding cakes of today. A simple recipe consisting of beaten egg whites and sugar, meringue can be chewy, crispy, or crunchy, depending on how it is prepared.

The origin of this basic recipe is widely disputed. Some say it is English; others claim it is French, Swiss, or Italian. We do know that in England in Elizabethan times it was mixed with flour and nuts to make bisket bread, a cookie cake similar to a biscotti that was flavored with anise seed, rosewater, and orange blossom. In the mid-1600s through the 1800s meringue's stiffness helped facilitate the fanciful decorations European pastry chefs used in sugar sculptures. These decorations made detailed and elaborate centerpieces for cakes, which inspired the meringue-covered wedding cakes of today.

Before electric mixers were invented, the creation of meringue was considered a true test of a pastry chef's skill. Always artful, the French developed a delicate meringue by adding sugar to whipped egg whites, 1 tablespoon at a time, until a smooth, glossy consistency was achieved. Usually this style of meringue is baked or toasted, which gives it a caramel flavor.

The Swiss make meringue by whisking egg whites and sugar over simmering water until the sugar has dissolved completely, then removing it from the heat and beating it until it's cool and firm. Since Swiss meringue is more stable and glossier than French meringue, it can be piped to create soft shapes.

Italian meringue is the strongest, which makes it ideal for frosting, torching, and piping. It is made by beating egg whites to the soft-peak stage, then folding in boiling-hot sugar syrup.

What's the chemistry? As the egg whites are beaten, proteins are separated into frothy bubbles that capture the air. Sugar helps create a thick structure that supports and stabilizes the proteins, until a moist and malleable texture is achieved. Cream of tartar is an extra stabilizer that holds the bubbles and maintains volume, making a light and fluffy meringue that is less likely to collapse. But some purists pooh-pooh the use of cream of tartar.

MERINGUE FAMILY TREE

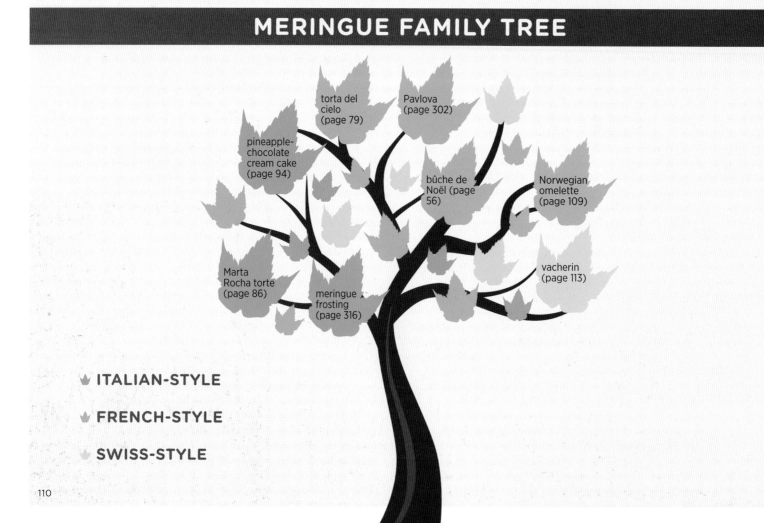

torta del cielo
(page 79)

Pavlova
(page 302)

pineapple-chocolate cream cake
(page 94)

bûche de Noël (page 56)

Norwegian omelette
(page 109)

Marta Rocha torte
(page 86)

meringue frosting
(page 316)

vacherin
(page 113)

🍂 **ITALIAN-STYLE**

🍂 **FRENCH-STYLE**

🍂 **SWISS-STYLE**

However it's made, silky, fluffy, melt-in-your-mouth meringue has many uses. It can be spread on top of cakes or piped into delicate designs. It may form an entire cake itself, or it may be used as a cake base, as in the case of macaroons and angel food cake. Dacquoise is a delightful nut meringue that is layered with whipped cream or buttercream in French cakes and pastries. Vacherin (page 113) is a Swiss or French cake made from meringue piped into discs. The Norwegian omelette (page 109) is an ice cream cake with a toasted meringue topping. In Mexico the tres leches cake (page 80) is hidden under a meringue topping. The Australian Pavlova (page 302) is a large meringue cake that is tender in the center and crisp on the outside. When it comes to meringue, there are a multitude of techniques and applications.

Want to make perfect meringue at home? Here are some tips from the pros:

- *Check the weather before embarking on a meringue-making session. Avoid humid days, as the extra moisture makes it difficult to achieve stiff peaks.*

- *Use a very clean, dry metal or glass bowl; any trace of fat will wreck the meringue. Fussy chefs say that copper bowls produce the fluffiest meringue.*

- *Use superfine or confectioners' sugar, as either will dissolve more easily than granulated sugar.*

- *Separate the eggs when they are cold, and set them aside to warm for 30 minutes before whipping them at room temperature.*

- *For French meringue, beat the egg whites until they are foamy before adding any sugar. Add the sugar 1 tablespoon at a time until stiff peaks form. Do not overbeat. The meringue should be smooth, glossy, and flexible. If egg-white foam appears, you have overbeaten. There is no way to fix meringue. Start over.*

- *For Swiss meringue, the water in the double boiler should not touch the bottom of the bowl, because this would make the mixing pan too hot. Test whether the sugar is dissolved by rubbing the mixture between your fingers to see if it is gritty.*

- *For Italian meringue, pour the hot sugar syrup slowly into the mixing bowl so it doesn't splash.*

- *Use whisk beaters, as they work faster and add more air to your meringue.*

- *When piping, hold the bag at the top and squeeze lightly.*

- *When baking meringue, you are really just drying it out. Either bake it at a low heat or leave it in a warm oven that is turned off. Baking for a short period will make it chewy, while baking for a long time will make it crisp.*

- *When toasting meringue, broil it in a high-heat oven (about 500°F) for just a few minutes. Meringue can also be browned with a handheld torch.*

- *Overcooking can cause meringue to bead with moisture. To correct this, slightly increase the oven temperature and decrease the baking time. Be careful not to overbrown.*

- *Don't spread meringue over a cold filling. This may cause weeping, a pool of liquid that will ruin the look of your cake. Of course when you're making a Norwegian omelette or baked Alaska, cold filling — in the form of ice cream cake — cannot be avoided. In this case, make the meringue extra thick and serve immediately.*

LEFT: *meringue mushrooms with a bûche de Noël (page 56);* CENTER: *meringue topping on a pineapple-chocolate cream cake (page 94);* RIGHT: *meringue filling and topping on a Marta Rocha torte (page 86)*

Apple-Lemon Charlotte Russe

Like trifles (page 140) and cassata (page 196), charlottes are layered arrangements of cake and filling. Warm charlottes are made by lining a mold with bread, filling it with a fruit purée, topping with more bread, and baking. Charlotte russe was the first chilled charlotte, said to have been invented by Frenchman Antoine Carême in the nineteenth century upon his relocation to Russia. In this version, ladyfingers line the mold and a cream filling is used. I like to make charlottes in individual serving sizes, but you could also use the recipe to make a larger one in an 8-inch square pan.

Ladyfingers

- 1 cup all-purpose flour
- 1⅓ cups confectioners' sugar
- ¼ teaspoon salt
- 6 eggs, at room temperature, separated
- 2 tablespoons dark rum

Apple-Raisin Filling

- 2 teaspoons unsalted butter
- 6 apples, peeled, cored, and sliced
- 2 teaspoons lemon juice
- ½ cup golden raisins
- ½ cup apple juice
- ¼ cup granulated sugar
- 1½ teaspoons freshly grated ginger

Lemon Cream

- 4 cups whipped cream (page 323)
- 2¼ cups lemon curd (page 321)

Makes 6 individual-serving cakes

TO PREPARE

Preheat the oven to 325°F. For baking the ladyfingers, line two baking pans with parchment paper. Line the inside of each compartment of a large muffin tin with plastic wrap, leaving a 2-inch overhang.

TO MAKE THE LADYFINGERS

Combine the flour, ⅔ cup of the confectioners' sugar, and the salt in a small bowl; set aside. In a separate large bowl, beat the egg whites until stiff peaks form; set aside. In a separate medium bowl, use a mixer to beat the egg yolks until soft peaks form, about 1 minute. Fold the yolks, the remaining ⅔ cup confectioners' sugar, and the rum into the egg whites. Carefully fold the flour mixture into the beaten egg mixture, a little at a time, until blended.

TO BAKE THE LADYFINGERS

Spoon the batter into a pastry bag fitted with a large writing tip, and pipe the batter onto the prepared baking sheets in fat lines, about 3 inches long and 1½ inches wide. Dust the tops with additional confectioners' sugar. Bake for about 10 minutes, until golden. Let cool.

TO MAKE THE FILLING

Melt the butter in a sauté pan over low heat. Raise the heat to medium, add the apple slices and lemon juice, and cook, stirring, for about 5 minutes, until the apples are browned and softened. Add the raisins, apple juice, sugar, and ginger; cover and cook for 5 to 7 minutes, until the sugar has dissolved. Remove from the heat and set aside.

TO MAKE THE LEMON CREAM

Blend half of the whipped cream with the lemon curd and set aside. Refrigerate the remaining whipped cream until needed.

TO ASSEMBLE

Stand the ladyfingers around the edge of each muffin cup. Line the bottom of each cup with ladyfingers cut to fill the space. Spoon 1 inch of lemon cream into each charlotte, followed by 1 inch of apple filling. Top with enough lemon cream to fill the cup. Refrigerate for at least 3 hours.

TO SERVE

Lift each charlotte out of its mold by pulling up the plastic wrap, and place it on a plate. Carefully peel off the plastic wrap. Pipe a dollop of the remaining whipped cream on top.

VARIATION

Blueberry–Peach Charlotte Russe
Replace the lemon curd with 2¼ cups blueberry sauce (page 320). Serve individual cakes with several slices of fresh peach on top.

Vacherin

A vacherin is a round meringue filled with fruit, sorbet, or ice cream. Looking a bit like the vacherin cheese that is made in Switzerland and France, the dense meringue is a perfect base for the cake. This recipe makes individual meringues that are not baked but simply dried in a heated oven. Vacherin makes a simple but impressive final course to serve to guests.

Meringues

- 6 egg whites, at room temperature
- ¾ cup superfine sugar
- ½ cup confectioners' sugar, sifted
- Pinch of cream of tartar

Toppings

- 2 cups fruit sorbet (mango and raspberry are a nice combination)
- Sprig of mint

Makes 6 individual-serving cakes

TO PREPARE

Preheat the oven to 300°F. Fill the bottom of a large double boiler with a couple inches of water and set over medium heat. Line a baking sheet with parchment paper. Draw six 4-inch circles on the paper. Fit a pastry bag with a star tip.

TO MAKE THE MERINGUES

Combine the egg whites and the superfine sugar in the double boiler over medium heat, and beat until foamy (a hand mixer with whisk beaters works well for this). Beat in the confectioners' sugar and cream of tartar a bit at a time. Continue beating until stiff, glossy peaks form. Remove from the heat and continue beating until the mixture is cooled and stiff.

Immediately spoon the meringue into the pastry bag, filling it halfway. Pipe the meringue into the circles you traced on the parchment paper, starting at the center and spiraling out to the edge. Add peaks to the outside of the circles to create raised edges.

TO BAKE

Turn off the oven, and place the meringues inside for 6 hours to dry. When ready, they will be white and crisp.

TO SERVE

Transfer the meringue disks to individual plates, and top with sorbet and mint leaves. Serve immediately.

VARIATIONS

Berry–Crème Anglaise Vacherin
Fill the vacherin with blackberries, raspberries, strawberries, and fresh currants. Top with lemon crème anglaise (page 102).

Japanese Green Tea Vacherin
Fill the vacherin with green tea ice cream and whole strawberries.

Vietnamese Mango Vacherin
Fill the vacherin with mango ice cream and sliced mangos and jackfruit. Top with 1½ cups coconut-peanut sauce (page 320).

Chocolate Fondue with Orange Cake

Dipping cake into a fondue pot is an experience that I needed to include in this book. These dense, bite-size orange cakes pair wonderfully with a chocolate and triple sec sauce. If you like experimenting, many of the other dense cakes and fruit glazes in this book can also be united for an instant party.

Orange Cake

- 2 cups all-purpose flour
- 1½ teaspoons baking powder
- ½ teaspoon baking soda
- 1 cup (2 sticks) unsalted butter, softened
- 1 cup sugar
- 4 eggs
- Juice and grated zest of 1 orange

Chocolate-Orange Fondue

- 12 ounces high-quality dark chocolate, chopped
- 1½ tablespoons unsalted butter
- Juice and grated zest of 1 orange
- ¼ cup chopped almonds
- ¾ teaspoon cornstarch
- 3 tablespoons triple sec

For Serving

- 2 oranges, segmented
- 2 clementines, segmented
- 2 tangerines, segmented
- ¼ cup chopped almonds

Makes approximately 12 servings

TO PREPARE

Preheat the oven to 350°F. Butter and flour either bite-size cake molds or two 7-inch square pans.

TO MAKE THE CAKES

Combine the flour, baking powder, and baking soda in a medium bowl. In a separate medium bowl, cream the butter and sugar until fluffy. Add the eggs one by one, beating well after each addition. Stir in the orange juice and orange zest. Gradually add the flour mixture until well blended.

TO BAKE THE CAKES

Transfer the batter into the prepared pans. Bake for 12 to 18 minutes (for bite-size cake molds) or 25 to 30 minutes (for 7-inch square pans), until a knife inserted in the center comes out clean. Let the cakes cool in their pans.

TO MAKE THE FONDUE

Combine the chocolate, butter, orange juice, and orange zest in a fondue pot and stir until the chocolate has melted. Stir in the chopped almonds. In a separate small bowl, stir the cornstarch into the triple sec until it dissolves, and then add the slurry to the fondue pot, stirring until the mixture has thickened.

TO SERVE

If you've used 7-inch square pans, cut the cakes into 1-inch cubes. Keeping the fondue warm, serve the cakes with the orange, clementine, and tangerine segments and almonds on the side. Using fondue forks, dip the orange slices and the cakes into the chocolate, then dip them in the almonds.

VARIATION

Chocolate-Amaretto Fondue

Replace the triple sec with amaretto. Prepare almond cake (page 104) and cut into 1-inch cubes for dipping.

Fondue Traditions

Derived from the French word *fondu*, meaning melted or blended, fondue has been a part of Swiss tradition since the eighteenth century, when villagers making good use of stale bread and cheese over the winter are said to have invented it. Many games are associated with the fondue pot. If a woman drops a cube into the fondue pot, for example, she must kiss all the men present, and if a man drops a cube he must buy a bottle of wine for each guest.

The communal nature of the dish made it popular at American dinner parties in the 1950s, and quickly the numbers of recipes for it grew. Then chocolate fondue hit the scene in the 1970s, and fondue fairly exploded in popularity. Though it fell out of fashion for a few decades, fondue has seen a recent rebirth in popularity, and fondue pots are now one of the top gift items on wedding registries.

Swiss Rolls

WITH SPONGE CAKE AND A JELLY ROLL PAN, almost any cake flavor and filling can take the form of a roll. The fillings are as varied as the cultures that make them, ranging from chocolate and whipped cream to fruits and vegetables, jams and compotes, and curds and creams.

Here are some tips for making perfect Swiss rolls:

- *Use a flat and shiny pan. Large 17- by 12-inch pans will make thinner jelly rolls with a tighter roll; smaller 15- by 10-inch pans will make a thicker Swiss roll.*

- *Line the pan with parchment paper and then grease the paper with butter or baking spray, which will make it easier to transfer the cake to your work surface.*

- *When preparing a sponge cake batter, focus on the eggs. Separate the eggs when they are cold; beat the eggs when they are at room temperature. For maximum volume, beat the whites separately from the yolks. Beat the whites until they form stiff peaks and the yolks until they are lemon colored.*

- *When pouring batter into the pan, spread it out gently; don't press out the air. Spread the batter higher on the sides than in the middle.*

- *Make sure the cake is done before removing it from the oven. You'll know it's done when it springs back when touched and pulls away from the sides of the pan.*

- *Increase the cake's flexibility by scoring a few slits halfway through it.*

- *When you're spreading the filling, leave open a 1-inch border on all the edges of the cake.*

- *Roll the cake away from you. Place it on a serving platter seam side down.*

- *Wrap the roll in plastic wrap and refrigerate for 2 hours to set.*

- *Serve the cake at room temperature. Cut the cake into slices using a serrated knife.*

Around the world, rolled cakes take on local flavors and ingredients. Here are some of my favorites:

ARROLLADO (rolled), an Argentine favorite usually filled with dulce de leche (page 92)

BOLU GULUNG (roll cake), an Indonesian specialty filled with buttercream, cheese, or fruit jam

BRAZO DE GITANO (gypsy's arm), a popular Spanish teatime snack filled with cream or jam and covered in chocolate

BRAZO DE REINA (queen's arm), a Chilean version filled with dulce de leche

BÛCHE DE NOËL ("Yule log"; see page 56), a Christmas version of a Swiss roll, with frosting that is textured like bark and adorned with chestnuts and meringue mushrooms

JELLY ROLL, an American classic, rolled up with jam

KÄÄRETORTTU (flan wrap), also known as sweet roll, a Finnish roll cake filled with cream and sometimes berries

RULLTÅRTA (roll cake), a Swedish roll cake filled with both buttercream and strawberry jam

TOP ROW: *Chocolate roll and lemon tiger roll;* MIDDLE ROW: *green tea roll, strawberry roll, and vanilla tiger roll;* BOTTOM ROW: *sponge roll with agar-agar, marble roll, and mocha roll;* FOREGROUND: *taro roll with whipped cream and buttercream*

SWISS ROLL FAMILY TREE

ASIA

🍁 MALAYSIA
🍁 PHILIPPINES
🍁 INDONESIA
🍁 JAPAN
🍁 CHINA
🍁 INDIA

tiger roll cake

gelatin roll cake

poppyseed roll cake

green tea roll cake

taro roll cake

egg roll cake

cream roll

chocolate egg roll cake

coconut roll cake

bolu gulung

pineapple roll cake

brazo de gitano

coffee roll cake

ube roll cake

jelly roll

mango roll cake

pandan roll cake

drömrulltårta

kuchen roll

brazo de reina

rulltårta

bûche de Noël (page 56)

almond roll (page 92)

kääretorttu

Swiss roll (page 116)

arrollado (page 92)

AMERICAS

🍁 ARGENTINA
🍁 MEXICO
🍁 CHILE
🍁 CANADA
🍁 UNITED STATES

EUROPE

🍁 ENGLAND
🍁 SPAIN
🍁 FRANCE
🍁 GERMANY
🍁 SWEDEN
🍁 FINLAND
🍁 CENTRAL EUROPE
🍁 EASTERN EUROPE

Swiss Roll with Bavarian Cream

Despite their impressive appearance, Swiss rolls are easy to make. The traditional Swiss roll is made with a sponge cake baked in a large rectangular pan. It is rolled while still warm, with a Bavarian cream filling, and served in round slices. The tighter the roll, the more impressive the cake.

Sponge Cake
- 4 eggs, separated
- ¾ cup granulated sugar
- 1 teaspoon vanilla extract
- ¼ cup milk, warmed
- 1⅓ cups cake flour

Bavarian Cream
- 8 egg yolks
- 1 cup granulated sugar
- Pinch of salt
- 4 tablespoons cornstarch
- 3 cups whole milk
- 4 tablespoons unsalted butter
- 2 teaspoons vanilla extract

Assembly
- 3 tablespoons confectioners' sugar

Makes 1 cake (serves 6 to 8)

TO PREPARE
Preheat the oven to 350°F. Line a 15- by 10-inch jelly roll pan with parchment paper, and butter the paper or spray it with baking spray.

TO MAKE THE SPONGE CAKE
Beat the egg whites in a large bowl with a mixer until foamy. Add the granulated sugar and beat until stiff, glossy peaks form. In a separate bowl, beat the egg yolks until lemon in color. In a separate small bowl, blend the vanilla with the milk. Fold the milk mixture into the yolks, alternating with the flour, until blended. Fold the egg whites into the yolk mixture, being careful not to deflate the whites.

TO BAKE
Spread the batter with a spatula into the prepared pan. Bake for 15 to 20 minutes, until the cake springs back when touched. Let cool just slightly.

TO MAKE THE BAVARIAN CREAM
Beat together the egg yolks, granulated sugar, and salt until blended. Gradually add the cornstarch, beating until the mixture is smooth; set aside. Pour the milk into a saucepan and warm over medium heat until bubbles form along the edges. Gradually add the milk to the yolk mixture, beating constantly. Transfer the mixture to the saucepan and warm over medium heat, stirring constantly, until it comes to a boil. Remove from heat and strain through a sieve. Add the butter and vanilla, stirring until the butter melts and the mixture is blended. Cover with plastic wrap, laying the plastic right on the surface of the pastry cream, and refrigerate for 2 to 3 hours, until thickened.

TO ASSEMBLE
While the cake is still warm, spread half the confectioners' sugar on a work surface and lay the cake on top of it. Sprinkle the top of the cake with the rest of the sugar. Spread the Bavarian cream over the cake, leaving a 1-inch border along all the edges. Roll the cake away from you into a cylinder. Place on a large platter with the seam on the bottom to serve.

VARIATIONS

American Jelly Roll
Fill the roll with 2 cups strawberry filling (page 322) instead of Bavarian cream.

Charlotte Royale
Fill the roll with 2 cups raspberry filling (page 322) instead of Bavarian cream. Line a 7-inch bowl with plastic wrap. Cut the Swiss roll into ½-inch-thick slices. Line the bowl with the slices, fitting them tightly next to each other. Fill the center with Bavarian cream and chill for at least 3 hours. When the cake is chilled, carefully invert it onto a serving plate and remove the plastic wrap.

Chinese Egg Roll Cake
In the cake batter, replace the vanilla extract with almond extract and add ¼ cup chopped almonds. Fill the roll with 2 cups whipped cream (page 323) instead of Bavarian cream.

French Coffee Swiss Roll
In the cake batter, replace the milk with ¼ cup double-strength espresso. Fill the roll with 3 cups coffee buttercream (page 316) instead of Bavarian cream.

Indian Mango Swiss Roll
Fill the roll with 3 cups mango buttercream (page 316) instead of Bavarian cream.

Japanese Green Tea Swiss Roll
Add 1 teaspoon matcha powder to the cake batter. Add 1 teaspoon matcha powder to the Bavarian cream.

Belgian Buns

These classic Belgian cakes are filled with currants and topped with icing and a candied cherry. The English Chelsea buns and hot cross buns — traditionally eaten on Good Friday — are similar.

Buns

- 1¼ cups all-purpose flour
- ½ cup granulated sugar
- 1 teaspoon salt
- 1½ tablespoons active dry yeast
- 1 cup water
- ½ cup milk
- 2 tablepoons vegetable oil
- 6 tablespoons unsalted butter, melted
- 2 eggs
- 1 cup dried currants
- ¼ cup light brown sugar

Toppings

- 1¾ cups lemon icing (page 316)
- ¼ cup candied cherries

Makes 6 buns

TO MAKE THE DOUGH

Combine ¼ cup of the flour, the granulated sugar, the salt, and the yeast in a large bowl; set aside. Combine the water, milk, and oil in a saucepan. Heat until hot to the touch, but do not boil. Stir the heated ingredients and 3 tablespoons of the melted butter into the flour mixture. Beat until combined. In a separate bowl, beat the eggs until foamy, then add to the batter. Gradually add the remaining 1 cup flour, mixing until the dough is no longer sticky. You may not need all of the flour.

Scrape the dough out onto a floured work surface. Knead ½ cup of the currants into the dough, and keep kneading for 8 to 10 minutes, until the dough is smooth and satiny. Place the dough in a bowl, cover, and let sit in a warm place for 30 to 45 minutes, until it has doubled in size.

TO BAKE

Preheat the oven to 350°F. Grease two 9-inch round springform pans with vegetable oil.

When the dough has risen, roll it out on a floured work surface into a large rectangle, about 16 inches by 12 inches. Brush the remaining 3 tablespoons melted butter over the dough, and top with the remaining ½ cup currants and the brown sugar. Roll the dough away from you into a tight log. Slice the log into 2-inch rounds. Fit them snugly into the prepared pans. Bake for 30 to 35 minutes, until golden.

TO SERVE

Spread the lemon icing over the buns. Break the buns apart. Top each with a maraschino cherry.

VARIATIONS

American Hot Cross Buns

Add ½ cup candied citron to the dough.

Chocolate Chelsea Buns

Add ¼ cup unsweetened cocoa powder to the dough. Top with 2½ cups semisweet chocolate icing (page 317) instead of lemon icing.

English Hot Cross Buns

After preparing the dough, shape it into rolls. Press a cross shape into the top of each bun with the back of a knife. After buns are baked, spread the icing in the crosses.

Jamaican Hot Cross Buns

Replace half the flour with corn flour or masa harina. Add ½ teaspoon ground ginger and ¾ cup chopped dried pineapple to the dough.

Black Forest Cake

The chocolate and cherry flavor of Black Forest cake is straight from the deep woods of Germany for which it's named. The Black Forest region of Germany is known for its sour cherries, which locals distill into kirsch, a clear brandy. This particular version of the cake has six thin layers, which allow the cherry juice and kirsch to soak in and moisten the cake. The sides are covered with chocolate bark and leaves, and the top is decorated with whipped cream and chocolate-covered cherries. Use fresh sour cherries if they're in season; otherwise, maraschino cherries will suffice.

Chocolate Cake

- ¾ cup water
- 10 ounces bittersweet chocolate, broken in pieces
- 12 eggs
- 1 cup plus 2 tablespoons sugar
- 1½ teaspoons kirsch
- ½ teaspoon vanilla extract
- 2¼ cups all-purpose flour

Sour Cherry Filling and Juice

- 3 pounds sour cherries, pitted
- ½ cup sugar
- 6 tablespoons lemon juice
- ¼ cup cherry juice
- ¼ cup kirsch

Kirsch Cream

- 7 cups heavy cream
- ¼ cup sugar
- ¼ cup kirsch

Toppings

- 4½ cups semisweet chocolate buttercream (page 317)
- Shaved chocolate (optional)
- Chocolate leaves (optional)
- Chocolate-covered cherries (optional)

Makes 1 cake (serves 6 to 8)

TO PREPARE

Preheat the oven to 350°F. Butter and flour three 9-inch round cake pans. Prepare a mixing-bowl double boiler by setting a heat-proof large mixing bowl in a larger saucepan. Fill the saucepan with water to just slightly below the lip of the bowl.

TO MAKE THE CAKE

Pour the ¾ cup of water into a saucepan and bring to a boil. Add the chocolate, stir until melted, and set aside to cool.

Bring the water in the mixing-bowl double boiler to a boil. Combine the eggs and sugar in the mixing bowl, and beat with a mixer until the mixture has doubled in volume and reached the ribbon stage (page 24). Remove from the heat and beat in the kirsch and vanilla. Gradually add the flour until blended. Stir in the chocolate until combined.

TO BAKE THE CAKE

Divide the batter evenly among the prepared pans and bake for 30 to 35 minutes, until a knife inserted in the center comes out clean. Let the cakes cool in the pans for 5 minutes, then remove them from the pans and set on a rack to finish cooling.

TO MAKE THE CHERRY JUICE

Combine the cherries, sugar, lemon juice, and cherry juice in a saucepan and simmer for 7 to 10 minutes, until the cherries are softened. Strain out the cherries, reserving them for use as a filling. Mix the kirsch into the cherry juice; set aside.

TO MAKE THE KIRSCH CREAM

Whip the cream and sugar until stiff peaks form. Stir in the kirsch. Divide the cream into two equal batches; one batch will be used for filling and the other for topping.

TO ASSEMBLE

Cut the three cakes in half crosswise, so that you have six layers. Brush the cherry juice mixture over the layers. Set one layer on a serving plate, and spread over it one-fifth of the cherries, followed by one-fifth of the kirsch cream filling. Stack the next layer on top, spread cherries and kirsch cream on it, and repeat until you've laid the final layer on top. Frost the entire cake with chocolate buttercream. Pipe the reserved kirsch cream decoratively around the cake edges, and chill for 1 to 2 hours, until set. If you're using them, press the shaved chocolate into the sides and decorate the top with chocolate leaves and chocolate-covered cherries.

VARIATIONS

Blackberry Forest Cake

Replace the cherries with an equal volume of blackberries. Replace the kirsch with blackberry brandy.

Individual Black Forest Cakes

Bake the batter in mini loaf pans; cut each loaf into three layers.

Loaf Black Forest Cake

Triple the recipe and bake the batter in a long loaf pan, as in the photograph; cut the cake into three layers.

Puritan Black Forest Cake

Replace the kirsch with cherry juice.

The World's Most Popular Cake

The flavors of the Black Forest cake bridge the cultural taste gap, making it the most recognizable cake in the world. You can find Black Forest cakes at weddings in India, picnics in Peru, tea shops in Japan, and coffeehouses in Egypt. As they are passed from one culture to the next, most other cakes have been adapted to suit local ingredients and regional palates. But the Black Forest cake has remained relatively unchanged, from its first creation in sixteenth-century Germany through its travels across the vast expanse of the rest of the globe.

Stollen

When Trader Joe's and Whole Foods started carrying stollen for Christmas, I knew this fifteenth-century treat was making a comeback. To spot a stollen, look for the confectioners' sugar glaze that coats the entire cake. It's a hearty fruitcake studded with almonds, raisins, currants, candied orange and lemon peels, and cherries and flavored with cinnamon, nutmeg, and cardamom. Traditionally it is soaked in butter, but I have lightened up the butter just a bit to better suit the sitting-at-the-computer life versus the working-the-fields diet.

Stollen

2¼ teaspoons active dry yeast

½ cup warm water

1 cup milk

¾ cup granulated sugar

½ teaspoon salt

1 tablespoon brandy

1 teaspoon almond extract

1 teaspoon vanilla extract

5 cups all-purpose flour

1 cup slivered almonds

½ cup raisins

½ cup dried currants

⅓ cup chopped candied citron

⅓ cup chopped candied cherries

⅓ cup chopped dried apricots

Zest of 1 lemon, grated

2 eggs, beaten

1 cup (2 sticks) unsalted butter, softened

1 teaspoon ground cinnamon

¼ teaspoon grated nutmeg

½ teaspoon ground cardamom

Glaze

1½ cups confectioners' sugar

¼ cup milk, warmed

1 teaspoon lemon juice

Toppings

¼ cup candied cherries

¼ cup slivered almonds

Makes 1 cake (serves 6 to 8)

TO MAKE THE DOUGH

Dissolve the yeast in the water in a large bowl; let the mixture rest for 5 minutes. Heat the milk in a small saucepan with 10 tablespoons of the sugar and the salt, stirring until the sugar is dissolved. Remove the milk from the heat and add the brandy, almond extract, and vanilla. Let cool.

Add the milk mixture to the yeast. Using a mixer, gradually mix in 1 cup of the flour, beating until smooth. Cover and let the dough rise in a warm place for at least 2 hours, until it has doubled in size.

When the dough has risen, punch it down and mix in the almonds, raisins, currants, citron, cherries, apricots, and zest. Add the eggs, ¾ cup of the butter, ½ teaspoon of the cinnamon, and the nutmeg. Stir in 3 more cups flour, and mix the dough until smooth. Transfer the dough to a lightly floured work surface. Knead in the remaining 1 cup flour until smooth.

TO SHAPE

Roll the dough into an oval about 10 inches long, 6 inches wide, and ½ inch thick, then fold it over lengthwise, folding the dough to look like draped fabric. Transfer the stollen to a buttered baking sheet and shape into a crescent. Melt the remaining ¼ cup butter and brush it over the loaf. Combine the remaining 2 tablespoons sugar, ½ teaspoon cinnamon, and the cardamom in a bowl. Sprinkle the stollen with the sugar-spice mixture. Cover and let rise for 1½ hours, until it has doubled in size.

TO BAKE

Preheat the oven to 350°F. Bake the stollen for 40 to 45 minutes, or until golden. Let cool on the baking sheet.

TO GLAZE

Combine the confectioners' sugar with the milk and lemon juice. Coat the stollen with the icing. Top with candied cherries and almonds.

VARIATION

Cranberry-Chip Stollen

Replace the raisins and currants with 1 cup dried cranberries. Replace the candied citron and cherries with ⅔ cup chocolate chips. Top with dried cranberries, chocolate chips, and almonds.

Stollen for the Holidays

Stollen is thought to have been first made in the early fifteenth century as a Christmas cake, and it is still being made for that holiday today. The folds of the cake, topped with white sugar, are said to represent the baby Jesus wrapped in swaddling blankets. Dresden is the epicenter of stollen preparation, with a huge festival called Stollen Days held at the beginning of December to launch the Christmas season.

Apple Strudel

This strudel is the perfect Sunday-morning brunch cake. Since the traditional dough is a bit complicated — the kind of dough professional pastry chefs pride themselves on — most home bakers use frozen phyllo, which is easier to work with.

Filling

- 6 large apples, peeled, cored, and diced
- 2 tablespoons unsalted butter
- 2 tablespoons lemon juice
- ¾ cup light brown sugar
- 1 teaspoon ground cinnamon
- ½ teaspoon ground ginger
- ¼ teaspoon grated nutmeg
- ⅛ teaspoon ground allspice
- ⅛ teaspoon salt
- 1 cup walnuts
- ½ cup golden raisins

Assembly

- ¼ cup all-purpose flour
- ⅓ cup water
- 8 (12- by 17-inch) sheets phyllo dough
- 1½ cups (3 sticks) unsalted butter, melted and cooled

Topping

- 1 cup lemon icing (page 316)

Makes 2 strudels (4 to 6 servings each)

TO PREPARE

Preheat the oven to 375°F. Butter two baking sheets.

TO MAKE THE FILLING

Combine the apples and 2 tablespoons butter in a pan over high heat, and sauté, stirring occasionally, for 5 to 7 minutes, until the apples begin to brown. Stir in the lemon juice, and continue to cook for 5 to 7 minutes, stirring often, until the apples have softened. Remove from heat and pour off any excess liquid. Stir in the brown sugar, cinnamon, ginger, nutmeg, allspice, salt, walnuts, and raisins; set aside.

TO ASSEMBLE

Mix together the flour and water to form a paste. On a floured work surface, lay out a sheet of phyllo. Brush with melted butter. Set another phyllo sheet on top of it, brush with melted butter, and repeat until you have stacked four sheets. Spread half the filling on top of the phyllo stack. Roll tightly, and seal the edges with a little of the flour-water paste. Flatten the roll and place on a prepared baking sheet. Brush with melted butter. Cut six slits across the top. Repeat with the remaining phyllo and filling.

TO BAKE

Bake the strudels for 20 to 25 minutes, until golden. Let cool.

TO FINISH

Scoop the lemon icing into a pastry bag fitted with a small tip, and pipe the icing over the strudels.

VARIATION

Peach Strudel

Replace the apples with peaches. Omit the nutmeg and allspice.

Strudel and Streusel

What's the difference between strudel and streusel? Both are popular breakfast cakes. But strudel, under the influence of Middle Eastern pastries such as baklava, is a sheet of thin pastry rolled up with a filling, usually fruit. Streusel is a coffee cake with a crumb topping; the topping may include nuts.

Rehruecken

A cake that no one should miss is the rehruecken. I got my first glance at this surreal cake in Vienna, where I saw it in a bakery window — but if I hadn't known about this cake, I would have mistaken the bakery for a butcher's shop. This classic Viennese chocolate cake is designed to look like meat. Its name translates as "saddle of venison" or "spine of the deer," and the semicircular, funky cake is designed to look like a rack of ribs. It is studded with almonds to represent the strips of bacon or salt pork used for curing venison.

Cake

1	cup sugar
8	eggs, separated
1	teaspoon ground cinnamon
¼	teaspoon salt
	Zest of ½ lemon, grated
½	cup ground almonds
1	cup semisweet chocolate chips
1½	cups all-purpose flour
1	cup double-strength espresso

Toppings

5	cups semisweet chocolate icing (page 317)
½	cup slivered almonds

Makes 1 cake (serves 6 to 8)

TO PREPARE

Preheat the oven to 375°F. Butter and flour a loaf pan approximately 10 by 6 by 3 inches.

TO MAKE THE BATTER

Beat the sugar, egg yolks, cinnamon, salt, and lemon zest in a large bowl with a mixer until blended. Add the ground almonds, chocolate, and flour, and stir in the espresso until blended. In a separate bowl, beat the egg whites until stiff peaks form; fold the whites into the batter.

TO BAKE

Spoon the batter into the prepared pan and bake for 40 to 50 minutes, until a knife inserted in the center comes out clean. Let the cake cool in the pan for 15 minutes, then remove it from the pan and set on a rack to finish cooling.

TO DECORATE

With a serrated knife, cut the cake into a half-cylinder shape. Spread the chocolate icing on the cake. Using a thin spatula, shape the frosting to demarcate the "ribs" extending across the width of the cake. Insert the slivered almonds in rows along the ribs.

VARIATION

Coffee Buttercream Rehruecken

Top the cake with 5 cups coffee buttercream (page 316) instead of chocolate icing.

Rehruecken Molds

For a truly realistic effect, use a rehruecken pan. This mold looks like a long loaf pan that is curved into a half-moon shape. It features evenly spaced grooves that not only mold the "ribs" on the cake but also demarcate the slices for serving. Another groove down the center molds the "bone" of the saddle of venison. If you're using a rehruecken pan, make the glaze a bit thinner or leave the cake plain so you can really show off the effect. The cake can also be made in a long loaf pan and shaped into a half cylinder, as I've done here. Simulate ribs by texturing the frosting.

Sachertorte

This famous Viennese cake is a dense, dry chocolate cake. Each layer is spread with a thin layer of apricot glaze, and the cake is topped with chocolate ganache. When I first tasted this torte its dryness was a surprise, but I soon learned to love it. It is meant to be dipped into fresh whipped cream, which moistens it.

Torte

10	ounces bittersweet chocolate, finely chopped
1	cup sugar
⅔	cup unsalted butter, softened
8	eggs, separated
2	teaspoons vanilla extract
1⅓	cups all-purpose flour

Fillings and Toppings

1¾	cups apricot glaze (page 318)
2¼	cups chocolate ganache (page 315)
2	cups whipped cream (page 323)

Makes 1 cake (serves 6 to 8)

TO PREPARE

Preheat the oven to 325°F. Butter and flour a 9-inch springform pan.

TO MAKE THE TORTE

Melt the chocolate in a double boiler or microwave; set aside. Beat the sugar and butter in a large bowl with a mixer until creamy. Add the egg yolks one at a time, blending after each addition. Add the vanilla. Fold in the chocolate and flour. In a separate bowl, beat the egg whites until stiff peaks form. Fold them into the batter.

TO BAKE THE TORTE

Pour the batter into the prepared pan and bake for 50 to 60 minutes, until a knife inserted in the center comes out clean. Let cool in the pan for at least 30 minutes.

TO ASSEMBLE

Cut the cake in thirds crosswise, making three layers. Stack the cake layers, spreading the apricot glaze as a filling between them. Set aside ¼ cup of the chocolate ganache and pour the rest over the cake. Let cool in the refrigerator for at least 1 hour, until set.

Scoop the reserved chocolate ganache into a pastry bag fitted with a small round tip. Use it to pipe a decorative border around the cake and in its center. Serve with whipped cream.

The Teen Pastry Chef

In 1832, when Franz Sacher was 16 years old, he worked as an apprentice in the kitchen of Prince Klemens Wenzel Lothar Metternich of Austria, and it was here that he invented this cake. He went on to become a well-known baker and the owner of several cafés and restaurants in Vienna. In 1876 his son, Eduard, opened the grand Hotel Sacher, where the Sachertorte was one of the beloved items on the menu for diplomats from around the world to enjoy. The original Sachertorte, decorated with a chocolate replica of the hotel's seal, is still being served there today. It is also packaged as a tourist cake in a beautiful wooden box.

Kugelhopf

This light, delicate yeast cake looks fantastic on a cake plate and doesn't require much fussing. It's customarily baked in a fluted ring mold, though it can also be baked in a plain tube pan or Bundt pan. In fact, it was German-Americans who invented the more streamlined Bundt pan because they couldn't find a kugelhopf pan in America. The trick to making a kugelhopf is to knead the dough well and to let it rise twice. This cake is best enjoyed the day it is made.

Cake

- ¾ cup golden raisins
- ½ cup dried currants
- Zest of ½ orange, grated
- 2¼ teaspoons active dry yeast
- 1 cup milk, warmed
- 4 cups all-purpose flour
- ¼ teaspoon salt
- 3 eggs, lightly beaten
- 3 tablespoons granulated sugar
- ½ cup (1 stick) unsalted butter, melted and cooled
- 3 tablespoons rum
- ⅓ cup slivered almonds

Toppings

- 2 tablespoons unsalted butter, melted
- ¼ cup confectioners' sugar

Makes 1 cake (serves 6 to 8)

Alsatian Kugelhopf

The kugelhopf, also known as the gugelhupf, originated in Austria but is best known as a specialty of French Alsace, where it is served for breakfast and brunch. In the United States this cake is especially popular in Castroville, Texas, where many Alsatians settled in the mid-1800s. Kugelhopf is a highlight of the city's 120-year-old St. Louis Day celebration.

TO PREPARE

Pour enough boiling-hot water over the raisins and currants to cover them, and let steep for 5 minutes to plump. Drain the water and pat them dry. Combine in a bowl with the orange zest.

TO MAKE THE DOUGH

Combine the yeast and milk in a large bowl, stir until the yeast is dissolved, and let sit for 5 minutes, until foamy. Add the flour and salt and stir to moisten the flour. Beat the eggs in one at a time, using a mixer. Beat in the sugar, butter, and rum. Mix the dough 5 to 7 minutes, until well kneaded. Stir in the dried fruit and slivered almonds.

Place the dough in a buttered bowl, cover, and let rise in a warm place for 1½ to 2 hours, until it has doubled in size. Punch down the dough to deflate, and put in the refrigerator for 1 hour.

Generously butter a 9-inch kugelhopf mold or tube pan. When the dough is chilled, place it in the pan. Cover, and let rise in a warm place for about 2 hours, until it has nearly doubled in size.

TO BAKE

Preheat the oven to 350°F. Bake the cake for 40 to 45 minutes, until a knife inserted in the center comes out clean. Let the cake cool in its pan for 15 minutes, then invert it onto a rack to finish cooling.

TO FINISH

Brush on the melted butter and sprinkle with confectioners' sugar.

VARIATIONS

Chocolate-Chip Kugelhopf

Replace the raisins with mini chocolate chips. Top the baked cake with 1 cup chocolate glaze (page 318) instead of butter and confectioners' sugar.

Cinnamon Streusel Kugelhopf

Add 1 teaspoon ground cinnamon to the cake dough. Combine ½ cup light brown sugar, ⅓ cup all-purpose flour, ¼ cup butter, and ½ teaspoon cinnamon in a food processor, and pulse until a crumbly streusel mixture forms. Line the baking pan with the streusel before pouring in the batter.

Luilakbollen (Lazybones Cake)

Maybe it's just me, but I don't think anyone would start celebrating this holiday by choice — but the cakes are good. In the Netherlands luilakbollen yeast cakes are traditionally given out to children on Lazybones Day. They are prepared in many ways, from ordinary buns to these more playful masklike faces. This recipe makes about 12 cakes.

Cakes

- 2¼ teaspoons active dry yeast
- ⅓ cup plus 2 tablespoons milk, warmed
- 2½ cups all-purpose flour
- ½ teaspoon salt
- ⅓ cup unsalted butter
- 1 egg
- 1 tablespoon grated orange zest
- 1 cup golden raisins
- ½ cup dried cranberries
- 2 egg whites, beaten

Toppings

- 1 cup royal icing (page 317)
- ¼ cup chocolate sprinkles
- 24 candy hearts
- ⅓ cup honey syrup (page 318), optional

Makes 12 individual-serving cakes

TO MAKE THE DOUGH

Dissolve the yeast in ⅓ cup of the warm milk and let sit for 5 minutes, until foamy. In a separate medium bowl, stir together the flour and salt; set aside. In a separate large bowl, beat the butter and the egg until combined. Add the remaining 2 tablespoons milk and the orange zest. Gradually mix in the flour mixture and then the yeast mixture, yielding a soft dough. If it is sticky, add more flour; if it's dry, add more milk. Knead in the raisins and cranberries. Cover and let rise in a warm place for about 1 hour, until it has doubled in volume.

TO SHAPE

Line two baking sheets with parchment paper. When the dough has risen, transfer it to a floured work surface and knead for 7 to 10 minutes, until smooth. Break the dough into 12 equal pieces, and form each into an oval. Use a small cookie cutter or knife to cut out eyes and mouths, reserving the trimmings. Place the cakes on the prepared baking sheets, spacing them about 2 inches apart. Shape the bits of dough you cut out into noses and ears, and press them into the faces to attach them. Let rise in a warm place for 1 hour, then brush the cakes with the beaten egg whites.

TO BAKE

Preheat the oven to 350°F. Bake the cakes 11 to 15 minutes, until golden. Let cool.

TO DECORATE

Brush royal icing over the forehead of each cake face, and attach the sprinkles as hair. Place a dot of royal icing on each cheek, and set a heart on top of it. Let set before serving.

TO SERVE

Wrap the cakes in waxed paper for handing out. If serving at home, dip the cakes in honey syrup.

Luilak (Lazybones Day)

How would you like to be woken up at 4 AM on a weekend morning by children squealing in the streets? That is exactly what this children's holiday is all about. In the western Netherlands, on the Saturday before Whitsunday, kids hit the streets. They whistle, screech, beat on pots and pans, ring doorbells, and clamor for lazybones cakes, waking up the neighborhood. Anyone who doesn't rise to join the fun is branded a lazybones and becomes the butt of jokes for the year to come.

CHAPTER 5

The British Isles
Comfort Cakes and High-Society Delights

BEFORE I STARTED RESEARCHING THIS BOOK, the only British cakes I knew of were tea cakes. When I asked friends from the United Kingdom to recommend their favorite traditional cakes, they looked at me as if I were insane and said, "We don't really have cakes, we have puddings." Well, I've done my research and I have to say, we all were mistaken. French, German, and Italian cakes may be more sophisticated, but I've discovered that the British Isles are home to a delightful selection of wholesome, robust cakes, and I'm excited to spread the sweet news.

Of course puddings really are an important part of British cake culture: their dessert puddings practically are cakes. But the region features many other homey comfort cakes and high-society cakes, too — so many, in fact, that choosing which recipes to include in this book had me spinning for weeks. (I still regret that I don't have more pages.)

From a sociological point of view, the cakes of the British Isles fall into two categories: the cakes of the common people

and the cakes of the upper class. What I call "high-society cakes" were developed exclusively for the aristocracy in the sixteenth through eighteenth centuries. These labor-intensive creations required lots of skill — and decadent amounts of sugar. In those days, long before KitchenAids or even rotary beaters, bakers had to beat eggs by hand for hundreds of strokes to get them fluffy enough to make sponge cakes rise. High society swooned over each new novelty cake, until the next new sugary confection took center stage.

Average farmers and workers had no time for such things, so they took a different approach to cake. Needing good, durable, healthy food that conserved time, energy, and calories, they concocted a wealth of wholesome and delicious common cakes. Jams, marmalades, and other preserved fruits were used as fillings. A trifle, originally made from stale cake, was created as a way to preserve perfectly good calories that would otherwise go to waste. Later, in the seventeenth and eighteenth centuries, trifles became fashionable, and many creative variations were developed. In fact, recently I saw a single-serving trifle served for high tea at a fancy hotel for the far-from-trifling price tag of $20.

The common cakes of England, Scotland, Ireland, and Wales are close relatives. Taste their fruitcakes and oatcakes, with the traditional preserves, clotted cream, and fruit curds, and you'll quickly see the resemblance. However, the Scots' cakes tend to show more French influences, thanks to the Scots' alignment with the Normans, and some Scandinavian influences, too, due to the geographical proximity. Hearty breakfasts are popular in Scotland, as are the scones and breakfast cakes that accompany the meal. Dundee cake (page 146) and Scottish scones (page 147) are staples at Scottish tea. English teatime, in contrast, features more delicate tea cakes, including Battenberg cakes (page 142) and Victoria sandwich cakes (page 136). The Irish and Welsh have a more rural culture, and their cake traditions reflect this. The Irish favor alcohol-soaked fruitcakes, and the Welsh favor rustic flat cakes, which are cooked on a griddle over an open fire, a practice that goes back to the time of their Celtic ancestors. These cakes are enjoyed today, along with the seasonal favorite bilberry jam, at the Celtic harvest festival Gwl Awst in August.

The pagan influence of the Druids also distinguishes the special-occasion cakes of Scotland and Ireland from those of England, and the Protestant-Catholic schism in the mid-sixteenth century further sliced up cake culture. Christmas is the most celebrated holiday in England, and the mostly Protestant population loves to celebrate all 12 days of the holiday. Plum pudding is the cake of choice at a traditional English Christmas. For those of you who have only heard of this dessert in Dickens's novels, plum pudding is a rich pudding-type cake filled with dried fruit (almost always including plums) that is steamed or broiled and served with a hard sauce.

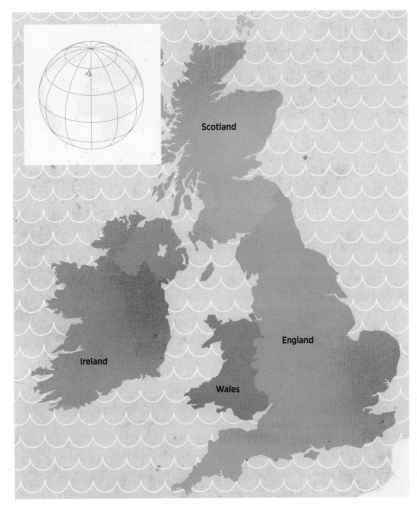

In Scotland, in contrast, Hogmanay, a Scottish New Year that dates back to the pagan era, is the most anticipated holiday. Any visitor who enters a Scottish house on the first day of the new year better be carrying some black buns, or else the entire year is said to be doomed. And in Ireland, Catholic holidays such as Easter and St. Patrick's Day are celebrated right alongside the Celtic harvest festivals and spring festivals.

The cake traditions of the British Isles are also heavily influenced by international travelers, whether immigrants to or explorers from the region. In ancient times Celts, Romans, Vikings, and Normans all conquered portions of the region, bringing with them their particular culinary and celebratory influences. Later waves of Jewish, African, Chinese, Pakistani, and other immigrants brought their own tastes and traditions with them. In turn, Britain was a powerful colonizer that spread its food traditions — including its favorite cakes — to the West Indies, Australia, New Zealand, Hong Kong, North America, and Africa. On each voyage, British explorers brought back spices and other ingredients from abroad, and local cake recipes, too. That, in short, is how cake culture spreads.

Parkin with Gooseberry Compote

This oatmeal ginger cake, thought to have originated in Yorkshire, is traditionally eaten on Bonfire Night (the evening of Guy Fawkes Day). Parkin is moist with a bit of texture from the steel-cut oatmeal and a bit of stickiness from the molasses. It is known to get tastier with age, so let it sit for a day or two in a sealed container. Traditionally it is eaten with a tart fruit compote made from gooseberries (as in this recipe) or Granny Smith apples (see the variation).

Parkin Cake

- 1 cup steel-cut oats
- ½ cup (1 stick) unsalted butter
- 1 cup all-purpose flour
- 1 teaspoon baking soda
- ¼ cup dark brown sugar
- 1 tablespoon ground ginger
- 2 teaspooons grated fresh ginger
- 1 teaspoon ground cinnamon
- 1 egg
- ¾ cup molasses, warmed
- ½ cup milk

Gooseberry Compote

- 1½ cups gooseberries
- ½ cup granulated sugar
- ¼ cup fresh orange juice
- ½ teaspoon grated orange zest
- 1 teaspoon vanilla extract

Makes 18 individual-serving cakes

TO PREPARE

Soften the oats by preparing them according to the package directions, but cooking them for only about three-quarters of the recommended time; drain any excess water. Preheat the oven to 300°F. Arrange square paper liners for 18 cakes, using two liners per cake and setting them 1½ inches apart on a baking sheet.

TO MAKE THE CAKE

Combine the softened oats, butter, flour, and baking soda in a medium bowl, and blend until they form a crumbly meal. Add the sugar, ground and fresh ginger, and cinnamon, and mix thoroughly. Add the egg, molasses, and milk and mix until well blended.

TO BAKE

Pour the batter into the prepared liners and bake 18 to 22 minutes, until a knife inserted in the center comes out clean. Let the cakes cool.

TO MAKE THE GOOSEBERRY COMPOTE

Reserve a few gooseberries for topping. Combine the sugar and the orange juice in a saucepan and bring to a boil. Add the remaining gooseberries and simmer until the berries have softened, about 5 minutes. Stir in the orange zest and vanilla, and let cool. Serve the cakes with fresh gooseberries and compote.

VARIATIONS

Large Parkin Cake

Instead of baking the batter in small cups, pour the batter into a buttered and floured 8-inch square pan, and bake for 50 minutes to 1 hour.

Rolled-Oat Parkin with Tart Apple Glaze

Prepare the Parkins with rolled oats instead of steel-cut oats, and do not soften them. Use tart Granny Smith apples to prepare an apple glaze (page 318). Serve the glaze alongside the cake.

Bonfire Night

Imagine Halloween and Mardis Gras rolled into one, and you have Bonfire Night in northern England. The streets feel medieval, filled with thousands of people carrying torches, burning barrels of tar, and setting off fireworks. A carnival with blazing floats parades from town to town, and papier-mâché effigies are carried through the streets.

This celebration is held on November 5 each year in commemoration of the foiling of a 1605 plot by Guy Fawkes to use gunpowder to blow up the houses of parliament (and King James I with them). Bonfire Night is also celebrated in South Africa, Australia, New Zealand, the Caribbean, and some parts of Canada as an excuse to let loose, eat some parkin, and set off fireworks.

THE WORLD TOUR OF
Sponge Cakes

WHISKING EGGS INTO A LIGHT AIRY CAKE with no shortening makes fluffy sponge cakes, now a base for many different cake and cupcake recipes around the world. This method for raising cakes was developed as an alternative to yeast sometime around the Renaissance. Though traditionally a sponge cake contains no fat, some of today's sponge cakes do include butter or oil — but purists would complain that these tiptoe into butter cake territory.

Spaniards were among the first to develop sponge cakes. In fact, when the technique was introduced to Italy in the sixteenth century, it became known as pan di Spagna ("bread of Spain"; see page 196). Italian cooks applied the technique with great inventiveness to their local cuisines. In the years that followed, many wealthy families in England and France began to employ Italian cooks, and they brought with them a variety of recipes for feather-light cakes and spongelike cookies, the precursors of the modern sponge cake. Because of their delightful ability to soak up liquid, these cakes and cookies were well suited for layering with creams and sauces, and they began to appear in custards, puddings, trifles, and fools.

Over time the early sponges and biscuits evolved into full-blown cakes: the génoise sponge (page 108), madeleines, and the opera cake (page 104) popped up in France, the cassata (page 196) and a number of other cream-filled cakes in Italy, the Victorian sponge in England, frog cakes (page 310) in Australia, and the Swiss roll (page 118) in Switzerland. Americans transformed the sponge cake into the egg-white-only cake known as angel food (page 34) and later the chiffon (page 89), an oil-based sponge cake.

The sponge cake traveled from West to East, too. In the sixteenth century, Portuguese sailors brought a sponge cake known as the bread of Castile to Japan, where the local culture transformed it into kasutera cake (page 280), which is still popular in Japan today. Other Asian cultures took the recipe and ran with it, steaming it, as they did their native cakes, to produce new favorites like steamed lemon cakes (page 272). Throughout Asia today, the sponge cake has been modified into a less sweet cake to suit palates less familiar with super-sugary desserts.

From the mid-1800s through the 1950s the ability to make a perfect sponge cake was a point of domestic pride in the British Isles, Australia, and the United States. After the 1950s it fell out of fashion for a few decades, replaced with richer, more decadent cakes containing shortening of some kind. But today sponge cakes are back in style, perhaps because they have less fat than butter cakes.

To make a perfect sponge, follow these tips:

* *Use fresh eggs, at room temperature.*

* *Whisk the eggs with sugar until they have increased in volume and are stiff enough to hold a peak for 30 seconds.*

* *Fold the flour into the mixture slowly to avoid clumps.*

* *When checking for doneness, look at the edges of the cake; they will shrink away from the baking pan when the cake is properly baked.*

* *When the cake is done baking, let it cool in the pan for 5 minutes. Then, while it is still warm, remove it from its pan by flipping it over onto a rack.*

* *Serve sponge cake the day you make it; it becomes stale quite quickly.*

LEFT: *cassata cake (page 196);* CENTER: *lamingtons (page 304);* RIGHT: *kasutera cakes (page 280)*

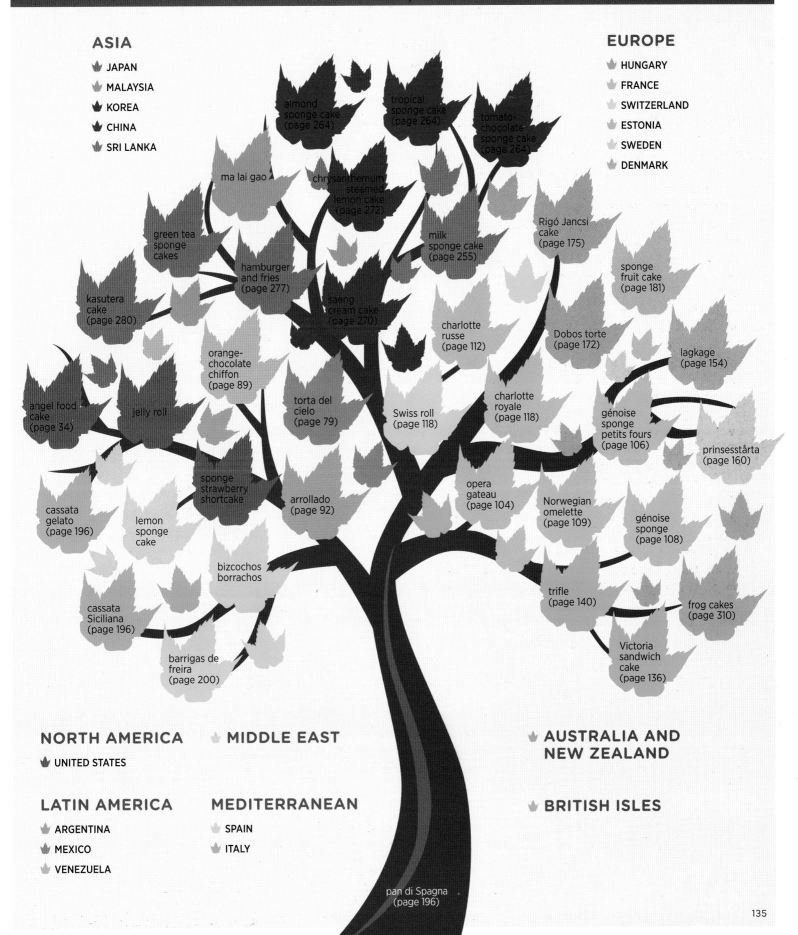

SPONGE CAKE FAMILY TREE

ASIA
- JAPAN
- MALAYSIA
- KOREA
- CHINA
- SRI LANKA

EUROPE
- HUNGARY
- FRANCE
- SWITZERLAND
- ESTONIA
- SWEDEN
- DENMARK

almond sponge cake (page 264)

tropical sponge cake (page 264)

tomato-chocolate sponge cake (page 264)

ma lai gao

chrysanthemum steamed lemon cake (page 272)

milk sponge cake (page 255)

Rigó Jancsi cake (page 175)

green tea sponge cakes

hamburger and fries (page 277)

saeng cream cake (page 270)

sponge fruit cake (page 181)

kasutera cake (page 280)

charlotte russe (page 112)

Dobos torte (page 172)

lagkage (page 154)

orange-chocolate chiffon (page 89)

angel food cake (page 34)

jelly roll

torta del cielo (page 79)

Swiss roll (page 118)

charlotte royale (page 118)

génoise sponge petits fours (page 106)

prinsesstårta (page 160)

sponge strawberry shortcake

arrollado (page 92)

opera gateau (page 104)

Norwegian omelette (page 109)

génoise sponge (page 108)

cassata gelato (page 196)

lemon sponge cake

trifle (page 140)

frog cakes (page 310)

cassata Siciliana (page 196)

bizcochos borrachos

Victoria sandwich cake (page 136)

barrigas de freira (page 200)

NORTH AMERICA
- UNITED STATES

MIDDLE EAST

AUSTRALIA AND NEW ZEALAND

LATIN AMERICA
- ARGENTINA
- MEXICO
- VENEZUELA

MEDITERRANEAN
- SPAIN
- ITALY

BRITISH ISLES

pan di Spagna (page 196)

Victoria Sandwich Cake

Queen Victoria is the woman who made "a spot of tea" all the rage in England. Her favorite tea accompaniment was this simple two-layer sponge cake, filled with a layer of raspberry jam and cream. This cake differed from other sponge cakes of the time in that it used butter. Today lemon curd, buttercream, and Devonshire cream are also used between the layers.

Sponge Cake
- 1¼ cups (2½ sticks) unsalted butter
- 1¼ cups granulated sugar
- 6 eggs, separated
- 3 cups cake flour
- 1¼ cups heavy cream
- 1 teaspoon vanilla extract

Assembly
- 2 cups vanilla buttercream (page 317)
- 1¼ cups lemon curd (page 321)
- 3 tablespoons confectioners' sugar

Makes 1 cake (serves 6 to 8)

TO PREPARE
Preheat the oven to 350°F. Butter and flour two 8-inch round cake pans.

TO MAKE THE CAKE
Cream the butter and sugar in a large bowl with a mixer for 2 to 3 minutes, until light and fluffy. In a separate bowl, beat the egg yolks until light yellow; add to the butter mixture. In another separate bowl, beat the egg whites for 3 to 5 minutes, until stiff peaks form. Fold 1 cup flour into the eggs. Stir the egg-white mixture into the butter-sugar mixture in batches, alternating with the remaining 2 cups flour, until well mixed. Beat well for 3 to 5 minutes, until fluffy and well blended. Mix in the cream and vanilla.

TO BAKE
Divide the batter between the prepared pans. Bake for 35 to 40 minutes, until a knife inserted in the center comes out clean. Let the cakes cool in the pans for 5 minutes, then remove from the pans and set on a rack to finish cooling.

TO ASSEMBLE
Set one of the cakes on a cake plate. Top with the buttercream, followed by the lemon curd. Top with the second cake, and sprinkle with confectioners' sugar.

VARIATIONS

Raspberry Victoria Sandwich Cake
Bake the cake in two 8-inch square pans. When the cakes have cooled, cut them into small rectangular pieces. Cut each piece in half crosswise, making two layers. Spread 2 cups raspberry filling (page 322) and buttercream on the bottom half, and set the upper half on top. Dust with confectioners' sugar.

Speedy Victoria Sponge Cake
Purchase a round sponge cake, high-quality raspberry jam, and Devonshire cream. Cut the cake in half crosswise, into two layers. Spread 1½ cups jam on top of the bottom layer, followed by 1½ cups cream. Top with the second cake and coat with confectioners' sugar.

Queen Victoria and Teatime

Teatime became an institution in the Victorian era. As 4:00 high-tea service was gaining popularity throughout Europe, so too was the practice of holding dinner late in the evening. Queen Victoria is said to have needed a pick-me-up in the late afternoon, and Anna, the Duchess of Bedford, her lady-in-waiting, began serving her tea with light snacks. The queen soon began inviting friends over to her rooms for tea and cakes. Over the years teatime gained popularity throughout England.

Sponge cakes were fashionable during this era, with makers of well-risen sponge cakes lauded for their baking skills. The Victoria sponge cake, also known as the Victoria sandwich cake, was a tremendously popular version. Even today, the Victoria sponge cake is a popular bake-off cake, with bakers still showcasing their skills for the best well-risen cake.

FRONT: *Queen Anne's cake (page 137)*; REAR: *Victoria sandwich cake*

Queen Anne's Cake
(Carrot Cake)

With all of my cake experimenting, you can only imagine the number of cakes that pop in and out of my oven over the course of a year. But on December 29, my husband Brian's birthday, the pressure is on to make a cake that is extra special, and this is it. The finely grated carrots soften while the cake is baking, giving the cake a soft, dense texture with a coarser crumb. I have added nuts, raisins, and pineapple to the traditional carrot-only cake, all of which fuse into a single sweet taste. The fluted pan is traditional, though of course any round pan would do.

Carrot Cake
- 2¾ cups all-purpose flour
- 1½ teaspoons baking soda
- 1½ teaspoons ground cinnamon
- ¼ teaspoon grated nutmeg
- ½ teaspoon salt
- 5 eggs
- 1¼ cups granulated sugar
- 1¼ cups light brown sugar
- 1½ teaspoons vanilla extract
- 1¼ cups corn oil
- 2½ cups finely grated carrots
- 1 (20-ounce) can crushed pineapple, drained
- 1¼ cups chopped walnuts
- ¾ cup golden raisins

Toppings
- 2 cups cream cheese frosting (page 316)
- ¼ cup walnut halves

Makes 1 cake (serves 6 to 8)

TO PREPARE
Preheat the oven to 350°F. Butter and flour an 8-inch fluted, round cake pan.

TO MAKE THE CAKE
Combine the flour, baking soda, cinnamon, nutmeg, and salt in a medium bowl. In a separate medium bowl, beat the eggs, granulated sugar, and brown sugar until thick, about 2 minutes, then stir in the vanilla. Slowly mix in the oil until blended. Add the flour mixture to the egg mixture, stirring until blended. Stir in the carrots, pineapple, walnuts, and raisins, and mix until evenly distributed.

TO BAKE
Pour the batter into the prepared pan. Bake for 50 to 60 minutes, until a knife inserted in the center comes out clean. Let cool in the pan for 10 minutes, then remove the cake from the pan and set on a rack to finish cooling.

TO ASSEMBLE
Pipe the frosting over the top of the cake, and top with walnut halves.

VARIATIONS

American Layered Carrot-Coconut Cake
Reduce the flour to 2½ cups, and add 1 cup shredded coconut to the batter. Bake the batter in three 8-inch round pans for 30 to 35 minutes. Prepare 4 cups cream cheese frosting, then use it as a filling between cake layers as well as a frosting over the entire cake.

Indian Carrot-Cardamom-Zucchini Cake
Reduce the cinnamon to ¾ teaspoon. Add ¾ teaspoon ground cardamom. Replace the pineapple with shredded zucchini.

The History of Carrot Cake

In medieval Europe, carrots were most commonly used as a sweetener, second only to sugar beets. In England, they were also known as Queen Anne's lace, for their ornamental flowers, and when cakes made from carrots were developed in the later Middle Ages, they were called Queen Anne's cakes. English cookbooks from the eighteenth and nineteenth centuries offer many variations on the recipe.

As Europeans made their way across the Atlantic, carrots came with them, and carrot cakes made their way to American tearooms. It is said that George Washington was served an English Queen Anne's tea cake on November 25, 1783, the day upon which the last British troops left the newly independent United States.

During World War II carrot cake experienced a revival in Britain, when sweeteners were scarce. And in the 1970s carrot cake became a veritable food fad, promoted as a healthy cake with whole-grain flour, nuts, grated vegetables, and dried fruits. Today it has surpassed its fad status to become a star in its own right, one of the most commonly requested cakes in restaurants high and low.

Queen Mother Cake

Dense and intense, this flourless chocolate cake has a soft center that is similar to that of a soufflé. Although it's sophisticated, because of its minimalism it tastes best with a childhood favorite — a tall glass of milk.

Chocolate Cake

- 8 ounces semisweet chocolate, finely chopped
- ½ cup (1 stick) unsalted butter
- 1 teaspoon instant coffee
- 2 teaspoons boiling water
- 4 eggs, separated
- 1 teaspoon vanilla extract
- ½ teaspoon cream of tartar
- ¾ cup sugar

Toppings

- 1½ cups chocolate ganache (page 315)
- ½ cup fresh raspberries
- Decorative chocolate pieces

Makes 6 individual-serving cakes

TO PREPARE

Preheat the oven to 325°F. Butter six 3½-inch Bundt pans, and dust them with cocoa powder.

TO MAKE THE CAKE

Combine the chocolate and butter in a double boiler over medium heat and cook, stirring, until the chocolate is melted. Remove from the heat and set aside to cool. Combine the coffee and the boiling-hot water in a small bowl, and stir until the coffee is dissolved. Set aside to cool.

When the coffee has cooled, add to it the egg yolks and vanilla, and stir until blended. Pour the coffee mixture over the melted chocolate and whisk until blended.

The Queen Mother

Just like me, Queen Elizabeth, the Queen Mother (the mother of Elizabeth II), was nicknamed Cake by family and friends. She revealed her enthusiasm for this sweet confection at the many weddings she attended, always complimenting and expressing excitement when the cake ceremony began. This was quite endearing for a woman who lived to be 101. Flourless chocolate cake was the Queen Mother's favorite. Her pianist friend Jan Smeterlin was the first to serve it to her, in the 1950s, and she enjoyed it so much that she began featuring it at royal parties and continued to do so for the next 50 years.

In a separate medium bowl, beat the egg whites and cream of tartar until soft peaks form. Gradually add the sugar, beating until stiff, shiny peaks form. Fold the egg whites into the chocolate mixture in three batches, blending thoroughly.

TO BAKE

Pour the batter into the prepared pans. Bake for 20 to 25 minutes, until the cakes jiggle just slightly when gently shaken. Let the cakes cool in the pans for 15 minutes, then remove from the pans and set on a rack to finish cooling. The cakes may sink a bit in the middle while cooling.

TO SERVE

Spread chocolate ganache over the cakes. Top with raspberries and chocolate pieces.

VARIATION

Flourless Peanut Cake

Reduce the butter to ⅓ cup. Add 2 tablespoons peanut butter and 1 cup ground peanuts to the cake batter. Top with 2¼ cups peanut frosting (page 316) instead of ganache.

Zabaglione Cream–Berry Trifle

The word *trifle* comes from the Old French term *trufle*, which translates as "whimsical" or "of little consequence." This term represents the fanciful nature of this cake, which is more custard, cream, and fruit than cake. Trifles are usually prepared in glass bowls that show off the colorful berry and cream layers. If your priority is an impressive presentation, use a tall bowl. If you want simplicity, so that you can scoop up all the flavors in a spoonful, use a shorter bowl. I like to prepare individual servings. However you prepare it, make sure the cake pan is slightly smaller than the serving bowl, so that your cake layers will fit easily inside.

Pan di Spagna

- 2 cups cake flour, sifted
- 2 teaspoons baking powder
- 12 eggs, at room temperature, separated
- 2 cups granulated sugar
- 1 tablespoon orange juice
- 2 teaspoons vanilla extract
- ¼ cup milk, warmed

Zabaglione Cream

- 8 egg yolks
- ½ cup sugar
- ¾ cup marsala
- Pinch of salt

Assembly

- ½ batch orange syrup (page 318)
- ¼ cup marsala
- 1 cup sliced strawberries
- 1 cup blueberries
- 1 cup raspberries
- 1 cup blackberries
- 1¼ cups sliced almonds
- 4 cups whipped cream (page 323)

Makes 6 servings

TO PREPARE

Fill a medium bowl half full with ice water. Set aside six individual glass serving bowls, each 3 to 4 inches wide.

TO MAKE THE CAKE

Prepare the pan di Spagna batter as directed on page 196. Divide the batter among the six cups of a muffin pan. Bake for 20 to 35 minutes, until the tops begin to brown and a knife inserted in the center comes out clean. Let the cakes cool in the pan for 5 minutes, then finish cooling on a wire rack. Cut each one in thirds crosswise, to make three layers.

TO MAKE THE ZABAGLIONE CREAM

Whisk together the egg yolks, sugar, marsala, and salt in a double boiler over medium heat. Cook for 5 to 7 minutes, whisking constantly, until thickened. Remove from the heat, set the top of the double boiler in the ice water, and continue whisking until the mixture has cooled.

Transfer half of the whipped cream to a bowl, cover, and refrigerate. Fold the cooled zabaglione cream into the remaining whipped cream. Cover and refrigerate.

TO ASSEMBLE

Combine the orange syrup with the marsala. Spread the syrup over all the cake layers with a brush. For each cake, set one layer in the bottom of a bowl. Top with a layer of mixed berries, a scattering of almonds, a layer of zabaglione cream, and then a layer of whipped cream. Set another cake layer on top, and repeat the fillings. Set the final cake layer on top.

Refrigerate the trifles for at least 3 hours. When they're set, top with the remaining almonds and berries.

VARIATIONS

American Corn and Cranberry Trifle

Replace the pan di Spagna with Cherokee corn-flour cake (page 42). Replace the berries with cranberry sauce (page 320). Top with orange slices.

Tipsy Parson

Replace the marsala in the cream and the orange syrup with rum.

Zuppa Inglese

Replace the berries with 2½ cups candied fruit. Add 1½ cups chocolate chunks to the filling.

A History of Trifles

During the Renaissance Italian cooks brought sponge biscuits to England to prepare pudding trifles. They were commonly prepared with leftovers as a way to finish up stale cake. Though trifles were very popular in the early seventeenth century, they eventually fell out of fashion until the nineteenth century, when the sponge cake was introduced into the trifle, and cut glass bowls were used for a beautiful presentation.

Trifles have traveled the globe and, as you might imagine, taken different paths in different regions. The Italian zuppa inglese trifle is made with chocolate chunks and candied fruit. In colonial America cornmeal cakes and cranberry sauce were made into trifles. The southern tipsy parson is an alcohol-laden trifle that is said to have lured visiting preachers. Today trifles are a common dessert in English households and are available in many department-store restaurants.

Battenberg Cake

A classic and elegant English tea cake, the Battenberg cake is now produced commercially and sold by the millions throughout England. Made from a butter cake (or sometimes a sponge cake), it has a recognizable pink and yellow checkerboard pattern. The segments are held together with apricot glaze and wrapped in a thin skin of marzipan. The traditional cake is entirely vanilla in flavor, with the pink part only being colored. Here I have poshed up the pink with some cherry juice, giving it a mild fruity flavor that complements the vanilla.

Cake

3	cups all-purpose flour
1½	teaspoons baking powder
¼	teaspoon salt
1½	cups (3 sticks) unsalted butter, softened
1½	cups granulated sugar
4	eggs
½	cup milk
1	teaspoon vanilla extract
¼	cup cherry juice
	Red food coloring (optional)

Assembly

1¾	cups apricot glaze (page 318)
	Confectioners' sugar
5½	cups marzipan (page 324)

Makes 2 cakes (each serving 4 to 6)

History of the Battenberg

It is thought that the Battenberg cake was created to celebrate the marriage of Princess Victoria of Hesse and by Rhine, granddaughter of Queen Victoria, to Prince Louis of Battenberg in 1884.

TO PREPARE

Preheat the oven to 350°F. Butter two 9-inch square cake pans.

TO MAKE THE CAKE

Mix together the flour, baking powder, and salt in a medium bowl. In a separate large bowl, cream the butter and sugar until light and fluffy. Beat in the eggs, one at a time, blending well after each addition. Stir in the milk and vanilla. Gradually add the flour mixture to the butter mixture.

Divide the batter into two batches. Add the cherry juice to one batch, and if needed add a few drops of food coloring to make it pinker. Transfer each batch of batter to a separate prepared pan.

TO BAKE

Bake for 25 to 30 minutes, until a knife inserted in the center comes out clean. Let the cakes cool in their pans for 10 minutes, then remove from the pans and set on a rack to finish cooling.

TO ASSEMBLE

Stack the two cakes on a work surface and trim them so they are both perfectly square. Measure the height of each, and trim where necessary so they are the same height and flat across the top. Cut each cake into strips that are just as wide as they are high. Each cake should yield four strips.

Coat one side of one golden cake strip with glaze. Set a pink cake strip next to it. Spread glaze over the top of both strips. Set another golden cake strip on top of the pink cake strip, and coat its inside edge with glaze. Set a pink cake strip next to it, on top of the first golden cake strip. The four cake strips should now form a checkerboard pattern, with apricot glaze between all their joined edges. Repeat with the remaining cake strips to make a second checkerboard cake.

Dust a work surface with confectioners' sugar. Divide the marzipan into two equal batches. Roll out one batch of marzipan to ⅛-inch thickness. Measure the cake carefully, and cut the marzipan so that it will wrap entirely around one cake, leaving the ends exposed. Allow ½ inch extra to overlap. Set the cake on one end of the marzipan, and wrap the marzipan around it. Pinch together the ends of the marzipan to seal the seam. Repeat with the remaining cake and marzipan.

___

VARIATION

Chocolate Battenberg Cake

Omit the cherry juice and red food coloring. Add ¼ cup unsweetened cocoa powder to one batch of batter. After wrapping the cakes in marzipan, cover them with 2¼ cups chocolate ganache (page 315).

Dorset Apple Cake

This apple cake will transport you to a fall day in the English countryside. Deliciously moist, it is traditionally served warm with clotted cream. Regional bakers all have their own special recipe, some more cakelike (like this recipe), others more puddinglike. Dorset apple cake and Somerset apple cake, both from England, and Kerry cake from Ireland are the most common variations of this cake. Whichever you decide to prepare, your home will smell warm and inviting while the cake is baking.

Apple Cake

- 1¾ cups all-purpose flour
- 1 teaspoon baking powder
- 1 teaspoon baking soda
- 1 teaspoon ground cinnamon
- ½ teaspoon ground cloves
- ¼ teaspoon grated nutmeg
- ¼ teaspoon salt
- 1¼ cups (2½ sticks) unsalted butter, softened
- 1 cup light brown sugar
- ¾ cup granulated sugar
- 4 eggs
- ⅔ cup buttermilk
- 1 teaspoon vanilla extract
- 1¼ pounds apples (about 5 apples), peeled and cut into chunks

Apple Rosettes

- 2 cups apple juice
- ¼ cup lemon juice
- 1 Granny Smith apple, cored and thinly sliced
- 1 Gala apple, cored and thinly sliced
- 1 Golden Delicious apple, cored and thinly sliced

Topping

- 3½ cups apple glaze (page 318)

Makes 1 cake (serves 4 to 6)

TO PREPARE

Preheat the oven to 350°F. Butter and flour a 10-inch square cake pan.

TO MAKE THE CAKE

Combine the flour, baking powder, baking soda, cinnamon, cloves, nutmeg, and salt in a medium bowl; mix together, and set aside. In a separate large bowl, cream the butter, ¾ cup of the brown sugar, and all of the granulated sugar with a mixer until fluffy. Add the eggs one at a time, beating well after each addition. Then mix in the buttermilk, alternating with the flour mixture, until combined. Stir in the vanilla and three-quarters of the apples.

TO BAKE

Pour the batter into the prepared pan. Place the remaining apples on top of the batter. Sprinkle with the remaining brown sugar. Bake for 55 minutes to 1 hour, until a knife inserted in the center comes out clean. Let the cake cool in its pan for 10 minutes, then remove from the pan and set on a rack to finish cooling.

TO MAKE APPLE ROSETTES

Combine the apple juice, 2 tablespoons of the lemon juice, and the sliced apples in a skillet over low heat. Cook for 5 to 7 minutes, flipping occasionally, until the apples have softened. Remove from the heat and let cool. Form the apples into rosettes by curling a small slice into a circle, then wrapping other slices around it, in a spiral pattern (see the photo opposite). Spritz with the remaining lemon juice.

TO ASSEMBLE

Set the cake on a serving plate. Spread the apple glaze over it, and top with apple rosettes. Serve with clotted cream and some port.

VARIATIONS

Jewish Apple Cake

Prepare with McIntosh apples. Douse with powdered sugar to serve.

Kerry Apple Cake

Serve warm with cream or Greek-style yogurt and Irish cheddar cheese.

Somerset Apple Cake

Add 1 cup walnuts and 1 teaspoon grated lemon zest to the batter. Top with 2 cups lemon cream cheese frosting (page 316) instead of apple glaze.

Jewish Apple Cake

Jewish apple cake is an American-style coffee cake based on apple kuchen. In America it is most often made with McIntosh and Rome apples. It is prepared the same way as this apple cake, with streusel or a healthy coating of confectioners' sugar on top.

About Dorset and Somerset Apples

Dorset and Somerset, adjacent counties in the south of England, have a rich soil and a climate well suited for apple orchards. Spartan, Russet, Early Windsor, Regal Prince, Meridian, Bramley, and Warrior apples are all flavorful varieties typical of the region. Golden-Skin Russet, in particular, is a regional specialty, with a distinctive nutty taste. If you're traveling through the area and happen to spot these apples at a farmers' market, be sure to pick up a few. Another option is to visit on Apple Day, a festival held in October to celebrate the apples of this region, with fresh cider mulled on bonfires, apple cake competitions, apple tastings, orchard walks, and games, including the longest peel competition.

FRONT: *Dorset apple cake;* REAR: *Dundee cake (page 146)*

Apple Crumble

Dundee Cake

The Dundee cake, named for the city of its origin, is the traditional Scottish Christmas cake. It is not as heavy as other fruitcakes, and it is easy to identify by its top, which is studded with concentric circles of blanched almonds. For a modern take I replaced the traditional candied fruit with fresh pineapple and cherries and the traditional Scotch whiskey with Irish Guinness stout. Though unique, this recipe retains the Dundee cake's classic flavor. (For a photo of this cake, see page 145.)

Cake

- ¾ cup Guinness stout
- ½ cup chopped blanched almonds
- ¾ cup fresh pineapple chunks
- ¾ cup fresh or frozen cherries, pitted
- ½ cup golden raisins
- 1¼ cups all-purpose flour
- 2 teaspoons baking powder
- 1 teaspoon ground cinnamon
- ½ teaspoon grated nutmeg
- ½ teaspoon ground cloves
- ½ teaspoon ground ginger
- ¼ teaspoon ground allspice
- 1 cup (2 sticks) unsalted butter, softened
- 1 cup light brown sugar
- 4 eggs

Guinness Icing

- 1¼ cups confectioners' sugar
- 3 tablespoons Guinness stout

Topping

¾ cup whole blanched almonds

Makes 1 cake (serves 4 to 6)

TO PREPARE

Preheat the oven to 325°F. Line an 8-inch tall, round cake pan with buttered parchment paper.

TO MAKE THE CAKE

Combine the Guinness with the chopped almonds, pineapple, cherries, and raisins in a medium bowl; set aside. In a separate small bowl, combine the flour, baking powder, cinnamon, nutmeg, cloves, ginger, and allspice; set aside. In another separate medium bowl, cream the butter and brown sugar until light and fluffy. Add the eggs one at a time, beating well after each addition. Stir in the fruit mixture, followed by the flour mixture. Mix until well blended.

TO BAKE

Transfer the batter to the prepared pan. Cover with foil and bake for 45 to 50 minutes, until a knife inserted in the center comes out clean. Let cool in the pan.

TO MAKE THE ICING

Combine the confectioners' sugar and the Guinness and mix until smooth.

TO ASSEMBLE

Spread the icing over the cake. Arrange the whole almonds in concentric circles on the top of the cake.

VARIATION
Classic Dundee Cake

Replace the fresh pineapple with dried pineapple and the fresh cherries with candied cherries. Replace the Guinness in the cake with ½ cup Scotch whiskey; replace the Guinness in the icing with 2 tablespoons Scotch whiskey.

Sweet Scottish Scones

Scones are the traditional breakfast cake of Scotland, and they serve that purpose in many other countries of the world as well, particularly those with large Scottish immigrant populations, such as New Zealand and Argentina. Traditionally they are served with strawberry jam, lemon curd (page 321), or clotted cream.

Scones

- ¾ cup chopped almonds
- 2 tablespoons sugar
- 2½ cups all-purpose flour
- 2½ teaspoons baking powder
- ½ teaspoon baking soda
- ½ teaspoon salt
- 4 tablespoons unsalted butter, chilled and cut into chunks
- ⅔ cup buttermilk
- 1 egg
- 1 cup dried currants or raisins

Accompaniments

- 2 cups clotted cream
- 2 cups jam of choice

Makes 8 scones

TO PREPARE

Preheat the oven to 375°F. Butter and flour two baking sheets.

TO MAKE THE DOUGH

Combine the almonds and sugar in a food processor, and grind. Add the flour, baking powder, baking soda, and salt and pulse to combine. Add the butter and pulse until the mixture is sandy and blended. Add the buttermilk and egg, and process for 30 seconds. Stir in the currants by hand.

TO BAKE

Roll out the dough on a floured work surface. Use a cookie cutter or knife to cut the dough into 3-inch rounds. Transfer to the prepared baking sheets, spacing them 3 inches apart. Bake for 15 to 20 minutes, until golden. Let cool.

TO SERVE

When the scones have cooled, cut them in half. Serve topped with clotted cream and jam.

VARIATIONS

American Blueberry Scones
Replace the currants with 1 cup blueberries.

Scottish Oat-Cherry Scones
Reduce the flour to 2 cups. Add ½ cup rolled oats to the dough. Replace the currants with dried cherries.

About Clotted Cream

Clotted cream is added to or eaten alongside baked goods. Clotted cream, also known as Devonshire cream, is made by allowing whole milk to stand, so that the cream rises, and slowly heating it. The cream forms small golden clumps of butterfat, called dots, which are skimmed off and packaged as clotted cream. It's a wonderful accompaniment to baked goods and is much favored in the British Isles.

Welsh Cakes

Whenever I eat Welsh cakes, I feel like I've stepped into a time warp. These sconelike flat cakes are baked on a lightly buttered baking stone, just as they have been for centuries. If you don't have a baking stone, bake them on a cookie sheet lined with parchment paper or cook them on a griddle.

Flat Cakes

3½	cups all-purpose flour
1	tablespoon baking powder
1	teaspoon ground cinnamon
1	teaspoon salt
¼	teaspoon ground mace
½	cup (1 stick) unsalted butter
½	cup shortening
1¾	cups sugar
2	eggs
½	cup milk
1	cup dried currants
¼	cup candied citrus peel (page 325)

Toppings

2	cups raspberry filling (page 322)
2	cups brandy whipped cream (page 323)

Makes 10 cakes

TO PREPARE

Dust a baking stone with cornmeal and place it in the oven. Preheat the oven to 350°F.

TO MAKE THE CAKES

Combine the flour, baking powder, cinnamon, salt, and mace in a medium bowl. In a separate large bowl, mix the butter, shortening, sugar, and eggs until blended. Gradually add the flour mixture to the butter mixture, alternating with the milk. Stir in the currants and citrus peel until combined.

Form the dough into a ball and roll out to ½-inch thickness on a floured work surface. Use a cookie cutter or knife to cut the dough into 3½-inch hexagons or rounds.

TO BAKE

Transfer the cakes to the heated stone and bake for 6 to 8 minutes, then flip and bake for an additional 6 to 8 minutes, until browned on both sides.

TO SERVE

Top the cakes with raspberry filling and a dollop of brandy whipped cream.

Holding On to History

According to popular theory, the Welsh were a bit isolated from the rest of England, and they continued to prepare these flat cakes in the ancient manner even while the rest of Europe had moved on to high-rising cakes. Even when the spices and baking influences of the wider world made their way into Welsh communities, Welsh bakers continued to prepare their stone cakes as part of their cultural identity. Traditionally these cakes are prepared on Shrove Tuesday, when the last bits of fat and all of the tasty foods are to be eaten up before beginning the sacrifices of Lent.

Simnel

Simnel is a marzipan-covered fruitcake, similar to an English Christmas cake, that is usually prepared for Easter in Ireland, the United Kingdom, and France. In Ireland and England simnel is prepared as a two-layer round cake, with marzipan sandwiched between the layers. Eleven marzipan balls line the cake's perimeter, symbolizing the eleven favored apostles (excluding Judas), and a twelfth marzipan ball placed at the center represents Christ. The French prepare simnel in cupcake-size servings, each bearing a sugar cross embossed in its marzipan top.

Fruitcake

- ⅓ cup prunes
- ⅓ cup raisins
- ⅓ cup dried apples
- ⅓ cup dried apricots
- ⅓ cup dried pears
- ⅓ cup dried figs
- ¾ cup dark rum
- ¾ cup brandy
- 2⅔ cups all-purpose flour
- ½ cup cornstarch
- 1 tablespoon baking powder
- 2½ teaspoons ground cinnamon
- 1½ teaspoons ground allspice
- 1 teaspoon grated nutmeg
- ¾ teaspoon ground coriander
- ¼ teaspoon salt
- 1⅓ cups unsalted butter, softened
- 1¾ cups confectioners' sugar
- 9 eggs
  Zest of 1 lemon, grated
  Zest of 1 orange, grated
- 2 cups chopped walnuts

Simnel Marzipan

- 4½ cups finely ground blanched almonds
- 3 cups granulated sugar
- 6 egg whites
- 1 teaspoon almond extract
  Confectioners' sugar
- 2 egg whites, lightly beaten

Topping

- 4½ cups vanilla buttercream (page 317)
  Two food colorings

Makes 1 cake (serves 4 to 6)

TO PREPARE

Preheat the oven to 350°F. Butter and flour two 10-inch round cake pans.

TO MAKE THE CAKE

Chop the dried fruit into small pieces and combine in a bowl with the rum and brandy. Soak for at least 2 hours, then drain, reserving the liquid.

Combine the flour, cornstarch, baking powder, cinnamon, allspice, nutmeg, coriander, and salt in a medium bowl. In a separate large bowl, cream the butter and confectioners' sugar with a mixer until light. Add the eggs one at a time, beating well after each addition. Gradually add the flour mixture, mixing until blended. Fold in the dried fruits, lemon zest, orange zest, and walnuts.

TO BAKE

Pour the batter into the prepared pans. Bake for 45 to 55 minutes, until a knife inserted in the center of the cakes comes out clean. Remove the cakes from the oven and drizzle with the reserved rum and brandy. Let cool in the pans.

TO MAKE THE SIMNEL MARZIPAN

Line two baking sheets with parchment paper. Remove one of the cakes from its pan and set on a baking sheet. Preheat the oven to 400°F.

Combine the ground almonds, granulated sugar, six egg whites, and almond extract; blend well. Divide the marzipan into two batches, and divide one of those batches in half. Set aside the larger batch.

Coat a work surface with confectioners' sugar, and roll out the two smaller batches to ⅛-inch thickness. Using a cake pan as a template, cut out two marzipan circles the same size as the cakes. Set one marzipan circle on one of the cakes; this will be the bottom layer, with the marzipan as a filling. Trim the other marzipan circle into a lattice pattern; set the lattice on the prepared baking sheet. Combine any remaining marzipan with the larger batch. Divide the larger batch into 12 equal balls. Set on the prepared baking sheet.

TO BROWN

Brush the beaten egg whites over all the marzipan (on the bottom cake layer, on the lattice, and on the balls), and bake for 3 to 5 minutes, until the marzipan is browned. Watch the oven carefully so the marzipan doesn't burn. Remove from the oven and let cool. (You could also brown the marzipan with a torch.)

TO ASSEMBLE

Remove about one-third of the butter-cream to a separate bowl, and color each portion separately with food coloring. Set the marzipan-topped bottom layer on a serving plate, and top with the second cake layer. Frost the entire cake with the larger batch of buttercream. Set the marzipan lattice on top of the cake. Scoop the smaller batch of buttercream into a pastry bag fitted with a star tip, and use it to pipe a decorative border around the cake. Set the marzipan balls on top of the cake, using a dab of buttercream on each one as glue.

VARIATIONS

English Christmas Cake

Prepare the cake in one 10-inch round cake pan. Roll out and wrap the marzipan around the sides and top of the cake. Brown the marzipan-topped cake; omit the frosting.

French Simnel Cake

Bake the cake batter in large six-cup muffin pans. Cut the marzipan to fit on the top of each cake. Emboss a cross on the marzipan rounds, then set on the cakes. Brown the marzipan-topped cakes; omit the frosting.

Mothering and Holy Humor Sundays

Since medieval times, simnel cakes have been prepared to celebrate the fourth Sunday in Lent. This special day is known as Mothering Sunday, the original Mother's Day. It is also Holy Humor Sunday, the day when Christians celebrate the "joke" that God played on Satan by resurrecting Christ. During services on this day, in a tradition dating back to the Greeks in the early days of Christianity, churchgoers may tell jokes or humorous stories, sing, dance, and otherwise merrily rejoice.

CHAPTER 6

Scandinavia
The Romance of Berries and Liqueur, Topped with Cream

SCANDINAVIA IS A RUGGED AND VARIED REGION encompass-ing the snow-crested peaks of Iceland, the glacier-born fjords of Norway, the icy lakes and moraines of Sweden and Finland, and the low-lying lands of Denmark, which serve as a bridge to the rest of northern Europe. Its short but delight-fully light-filled summers are highlighted by white nights — an enchanting period when the sun never sets — which are a welcome reprieve from the region's long, dark winters.

Venturing into this northland, visitors find that here any cake goes at any time. No meal is complete without coffee and a sweet at the end. Bakeries can be found in almost every neighborhood — just look for the golden pretzel, the symbol of the baker's trade, hanging above a door or window.

If you want to know what a "typical" Scandinavian cake is like, think fruity with vanilla cream. Native wild berries — lingonberries, strawberries, Arctic cloudberries,

blueberries, honeyberries, and rowanberries — are all used in the batter and as toppings for cakes. Cakes may be served with fruit soups on the side, from warm rose hip soup in winter to chilled bilberry soup in summer. Spices used in cakes also tend to be fruity; juniper berries, allspice, anise seed, citrus peel, and lemon are all popular cake flavorings, as are almonds, hazelnuts, and chocolate.

For the months when fresh fruits are not available, Scandinavians may use traditional Viking-influenced tech-niques to dry fruits or preserve them in honey. Making jam is another popular preservation technique, extending a fruit's season as a jam layer in a sandwich cake. Scandinavians are also known for their herb- and berry-based liqueurs, which they make plentiful use of in baking. Aquavit is a tra-ditional potato spirit spiced with anise and caraway. Lakka is a strong, sweet liqueur made with Arctic cloudberries and

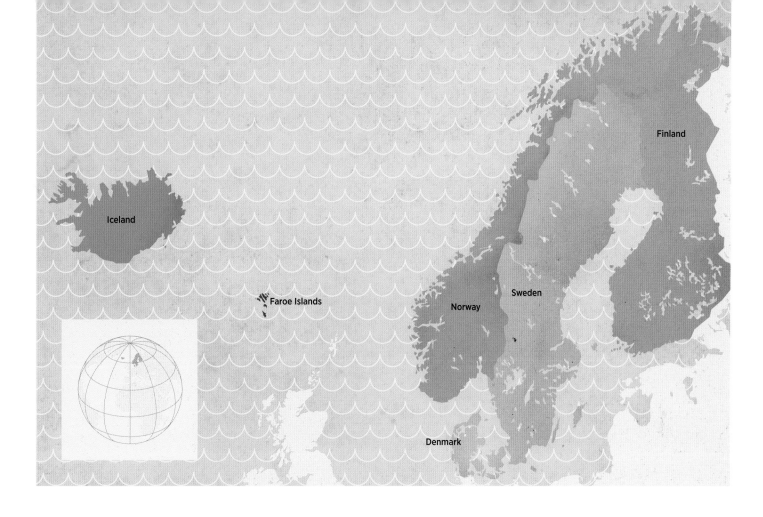

orange berries. And as the punsch in Runeberg cake (page 164) shows, liquor-soaked cakes are welcome at any time, even breakfast.

Dough sweetened with honey and sugar is known by the Viking name "kaka," a term that later morphed into the English word "cake." Like the word, most cake recipes in this region have crossed borders and seas, spreading from country to country. Over time, each region developed its own names for and customs around the cakes. For example, the kransekake (page 162), the ultimate celebration cake, is a tower of rings that may be filled with candy in Norway and a bottle of champagne in Finland. The surprises are revealed as you start cutting into the rings.

While thanks to global commerce Scandinavians may no longer lack for fresh fruits and vegetables in winter, potatoes and other root vegetables continue to be staples in their diet, and their cooking traditions are strongly rooted in wheat and oats. These homely staples are all used in their cakes. In Norway the julekake, a potato fruitcake, is prepared for Christmas, and the sandkake, a potato pound cake, is the traditional butter cake. Imagine a fruitcake even more dense and earthy than an English fruitcake and a butter cake more dense and earthy than a quatre quarts (page 54), if you can believe that such a thing is even possible.

Scandinavian cooking also incorporates a lot of dairy products, from milk, buttermilk, butter, cream, and cheese to skyr (similar to yogurt) and curds. The dome-shaped prinsesstårta (page 160), with its custard pastry cream and whipped cream center, is the most popular cake in Sweden. Most cakes are served with a vanilla cream, whether vanilla custard, vanilla sauce, vanilla ice cream, or vanilla whipped cream.

Scandinavians are notorious for their coffee drinking. They drink coffee for breakfast, after lunch, during breaks at work, and at parties. And where there is coffee, there are cakes, buns, and pastries. They are famed for coffee table entertaining, a charming style of hospitality in which seven courses are laid out in ceremonious fashion. Each serving is accompanied by a fresh cup of coffee. The first cup of coffee is served with small yeast cakes or butter cookies. The second cup is enjoyed with a sponge cake and more cookies. The third cup is accompanied by a richer cake, such as a cream-covered cake or torte, and so on, until all seven courses have been served and guests and hosts alike are warm and well fed.

Lagkage (Layer Cake)

The traditional birthday cake in Denmark is the lagkage, a white layer cake filled with jam, custard, or both. The sides are decorated with squiggly lines of whipped cream piped from a pastry bag. The top may have whipped cream or icing. Fresh fruit and tiny Dannebrog (Danish flags) traditionally decorate the cake. Hot cocoa is a favorite birthday drink and accompaniment. (For a photo of lagkage, see page 157.)

Cake

- 1 cup all-purpose flour
- 1½ tablespoons cornstarch
- 1½ teaspoons baking powder
- ½ teaspoon salt
- 4 eggs, separated
- 1 cup sugar
- 3 tablespoons cold water
- 1 teaspoon vanilla extract

Custard Filling

- ¾ cup sugar
- 1½ tablespoons cornstarch
- ¼ teaspoon salt
- 3 eggs
- 2¼ cups milk
- 2 teaspoons vanilla extract

Fresh Strawberry Sauce

- 1 cup sugar
- 1 cup water
- 2 cups halved fresh strawberries

Toppings

- 4 cups whipped cream (page 323)
- 1 cup fresh berries
- Sprig of mint

Makes 1 cake (serves 6 to 8)

TO PREPARE

Preheat the oven to 450°F. Butter and flour four 9-inch round cake pans. (You can prepare the cakes in two batches if your oven is too small or you don't have four pans.)

TO MAKE THE CAKE BATTER

Mix the flour, cornstarch, baking powder, and salt in a medium bowl; set aside. In a separate large bowl, beat the egg yolks with a mixer until light. Add the sugar, water, and vanilla and beat for an additional 2 to 3 minutes, until foamy. Gradually add the dry ingredients to the egg yolk mixture, and beat well. In a separate small bowl, beat the egg whites until stiff peaks form. Fold the egg whites into the batter.

TO BAKE

Pour the batter into the prepared pans. Bake for 10 to 12 minutes, until a knife inserted in the center comes out clean.

TO MAKE THE CUSTARD FILLING

Combine the sugar, cornstarch, and salt with the eggs in a saucepan over medium heat. Stir in the milk and vanilla, bring to a simmer, and cook, stirring, until the custard is thick. Remove from the heat and let cool.

TO MAKE THE STRAWBERRY SAUCE

Combine the sugar and water in a medium saucepan over medium heat, stirring until the sugar is dissolved. Add the strawberries and cook for 5 to 7 minutes, stirring, until the berries break apart and the mixture thickens. Remove from the heat and let cool.

TO ASSEMBLE

Place one cake layer on a serving plate and top with custard. Place a second cake layer on top, and top with strawberry sauce. Place a third cake layer on top, and top with custard. Place the fourth cake layer on top, and cover the entire cake with half of the whipped cream. Scoop the rest of the whipped cream into a pastry bag fitted with a large star tip. Use it to decorate the sides of the cake with squiggly lines running from the top of the cake to the bottom. Top the cake with fresh berries and a sprig of mint.

VARIATIONS

Brandy Lagkage

Brush each cake layer with brandy before assembling.

Bittersweet Frosted Lagkage

Prepare 2 cups bittersweet chocolate buttercream (page 315). Frost the top of the cake with the buttercream and the sides with whipped cream.

Kagemands and Kagekones

The brunsviger is an everyday Danish cake that is well known for the delicious, gooey mess of its burnt-sugar topping. For children's birthdays — and for those adults who can't bear to give it up — the brunsviger is shaped like a boy or a girl and called a kagemand (cake man) or kagekone (cake woman). The boy or girl cake is decorated with candy to look like the lucky birthday child in his or her favorite outfit. Kagemands and kagekones have less burnt-sugar topping than the classic brunsviger to allow space for these candy decorations. Following the nationalistic Danish birthday tradition, the cake is often surrounded with Dannebrog (Danish flags) for presentation.

Brunsviger

2½ tablespoons active dry yeast

1 cup milk, warmed

3 cups all-purpose flour

2 tablespoons granulated sugar

½ teaspoon salt

2 eggs

½ cup (1 stick) unsalted butter, melted and cooled

1 teaspoon vanilla extract

Brown-Sugar Topping

1 cup (2 sticks) unsalted butter

1¼ cups light brown sugar

Decorations

Assorted candies (candy-coated chocolate, licorice, gummies, jelly beans, caramel, gumdrops)

Colored sugars and nonpareils

2½ cups royal icing (page 317)

TO MAKE THE DOUGH

Dissolve the yeast in the milk and set aside for 5 minutes. Combine the flour, sugar, and salt in a medium bowl. Add the eggs, butter, and vanilla, and beat well. Transfer the dough to a floured work surface and knead for 7 to 10 minutes, until it is glossy and slightly sticky. Add some flour or milk if necessary to achieve the correct consistency. Transfer the dough to a bowl, cover, and let rise in a warm place until it has doubled in size, about 1 hour.

TO SHAPE

Butter a large baking sheet. When the dough has risen, punch it down with a quick blow. Roll it out on a floured work surface to the dimensions of your baking sheet and about ⅜ inch thick. Use a knife to cut the dough into the shape of a boy or a girl. Use the scraps to make a face, hair, or clothing designs. Carefully transfer the cut-out girl or boy to the baking sheet. Cover and let rise again for 1 hour.

TO MAKE THE TOPPING

Combine the butter and the brown sugar in a saucepan over high heat, and cook, stirring, for 4 to 6 minutes, until the butter is melted and the mixture is brown. Remove from the heat and let cool.

TO BAKE

Preheat the oven to 400°F. Dimple the dough all over the figure by pressing into it with your fingers. Pour the topping over the dough. Bake for 25 to 30 minutes, until the dough is lightly browned. Decorate the cake with assorted candies, using royal icing as a glue.

THE WORLD TOUR OF
Birthday Cakes

BIRTHDAY CAKES HAVE BEEN PART OF WESTERN CULTURE for almost as long as culture has been recorded. Ancient Greeks celebrated birthdays with honey and nut cakes. For Romans, birthdays were a family occasion, celebrated privately with sweet breads and fruitcakes.

Today's birthday cakes have their roots in the fifteenth and sixteenth centuries, when decorations developed into an art form that overshadowed cake flavors, which were still limited. The multilayered, heavily decorated birthday cakes resembled today's wedding cakes and became a venue for bakers to showcase their sugar and marzipan creations. These elaborately designed birthday cakes were, of course, a privilege of the wealthy. As the sugar trade routes expanded and sugar became more readily available, more modest versions of these grand birthday cakes soon became within reach of the working classes.

In the nineteenth century European colonies around the globe exported Western-style birthday cakes to Australia, India, Africa, and the Americas. Since that time, the birthday cake has been a universal component of birthday celebrations in both Western and Eastern cultures.

The familiar layered birthday cake originated in the United States in the midnineteenth century. Since America lacked the professional bakers that were commonplace in Europe, homemakers developed the easy-to-make layered butter cake, filled and frosted with boiled icing. These golden cakes soon became popular birthday cakes, and their simplicity helped them spread throughout the world.

Decorative presentation was a hallmark of the traditional American layer cake, and by the late 1800s cake decorating at bakeries had become an elaborate art. Inscriptions became common, especially "Happy Birthday," after the now-classic birthday song became popular in the early 1900s. Home bakers of the time would often bake their cake at home and bring it to a bakery to be decorated. Others purchased style guides with suggestions for decorating, mostly using colored candies. By the 1950s there were numerous cookbooks with decorating instructions, and cake decorating tools and ingredients became readily available for the home baker. Today cake decorating is a profitable industry with a seemingly limitless supply of cookbooks, classes, and TV shows to lend a helping hand to anyone who is interested in sharpening his or her skills.

Candles are another hallmark of the traditional birthday cake, in ancient as well as modern times. The Greeks were said to have placed candles around a birthday cake to make it glow like the moon. Germans popularized the addition of candles on top of children's birthday cakes for the fifteenth-century celebration known as Kinderfest. The candles were said to protect children against evil spirits, and the smoke was said to carry birthday wishes up to God.

Today a candle is commonly placed on the cake to represent each year a person has been alive, plus one for good luck.

Here's a sampling of some of the more interesting birthday cake traditions from around the world.

AUSTRALIA
In Australia, special cupcakes called butterfly cakes (page 52) are made to celebrate a child's birthday; they're cut and shaped to look like butterflies. Fairy bread is also traditional; this treat is nothing more than white bread cut into triangles and sprinkled with sparkly sugar, but children adore it.

BRAZIL
Brazilian birthday candies are made from marzipan to look like fruits and vegetables. These sweets are used to decorate the top of the cake.

CANADA
On a child's birthday, Canadians traditionally place a wrapped coin in the cake. Whoever finds it is first to play the party games.

CHINA
Traditionally longevity peach buns (page 268) are served to each guest at a Chinese birthday celebration. Today a layer cake with non-dairy topping is frequently served as well. In China tigers are believed to protect children, so an image of a tiger created from colored frosting sometimes adorns children's cakes.

DENMARK
The lagkage (page 154) is traditionally eaten as the birthday cake.

EGYPT
Egyptian birthday cakes are topped with fruits and flowers, which symbolize life and growth.

GERMANY
A member of the birthday person's family rises at sunrise to light the candles on the cake, and they stay lit all day long. Black Forest cake (page 120) is a regional favorite.

HOLLAND
Fruit tarts topped with whipped cream are served at birthday parties, alongside lemonade and hot chocolate. Ages 5, 10, 15, and 21 are considered special birthdays, celebrated with large gifts and a crown for the honored guest.

INDIA

On a child's birthday in India, traditionally chocolates are passed out to his or her entire class at school; today cupcakes accompany the chocolates.

JAMAICA

In Jamaica birthdays are celebrated with planter's cake, a simple peanut-lime cake topped with mocha icing.

KOREA

Steamed rice cakes made of layers from ground rice and bean paste are traditionally served on Korean birthdays. Today saeng cream cake (page 270) — a Western-style sponge cake topped with buttercream and fruit — and roll cakes are also popular for birthday celebrations.

MEXICO

On a Mexican girl's quinceañera, or 15th birthday, a special mass is given to celebrate her coming of age. The reception features a large tiered cake that looks like a wedding cake. Sometimes small wrapped cakes are placed inside a piñata along with candy and toys.

NEW ZEALAND

Since it is warm most of the year in New Zealand, ice cream cake is often served at birthday parties, along with barbecue. As part of the cake-cutting ceremony, the guest of honor receives a clap for each year he or she has been alive, plus one for good luck.

NORWAY

Chocolate cake with chocolate frosting is traditional. At a child's birthday party, the child chooses a friend to dance with to the birthday song, then the cake is served alongside red gelatin and vanilla sauce. At the birthday party guests play a fishing game, trying to catch ice cream treats attached to a string.

PERU

Peruvian guests receive two types of party favors, a goodie sweet and a pin to honor the event. The sweet can be candy or cake.

PHILIPPINES

In the Philippines not just one but several birthday cakes are made in various sizes and shapes. The outside of the honoree's house is decorated with lights.

RUSSIA

At birthday parties Russian children are served fruit pies with their names or a greeting embossed in the crust.

SWEDEN

On their birthdays Swedes enjoy a pound cake topped with marzipan and decorated with the national flag.

UNITED STATES

In the United States children often choose a novelty character cake decorated with the image of their favorite cartoon character or superhero. Another favorite is a large sheet cake or a layer cake in the birthday person's favorite flavor.

The Native American Winnebago throw a large word-of-mouth party, meaning if you hear about it, you are invited. The birthday girl or boy chooses the cake for the party, and also the guest who will cut the cake, a great honor.

Lagkage shown at left

157

Saffransbullar
(Saffron Buns or Lucia Cats)

Lucia cats, flavored with golden saffron and dark raisins, pivot on that narrow divide between sweet bun and cake. They are most commonly shaped into a figure eight, though many bakers form them into other shapes as well. They make a really good light breakfast cake. For special occasions they are often topped with rock candy.

Dough

- 2½ teaspoons active dry yeast
- ¼ cup plus 2 tablespoons sugar
- ½ cup warm water
- ½ teaspoon saffron threads
- ½ cup (1 stick) unsalted butter
- ¾ cup hot water
- ⅓ cup dry milk
- ½ teaspoon salt
- 1 egg, beaten
- 3½ cups all-purpose flour
- ¼ cup raisins (or dried currants, candied fruit, or nuts)

Glaze

- 1 egg
- 2 teaspoons cognac

Makes 12 individual-serving cakes

TO PREPARE

Combine the yeast, 1 tablespoon of the sugar, and the warm water in a small bowl. Stir until the yeast is dissolved, and let sit for 5 minutes, until foamy. Finely grind the saffron and 1 tablespoon of the sugar with a mortar and pestle.

TO MAKE THE DOUGH

Combine the butter with the hot water in a large bowl to melt. Stir in the dry milk, the remaining ¼ cup sugar, the salt, the saffron mixture, and the egg. Gradually add the flour, mixing until the dough starts to pull away from the sides of the bowl.

Transfer the dough to a floured work surface and knead for 7 to 10 minutes, until soft, smooth, and shiny. Add more flour if needed, but not so much that the dough dries out. Transfer the dough to a bowl, cover, and let rise in a warm place for 1 to 1½ hours, until the dough has doubled in size.

TO SHAPE

When the dough has risen, punch it down and transfer it to a floured work surface. Knead for 1 minute. Divide the dough into 12 equal pieces, and roll each into an oblong rope about 4 inches long. Cover and let rise for 1 hour, until the ropes have doubled in size.

When the dough ropes have risen, roll them again, now to about 8 inches in length. Twist the ends to form each rope into a figure eight. Place a raisin in the center of each end. Cover and let rise for 90 minutes, or until they have doubled in size.

TO BAKE

Set a rack in the upper third of the oven, and preheat to 350°F. Line two baking sheets with parchment paper.

Whisk the egg and cognac together in a small bowl. Brush the tops of the Lucia cats with the egg mixture. Bake for 10 to 15 minutes, until golden. Cool on the baking sheet.

St. Lucia's Day

St. Lucia, a Christian martyr known as the queen of light, is said to symbolize hope. On December 13 each year — a time of darkest winter in the northern country of Sweden — St. Lucia Day and Lucia cats kick off the Christmas season. First thing in the morning, children carry a tray of Lucia cats and coffee to awaken their parents. And in towns across the country, a young girl dresses up in a white dress or robe and wears a crown with seven lit candles. She visits homes, churches, shopping malls, and other locations, singing and handing out pepparkakor (gingersnaps).

VARIATIONS

Cinnamon Buns

For the dough, replace the saffron with cinnamon, and add 1 cup raisins. Prepare a filling by blending ½ cup sugar, 1 table-spoon ground cinnamon, and ½ cup chopped raisins. Divide the dough into 12 equal pieces, and roll each out into strips approximately ¼ inch thick, 12 inches long, and 2½ inches wide. Spread the filling over the strips and roll them up. Place the rolls in a 9-inch round pan and let rise for about 30 minutes, until they have doubled in size. Brush with the cognac mixture and bake for 15 to 20 minutes, until golden. Let cool, then top with ¾ cup lemon glaze (page 318).

Rock Candy Lucia Cats

After the buns are baked, top them with 1¾ cups lemon icing (page 316) and ¼ cup chopped rock candy.

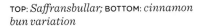

TOP: *Saffransbullar;* BOTTOM: *cinnamon bun variation*

Prinsesstårta (Princess Cake)

The prinsesstårta is a dinner-party dream cake, like something out of a fairy tale. It is most recognizable by its dome shape and bright marzipan topping, with a marzipan flower in the center. Wrapping the marzipan around the cake tightly takes a bit of skill, so practice a few times on a bowl before putting it on the cake. The prinsesstårta is most commonly made with sponge cake, apricot glaze, pastry cream, and whipped cream, although other fruit preserves and custardy creams are also common.

Génoise Sponge Cake

- 1⅓ cups cake flour
- 1 cup cornstarch
- 12 eggs
- 1½ cups superfine sugar
- ⅔ cup unsalted butter, melted and cooled
- 2 teaspoons vanilla extract

Assembly

- 1¾ cups apricot glaze (page 318)
- 2 cups rum whipped cream (page 323)
- 1¾ cups pastry cream, any kind (page 323)
- 8 cups marzipan (page 324), at room temperature
- Food colorings of choice
- Confectioners' sugar

Topping

- 6 ounces chocolate, melted

Makes 1 cake (serves 6 to 8)

TO PREPARE

Prepare the sponge cake as directed on page 108, baking it in a 9-inch domed cake pan for 40 to 50 minutes, until the cake is golden brown and shrinks away from the sides of the pan. Cut the cake in thirds crosswise, making three layers.

TO ASSEMBLE

Set one of the flat cake layers on a serving plate, and spread a thin layer of apricot glaze over it. Top with the second flat cake layer, and spread a ⅜-inch layer of whipped cream on it, followed by the pastry cream. Top with the domed cake layer. Coat the sides of the cake with a ¼-inch layer of whipped cream.

TO TOP WITH MARZIPAN

Remove a 2-inch ball of marzipan from the total amount, and set aside. Use food coloring to dye the remaining marzipan. (See the instructions on page 324 for dyeing marzipan.)

Dust a work surface with confectioners' sugar. Roll out the marzipan into a 16-inch circle, about ⅛ inch thick. Drape the marzipan over the top of the cake; some will extend onto the plate. If the marzipan is folded or creased, gently stretch it flat, working your way around the cake. Trim the marzipan even with the bottom of the cake.

TO DECORATE

Scoop the melted chocolate into a pastry bag fitted with a small tip. Pipe the chocolate in a decorative pattern over the cake. Dust the cake with confectioners' sugar.

Divide the reserved marzipan into two small batches. Use food coloring to dye one small batch the color of a flower, and dye the other small batch the color of leaves. (See the instructions on page 324 for dyeing marzipan.) Roll out the leaf marzipan to ¹⁄₁₆-inch thickness. Cut three leaf shapes, and score the leaves with a knife to create veins. Curve each leaf so that it arches slightly. Place the leaves on the center of the cake, and press down to affix.

Roll out the flower marzipan to ¹⁄₁₆-inch thickness. Cut into ten thin strips. Curl one small slice into a circle, then wrap other slices around it, in a spiral pattern, to make a flower. Set the flower with the leaves on the center of the cake, and press down to affix.

VARIATION

Chocolate-Almond Prinsesstårta
Replace the génoise sponge cake with devil's food cake (page 52). Replace the apricot glaze with 1¾ cups orange glaze (page 319).

Princess Cakes for All

In Sweden you can find the prinsesstårtas everywhere, in every variation, and for every holiday: birthdays, anniversaries, national holidays, and more. For Father's Day the central flower is removed so it has a manlier presence — and we might safely assume the cake is no longer called a "princess" cake.

Bakelser are made in the same way as prinsesstårtas, but they are individual-size. They are often decorated to resemble cutesy frogs, the idea being that if you kiss one, it will grow into a prince. These cakes inspired the frog cakes of southern Australia (page 310).

Kransekake (Wreath Cake)

There is nothing quite like this Scandinavian-style cake tower. Rings of cookielike marzipan are baked to be firm on the outside, soft and chewy on the inside. The marzipan has a rich almond, orange, rosewater flavor. The rings are stacked into a steeply sloped pyramid and then decorated with royal icing and miniature flags. (For Christmas the cake is decorated to look like a Christmas tree.) A bottle of champagne, chocolates, cookies, or candies may be hidden in the center of the tower. Special pans are available to make the rings, although here I have shown you how to make them with standard equipment.

Cake Rings

3¾	cups finely ground blanched almonds
3¾	cups finely ground unblanched almonds
6¾	cups confectioners' sugar, sifted
6	egg whites
2	teaspoons rosewater
1	teaspoon almond extract
3	tablespoons orange juice

Assembly

2¼	cups royal icing (page 317)
	Bottle of champagne or candies of choice

Makes 1 cake (serves 6 to 8)

TO PREPARE

Preheat the oven to 250°F. Cover three baking sheets with parchment paper. Use a compass to draw 18 circles on the parchment, in the sizes specified opposite. Then butter the parchment.

TO MAKE THE DOUGH

Combine the ground almonds with the confectioners' sugar in a large bowl. Add the egg whites, rosewater, almond extract, and orange juice and mix well. Transfer the dough to a double boiler, and heat until it is warm. Then transfer it to a work surface dusted with confectioners' sugar and knead for 2 to 3 minutes, until smooth.

TO SHAPE

Dust a work surface with confectioners' sugar. Roll out the dough into ½-inch-thick logs in the lengths that you need to fit the circles you drew. Form each log into a ring, smoothing the seam as best you can. Flatten the tops of each ring, to provide a stable surface for the ring that will sit on top of it.

TO BAKE

Bake the rings for 12 to 15 minutes, until dry and firm on the outside but soft on the inside. Cool for 10 minutes on the baking sheets, then transfer to racks to finish cooling.

TO ASSEMBLE

Scoop the royal icing into a pastry bag fitted with a medium tip, and pipe squiggly lines onto each ring. If you will fill the tower with a champagne bottle, set it on a serving plate and slide the rings in order of size over it. If you will fill the tower with candy, stack the rings on a serving plate, holding them together with the remaining icing and miniature toothpick flags, and fill the tower with candy before placing the last ring on top.

TO SERVE

Disassemble the rings and cut into segments, or cut in long slices from the top down.

VARIATION

Chocolate Mini Kransekake

Prepare the dough and roll into logs. Instead of forming the logs into rings, cut them into 3½-inch segments. Bake for 10 to 12 minutes, until dry and firm on the outside. Remove from the oven and let cool. Dip the bottom half of each segment into 1 cup chocolate glaze (page 318), and pipe ½ cup royal icing on top.

Wreath Cake Traditions

Norwegians call it *kransekake*, Danes call it *kransekage*, Swedes call it *kranskaka*. Whatever the name, the wreath cake is the same throughout Scandinavia, but what goes inside differs depending on the culture and the event. In Finland a bottle of champagne is placed inside for weddings. Guests break off pieces, and when the bottle is uncovered, everyone shares the champagne for a toast. In other countries candy, cookies, or chocolates are placed inside. The rings are usually formed into a tower shape but may also be formed into a basket or even an impressive cornucopia, called "the horn of abundance."

KRANSEKAKE RINGS

To make the kransekake, prepare 18 dough
rings with the following diameters:

2¼ inches →

2½ inches →

2¾ inches →

3 inches →

3½ inches →

3¾ inches →

4¼ inches →

4½ inches →

4¾ inches →

5 inches →

5¼ inches →

5½ inches →

5¾ inches →

6 inches →

6½ inches →

7 inches →

7½ inches →

8 inches →

Runeberg Cakes

National pride led the Finns to name a cake after a literary genius, Johan Ludvig Runeberg, a famous nineteenth-century Finnish poet. These were his favorite breakfast cakes. These little almond cakes are easily identified because they are topped with raspberry jam or red currant jelly, surrounded by a ring of pink icing. The unique texture comes from crumbled cookies (I used gingersnaps) and breadcrumbs mixed into the batter. Most Runeberg cakes are made in tall, cylindrical pans called Runeberg forms, but you can use cupcake pans or baba forms instead.

Cake

- 2 cups all-purpose flour
- 1 teaspoon baking powder
- 1 teaspoon baking soda
- 1 teaspoon ground cardamom
- ½ teaspoon salt
- 1 cup (2 sticks) unsalted butter, softened
- 1 cup dark brown sugar
- ½ cup granulated sugar
- 1 tablespoon grated orange zest
- 3 eggs
- ¾ cup orange juice
- ¾ cup crushed gingersnaps
- ¼ cup breadcrumbs
- 1 cup ground almonds

Pink Icing

- ⅓ cup confectioners' sugar
- 2 teaspoons orange juice
- Red food coloring

Assembly

- ¼ cup punsch liquor, rhum agricole, or cognac
- 1¾ cups raspberry glaze (page 319)

Makes 12 individual-serving cakes

TO PREPARE

Preheat the oven to 350°F. Butter and flour 12 Runeberg pans or two six-cup cupcake pans.

TO MAKE THE CAKES

Combine the flour, baking powder, baking soda, cardamom, and salt in a medium bowl. In a separate large bowl, cream the butter with the sugars and orange zest until light and fluffy. Mix in the eggs one at a time, beating well after each addition. Gradually add the flour mixture, alternating with the orange juice. Stir in the gingersnaps, breadcrumbs, and almonds.

TO BAKE

Fill the prepared pans half full with batter. Bake for 18 to 22 minutes, or until the tops of the cakes are golden brown and a knife inserted in the center comes out clean.

TO MAKE THE ICING

While the cakes are baking, combine the confectioners' sugar with the orange juice. Add a drop of red food coloring to make the icing pink.

TO ASSEMBLE

When the cakes are baked, brush their tops with punsch. Let cool in their pans for 10 minutes, then run a knife around the edges of the cakes to release them, remove from the pans, and set on a rack to cool. Top each cake with a round dollop of raspberry glaze, leaving ½ inch around the edges. Pipe pink icing around the raspberry glaze atop each cake.

VARIATION

Red Currant Runeberg Cakes
Replace the raspberry glaze with red currant jelly. Omit the punsch.

History of the Runeberg Cake

These breakfast cakes were the invention of Runeberg's wife, Fredrika, who took creative license with her recipes. Runeberg favored his breakfast cakes flavored with punsch and topped with fruit jam. Frederika used leftover bread, cake, and cookies to extend the dough, due to the home economics of the poet's modest income. These cakes are now such a strong part of Finnish tradition that the populace consumes more than 1.4 million of them each year between New Year's Day and February 5 (Runeberg Day), the poet's birthday.

THE WORLD TOUR OF
Breakfast Cakes

BREAKFAST IS ABOUT BREAKING THE FAST after a long night. Throughout most of history, around the globe this meal has been simple and quick. It usually consists of a warm drink (coffee, tea, soup, hot chocolate) and a simple grain (bread, cake, cereal, rice). In Latin America sweet bread or churros (page 78) are eaten with some thick chocolate to drink. In Asia, dim sum (savory and sweet dumplings and cake) are eaten with tea. And in many Western countries, coffee and pastry are the breakfast norm.

You can recognize a breakfast cake not only by the time of day when it is usually eaten but also by the casual nature in which it can be consumed. Whole breakfast cakes, such as pound cakes and coffee cakes, are generally made in loaf or ring pans, and individual wedges make sturdy travel food. Individual-size cakes such as doughnuts, scones, and Runeberg cakes are natural grab-and-go mini meals.

These on-the-go cakes have taken journeys much longer than your morning commute. Tasty delights like beignets have become so ubiquitous in New Orleans that you'd most certainly forget their French origins if it weren't for the name, and the common Danish sold off street trucks in New York City has traveled even further, migrating from Austria to Denmark to the world around. Even in regions of the world where coffee and pastry are not traditions, including Japan, Africa, and the Middle East, the Western style has recently been taking hold. Witness a recent bumper crop of Starbucks and other Western coffee chains in cities everywhere from Bangkok to Dubai — and it's not just the tourists who are imbibing.

Here's a sampling of breakfast cakes from around the globe, with their country of origin:

LEFT: *lemon poppyseed cake (page 177);*
CENTER: *kugelhopf (page 127);*
RIGHT: *apple strudel (page 123)*

BEIGNET (FRANCE)

In America this French fried choux pastry is made into a doughnut and covered with confectioners' sugar. In France the term *beignet* refers to a whole category of fried pastries.

BUCKLE (UNITED STATES)

This single-layer old-fashioned coffee cake is made with fruit and streusel topping. It is the American version of the German streusel.

BUNDT (UNITED STATES)

Based on the yeast kugelhopf/gugelhupf from Austria/Germany (page 127), Bundt cakes are buttery rich and very retro chic.

CHURROS (SPAIN)

These crunchy fried doughnuts (page 78) made of choux pastry are popular in all of Latin America. They are eaten with thick, syrupy hot cocoa.

COFFEE CAKE (RUSSIA)

Traditional Russian coffee cake is flavored with cinnamon, nuts, and fruit. The now classic coffee cake is the German kuchen.

CROISSANT (AUSTRIA)

These cakes are made from a buttery puff pastry in a classic crescent shape. The French adapted it and made it their own in their famous boulangerie. Medialunas are small croissants prepared in South America.

DANISHES (AUSTRIA)

Inspired by the same dough as croissants and strudel, Danishes have traveled the globe and can now be found in endless variety, stuffed with marzipan, custard, or fruit and topped with chocolate or icing.

DOUGHNUTS (UNITED STATES)

Both ring and filled doughnuts (page 44) are fabulous. Dutch settlers in America adapted their traditional oliebollen with a hole to help with the preparation process.

IDLI (SOUTHERN INDIA)

These small, savory steamed cakes are made with rice and fermented split peas. They are served for breakfast with a side of chutney.

LEMON POPPYSEED CAKE (RUSSIA)

Poppyseeds and lemon are common butter cake combinations (page 177), especially in Jewish households, where the seeds contain religious symbolism

MUFFINS (UNITED STATES)

Muffins are individual, cupcake-shaped quick breads. They tend to be denser than cakes, and traditionally they lack the frosting cupcakes are famous for. Muffins can be found in flavors such as corn, blueberry, pumpkin, apple, and date-nut.

OATMEAL CAKES (SCOTLAND)

Made with oats, these breakfast cakes can also be dressed up with icing.

PAN DULCE (LATIN AMERICA)

This chewy sweet bread comes in many different shapes and sizes. Stop by a local panadería to find it.

LEFT: *quatre quarts (page 54);* CENTER: *vasilopita (page 202);* RIGHT: *sweet scones (page 147)*

QUATRE QUARTS (CANADA)

The classic pound cake (page 54) traditionally contains a pound each of all of the major ingredients.

RUNEBERG CAKES (FINLAND)

These cakes (page 164) are easy to identify, carrying a circle of jam with a ring of pink icing around the tops.

SESAME BALLS (CHINA)

These dim sum rice cakes are filled with adzuki bean or lotus seed paste and covered with sesame seeds. They are sweet and chewy all at once. Miniature egg tarts similar to the Portuguese pastéis de nata (page 201) are also a favorite.

SODA BREAD (IRELAND)

The ultimate quick bread; it even has the fast-acting agent in its name. Although called bread, soda bread has a lot of sugar and usually dried fruit, making it a close cousin of fruitcakes.

STRUDEL (HUNGARY)

Strudel derives from the puff pastry dough developed in the ancient Byzantine empire. Apple (page 123), cherry, and cheese are favorite flavors.

SWEET BAKIRKHANI (INDIA)

When molasses and sesame seeds are added to this table bread, it becomes a sweet breakfast cake.

SWEET SCONES (SCOTLAND)

These dense, flaky biscuit cakes (page 147) are traditionally prepared with dried fruits, but now almost anything goes.

VASILOPITA (GREECE)

This coffee cake (page 202) has an extra special treat inside: on New Year's, a trinket reveals who will have the best luck of the year.

Vatnsdeigsbollur (Carnival Cakes)

In Iceland these sweet cakes are prepared for Bolludagur (Bun Day), the Monday before Lent begins. Similar to cream puffs, they are filled with sweetened fruit, whipped cream, or both, and topped with chocolate and confectioners' sugar. Although it can be hard to find many native fruits and vegetables in Iceland, rhubarb is a national favorite, so I have filled these with a rhubarb jam.

Buns

- ⅔ cup unsalted butter
- 1⅓ cups water
- ⅔ cup all-purpose flour
- ½ teaspoon salt
- 5 eggs, beaten

Rhubarb Jam

- 1 cup water
- 2¼ cups sugar
- 1 teaspoon cornstarch
- 3 cups chopped red rhubarb
- 1 tablespoon vanilla extract

Toppings

- 4 cups whipped cream (page 323)
- 1½ cups chocolate glaze (page 318)
- Confectioners' sugar

Makes 8 buns

TO PREPARE

Preheat the oven to 375°F. Butter two baking sheets.

TO MAKE THE BUNS

Combine the butter and water in a medium saucepan over low heat, and stir until the butter is melted. Add the flour and salt, and stir until thick. Remove from the heat. Add the eggs and mix well.

TO BAKE

Scoop up the dough with a tablespoon and drop onto the baking sheets, spacing the cakes about 2½ inches apart. Bake for 15 to 20 minutes, until golden. Turn off heat, open the oven door slightly, and let cool in the oven for 15 minutes. Then remove the buns from the oven and transfer to a rack to finish cooling.

TO MAKE THE RHUBARB JAM

Pour the water into a large saucepan over medium heat. Stir in the sugar and cornstarch, bring to a boil, and stir until the solids are dissolved. Add the rhubarb, reduce the heat, and simmer, stirring occasionally, until the mixture thickens, 20 to 30 minutes. Remove from the heat and stir in the vanilla. Let cool.

TO ASSEMBLE

Slice three-quarters of the way through each bun. Fill with rhubarb jam and whipped cream. Top with chocolate glaze and confectioners' sugar.

VARIATIONS

Blueberry-Peach Cream Vatnsdeigsbollur

Omit the rhubarb jam. Add 1½ cups chopped fresh peaches and 1 cup blueberries to the whipped cream. Fill the buns with the fruit-cream mixture.

Chocolate-Chip Vatnsdeigsbollur

Omit the rhubarb jam. Add 1 cup mini chocolate chips to the whipped cream.

Japanese Cream Puffs

Omit the rhubarb jam and whipped cream. Fill the buns with chocolate or vanilla pastry cream (page 323).

Strawberry-Banana Vatnsdeigsbollur

Omit the rhubarb jam. Mash 2 ripe bananas and stir into the whipped cream (page 323). Fill each bun with banana pastry cream (page 323) and sliced strawberries.

Hazelnut Oatcake with Vanilla Sauce

Quite isolated, quite cold, and quite unique. I had never heard of the Faroes until I began researching cakes of Scandinavia and interesting cakes from these islands kept popping up. Also known as the Sheep Islands, the 18 Faroes are halfway between Scotland and Iceland. This cake recipe includes oats, which are common in Scottish breads, and cardamom, caraway, currants, and hazelnuts, which are common in Scandinavian cuisine. The vanilla sauce is also very Scandinavian. Traditionally these cakes are served with a fruity dessert soup.

Hazelnut Oatcake

- 1¼ cups water
- 1½ cups rolled oats
- 1⅓ cups all-purpose flour
- 1 teaspoon ground cardamom
- ½ teaspoon caraway seeds
- 1 teaspoon baking powder
- ½ teaspoon salt
- 1½ cups light brown sugar
- ½ cup granulated sugar
- 1 cup (2 sticks) unsalted butter, melted and cooled
- 2 eggs
- ¾ cup chopped hazelnuts

Toppings

- 1¼ cups vanilla sauce (page 320)
- 2 cups fresh currants, cloudberries, or golden raspberries
- ¼ cup whole hazelnuts

Makes 1 cake (serves 6 to 8)

TO PREPARE

Preheat the oven to 350°F. Butter and flour a 9-inch round cake pan, and line it with parchment liner.

TO MAKE THE CAKE

Bring the water to a boil and pour over the oats in a small bowl. In a separate bowl, combine the flour, cardamom, caraway, baking powder, and salt; set aside. In a separate large bowl, mix the sugars with the melted butter until blended. Add the eggs, one at a time, beating well after each addition. Gradually add the flour mixture, the oats, and the hazelnuts, stirring until blended.

TO BAKE

Pour the batter into the prepared pan and bake for 50 minutes to 1 hour, until a knife inserted in the center comes out clean. Remove from the pan and let cool in the liner.

TO SERVE

Pool the vanilla sauce on the cake. Top with fresh berries and hazelnuts.

St. Olaf's Wake

Ólavsøka (St. Olaf's Wake) on July 29 is a national holiday in the Faroes. It's celebrated in the height of summer, which in this cold region is the best time to enjoy the outdoors. National rowing and sports competitions are held, as well as arts and music festivals, and food vendors across the islands sell various versions of these oatcakes, a common festival food.

FRONT: *hazelnut oatcake;*
BACK: *vatnsdeigbollur (page 168)*

CHAPTER 7

Eastern Europe
Marzipan, Gingerbread, and Other Fairy-Tale Cakes

THE PROUD SPIRIT OF MANY CULTURES SHINES THROUGH in their baking traditions. During a stay in Budapest, while backpacking across Europe, I rented a room from a family for one week. Their home was so modest that almost all of the family's possessions could have fit into my backpack. Yet every morning the mother and her two daughters baked enough strudel and kuchen for ten visitors and set it outside my door. They took such great care and pride in showing off their cultural heritage through baking. It blew me away! Plus backpacking burns lots of calories, so I was especially delighted to gorge on homemade cake every morning.

If cake is your priority, it is well worth your while to leave the well-trodden tourist paths to explore out-of-the-way parts of eastern Europe. In some areas of this region where the Ottoman Empire once ruled, baking traditions carry distinct Middle Eastern influences, with phyllo, tropical fruits, and nuts being common ingredients. Baklava (page 235), for example, is well loved in Albania, though Greeks, Armenians, Turks, and Iranians all claim to have invented it. Poppyseed fillings are popular in cakes and pastries, such as the kolache

(page 178). Also popular are various traditional Middle Eastern spices such as saffron, juniper, pepper, cinnamon, and nutmeg, used in cakes ranging from Slovenian potica (nut roll; see page 182) to Russian saffron cake (page 176).

Marzipan, made from crushed almonds, becomes a work of art in the hands of eastern European bakers, who use it in cake batters as well as for decorative toppings. Estonia, for one, is well known for its marzipan decorations. While walking through the streets of its cities, you will see window displays filled with marzipan creations showcasing bakers' skills through hand-painted details.

In western parts of the region, cakes are more central European in style, often featuring chocolate in sophisticated presentations, such as the Dobos torte (page 172) and the Rigó Jancsi cake (page 175) of Hungary. As in northern European countries, dairy ingredients such as sweet cream, clotted cream, and cheese find their way into cheesecakes, buttercream toppings, and other delights.

Gingerbread is a staple of the region, appearing in various forms depending on the culture of origin. Polish gingerbread,

for example, is piernik — soft gingerbread cakes iced or filled with preserves and covered with chocolate — while Russian gingerbread is a rich, buttery confection usually served with strong black tea.

Dumplings and other filled cakes are also popular. In the Czech Republic and Slovakia dumplings are filled with strawberry, cherry, apricot, bilberry, or peach preserves, while in Poland paczki — doughnuts filled with jam — are famous as street food.

The countries of the Balkan Peninsula have been influenced by traditions from ancient Rome, Greece, and Byzantium, and their cakes are regionally diverse. Bulgarian cakes, for example, often contain maize, apples, cherries, yogurt, peanuts, and chocolate, while Romanian cakes often feature phyllo, sunflower oil, sesame seeds, and poppyseeds.

The foundations of Russian and Polish cuisine are peasant food, and here you will find very simple cakes made from hearty ingredients like potatoes and cottage cheese. There are also many cakes inspired by Jewish tradition, such as the lemon poppyseed cake (page 177) that you find at many Jewish delis in the United States. Others reflect the traditions of the Eastern Orthodox church, such as the kulich, a saffron-flavored cake filled with brightly colored hard-boiled eggs, and the folk-art-decorated mazurek (page 180), which is as much fun to design as to eat at Easter brunch.

As in Russia, traditional cakes of the Baltic states tend to be rustic affairs. Fruits are common ingredients; in fact, some cakes are even shaped to look like fruits (page 181). Lithuanian pyraga cakes often have apples or plums baked into the batter, while spurgo doughnuts are filled with preserves. Scandinavian influences can also be seen in the regional Danishes, cream cakes, and oatcakes.

Russia's southern neighbors make great use of honey as a sweetener. Ukraine produces rich, dark honey cakes, while Georgia combines walnuts and honey in coffee cakes that taste just like the ones I grew up with in New York. Ukraine is considered the breadbasket of the region, and its people are known for their baking, mostly breads and sweet breads that they make for festivals throughout the year, shaping the dough to symbolize the celebration. Their ultimate bread-making skill is shown off in the multitiered wedding bread known as korovai, which is braided to symbolize the families coming together.

Dobos Torte

The wow factor of the Dobos torte is in the top layer, in which caramel-glazed wedges are propped up by hazelnuts to delineate the cake slices. The cake is made with five or more thin layers of golden sponge cake, filled and topped with chocolate buttercream. Chopped hazelnuts adorn the sides. When preparing this cake, measure the batter for the layers in a measuring cup so that they will be perfectly uniform.

Sponge Cake
1½ cups cake flour

¼ teaspoon salt

9 eggs, separated

2¼ cups confectioners' sugar

1½ teaspoons vanilla extract

Caramel Glaze
1½ cups granulated sugar

¼ cup water

1½ tablespoons unsalted butter

1 tablespoon lemon juice

Toppings
6 ounces chocolate, melted

6 cups bittersweet chocolate buttercream (page 315)

1 cup hazelnuts

Makes 1 cake (serves 6 to 8)

TO PREPARE
Preheat the oven to 350°F. Butter and flour four 9-inch round cake pans.

TO MAKE THE SPONGE CAKE
Combine the flour and salt in a large bowl; set aside. In a separate large bowl, beat the egg yolks, 1 cup of the confectioners' sugar, and the vanilla with a mixer until pale and thick. Add the egg yolk mixture to the flour mixture. In another separate large bowl, beat the egg whites until frothy but not stiff. Add the remaining 1¼ cups confectioners' sugar and continue to beat until stiff peaks form. Fold the egg whites into the batter.

TO BAKE
Pour 1 cup batter into each of the prepared pans and bake for 5 to 8 minutes, or until springy to the touch. Let the cakes cool in their pans for 5 minutes, then remove them from the pans and set them on a rack to finish cooling. Repeat until the batter is used up, washing and regreasing and flouring the pans if necessary.

TO MAKE THE CARAMEL-GLAZED LAYER
Bring the sugar, water, butter, and lemon juice to a boil in a small saucepan. Cook, stirring, until the sugar is dissolved and the mixture is caramel colored. Spread the caramel over one cake layer and let set for 30 seconds. Then cut with a sharp knife into 8 wedge shapes. When they're cooled, drizzle the glazed wedges with melted chocolate.

TO ASSEMBLE
Set one cake layer on a large plate, and spread with chocolate buttercream. Top with another cake layer, and repeat until you've used up all the layers. Frost the top and sides of the stacked cake with chocolate buttercream.

Reserve eight hazelnuts and chop the rest. Coat the sides of the cake with the chopped nuts.

Using the remaining hazelnuts and dollops of buttercream as props, arrange the glazed wedges on the top of the cake, overlapping one another. Cut in between the wedges to serve.

VARIATION
Chocolate-Walnut Dobos Torte
Prepare the Rigó Jancsi chocolate sponge cake (page 175), and replace the hazelnuts with walnuts.

THE WORLD TOUR OF
Famous People Cakes

NAMING A CAKE AFTER A FAMOUS PERSON is a savvy strategy for making its popularity skyrocket. In the West, this flattery has been a custom for centuries. Some popular cakes have been renamed after a royal figure who loves it, such as the Victoria sponge cake, Queen Mother cake, and Queen Elizabeth cake. Others honor the superstar bakers who invented them, including the Sachertorte, named after the baker Franz Sacher, and the Martha Washington fruitcake, developed by the first First Lady of the United States. Cakes honor celebrities, such as the Pavlova of Australia, which was renamed after the Russian prima ballerina visited that country. Picking a sexy person is a good way to popularize a cake: just look at the Robert Redford cake, a chocolate cake sweetened with honey and named after the American actor, or the Marta Rocha torte, named after the 1950s Brazilian beauty who disputably lost the Miss Universe pageant.

Read on for more cakes named after famous people.

CAKES NAMED FOR ROYALTY OR POLITICAL LEADERS

Battenberg Cake: This multiple-flavored checkered cake (page 142) is named in honor of the marriage of Queen Victoria's granddaughter to Prince Louis of Battenberg in the late nineteenth century.

Betsy Ross Cake: This vanilla-frosted sheet cake is decorated with strawberries and blueberries to form the stars and stripes of the American flag, which Betsy Ross (1756–1836) is credited with designing. Though not an elected official, her supposed contribution has made her an American legend.

Gâteau Alexandra: This chocolate cake was named after Alexandra of Denmark (1844–1925) when she became the Princess of Wales by marrying Edward VII.

Lady Kenny: This Bengali milk-based fried pastry stuffed with raisins is named after Lady Charlotte Canning (1817–1861), lady-in-waiting to Queen Victoria and the wife of the governor general of India.

(continued on next page)

József Dobos

József Dobos, the Hungarian chef who invented this cake, was quite a character. He became famous for his culinary inventiveness and showmanship in the late nineteenth and early twentieth centuries. He owned a gourmet shop near Budapest, where he created his own specialties and sold delicacies from around the globe. He arranged stunts and performances to highlight the food and filled his store with unique displays and presentations.

The Dobos torte is one of József's masterpieces. He created unique packaging for transporting the cake, encouraging many people to buy it as a gift and send it abroad. As the word spread about this cake, many imitators tried to replicate his recipe, with inferior results. In 1906, to protect the cake's identity, he decided to donate the recipe to the Budapest Pastry and Honey Breadmakers Guild and make it public for everyone to share and enjoy.

Lamingtons: These small, coconut-covered sponge cakes (page 304) were named after Charles Cochrane-Baillie, Baron Lamington, who was governor of Queensland, Australia, at the turn of the twentieth century.

Martha Washington's Cake: This is the famous fruitcake recipe of Martha Washington (1731–1802), George Washington's wife. She often made these "Great Cakes" for large crowds.

Queen Elizabeth Cake: Named after the queen of England, this date cake with coconut topping is popular in Canada.

Queen Mother Cake: The Queen Mother loved this flourless chocolate cake (page 138) and served it at many royal parties.

Queen of Sheba Cake: This French chocolate almond cake (page 101) is named for the African Queen of Sheba, a famous guest of King Solomon of Israel in the tenth century.

Rissoles Pompadour: This fried pastry is named after Jeanne Poisson (1721–1764), the official paramour of Louis XV.

Victoria Sponge Cake: Many foods are named after Queen Victoria (1819–1901). This raspberry cream sponge cake (page 136) was her favorite teatime cake.

Washington Pie: Named after George Washington (1732–1799), the first president of the United States, this dessert is actually a sponge layer cake with fruit or cream filling, not a pie.

CAKES NAMED FOR ARTISTS, ENTERTAINERS, AND WRITERS

Bobby Deol Cake: Named after Bollywood star Bobby Deol, this cake is made of brownie cake topped with walnuts, chocolate mousse, and cheesecake.

Marta Rocha Torte: This rich, sweet cake featuring layers of custard and meringue (page 86) is named after the model and Brazilian beauty who lost the Miss Universe contest in the 1950s because her hips were supposedly too big.

Pavlova: This Australian fruit-topped meringue cake (page 302) is named after the Russian prima ballerina Anna Matveyevna Pavlova (1881–1931).

Ray Ventura Cake: This is a génoise layer cake with kirsch-flavored cream and strawberries. Popular in the post–World War II era, it is named after the French bandleader Ray Ventura (1908–1979).

Robert Redford Cake: Famous baker Maida Heatter created this chocolate cake sweetened with honey after reading about how much the American actor likes chocolate.

Runeberg Cake: This almond cake (page 164) was created by Finnish poets Johan Ludvig Runeberg (1804–1877) and his wife, Fredrika. There is also a variation called the Fredrika pastry.

Sarah Bernhardt Cake: This chocolate-almond macaroon pastry is named after the famous French actress Sarah Bernhardt (1844–1923).

Schillerlocken: This cream-filled pastry is named after the curly hair of the German poet Friedrich von Schiller (1759–1805).

CAKES NAMED FOR PASTRY CHEFS

Chiboust Cream: This cream filling was invented by the French pastry chef Chiboust in the midnineteenth century to fill his gâteau Saint-Honoré.

Dobos Torte: This multilayered chocolate torte (page 172) was created by Hungarian pastry chef József Dobos (1847–1924).

Sachertorte: This chocolate cake with apricot preserves (page 126) was named after its Viennese creator, Franz Sacher (1826–1907).

CAKES NAMED FOR INVENTORS AND DISCOVERERS

Frangipane: This almond-cream-filled tart is named for Marquis Muzio Frangipani, a sixteenth-century Italian living in Paris. He invented a well-known bitter-almond-scented glove perfume that was used by Louis XIII.

German Chocolate Cake: This chocolate layer cake topped with coconut-pecan frosting (page 48) is named after Sam German, who invented the chocolate it's made from.

CAKES NAMED FOR OUTLAWS AND SCOUNDRELS

Hamentashn: This filled pastry was named for the cruel Persian official outwitted by Queen Esther and hanged in the Book of Esther. Hamentashn are traditionally eaten for the Jewish holiday Purim.

Rigó Jancsi: This Viennese chocolate and cream cake (page 175) is named after the famous Gypsy violinist Rigó Jancsi, who is known for running off with the Princess de Chimay.

CAKES NAMED FOR SAINTS AND POPES

Gâteau Saint-Honoré: This pastry was named for the French patron saint of bakers, confectioners, and pastry chefs, St. Honoré, or Honorius, the seventh-century bishop of Amiens.

Lucia Cats: These Swedish saffron buns (page 158) are named for St. Lucia of Syracuse (283–304). The Swedish name, Lucia's cats, refers to the bun's curled shape.

Pio Quinto: This Nicaraguan cake is soaked in rum and topped with custard and cinnamon. It is named after Pope Pius V (1504–1572).

CAKES NAMED FOR MILITARY FIGURES

General Robert E. Lee Cake: This sponge cake is named after the Confederate U.S. general (1807–1870) who was revered in the South during the Civil War.

Kossuth Cake: A variation of the charlotte, this sponge cream cake is named for Hungarian Lajos Kossuth (1802–1894), the leader of the 1848 Hungarian Revolution. He visited the United States in 1851–1852, and this cake was created in his honor in Baltimore, Maryland.

Marshal Ney Cake: Named after the commander at Waterloo, Napoléon's marshal, this cake contains molded tiers of meringue shells, vanilla custard, and marzipan.

Rigó Jancsi Cake

This is my favorite chocolate cake from eastern Europe. Chocolate sponge cake, chocolate mousse, apricot sauce, and dark chocolate ganache make a richly satisfying dessert. Traditionally servings are cut from a large sheet in cubes, but I use mini loaf pans to make the edges perfect and extra tall.

Chocolate Sponge Cake
- ¼ cup water
- 8 ounces semisweet chocolate, chopped
- 8 eggs, separated
- ⅔ cup sugar
- ¼ teaspoon salt
- 1 cup all-purpose flour

Chocolate Mousse
- 2 tablespoons unsalted butter
- 2 tablespoons light corn syrup
- 1¾ cups heavy cream
- 16 ounces semisweet chocolate, chopped
- ¼ cup dark rum
- 1 teaspoon vanilla extract

Other Fillings and Toppings
- 2 cups apricot glaze (page 318)
- 1½ cups chocolate ganache (page 315)
- 1 cup whipped cream (page 323)
- Chocolate strips or shavings

Makes 8 individual-serving cakes

TO PREPARE
Preheat the oven to 350°F. Butter and flour eight mini loaf pans.

TO MAKE THE CAKES
Bring the water to a boil. Pour the hot water over the chocolate, stir until melted, and set aside. Beat the egg yolks and ⅓ cup of the sugar in a medium bowl with a mixer until light and thickened. In a separate medium bowl, beat the egg whites and salt until they hold a soft peak. Add the remaining ⅓ cup sugar to the egg whites and beat until firm peaks form. Add the chocolate and one-quarter of the egg-white mixture to the egg-yolk mixture and stir. Fold in the flour and then the remaining egg whites.

TO BAKE
Divide the batter among the prepared pans. Bake for 25 to 30 minutes, until a knife inserted in the center comes out clean. Remove the cakes from their pans and set on a rack to cool.

TO MAKE THE MOUSSE
Melt the butter in a medium saucepan. Add the corn syrup and cream and heat to a boil. Place the chocolate in a mixing bowl. Pour the boiling mixture over the chocolate and let sit 5 minutes, until melted. Stir until smooth. Stir in the rum and vanilla, and refrigerate for about 30 minutes, just until cool. When it's cool, whip the mousse until fluffy.

TO ASSEMBLE
Cut each cake in half, forming two layers. For each cake, spread apricot glaze over the bottom layer, followed by chocolate mousse, and set the top layer on top. Press down gently to help the top layer adhere. Spread the chocolate ganache on the top of the cakes and refrigerate until set. Serve topped with a rosette of whipped cream and chocolate pieces.

The Gypsy Violinist

This famous cake was created in the late nineteenth century by a Budapest pastry chef and named for the romantic scandal of the day: the Hungarian Gypsy violinist Rigó Jancsi luring the princess of Chimay, Clara Ward (daughter of an American billionaire), from her husband, the prince of Belgium. Clara fell in love with Rigó's music and alluring black eyes. They began an affair, and when their secret meetings were discovered and made public, they became the hottest story of the time. Clara left her family to live a bohemian lifestyle with Rigó. Though they married, the romance didn't last; Clara eventually left him. Thankfully the cake is here to stay.

Saffron Cake

Russian Jews celebrate weddings with saffron cakes, and Christians eat them for Easter. Heat releases the flavor from saffron threads, so it is important to saturate them with boiling water and let them sit all night. I have gone light on all of the other spices so that they enhance the saffron, rather than competing with it. The saffron flavor in the buttercream frosting gives it a touch of extravagance.

Saffron Water
- ¾ cup boiling water
- ¾ teaspoon saffron threads

Cake
- 2 cups all-purpose flour
- 1 teaspoon baking soda
- 1 teaspoon baking powder
- ¼ teaspoon salt
- ¼ teaspoon grated nutmeg
- ½ cup (1 stick) unsalted butter, softened
- 1 cup granulated sugar
- 2 eggs
- ¼ cup buttermilk
- ½ cup raisins
- ½ cup fresh red currants
- ½ cup pistachio nuts
- 1 teaspoon lemon juice

Saffron Buttercream
- ½ cup (1 stick) unsalted butter
- 2 cups confectioners' sugar
- 1 teaspoon vanilla extract
- Milk (as needed)

Topping
- ¼ cup fresh currants

Makes 1 cake (serves 6 to 8)

TO PREPARE
The night before baking, pour the boiling water over the saffron threads and let soak overnight. The next day, preheat the oven to 350°F. Butter and flour a 9-inch square cake pan. Reserve 3 tablespoons saffron liquid for the frosting, placing it in a small bowl.

TO MAKE THE CAKE
Stir together the flour, baking soda, baking powder, salt, and nutmeg in a medium bowl. In a separate medium bowl, cream the butter and sugar with a mixer until fluffy. Add the eggs one at a time and beat well. Add the flour mixture to the butter mixture, alternating with the buttermilk. Stir in the raisins, currants, pistachios, lemon juice, and the larger portion of saffron water.

TO BAKE
Pour the batter into the prepared pan and bake for 30 to 35 minutes, until a knife inserted in the center comes out clean. Let cool in its pan for 10 minutes, then remove from the pan and set on a rack to finish cooling.

TO MAKE THE SAFFRON BUTTERCREAM
Use a mixer to beat together the butter and confectioners' sugar. Add the reserved saffron water and the vanilla. Add more confectioners' sugar or milk as needed to reach a spreadable consistency.

TO ASSEMBLE
Measure the height of the cake, and cut it in portions that are the same width and depth, forming cubes. Frost the cubes with the saffron buttercream, and top with fresh currants.

About Saffron
Saffron is not your everyday baking spice — it is the most expensive spice in the world. The deep orange saffron threads are actually the stigma of a purple-flowered crocus (*Crocus sativa*). Harvesting them is extremely labor-intensive; you need 4,300 stigmas to make just an ounce of saffron. The crocus is native to Asia Minor, where it has been cultivated for thousands of years. Phoenician sailors used saffron as currency and spread the delight around the world. Know your source when purchasing saffron; it is the most common counterfeited commodity on the market.

Lemon Poppyseed Cakes

Eastern European Jews have created many interesting recipes with seeds of the local poppy flower, perhaps because the Jewish holiday Purim requires worshippers to eat seeds as part of the celebrations. In this traditional recipe, the satisfying toasted flavor of poppyseed combines well with lemon for a light breakfast or dessert cake. (For a photo of these cakes, see page 179.)

Poppyseed Cake

- 2¾ cups all-purpose flour
- 2 teaspoons baking powder
- ¼ teaspoon baking soda
- ¼ teaspoon salt
- ¾ cup (1½ sticks) unsalted butter, softened
- 1¾ cups sugar
- 3 eggs
- 1 teaspoon vanilla extract
  Zest of 1 lemon, grated
- 1 tablespoon lemon juice
- 1¼ cups buttermilk
- 1¼ cups poppyseeds

Toppings

- 1¾ cups lemon icing (page 316)
- 6 lemon slices

Makes 6 individual-serving cakes

TO PREPARE

Preheat the oven to 350°F. Butter and flour six 3- to 4-inch ceramic or porcelain ramekins.

TO MAKE THE CAKES

Combine the flour, baking powder, baking soda, and salt in a medium bowl; set aside. In a separate large bowl, beat the butter and sugar with a mixer until fluffy. Add the eggs one at a time, beating well after each addition. Stir in the vanilla, lemon zest, and lemon juice. Add the flour mixture, alternating with the buttermilk, until blended. Stir in the poppyseeds.

TO BAKE

Divide the batter among the pans and bake for 25 to 30 minutes, until a knife inserted in the center comes out clean. Let the cakes cool in their pans for 10 minutes or so.

TO ASSEMBLE

While the cakes are still warm, top each with lemon icing and a lemon slice. Serve in the pans.

VARIATIONS

Large Lemon Poppyseed Cake

Bake the cake in two 9-inch round cake pans for 30 to 35 minutes. Stack the cakes, spreading 1¼ cups lemon curd (page 321) as a filling between them. Top with 1¾ cups lemon icing and more poppyseeds.

Lime Poppyseed Cake

Replace the lemon zest and juice with lime zest and juice. Top with 1¾ cups lime icing (page 316) instead of lemon icing.

Orange-Poppyseed Cake

Replace the lemon zest and juice with orange zest and juice. Top with 1¼ cups orange glaze (page 319) instead of lemon icing.

Poppyseed Varieties

Poppyseeds come from *Papaver somniferum*, the same poppy from which opium is derived. But not all poppyseeds are the traditional blue-black color Westerners are accustomed to. The variety *P. somniferum* var. *album* bears white seeds, which have a milder flavor than their blue-black cousins. These white seeds are popular in Indian, Middle Eastern, and Scandinavian cooking.

Kolache

Making kolaches is an old-world craft. Prepared from a sweet dough, they are stuffed with fruits, seeds, nuts, and cheeses. This particular recipe uses a poppyseed filling common in eastern European pastries and cakes. It is topped with posypka, a crumb mixture made with butter, flour, and sugar.

Dough
- 1 cup milk, warmed
- ⅓ cup sugar
- 2 teaspoons active dry yeast
- 3½ cups all-purpose flour
- 1 egg
- ⅓ cup unsalted butter, melted
- 1 teaspoon salt

Filling
- 2¾ cups poppyseed filling (page 322)

Posypka
- ½ cup (1 stick) unsalted butter, softened
- 1 cup sugar
- 1½ cups all-purpose flour

Topping
Melted butter, for brushing

Makes 24 individual-serving cakes

TO MAKE THE DOUGH
Combine ⅓ cup of the milk and 1 teaspoon of the sugar in a small bowl; stir to dissolve. Stir in the yeast and let stand for 5 minutes. Add the flour to a large bowl, making a well in the middle. Pour the remaining ⅔ cup milk, the egg, the remaining sugar, the melted butter, the salt, and the yeast mixture into the well. Mix until smooth.

Form the dough into a ball and place in a greased bowl. Cover and place in a warm spot to rise until doubled in size, about 2 hours.

TO MAKE THE POSYPKA
Combine the butter, sugar, and flour in a bowl and mix until it resembles a coarse meal.

TO BAKE
When the dough has risen, preheat the oven to 350°F. Butter and flour two baking sheets.

Punch down the dough to get rid of some air. Scoop out 2-inch balls of dough with a tablespoon and drop them onto a floured work surface. Roll each scoop of dough into a ball, then press them down into a disk or a square. Press a finger into the center of each disk, and fill the indentation with 1 to 2 teaspoons of poppyseed filling. Place the disks on the baking sheets, spacing them 2 inches apart. Let rise for 10 minutes.

Brush the tops lightly with melted butter. Sprinkle the kolaches with posypka. Bake for 15 to 20 minutes, until light golden brown. Remove the kolaches from the baking sheets, and let cool. Brush the tops with additional butter if you like.

Kolaches in the United States

First created in the Middle Ages, kolaches have evolved over the years to incorporate many kinds of doughs and fillings throughout the Slavic nations. Between the 1850s and 1920s thousands of Czechs immigrated to the United States, with large populations moving to Texas, Minnesota, Oklahoma, and Nebraska. They were known as hardworking farmers with a love for celebrations. Today kolache remains a tradition for Czech-Americans, served at weddings and agricultural fairs. Caldwell, Texas, hosts an annual kolache festival in which you can enter a kolache bake-off, with the winner taking home a prize. Montgomery, Minnesota, claims to be the kolache capital of the world, while Prague, Nebraska, is home to the world's largest kolache.

OPPOSITE PAGE: *The cakes in dishes are lemon poppyseed cakes, page 177; all other cakes are kolaches.*

Alternative Fillings

Poppyseed (page 322) is not the only traditional kolache filling. Here are a few others to try.

Peach-Cheese Filling

1¾ cups small-curd cottage cheese, drained in a sieve or cheesecloth
1 egg
2 tablespoons sugar
1 tablespoon unsalted butter, melted
½ teaspoon grated nutmeg
¾ cup peach jam

Combine all ingredients in a medium bowl. Use as the kolache filling.

Prune Filling

1½ cups pitted prunes
Boiling water
½ teaspoon ground cinnamon
½ cup sugar
½ teaspoon grated lemon or orange zest

Place the prunes in a bowl and cover them with boiling water. Let sit overnight. Then drain off the liquid and mash prunes in a food processor or blender. Add the cinnamon, sugar, and lemon zest. Mix thoroughly. Use as the kolache filling.

Other Kolache Fillings

- *Cherry filling (page 321)*
- *Cream cheese filling (page 321)*
- *Date filling (page 321)*
- *Raspberry filling (page 322)*

Mazurek

I am so glad that I embarked on this tour of cakes from around the world, because otherwise I would never have experienced the amazing Polish folk art otherwise known as mazureks. The traditional mazurek is a flat pastry cake topped with chocolate and highly decorated. Though modern mazureks come in all forms, from flat cakes to layer cakes, you know a mazurek is a mazurek by its decorations. This cake is a blast to make and to eat.

Mazurek

- 1½ cups (3 sticks) unsalted butter, softened
- 1⅔ cups sugar
- 1¼ cups ground almonds
- 2 teaspoons vanilla extract
- Zest of 1 orange, grated
- 9 egg whites
- 2¼ cups all-purpose flour

Toppings

- 1½ cups chocolate ganache (page 315)
- Cookies, nuts, marzipan, poppyseeds, candied fruits, dried fruits, cheese, jams, chocolate, icing, or other decorations

Makes 1 cake (serves 6 to 8)

TO PREPARE

Preheat the oven to 350°F. Butter and flour a 10-inch square or round baking pan.

TO MAKE THE CAKE

Cream the butter and sugar in a medium bowl until fluffy. Add the ground almonds, vanilla, and orange zest; set aside. Beat the egg whites in a medium bowl until stiff. Stir the flour into the butter mixture. Fold the egg whites into the batter.

TO BAKE

Pour the batter into the pan and bake for 30 to 35 minutes, until lightly browned. Let the cake cool in its pan for 10 minutes, then remove it from its pan and set on a rack to finish cooling.

TO DECORATE

Set the cake on a serving tray, and top with chocolate ganache. While the ganache is still wet, press in the decorative toppings. If you want to write a message with icing, wait until the ganache has dried before piping it on.

It's in the Decorating

Mazureks, the traditional Polish Easter cakes, are all about the decorating. The toppings on each one are unique, but the decorator's palette usually includes nuts, figs, marzipan, poppyseeds, candied fruits, dried fruits, jams, cheeses, and chocolate. These ingredients are used to make flowers, trees, landscapes, or patterns or to write messages. "Hallelujah" is one popular phrase seen on mazureks — and though I know it's a reference to the joy of Easter, I'd like to think it has more to do with how great the cake is.

Sponge Fruit Cakes

Cakes shaped like fruits are common from East to West. In Estonia, where shaping marzipan is a form of national pride, confectioners' skills expand into shaping cakes during the spring harvest festival season. These realistic fruit-shaped sponge cakes are filled with fruit-flavored cream. I am lucky enough to have fruit-shaped cake pans, but if you don't, you can cut the shapes from domed or sheet cakes. I like to leave the batter its natural yellow color and then color the baked cakes by spraying on coloring with a small spray bottle, brushing in some details, and topping with crystal sugar. This technique gives a very realistic effect.

Génoise Sponge Cake
- 1⅓ cups cake flour
- 1 cup cornstarch
- 12 eggs
- 1½ cups superfine sugar
- ⅔ cup unsalted butter, melted and cooled
- 2 teaspoons vanilla extract

Toppings
- Food colorings of choice
- Water, to dilute food colorings
- Crystal sugar

Fillings
- 3½ cups pastry cream, any kind (page 323)
- 2 peaches, chopped
- 1 large banana, mashed
- 2 pears, chopped

Makes 6 individual-serving cakes

TO PREPARE
Preheat the oven to 375°F. Butter and flour twelve 3- to 4-inch fruit-shaped cake molds (or two 8-inch dome cake pans or one 9- by 13-inch sheet cake pan). You'll want two fruit halves for each fruit-shaped cake you intend to make.

TO MAKE THE CAKES
Prepare the génoise sponge cake batter as directed on page 108, baking it for 20 to 25 minutes, until the cake is golden brown and shrinks away from the sides of the pan. (If you're using dome or sheet cake pans, bake for 30 to 40 minutes.) Remove the cakes from the pans and set on a rack to cool.

TO COLOR THE CAKES
If you've prepared dome cakes or a sheet cake, cut the cake into half-fruit shapes. Add 1 tablepoon water to each drop of food coloring to dilute. Color the cakes to look like the actual fruits by spraying or brushing diluted food coloring onto them. While the coloring is still damp, top with crystal sugar.

TO MAKE THE CREAM
Divide the cream into three batches. Add the peaches to one, the banana to another, and the pears to the last.

TO ASSEMBLE
For each fruit-shaped cake, spread cream on one cake half, then top with the other cake half. Sprinkle with crystal sugar.

VARIATION

Malaysian Banana Cake
Soak ½ cup raisins in ¼ cup very warm apple juice for about 15 minutes, until plump, then drain. Add the raisins, half a banana (mash well), and 2 teaspoons banana extract to the cake batter. Bake in a banana-shaped cake mold. For the cream filling, omit the peaches and pears and use three bananas instead. (For a photo of this cake, see page 286.)

Potica (Nut Roll)

The potica embodies Slovenian food at its finest. This iconic old-world cake is made by stretching the dough so thin that you can almost see through it; it may become so stretched that it takes up the entire table. With a walnut filling, it is rolled into a long log, placed in a tube pan, and baked at low heat for a long time to create a breadlike pastry. The walnuts take on a lightly toasted flavor.

Potica

- 1 tablespoon active dry yeast
- ¼ cup milk, warmed
- ⅓ cup sugar
- ¼ cup sour cream
- 3 egg yolks
- 1 cup evaporated milk
- 6 tablespoons unsalted butter, softened
- 4 cups all-purpose flour
- 1 teaspoon salt

Nut Filling

- 4 tablespoons unsalted butter, melted
- ½ cup milk
- ½ cup honey
- 2 cups sugar
- 1½ teaspoons ground cinnamon
- ½ teaspoon grated nutmeg
- ¼ teaspoon ground cloves
- 3 egg whites
- 1¾ cups finely ground walnuts
  Zest of ½ lemon, grated
- 1 tablespoon vanilla extract

Glaze

- 2 egg whites, lightly beaten

Makes 1 cake (serves 6 to 8)

TO MAKE THE DOUGH

Stir together the yeast, milk, and 1 tablespoon of the sugar, and set aside for 10 minutes, until foamy. Mix the sour cream, egg yolks, and evaporated milk in a bowl; set aside. In a separate medium bowl, use a mixer to cream the butter with the remaining sugar until light and fluffy. Add the flour and salt to the butter mixture, alternating with the sour cream mixture. Stir in the yeast mixture and set the dough aside.

TO MAKE THE FILLING

Combine the butter, milk, honey, sugar, cinnamon, nutmeg, and cloves in a medium saucepan over low heat; stir until dissolved. Remove from the heat and set aside, until cool enough to touch.

In a separate bowl, beat the egg whites until soft peaks form. Fold into the milk mixture, then stir in the walnuts, lemon zest, and vanilla.

TO ASSEMBLE

Butter and flour a 10-inch tube pan. Roll out the dough to about 22 inches in length and ¼ inch or less in thickness. (The thinner your dough, the more impressive the design.) Spread the filling over the dough, and carefully roll up the cake. If the dough tears, patch the hole with dough from the edges. Place the dough in the prepared pan. Cover and set in a warm spot to rise for 3 to 4 hours, until it has doubled in volume.

When the dough has risen, preheat the oven to 325°F. Brush the potica with egg whites. Bake for 50 minutes to 1 hour, until a knife inserted in the center comes out clean. Let cool in its pan. Slice thinly to serve.

TO SERVE

Potica is cut into thin slices, with several slices per serving. When made for an Easter brunch it's served with a slice of ham, with cheese melted on its top, or on the side of bacon and eggs. On other occasions it may be spread with butter or honey or sprinkled with cinnamon. When served as dessert potica is topped with ice cream, vanilla custard, whipped cream, or fresh fruit.

VARIATIONS

Almond-Peach Potica
In the filling, replace the ground walnuts with ground almonds. Spread 1½ cups peach preserves over the rolled-out dough before adding the nut filling.

American Coffee Potica
For the filling, reduce the milk to ¼ cup and add ¼ cup double-strength espresso.

Chocolate Potica
For the filling, replace the cinnamon, nutmeg, and cloves with ½ cup Dutch-processed cocoa powder, reduce the nuts to 1 cup, and add ¾ cup ground chocolate.

Cream Cheese–Pine Nut Potica
Replace the nut filling with cream cheese filling (page 321) mixed with ½ cup ground pine nuts.

Poppyseed Potica
Replace the nut filling with 3¾ cups poppyseed filling (page 322).

Strawberry–Cream Cheese Potica
Replace the nut filling with 3 cups cream cheese filling (page 321) mixed with 1 cup mashed and strained strawberries.

VARIATIONS, CONTINUED
Walnut-Raisin Potica

For the filling, reduce the nuts to 1 cup and add 1 cup soaked raisins.

Potica Traditions

Potica (from the verb *poviti*, "to roll up") is a symbol of Slovenian national identity. Making this walnut roll is an elaborate process, and the preparation of the cake is a major part of special occasions and holidays. At weddings you may find dozens of potica towering in the center of the tables, sometimes as many as one per person, so that all guests will get their share. On Easter morning, families bring potica, ham, bread, and eggs to be blessed at church. They are then served to the family at Easter breakfast.

FRONT TO BACK: *walnut, strawberry–cream cheese, cream cheese–pine nut, and almond-peach potica*

CHAPTER 8

The Mediterranean
Epic Confections from Balmy Climates and Ancient Cultures

THANKS TO AN ANCIENT HISTORY and rich cultural heritage — not to mention some of the best ingredients in the world, due to the wonderful temperate climate — the countries surrounding the Mediterranean Sea offer a wealth of baking traditions. Whether you're traveling in the rolling hills of the Italian countryside or the sun-drenched Greek islands, the teeming ports of Portugal or the picturesque orchards of the Basques in Spain, the cake culture of each area reflects a strong identity.

Cake culture as a whole has its roots in Greece. Though ancient Greeks learned to bake from the Egyptians, once they'd seen the technique, they really ran with it. Greeks were the inventors of the front-loading bread oven, and with it many of the world's early sweet breads, fritters, and cheesecakes. They also developed the bakers' trade. These progenitors of modern professional bakers were specially trained to work the hot and often dangerous ovens.

The Romans learned to bake from the Greeks, and as they expanded their empire, they brought Greek baking traditions with it. Soon other European cultures were experimenting with baking techniques, each creating cakes using their own local ingredients. Today, though cake culture has spread far and wide, Greeks are still renowned for their native baked goods. Their cakes are generally fresh and unfussy and make use of phyllo, nuts, sesame seeds, honey, eggs, lemons, and feta and goat cheeses. The classic Greek cheesecake, tiropita (page 205), for example, features a filling of feta, cottage cheese, and yogurt seasoned with orange zest, cinnamon, and sugar, sandwiched between sheets of phyllo, while the Greek lambropsomo (page 204), a braided Easter sweet bread, is baked with hard-boiled eggs nested right inside it.

Like the Greeks, Italians generally aim to make homey, simple, fresh cakes. Their nation boasts not one cake culture but two, that of the north and that of the south, with Rome in

the center picking and choosing the best of each. The main difference between the regions is the ingredients: in the north butter and cornmeal are more widely used, while in the south olive oil and wheat are key ingredients in cakes.

Cheese making has been an important part of Italian culture for thousands of years, and it has made its way into cakes in the traditional Roman-style cheesecakes made from ricotta (page 190) and the modern cheesecakes made from mascarpone. Where Italy borders Austria and Switzerland, local cake culture has been inspired by Germanic and Swiss influences; recipes here often feature chocolate, ginger, and spiced apples and nuts. On the east coast Italian cakes share commonalities with cakes of eastern Europe; for example, the Italian version of potica, a Slovenian nut roll cake, is made with cream cheese and local pine nuts (page 182). Sicily in particular, being a historical crossroads between Asia Minor, northern Africa, and the rest of southern Europe, is home to fusion cake culture, reflected in offerings such as the cassata Siciliana (page 196), a sponge cake moistened with orange liqueur and layered with ricotta, candied citrus peel, fruits, and chocolate.

The cakes of Spain and Portugal are similar to each other, incorporating influences from western Europe and northern Africa. The cake culture of both nations profits from the produce that flourishes on the Iberian Peninsula, from dates, pomegranates, and peaches to bananas, apricots, and grapes. Almonds, citrus fruits, and a wide range of international spices, such as cinnamon, nutmeg, sesame, anise seed, coriander, and saffron, all shape the flavor profiles of traditional Spanish cakes. The tarta de Santiago (St. James' cake; see page 199), for example, is an orange-almond confection often prepared to celebrate St. James' Day, while the traditional Catalan cheesecake (page 198) is flavored with orange and cinnamon, and bizcochos borrachos are "drunken" sponge cakes spiced with cinnamon, nutmeg, and orange juice and drenched with a sweet Madeira syrup featuring lemon juice and more cinnamon.

The Portuguese, in turn, can boast of their rich and custardy cakes made from egg yolks. Nuns' bellies (page 200), for example, are individual custard-soaked sponge cakes, and pastéis de nata (page 201) are vanilla custards in a puff pastry crust with a cinnamon sugar topping. Portuguese bakers also make great use of quince and quince preserves and find creative ways to exploit maize.

Panforte

I took a trip to Italy while writing this book, and I had the opportunity to taste and write about panforte on location in the quaint city of Siena, where it was created. A combination of spices, fruit, nuts, and honey, with just enough flour to hold everything together, this cake is dense, chewy, and delicious. Serve panforte in thin wedges with espresso or a dessert wine. (For a photo of this cake, see page 189.)

Panforte

- 1¼ cups shelled hazelnuts
- 1 cup all-purpose flour
- 1 tablespoon breadcrumbs
- ¾ cup chopped candied citrus peel (page 325)
- ¼ cup unsweetened cocoa powder
- ½ teaspoon ground cinnamon
- ¼ teaspoon ground cloves
- ¼ teaspoon ground coriander
- ¼ teaspoon grated nutmeg
- ¾ cup granulated sugar
- ¾ cup honey
- 3 tablespoons unsalted butter

Spice Topping

- ¼ cup confectioners' sugar
- 3 tablespoons ground cardamom
- 1 tablespoon ground cinnamon

Makes 1 cake (serves 6 to 8)

TO PREPARE

Preheat the oven to 300°F. Butter and flour a 7-inch round springform pan.

TO MAKE THE CAKE

Place the hazelnuts on a baking sheet and toast in the oven for 7 to 10 minutes, until fragrant. Chop finely. Combine 2 tablespoons of the chopped hazelnuts, 1 tablespoon of the flour, and the breadcrumbs in a small bowl. Sprinkle the mixture on the bottom of the springform pan.

Combine the remaining nuts, candied citrus peel, remaining flour, cocoa powder, cinnamon, cloves, coriander, and nutmeg. Stir to mix and set aside. Combine the granulated sugar, honey, and butter in a small saucepan over low heat, and stir until melted. Continue cooking, stirring, for 3 minutes, until the butter is slightly browned. Add the melted butter mixture to the nut mixture, stirring to combine.

When the mixture has cooled enough to touch, press it into the prepared pan to form a thin layer. Bake for 45 to 55 minutes, until it's firm and a knife inserted in the center comes out clean. Let cool in its pan for at least 30 minutes.

TO MAKE THE SPICE TOPPING

Combine the confectioners' sugar, cardamom, and cinnamon in a small bowl. Sprinkle on top of the cooled cake.

VARIATIONS

Apricot-Peach-Pecan Panforte

Replace the hazelnuts with pecans and the candied citrus peel with 6 tablespoons each chopped dried apricots and dried peaches.

Cherry-Currant Panforte

Replace the candied citrus peel with 6 tablespoons each candied cherries and dried currants.

Chocolate-Raisin Panforte

When you add the candied citrus peel, add ⅓ cup golden raisins as well. When you warm the honey, add 6 ounces chopped chocolate and stir to melt.

Date-Walnut Panforte

Replace the hazelnuts with walnuts and the candied citrus peel with chopped dates.

Orange-Almond Panforte

Replace the hazelnuts with almonds. Add 2 tablespoons orange juice to the dough.

Pine Nut–Pineapple Panforte

Replace the hazelnuts with toasted pine nuts. Replace the candied citrus peel with chopped candied pineapple.

The History of Panforte

Throughout Italy panforte is called Siena cake, after the city of its origin in Tuscany. Its creation can officially be traced back to 1205, when records first mention it as a tax payment made to the monasteries. Soon after it was on the menu for every feast given by Italian nobility. Crusaders are said to have carried the durable panforte with them. Today many shops in Tuscany sell panforte by the slice or packaged in a traditional octagonal box or wrapper. Panforte is prepared today much like the original recipes. The only exception is that warmer spices, such as cinnamon, nutmeg, and coriander, have replaced pepper, which was the most widely available spice at the time of the cake's invention.

Panettone versus Panforte

Though these two cakes have names that sound alike, they definitely do not taste alike. Panettone (page 188) (from Milan) is a very bready cake, while panforte (from Siena) is a very spicy, candylike cake. To avoid confusion, try to remember the roots of their names: *Panettone* is a variation of *panetto*, "small bread," with the suffix *-one* (pronounced "o-neh") changing the meaning to "large bread." *Panforte* translates as "strong bread," in reference to its spicy flavors.

Panettone

Christmastime in Milan means both shopping and panettone, the bready cake with a sweet flavor and soft texture. It is made by curing the dough with a starter, similar to sourdough. Candied orange, citron, lemon, and raisins all sweeten the cake, and it is served with crema di mascarpone and sweet dessert wine. Store-bought panettone is often molded into a cupola shape with an octagonal or cylindrical base.

Starter

- 1½ tablespoons active dry yeast
- 1 cup milk, scalded and cooled to lukewarm
- 1 tablespoon granulated sugar
- 1 cup bread flour

Cake

- 6 tablespoons unsalted butter
- ½ cup granulated sugar
- ½ teaspoon salt
- 2 teaspoons vanilla extract
- 1 teaspoon grated lemon zest
- 3 eggs
- 2 cups bread flour
- 1 cup golden raisins
- ½ cup dark raisins
- ½ cup candied orange peel (page 325)
- ½ cup candied citron
- ½ cup candied red and green cherries

Almond Glaze

- 1 cup sliced almonds
- 1 cup confectioners' sugar
- 1 egg white
- 1 tablespoon amaretto
- 1 teaspoon cornstarch

Crema di Mascarpone

- 1 pound mascarpone cheese
- ½ cup granulated sugar
- 4 egg yolks
- 2 tablespoons heavy cream
- 2 tablespoons amaretto

RAW EGGS: *The mascarpone cream in this recipe calls for using raw egg yolks. You can use pasteurized eggs here or replace the eggs with 2 tablespoons (¼ cup total) heavy cream. If you opt not to, do not serve this recipe to those for whom the consumption of raw eggs poses a serious health risk, including children under the age of four, the elderly, pregnant women, and anyone with a compromised immune system.*

Makes 2 cakes
(each serving 4 to 6)

TO PREPARE

Spray two 4-inch-tall, 7-inch-diameter round parchment liners with baking spray. Set the liners in two 7-inch round pans.

TO MAKE THE STARTER

Dissolve the yeast in the warm milk. Add the sugar, stir, and let rest for 5 minutes. Combine the yeast mixture with the flour, mixing with a wooden spoon until smooth. Cover and let rest in a warm place until tripled in volume, about 45 minutes to 1 hour.

TO MAKE THE CAKE

Gently beat together the butter, sugar, and salt. Stir in the vanilla and lemon zest. Add the eggs one at a time, alternating with portions of the flour, beating well after each addition. Blend in the starter. Stir in the raisins, orange peel, citron, and cherries. Cover the dough with plastic wrap and let rise in a warm place until doubled in volume, about 1 hour.

Punch down the dough to let the air out. Divide the dough in half and set in the prepared pans, pushing the dough out to the edges. Cover the dough with plastic wrap and let rise in a warm place until doubled again, about 2 hours.

TO MAKE THE GLAZE

Combine the almonds, confectioners' sugar, egg white, amaretto, and cornstarch, and stir until the sugar and cornstarch are dissolved. Refrigerate until ready to use.

TO BAKE THE CAKE

When the dough is risen, preheat the oven to 325°F, and set the cakes on a baking sheet. Bake for 40 minutes, and then stir up the glaze and spread it evenly across the cakes' tops. Bake for an additional 5 to 10 minutes, until the almonds in the glaze are toasted and a knife inserted in the center of the cakes comes out clean. Let cool in the pans.

TO MAKE THE CREMA DI MASCARPONE

Blend the mascarpone with a mixer until smooth. Beat in the sugar, egg yolks, cream, and amaretto until the mixture is thick, about 5 minutes. Refrigerate until chilled. Serve a dollop of cream next to each slice of cake.

VARIATIONS
Chocolate Panettone

Add ¼ cup unsweetened cocoa powder and 1½ cups chocolate chips to the dough.

Colomba Pasquale (Easter Dove)

Omit the raisins. Shape the dough like a dove by forming it into two logs, one about 12 inches long, the other 8 inches long. Arrange the logs in a cross, like a dove with wings outstretched. You could also bake the cake in a dove-shaped pan.

Colomba Pasquale

Colomba pasquale is a dove-shaped cake that is eaten for Easter in Italy. It is made with the same recipe as panettone, but without the raisins, and it is flavored with amaretto and topped with an almond amaretto glaze. (I like my panettone sweet, so I use the glaze on it as well.) It is said the sixth-century king Alboino, king of the Lombards, had a conflict with the city of Pavia. A baker from Pavia sent him this sweet bread as a peace offering, and the dispute was resolved. The cake declined in popularity over the following centuries, but in the early 1900s a Milanese manufacturer of panettone decided to revive the tradition to extend his panettone business into the spring. It worked. Colomba pasquale is now sold throughout the world for Easter.

LEFT: *panforte;* RIGHT: *panettone (page 188)*

Crostata di Ricotta
(Roman Ricotta Cheesecake)

Although ancient Greeks made the first cheesecakes, the Roman Empire gets our thanks for spreading this custardy cake throughout Europe. This cheesecake is not that different from the one the Romans popularized, though it has a modern-style biscotti crust. The cake has a crumbly texture and is flavored with orange zest and dried fruits. The old-fashioned way to prepare this cake is in a skillet over an open fire. I like to start it on the stove top in a skillet and finish it in the oven. Serve the cake right in the skillet, or carefully invert it onto a serving plate to show off the crust.

Almond Biscotti Crust

- 2 cups ground biscotti
- ¼ cup ground almonds
- ¼ cup sugar
- ½ cup (1 stick) unsalted butter, melted

Cheesecake

- 2 pounds ricotta cheese
- ½ cup sugar
- 2 tablespoons cornstarch
- 4 eggs, beaten
- Zest of 1 orange, grated
- 1 teaspoon vanilla extract
- 1 cup chopped dried fruit (such as raisins, apricots, pineapple, and mango)

Makes 1 cake (serves 6 to 8)

TO PREPARE

Coat an ovenproof 10-inch skillet generously with butter.

TO MAKE THE CRUST

Stir together the ground biscotti, ground almonds, sugar, and melted butter. Press the crumbs into the bottom and sides of the skillet and set aside.

TO MAKE THE FILLING

Mix together the ricotta, sugar, and cornstarch. Add the eggs, orange zest, vanilla, and dried fruit. Stir to combine. Spread the mixture over the crust.

TO BAKE

Preheat the oven to 350°F. Place the skillet on a stove top over medium heat and cook, covered, for 15 to 20 minutes, until the outer edges begin to set. Uncover the skillet, transfer to the oven, and bake for 25 to 30 minutes, until the cake is puffy and golden. Let cool in the skillet.

VARIATIONS

Chocolate-Ricotta Cheesecake

Add ¼ cup chopped chocolate and 1 tablespoon rum to the filling. Dust the cake with unsweetened cocoa powder before serving.

Torta di Ricotta

Prepare the recipe without the crust and dried fruit. Once it's been baked and cooled, invert the cheesecake onto a plate. Top the cake with 1 cup whole strawberries and ¾ cup chopped fresh pineapple.

THE WORLD TOUR OF
Cheesecakes

THE FIRST CHEESECAKES WERE PREPARED by the ancient Greeks for the Olympics. The cheese was thought to strengthen the athletes, and the cakes were also enjoyed as tasty festival food by the attendees. The Romans are credited with spreading a taste for cheesecake around Europe. Early Roman cheesecakes were loaves made of ricotta and honey and flavored with bay leaf, which also served as a preservative. Although the methods of baking these early cheesecakes were primitive, if you followed an ancient recipe today it would yield a cake with a taste very similar to that of the cheesecakes we all know and love.

Although relatively simple to bake, cheesecakes can be a bit fussy, and sometimes the top may crack. Here are some cheesecake tips to ensure a perfect cake:

- *Use a springform pan. It makes it easy to remove cheesecakes from the baking pan.*

- *Mix the batter gently. Too much air in the batter will cause the cake to deflate and flatten or crack.*

- *Cook slowly. Slow cooking allows air and extra moisture to escape.*

- *Do not overcook. This causes the cheesecake to shrink and dry out.*

- *Cool slowly. This prevents shocking from a change in temperature. Cool the cheesecake in the oven with the door slightly ajar.*

Today almost every culture in the world has a cheesecake specialty invented from local cheeses and ingredients. Each cheese gives a unique flavor, from sweet to tangy, and texture, from soft and silky to crumbly. Here's a quick tour of some of the better-known styles.

AUSTRIA
Cheesecakes from this country are often made with cottage cheese or quark, a fresh (unaged) cheese with no salt and less fat than most other cheeses. Almonds are a common ingredient.

BELGIUM AND THE NETHERLANDS
Their fantastic chocolates are the pride of the Belgian and Dutch people, and they often feature them in their cheesecakes. The cakes often have a crust of speculaas, a kind of shortbread biscuit.

BRAZIL
Cream cheese and cottage cheese form the base of cheesecakes in Brazil. They're often made with a crust of digestive biscuits and a guava marmalade or cashew-butter topping.

CARIBBEAN
Coconut milk, fresh coconut, sweet potatoes, bananas, and rum are common cheesecake ingredients, and cream cheese tends to be the cheese of choice.

(continued on next page)

LEFT: *baked cheesecake with coffee jelly (page 278);* CENTER: *tiropita (page 205);* RIGHT: *New York cheesecake (page 38)*

ENGLAND, AUSTRALIA, AND NEW ZEALAND

No-bake cheesecakes are popular in these countries. They are made with cream cheese and sour cream and have a biscuit crust. They are often topped with fresh fruit.

FRANCE

Classic French cheesecake is made with Neufchâtel cheese, also known as farmer's cheese, a style that dates back to the sixth century. It yields a cheesecake with a creamy texture and mild flavor.

GERMANY

In Germany as well as many other regions of central and eastern Europe, quark is the traditional base for cheesecakes.

GREECE

Greek mizithra cheesecake uses sheep's milk cheese, which gives it a slightly sour flavor and a granular texture, similar to that of ricotta. Tiropita (page 205), a cheesecake pastry eaten during Lent, is made with feta and phyllo, which can give it a slightly salty flavor, depending on the saltiness of the cheese.

ISRAEL

Kosher cheesecakes are prepared with cottage cheese and matzo-meal crusts.

ITALY

There are two predominant variations in Italian cheesecakes. Roman-style cheesecake is a modern version of the ancient ricotta cake; it is crumbly in texture and flavored with zests and dried fruits. Modern-style cheesecake is made with mascarpone cheese, which gives it a creamy interior, and it has a biscotti crust. (The recipe for Roman ricotta cheesecake on page 190 combines the two styles, with a ricotta-based filling and biscotti crust.)

JAPAN

Japanese cheesecakes (page 278) are a bit softer, lighter, and less sweet than many Western cheesecakes. Matcha powder and white chocolate are often used as flavorings.

MIDDLE EAST

Ricotta forms the base of traditional cheesecakes from the Middle East. They often have an almond crust and include dried fruits.

SOUTH AFRICA

Cream-cheese cheesecakes with shortbread pastry or oat-based crusts are popular here, with nuts and warm spices as common additives.

SPAIN

Pot cheese forms the base of many Spanish cheesecakes, including the Catalan version (page 198). Raisins and rum are common additions, and often the pastry crust is prebaked.

SWEDEN

Ostkaka is a uniquely Swedish cheesecake made from curdled milk. It is eaten warm with jam, whipped cream, and ice cream. Sometimes cottage cheese is substituted for the curdled milk.

UKRAINE

Syrnik is the Ukrainian version of cheesecake, made with farmer's cheese. It's fried rather than baked, so that it is crispy on the outside and warm and creamy on the inside. It's eaten for breakfast as well as dessert.

UNITED STATES

Today the most widely recognized cheesecake in the world is the New York cheesecake (page 38). Its base is cream cheese, which yields a creamy cake that crumbles a bit when cut. A graham cracker crust is traditional, though certainly other types are used. Flavorings, additions to the filling, and toppings are manifold, depending on the creator. Philadelphia-style cheesecake also uses cream cheese, but it is lighter and creamier. Pennsylvania Dutch cheesecake uses quark. Chicago-style cream-cheese cheesecake is firmer on the outside but still creamy on the inside. Ann Arbor–style cheesecake has a crust on its sides as well as its bottom and uses sour cream. Country-style cheesecake uses buttermilk.

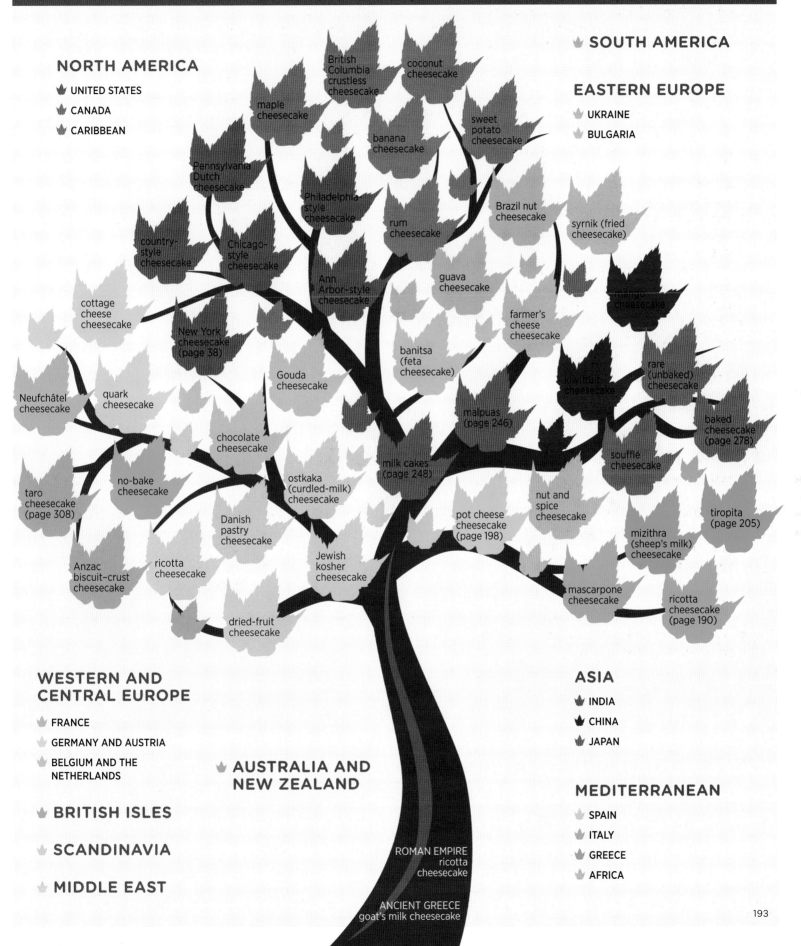

CHEESECAKE FAMILY TREE

NORTH AMERICA

- UNITED STATES
- CANADA
- CARIBBEAN

SOUTH AMERICA

EASTERN EUROPE

- UKRAINE
- BULGARIA

WESTERN AND CENTRAL EUROPE

- FRANCE
- GERMANY AND AUSTRIA
- BELGIUM AND THE NETHERLANDS

BRITISH ISLES

SCANDINAVIA

MIDDLE EAST

AUSTRALIA AND NEW ZEALAND

ASIA

- INDIA
- CHINA
- JAPAN

MEDITERRANEAN

- SPAIN
- ITALY
- GREECE
- AFRICA

British Columbia crustless cheesecake

coconut cheesecake

maple cheesecake

banana cheesecake

sweet potato cheesecake

Pennsylvania Dutch cheesecake

Philadelphia-style cheesecake

Brazil nut cheesecake

syrnik (fried cheesecake)

country-style cheesecake

Chicago-style cheesecake

rum cheesecake

guava cheesecake

mango cheesecake

cottage cheese cheesecake

Ann Arbor-style cheesecake

farmer's cheese cheesecake

New York cheesecake (page 38)

banitsa (feta cheesecake)

rare (unbaked) cheesecake

Neufchâtel cheesecake

quark cheesecake

Gouda cheesecake

kiwifruit cheesecake

chocolate cheesecake

malpuas (page 246)

baked cheesecake (page 278)

taro cheesecake (page 308)

no-bake cheesecake

ostkaka (curdled-milk) cheesecake

milk cakes (page 248)

soufflé cheesecake

nut and spice cheesecake

tiropita (page 205)

Danish pastry cheesecake

pot cheese cheesecake (page 198)

mizithra (sheep's milk) cheesecake

Anzac biscuit-crust cheesecake

ricotta cheesecake

Jewish kosher cheesecake

mascarpone cheesecake

ricotta cheesecake (page 190)

dried-fruit cheesecake

ROMAN EMPIRE
ricotta cheesecake

ANCIENT GREECE
goat's milk cheesecake

Bolognese Rice Cake

Rice cakes are prepared throughout Italy. Unlike most rice cakes from the Far East, which are prepared with rice flour, Italian rice cakes are made with Arborio rice, the same short-grain rice used for risotto. While staying true to the Bolognese original, I have given this uniquely textured cake a new twist by flavoring it with fresh currants, rum, and pistachios. It is topped with a light mascarpone-rum cream.

Rice Cake

- 2 tablespoons breadcrumbs
- 1 cup dried currants
- ¼ cup light rum
- ½ cup chopped pine nuts
- 4 cups milk
- ⅛ teaspoon salt
- 1 cup uncooked Arborio rice
- 4 tablespoons unsalted butter
- 3 tablespoons granulated sugar
- 1 teaspoon vanilla extract
- 3 tablespoons lemon juice
  Zest of 1 lemon, grated
- 3 eggs

Mascarpone-Rum Cream

- ¼ cup pine nuts
- 2 tablespoons granulated sugar
- 8 ounces mascarpone cheese
- 3 tablespoons rum
- 3 tablespoons heavy cream

Toppings

- 2 tablespoons confectioners' sugar
- ¼ cup whole pine nuts

Makes 1 cake (serves 6 to 8)

TO PREPARE

Butter an 8-inch round springform pan and dust its inside with breadcrumbs; reserve any breadcrumbs that don't stick.

TO MAKE THE CAKE

Combine the currants and rum in a small saucepan over medium heat, and cook until the rum is partially absorbed. Remove from the heat, stir in the pine nuts, and set aside.

Bring the milk and salt to a boil in a large saucepan. Add the rice and return to a boil, then reduce the heat and let simmer, covered, for about 30 minutes, or until the rice has absorbed all the milk, stirring occasionally. Remove the rice from the heat and stir in the butter, 2 tablespoons of the granulated sugar, vanilla, and lemon juice and zest. Let the mixture cool to room temperature. Stir in the currant mixture.

Using an electric mixer, beat the eggs for about 2 minutes, until they are light and foamy. Stir half the rice mixture into the eggs. Fold in the remaining rice mixture until the batter is well blended.

TO BAKE

Preheat the oven to 300°F. Pour the batter into the prepared pan and smooth out the top. Sprinkle with the remaining 1 tablespoon granulated sugar. Bake for 40 to 45 minutes, until the cake is golden and firm. Let cool in the pan.

TO MAKE THE MASCARPONE-RUM CREAM

Grind the pine nuts with the sugar in a food processor or blender. Combine the mascarpone, rum, cream, and ground pine nuts, and stir until blended.

TO SERVE

Remove the cake from the pan, and sprinkle it with confectioners' sugar. Scoop the cream into a pastry bag fitted with a medium star tip, and use it to pipe a spiral on top of the cake. Sprinkle with the remaining breadcrumbs and whole pine nuts.

VARIATIONS

Candied Sicilian Rice Cake

Replace the currants with ½ cup candied citron and ½ cup candied cherries. Replace the pine nuts with almonds. Replace the lemon juice and zest with orange juice and zest.

Muscat Italian Rice Cake

Replace the currants with raspberries. Replace the rum with muscat wine and the pine nuts with almonds. Top the cake with fresh raspberries.

Name-Day Cakes

Like birthday cakes, name-day cakes are made to celebrate a special day: in this case, the day of the saint for whom the recipient is named. Traditional Catholics name their children after saints. Since every day of the year has a particular saint associated with it, everyone has a name day. That's two special cake days a year, not just one. In Bologna this rice cake is prepared to celebrate St. Joseph's day on March 19. Tradition would give anyone named for St. Joseph — whether Joseph, Josephine, Giuseppe, or so on — a Bolognese rice cake on this day.

Zeppole

After becoming obsessed with these sugared fried cakes at the St. Joseph's Day festival at our church in Staten Island, New York, when I was about five, I insisted that we make them at home. So my mother taught me how to make zeppole, and one day in college, in my tiny, standing-room-only kitchen, I taught some friends to prepare them. One friend insisted that they weren't Italian zeppole but Greek loukoumathes, prepared for Hanukkah only. Another said they were Mexican fritters, although they should be topped with cinnamon-honey syrup instead of confectioners' sugar. Another said he had eaten them on a trip to New Orleans, but they had had rice in them. And that was when the seed for this book was planted in my mind. Find a photograph of zeppole on page 217.

Fried Cakes

- 2¼ teaspooons instant yeast
- 1 cup warm water
- 3 cups all-purpose flour
- 2 tablespoons plain breadcrumbs
- 3 tablespoons granulated sugar
- 1 teaspoon salt
- 3 eggs
- 4 cups vegetable oil, for frying

Topping

- ⅓ cup confectioners' sugar

Makes 18 zeppole

TO MAKE THE DOUGH

Combine the yeast and water in a small bowl, mix to dissolve, and let sit for 5 minutes. In a large bowl, combine the flour, breadcrumbs, sugar, and salt. When the yeast mixture is bubbly, blend it into the flour mixture. Add the eggs one at a time, beating well after each addition. Set the dough in a bowl, cover, and let rise in a warm spot for 30 minutes. Punch down, cover, and let rise for an additional 30 minutes.

TO FRY THE ZEPPOLE

Pour the 4 cups oil into a deep, heavy-bottomed pot, and warm it over medium heat. Line two plates with paper towels for draining the fried cakes.

Drop a piece of bread into the oil to test it; if it browns, the oil is ready for frying. Add the dough to the oil, 1 heaping tablespoon at a time. Fry the dough, flipping to brown both sides. When the zeppole are golden brown, transfer them to the prepared plates to drain. Continue frying, in batches, until the batter is used up.

TO SERVE

Sprinkle the zeppole with confectioners' sugar. Serve while still warm.

VARIATIONS

Dutch Apple Fritters

Add 1½ cups chopped apples and 1 teaspoon ground cinnamon to the batter. Roll the zeppole in powdered sugar.

Greek Loukoumathes

Combine ½ cup honey, 1 tablespoon lemon juice, ¼ cup water, and 1 teaspoon ground cinnamon in a saucepan over medium heat and cook, stirring, until the mixture thickens into a syrup. To serve, dip the fried cakes in the honey syrup and top with finely chopped walnuts.

Mexican Honeyed Fritters

Combine 2 tablespoons honey, 1 tablespoon rum, ½ teaspoon ground cinnamon, and 1 tablespoon butter in a saucepan over medium heat and cook, stirring, until the mixture thickens into a syrup. To serve, drizzle the syrup over the fried dough.

New Orleans Zeppole

Reduce the flour to 2 cups. Add 1 cup cooked rice and 1 teaspoon ground cinnamon to the batter.

Turkish Fritters

Top the fried cakes with ¾ cup rosewater-saffron syrup (page 319).

St. Joseph's Day

Joseph, husband to Mary, the mother of Jesus, is widely revered by Catholics around the world. From Italy to Malta to the Philippines, St. Joseph's Day is a festival day, and fried zeppole are popular at these festivals. Breadcrumbs are a traditional ingredient in St. Joseph's Day treats, representing sawdust, in homage to Joseph's trade as a carpenter. In the United States, St. Joseph's Day is widely celebrated in Italian-American communities. In New Orleans the festival includes city-wide parades.

Cassata Siciliana

As a kid I experienced two types of cassata on holidays, depending on which side of the family was hosting the event. My father's family is from Sicily and served cassata Siciliana, while my mother's is from Naples and served cassata gelato. Both types are based on pan di Spagna, a traditional sponge cake (for more on sponge cakes, see page 134). What differentiates the two is the filling. Both varieties are described here.

Pan di Spagna

- 2 cups cake flour, sifted
- 2 teaspoons baking powder
- 12 eggs, at room temperature, separated
- 2 cups granulated sugar
- 1 tablespoon orange juice
- 2 teaspoons vanilla extract
- ¼ cup milk, warmed

Filling

- 2 cups ricotta cheese
- ¾ cup confectioners' sugar
- 2 tablespoons cherry liqueur or kirsch
- 2 tablespoons orange liqueur (Grand Marnier, triple sec)
- ½ teaspoon vanilla extract
- ¼ cup grated sweet chocolate or tiny chocolate bits
- ¼ cup chopped candied citrus fruit

Toppings

- 5½ cups marzipan (page 324)
- 3 drops green food coloring
- ½ cup almond whipped cream (page 323)
- 1 cup royal icing (page 317)

   Candied and dried fruits to decorate (such as cherries, apricots, pineapple, and citrus peel)

Makes 1 cake (serves 6 to 8)

TO PREPARE

Preheat the oven to 350°F. Butter and flour two 8-inch round cake pans. (For a cake with rounded top, use a dome pan for the top layer.)

TO MAKE THE PAN DI SPAGNA

Combine the flour and baking powder; set aside. In a large bowl, beat the egg yolks slightly. Add the sugar and continue to beat for 2 to 3 minutes, until soft ribbons form. In a separate bowl, beat the egg whites with a mixer at high speed until stiff. Fold the whites into the yolks, then stir in the orange juice and vanilla. Add the flour mixture to the egg mixture, alternating with the milk, stirring to combine.

TO BAKE

Pour the batter into the prepared pans and bake for 30 to 35 minutes, or until the tops begin to brown and a knife inserted in the center comes out clean. Let the cakes cool in their pans for 10 minutes, then remove them from their pans and set on a rack to finish cooling.

TO MAKE THE FILLING

Combine the ricotta, confectioners' sugar, cherry liqueur, orange liqueur, and vanilla and blend until smooth. Add the chocolate and candied fruit and mix well.

TO ASSEMBLE

Cut the cakes in half crosswise to make four layers. Stack the four layers, spreading the filling between them.

   Separate about two-thirds of the marzipan from the full batch, and use the food coloring to dye it green; leave the remaining marzipan white. Roll the green marzipan out into a strip roughly 4 inches wide, 22 inches long, and ¼ inch thick. Reserve some green marzipan for the trim. Trim away any extra marzipan, and roll the trimmings into a log roughly ¼ inch wide and 22 inches long. Roll out the white marzipan into a 9-inch circle, ¼ inch thick.

   Cover the top of the cake with the white marzipan circle, and wrap the long green strip of marzipan around the cake's sides. Smooth and stretch the marzipan to get rid of any wrinkles. Shape the marzipan log around the base of the cake as trim. Spoon a dollop of almond whipped cream onto the center of the cake, and use royal icing to attach candied fruits and trace decorative patterns on the marzipan. Refrigerate until ready to serve.

VARIATION

Cassata Gelato

The traditional cassata gelato is made in a dome-shaped bowl. Bake the pan di Spagna in an 11- by 15-inch jelly roll pan at 325°F for 10 to 15 minutes, until it is springy. When cool, cut into strips roughly 1 inch wide and the length of the bowl. Line the bottom and sides of the bowl with overlapping strips of cake, leaving a cavity in the center. Spread a 1-inch layer of your favorite gelato over the cake strips, cover, and freeze for at least 2 hours. Then fill the cavity with the cassata Siciliana filling, just to the rim of the bowl, and freeze overnight. To serve, invert the cake onto a plate and top with almond whipped cream and candied fruits.

Convent Cakes

We can thank Arabic influences for Italian cassata, as Arabs first introduced citrus, apricots, almonds, and frozen desserts to the country. Italian nuns took these ingredients and perfected the cassata recipes. In fact, the nuns were such fans of cassata that church fathers of the sixteenth century thought they had become overzealous, and they banned cassata during Holy Week so that the nuns would not be distracted from their godly duties.

Catalan Cheesecake

I want to share a cheesecake secret with you: Use pot cheese, a soft, crumbly cheese traditionally used in Spanish cheesecakes. Its texture is halfway between that of cottage cheese and farmer's cheese. If you can't find pot cheese, substitute ricotta, and the cheesecake will have a bit more of an Italian flair. This Catalan version of cheesecake has a yeast-bread pastry crust and is topped with peaches, pomegranate seeds, and grapes.

Crust

- 1 cup warm milk
- 2 teaspoons active dry yeast
- 1 tablespoon sugar
- 1 cup all-purpose flour
- 1 cup whole-wheat flour
- 4 tablespoons unsalted butter, melted
- 1 teaspoon ground cinnamon
- ¼ teaspoon salt

Filling

- ½ cup golden raisins
- 3 tablespoons rum
- ¾ pound fresh pot cheese
- ¾ cup sugar
- 4 eggs
- 2 tablespoons orange juice
- 1 teaspoon cornstarch
- 1½ cups heavy cream
- 2 teaspoons grated orange zest

Toppings

- Seeds from 1 small pomegranate
- 1 peach, sliced
- ½ cup red grapes

Makes 1 cake (serves 6 to 8)

TO PREPARE THE CRUST

Combine the milk, yeast, and sugar in a medium bowl; stir together, then let sit for 5 minutes. Add the all-purpose flour, whole-wheat flour, butter, cinnamon, and salt and stir until blended. Transfer the dough to a floured work surface and knead until smooth. Cover the dough and let it rise in a warm place for about 1 hour until it has doubled in size.

Butter and flour a 10-inch round spring-form pan. When the dough has risen, turn it out onto a floured work surface. Press into a ¼-inch-thick disk, about 10 inches round. Press the disk into the prepared pan to cover the bottom. Cover and set in a warm place to rise for 20 minutes.

Preheat the oven to 350°F. Bake the crust for about 20 minutes, until firm.

TO PREPARE THE CHEESECAKE

Combine the raisins and rum in a small bowl and let sit for 20 minutes, until the raisins are plump. Beat the cheese, sugar, and eggs in a medium bowl. In a separate small bowl, whisk together the orange juice and cornstarch to dissolve, then blend into the cheese mixture. Add the cream, orange zest, and raisin mixture and mix until well blended. Pour the filling into the prebaked crust.

TO BAKE THE CHEESECAKE

Preheat the oven to 350°F. Bake for 30 to 40 minutes, or until the filling is set. Let cool in its pan. To serve, remove from the pan and top with fresh fruits.

Tarta de Santiago (St. James' Cake)

Spain

This tangy orange-almond cake is named for St. James, the patron saint of Spain. Traditionally it is decorated with a stenciled cross of confectioners' sugar on its top. The iconic cross makes this cake a good choice for christenings, communions, confirmations, and other Christian holidays.

Orange-Almond Cake

1½ cups ground almonds

1 cup granulated sugar

⅔ cup potato flour

5 eggs, separated

¾ cup orange juice

Zest of 1 orange, grated

Topping

2 tablespoons confectioners' sugar

Makes 18 individual-serving cakes

TO PREPARE

Preheat the oven to 300°F. Butter and flour two muffin-top pans.

Tartas de Santiago have a cross on top. Barrigas de freira (page 200) have the almonds.

TO MAKE THE CAKES

Combine the ground almonds with ⅓ cup of the granulated sugar and the potato flour, and set aside. Beat the egg whites until stiff and glossy, and set aside. In a large bowl, beat the egg yolks until light. Gradually add the remaining ⅔ cup granulated sugar to the yolks, beating until incorporated. Fold in the almond mixture, the orange juice, and the zest. Gently fold in the egg whites, taking care not to deflate them.

TO BAKE

Pour the batter into the prepared pans and bake for 20 to 25 minutes, until a knife inserted in the center comes out clean. Transfer the cakes to a rack to cool.

TO DECORATE

Using a stencil with a cross cutout, sprinkle confectioners' sugar on top of each cake.

VARIATIONS

Chilean Cherry St. James' Cake

Replace the orange juice with cherry juice. Add ¾ cup chopped cherries to the batter. Serve with cherry ice cream.

Full-Size St. James' Cake

Bake the batter in a 10-inch round cake pan for 40 to 45 minutes.

St. James

James, brother of the disciple John, was one of Jesus' closest friends. He spent many years proselytizing in Spain, and his remains are buried in the Spanish city of Santiago de Compostela. During the Middle Ages the pilgrimage to Santiago was the most important journey in the Christian world. Today, St. James' cake is sold throughout Santiago de Compostela and is popular with tourists, whether they are on a religious pilgrimage or simply vacationing in the region. Portuguese Jews brought St. James' cake to Italy in the late 1400s, where it became known as *focaccia alla portoghese*, or "Portuguese-style cake." St. James is also the patron saint of Chile, and there this cake is prepared (sometimes with cherry flavoring) to celebrate his feast day, July 25.

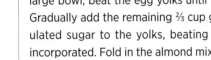

Barrigas de Freira (Nuns' Bellies)

Simple, sweet, and mellow, nuns' bellies are individual custard-soaked cakes. The almond on top looks somewhat like a belly button, hence the name. (Though the nuns reference is not to nuns' belly buttons but to the fact that nuns were the original creators of this recipe.) Nuns' bellies are sometimes made with day-old bread or cake, though I have used pan di Spagna sponge cake. They are prepared each year for the Festa do São João (Festival of St. John). (For a photo of these cakes, see page 199.)

Pan di Spagna
- 2 cups cake flour, sifted
- 2 teaspoons baking powder
- 12 eggs, at room temperature, separated
- 2 cups granulated sugar
- 1 tablespoon orange juice
- 2 teaspoons vanilla extract
- ¼ cup milk, warmed

Custard
- 1 cup sugar
- ¾ cup water
- Zest of 1 lemon, grated
- 2 tablespoons unsalted butter
- 5 egg yolks
- ¾ cup ground almonds
- 2 teaspoons ground cinnamon

Topping
- Handful of whole almonds

Makes 12 individual-serving cakes

TO PREPARE
Preheat the oven to 350°F. Butter and flour two six-cup muffin pans, or line the cups with wrappers.

TO MAKE THE CAKES
Prepare the pan di Spagna batter as directed on page 196. Pour into the prepared pans, filling each cup half full. Bake for 20 to 25 minutes, until golden. Remove the cakes from the pans and set on a rack to cool.

TO MAKE THE CUSTARD
Combine the sugar, water, and lemon zest in a saucepan over low heat, and stir until the sugar is dissolved. Add the butter, and stir until it's melted. Whisk in the egg yolks and cook, stirring until the mixture thickens. Remove from the heat and stir in the ground almonds and cinnamon.

TO ASSEMBLE
Cover the cakes with the hot custard and place a whole almond in the center of each. Let cool in the refrigerator for 1 hour.

The Festa do São João

The Festa do São João (Festival of St. John), celebrated on June 24 in the city of Porto in northern Portugal, combines sacred and profane traditions, much like the Mardi Gras of New Orleans. It has been held annually for more than six centuries and is known as Europe's craziest and liveliest street festival. You'll find swinging concerts, wild dancing, and lots of flames being shot around in the form of street fires and fireworks. Nuns' bellies are common street food at the festival, sold by vendors around the city.

Portuguese Nun Cakes

In the eighteenth century Portuguese nuns, who kept chickens in the monasteries, invented many egg-based custardy cakes and pastries with names like barrigas de freira (nuns' bellies), papos de anjo (angel's chests), and toucinho do céu (bacon from heaven). They sold their cakes at church festivals and fairs to pay their taxes and living expenses. Convents would enter into great competitions to see which could produce the best sweets and desserts. Which do you think is better: nuns' bellies or pastéis de nata (page 201)?

Pastéis de Nata (Cream Tarts)

Custardy is what I think when I think of cakes of Portugal. With their pastry crust, you may consider these creamy tarts to be more custard pies than cakes, but cakes they are called in Portugal, and so cakes we will consider them. They are traditionally used to celebrate birthdays, making their appearance with a bright pink candle in their center.

Pastry

2	cups all-purpose flour
3	tablespoons granulated sugar
1	teaspoon salt
10	tablespoons unsalted butter, chilled, cut into tablespoon pieces
5–7	tablespoons cold water

Vanilla Custard

6	egg yolks
1½	cups heavy cream
1	cup granulated sugar
1	tablespoon cornstarch
1	teaspoon vanilla extract

Toppings

¼	cup light brown sugar
½	teaspoon ground cinnamon
1	cup whipped cream (page 323)

Makes 24 individual-serving cakes

TO MAKE THE PASTRY

Combine the flour, sugar, and salt in a food processor or blender. Add the butter and pulse to form a coarse meal. Gradually add the water, pulsing, until the dough begins to hold together. Refrigerate the dough for 30 minutes.

TO BAKE THE PASTRY CUPS

Preheat the oven to 350°F. Butter and flour two cupcake pans. Transfer the dough to a floured work surface, and roll it out to ⅛-inch thickness. Cut the dough into 4½-inch rounds. Set each round in a cup in the prepared pans, pressing and shaping it so that the dough completely lines the cup. Bake for 8 to 10 minutes, until lightly browned. Let cool in the pans.

TO MAKE THE CUSTARD

Beat the egg yolks with an electric mixer for 2 to 3 minutes, until light. In a separate bowl, combine the cream, sugar, cornstarch, and vanilla, and stir until the cornstarch and sugar dissolve. Beat in the egg yolks.

TO BAKE THE CAKES

Preheat the oven to 350°F. Mix together the brown sugar and cinnamon. Fill the pastry cups (in the cupcake pans) two-thirds full with the custard. Bake for 10 minutes, then pull them out of the oven and sprinkle them with the sugar mixture. Return to the oven and bake for an additional 10 to 15 minutes, until the custardy centers are puffy but still jiggly when shaken. Let cool in the pans.

TO SERVE

Remove the cakes from the pans, top with whipped cream, and serve.

Pastéis de Belem

Pastéis de nata has its roots in a nineteenth-century Portuguese convent. In the mid-1800s two nuns at Jerónimos Monastery opened a bakery to sell delicious custardy tarts they called pastéis de belem. Visitors enthusiastically devoured them, and the tarts were soon recognized worldwide. The nuns' original recipe for pastéis de belem is still a guarded secret today; derivative recipes are known as pastéis de nata.

Vasilopita

Best served at a big family breakfast, this coffee cake rings in the first morning of the new year in Greece. You can easily recognize the cake by its tiered shape, with a small round cake set on top of a large round cake. It is usually flavored with anise seed or mahlab (the ground pit of a Mediterranean wild cherry). The Greek tradition is to serve the cake to the youngest first, then the next to youngest, and so on, working up in age, and the person who finds the hidden coin or trinkets will have good luck for the year.

¾ cup blanched, slivered almonds

⅓ cup light brown sugar

1 tablespoon honey

3 cups all-purpose flour

2 teaspoons baking powder

½ teaspoon baking soda

1 teaspoon mahlab or 1 tablespoon anise seed

1 cup (2 sticks) unsalted butter, softened

2 cups granulated sugar

6 eggs

2 teaspoons lemon juice

1 teaspoon vanilla extract

1 cup milk

A coin or hard candy

Makes 1 cake (serves 8 to 10)

TO PREPARE

Preheat the oven to 350°F. Butter a 9-inch round cake pan and a 4-inch round cake pan.

TO MAKE THE CAKE

Combine the almonds, brown sugar, and honey in a small bowl, and set aside. Mix the flour, baking powder, baking soda, and mahlab in a medium bowl, and set aside. In a large bowl, cream the butter and granulated sugar until light and fluffy. Add the eggs one at a time, beating well after each addition. Stir in the lemon juice and vanilla. Add the flour mixture to the butter mixture, alternating with the milk, and mix well.

TO BAKE THE CAKE

Divide one-third of the nut mixture between the two prepared pans, scattering it in an even layer over their bottoms. Fill the smaller (4-inch) pan two-thirds full of batter, then pour half of the remaining batter into the larger (9-inch) pan. Bake both layers for 20 minutes, until the cakes become a bit firm. Sprinkle half of the remaining almond mixture in an even layer over both cakes, and lay the coin on top of one of the partly baked cakes. Pour the remaining batter on top of each cake. Bake for another 20 to 25 minutes, until a knife inserted in the center of each comes out clean. Let the cakes cool in their pans for 10 minutes.

TO SERVE

Remove the cakes from their pans, and place the smaller one on top of the larger. Top with the remaining almond mixture, and serve warm.

VARIATIONS

Hazelnut–Anise–Chocolate Chip Vasilopita

Replace the almonds with chopped hazelnuts and the mahlab with anise seed. Add ½ cup chocolate chips to the nut mixture.

Raspberry-Yogurt Vasilopita

Replace the milk with yogurt. Add 1 cup fresh raspberries to the center of the cakes, along with the almond mixture and coin, during the baking.

Seed Wedding Cake

In Greece everyone is required to eat seeds at weddings to wish the happy couple a fertile life. Replace the nuts with ¾ cup sunflower seeds or poppyseeds and serve the cake at a wedding brunch.

St. Basil's Day

January 1 is the feast day of St. Vasili (St. Basil), the first saint's day of the year. In Greece the celebration of St. Basil's day is a grander event than Christmas. St. Basil, rather than St. Nicholas, is the gift-bringer, delivering presents for children on New Year's Eve. Basil was known for his work on behalf of the poor, and the coin baked in the vasilopita commemorates his charity.

The cake's sweetness is said to symbolize the sweet things in life: liberty, health, and happiness. Eating it on the first day of the year is a sign of hope that all these sweet things will come in the year ahead. In some rural areas, while the cake is being cut a pomegranate is violently thrown to the ground to scatter the seeds for a fruitful year.

Lambropsomo

The dyed hard-boiled eggs in this cake are the giveaway: this is the traditional Greek Easter sweet bread, braided into a ring. Lambropsomo has been adopted and adapted by many cultures. You can find Jewish versions made with challah bread and Russian versions with beautifully dyed Ukrainian eggs. There is even a spring festival version made in Egypt. The foundation of flavor comes from mahlab essence, extracted from the seeds of Mediterranean wild cherries.

Sweet Bread

- 1 tablespoon active dry yeast
- ½ cup sugar
- ½ cup milk, warmed
- 4¾ cups all-purpose flour
- 2 teaspoons salt
- 1 teaspoon grated nutmeg
- 1 teaspoon ground cinnamon
- 1 teaspoon grated lemon zest
- ½ cup (1 stick) unsalted butter
- 5 egg yolks
- 1 egg white
- 1 tablespoon mahlab essence or 2 tablespoons cherry juice
- 6 eggs, hard-boiled and dyed

Toppings

- 2 egg whites
- 1 tablespoon water
- 3 tablespoons sugar

Makes 1 cake (serves 8 to 10)

TO MAKE THE CAKE

Prepare the dough as for the king cake on page 50, adding the egg white and mahlab essence along with the yolks. Cover and set in a warm place to rise for about 2 hours, until doubled in size.

TO SHAPE

Butter a baking sheet. When the dough has risen, divide it into two loaves. Stretch each loaf into a long rope from 1½ to 2 feet long. Twist the loaves around each other, forming a braid. Set the braid on the prepared baking sheet and shape into a circle, pinching the ends together. Evenly distribute the eggs in the spaces between the coils, tucking them in deep so they don't pop out while the cake is baking. Cover and set in a warm place to rise for about 1 hour, until the dough has doubled in size.

TO BAKE

Preheat the oven to 350°F. Lightly beat the egg whites with the water, and brush the mixture over the cake. Sprinkle with the sugar. Bake for 50 minutes to 1 hour, until golden brown. Set on a rack to cool.

Easter Lambropsomo

The egg-glazed surface of lambropsomo gives it its name, which translates as "shining bread." It is eaten at the Easter meal after the forty-day fast of Lent. The eggs embedded in the cake represent the new life of springtime. They are often dyed red, symbolizing the blood of Christ. Greeks hand the eggs out to guests, and they crack the eggs against each other. The ones whose eggs stay intact will have good luck.

Tiropita

An adaptation of the classic Greek cheesecake, tiropita is usually eaten as an accompaniment to a main course during Lent. The type of feta you include will make a big difference in the taste. Choose your feta by the amount of saltiness you prefer. In Lebanon the same cake is topped with rosewater syrup.

Cheesecake

- 2 cups feta cheese, crumbled
- 2 cups small-curd cottage cheese
- ¼ cup granulated sugar
- 3 tablespoons yogurt
- 1 teaspoon grated orange zest
- ¼ teaspoon ground cinnamon
- 4 eggs
- 20 (12- by 17-inch) sheets phyllo dough
- 1 cup (2 sticks) unsalted butter, melted

Topping

- 2 tablespoons confectioners' sugar

Makes 1 cake (serves 6 to 8)

TO PREPARE

Preheat the oven to 350°F. Butter an 8-inch square baking pan.

TO MAKE THE BATTER

Combine the feta cheese, cottage cheese, granulated sugar, yogurt, orange zest, and cinnamon in a large bowl. In a separate bowl, beat the eggs until foamy, then add them to the cheese mixture.

TO ASSEMBLE

Fold a sheet of phyllo to fit the bottom of the prepared pan, and brush with butter. Repeat with four more sheets of phyllo, so that you have five sheets total, each brushed with butter. Spread one-third of the cheese mixture over the phyllo. Top with five more sheets of folded phyllo, each brushed with butter, and another third of the cheese mixture. Repeat, and top with a final layer of five buttered sheets of phyllo.

TO BAKE

Bake for 50 to 60 minutes, until the cheese is firm and set. Let cool in its pan for 20 minutes. Sprinkle with confectioners' sugar, cut into squares, and serve warm.

VARIATION

Lebanese Tiropita

Top the tiropita with ½ cup rosewater syrup (page 319).

Fasting for Lent

Pascha (Easter) is the most important holiday in the Greek Orthodox calendar, combining Jewish customs from Passover and Christian customs from Easter. Lent, the forty days before Pascha, is a time of fasting and ritual. Meat is not eaten during Lent, so the feta cheese and eggs in tiropita are a tasty source of protein.

CHAPTER 9

Africa
Deep-Fried Nibbles and Crunchy Bananas

DID YOU EVER HAVE THAT SOCIAL STUDIES ASSIGNMENT where you have to prepare a recipe from another culture and present it to your class? I was assigned to prepare fruit and vegetable fritters from Africa. Even as a sixth grader I knew it would be a disaster, since fritters are of course meant to be eaten crispy and hot immediately after they are made, not cold and soggy 24 hours later. I was already an aspiring baker and pleaded with my teacher for another recipe that would show off my skills but did not win that battle. The fritters were as soggy, mushy, and greasy as I had feared, and nobody ate them, although I compensated by delivering my oral presentation with gusto, and I passed. Here is a recommendation for any kids out there with the same assignment: if you get to choose your recipe, pick a baked cake to bring to school — preferably one topped with lots of crowd-pleasing frosting — but try these African fritters (page 214) at home. They are fantastic.

There are more than 50 nations in Africa, and they vary in every way possible: culturally, politically, agriculturally, economically, demographically, and more. But like people everywhere around the world, the peoples of Africa have one thing in common: they love cake.

Snack cakes are a real phenomenon in Africa, where having many small meals throughout the day, rather than a few large sit-down meals, is the eating pattern for many cultures. Many African snack cakes are fried in oil, including the fruit and vegetable fritters of Mali (page 214), cassava sweet balls of Ghana, chin-chin caraway cakes of Nigeria (page 209), and Cameroonian akkra (bean) fritters. Frying evolved as a common method of preparing cakes because indoor ovens for baking are not a part of traditional African food preparation. Instead, foods were prepared outdoors, over an open fire, in a barbecue pit, or even smoked in a tall termite hill. Though modern homes may have state-of-the-art kitchens, the technique of frying cakes prevails.

African cakes make great use of native ingredients, such as carob, palm oil, yams, bananas, melons, and squashes. They also make use of the many imported ingredients that are now important crops for the region, such as coconut, peanuts, vanilla, coffee, sugarcane, wheat, and cocoa. Some of these crops have been cultivated in Africa since the time of the Roman Empire.

Of course, crops aren't the only imports and exports from the continent. North African cuisine has been strongly influenced by Middle Eastern, Italian, Greek, and French cuisines, and vice versa. Check out the Mediterranean cakes in chapter 8, and you will notice crossovers in both flavors and techniques. The use of phyllo, dried fruits, almonds, and honey is widespread in northern African cakes. These flavors have filtered north to Italy, France, and Spain and south through the continent. Arabic spices like cinnamon, ginger, saffron, cumin, and caraway have put their stamp on north African cakes, and the regional use of orange-flower water, rosewater, and verbena in cakes gives a nod to the region's ties to ancient Persia.

Travel south to the Cape, which was heavily colonized by Germany, Holland, and England, and you will find many cakes familiar to Westerners, from dumplings to doughnuts. The country of South Africa is very cosmopolitan; star chefs and New York cheesecakes made in hundreds of different flavors are the order of the day. And if you visit Botswana, a region rich with diamonds, gold, wildlife, and tourists, you will discover many European and American influences reflected in the country's cake culture.

The great ancient trade routes established as early as the first century swept into Africa the spices, crops, and culinary techniques of Asia, India, and Indonesia. Indonesians, for example, set up shop on Madagascar, bringing their own sensibilities to the local spice cakes. Later European traders brought their own influences — and colonists. Tanzania is home to many descendants of German immigrants, for example, along with cakes of German tradition, such as Black Forest cake (page 120). The citizens of Mozambique and Angola bake Portuguese-influenced egg custard cakes similar to nuns' bellies (page 200). The Portuguese introduced buttery cakes and citrus fruits to the Ivory Coast in the sixteenth century, and the local culture soon combined the two in recipes such as lime loaves, a sweet-tart lime-flavored cake with a lime glaze. South African souskluitjies (page 219) are dumpling cakes cooked in a pot of boiling water, a preparation method brought to Africa by the Dutch from Indonesia.

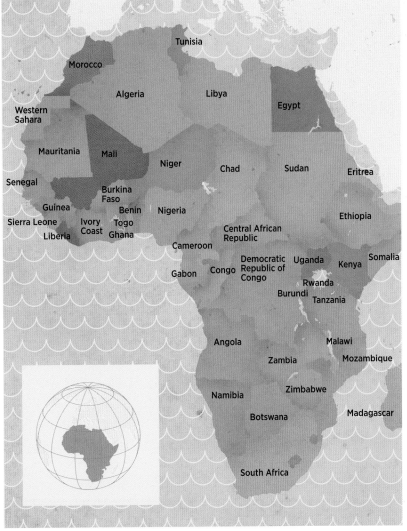

Basbousa

The sweetness of lemon-honey syrup is captured in the crispy texture of this semolina cake. It's flavored with almonds and yogurt, though variations found in Greece and Turkey use hazelnuts and coconut.

Lemon Semolina Cake

1	cup sugar
10	tablespoons unsalted butter, softened
2	tablespoons lemon juice
2	teaspoons vanilla extract
3	eggs
2	cups white semolina flour
⅓	cup all-purpose flour
½	cup ground almonds
2	teaspoons baking powder
1	cup plain yogurt

Toppings

¾	cup whole almonds
¾	cup lemon syrup (optional; see page 318)

Makes 1 cake (serves 6 to 8)

TO PREPARE

Preheat the oven to 375°F. Butter and flour a 10-inch square cake pan or an animal-shaped pan.

TO MAKE THE CAKE

Beat the sugar and butter in a large bowl until light and fluffy. Beat in the lemon juice and vanilla. Add the eggs one at a time, beating well after each addition. Slowly stir in the semolina, flour, almonds, and baking powder. Mix in the yogurt and stir until smooth.

TO BAKE

Pour the batter into the prepared pan. Place the whole almonds on top of the batter. Bake for 35 to 40 minutes, until a knife inserted in the center comes out clean.

TO SERVE

If you're serving the cake at home, top it with lemon syrup while it's still warm, and serve immediately. To take it on a "smell-the-spring" picnic, skip the sticky syrup, and wrap up the cake in a basket with fresh fruit and hard-boiled eggs.

VARIATIONS

Egyptian Basbousa with Fig Balls
Combine ½ cup ground almonds, ½ cup dried, chopped figs, ¼ teaspoon ground cinnamon, and a pinch of grated nutmeg in a food processor or blender, and pulse to blend. Add a bit of water to the mixture if it is not sticky. Roll the mixture into bite-size (¾-inch) balls. Dip the balls in honey, and stud with whole almonds. Set the balls on top of and around the basbousa.

Greek Hazelnut Basbousa
Replace the almonds with equal amounts of ground and whole hazelnuts. Replace the white semolina (farina) with yellow semolina (durum).

Turkish Coconut Basbousa
Add ¼ cup milk and 1 cup shredded unsweetened coconut to the batter.

Animal Cakes

In ancient Egypt sweetened doughs and cakes were treasured as food for the gods. These ancient cakes were made by combining honey, dates and other fruits, spices, and nuts with the dough. They were baked in the shapes of animals and birds. If you happen to have an animal-shaped pan, bake this cake in it for a truly authentic Egyptian experience.

Sham al Nessim

Sham al Nessim (smell the spring day) is a national holiday in Egypt celebrating the arrival of spring. It is rooted in the ancient Egyptian belief that this was the day the earth began. To celebrate, Egyptians have picnics with sweet basbousa cakes and hard-boiled eggs to enjoy in nature.

Chin-Chin

Enjoying African cakes prepared in Los Angeles by a Korean woman epitomizes the global cake experience. I found these fried twisted caraway cakes at the corner Korean grocery near my former design studio, where a very nice woman prepared them on the spot for customers, very much as they are prepared by street vendors at train stations in Nigeria.

1½ cups all-purpose flour

3 tablespoons sugar

3 tablespoons unsalted butter

¼ teaspoon ground cinnamon

2 eggs

1½ teaspoons caraway seeds

1 teaspoon grated orange zest

Vegetable oil for frying

Makes 12 cakes

TO MAKE THE DOUGH

Combine the flour, sugar, butter, and cinnamon in a food processor or blender, and pulse until the mixture forms a coarse meal. Add the eggs, caraway seeds, and orange zest and process until the dough stiffens. Transfer the dough to a floured work surface and knead until smooth.

TO SHAPE

Roll out the dough to ¼-inch thickness. Cut the dough into strips ¾ inch wide and 5 inches long. Cut the edges of the strips on an angle, and cut a ¾-inch slit in the center of each strip. Twist the dough a few turns, then slide one end through the slit to make a bow. Press the dough together at the intersection.

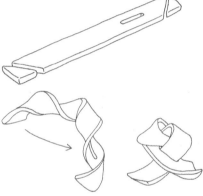

TO FRY

Fill a heavy-bottomed pot with 1½ to 2 inches of oil, and warm over medium heat. Drop a small piece of bread into the oil to test it; if the bread browns, the oil is ready for frying. Line plates with paper towels for draining the fried cakes.

Drop the knots into the oil and fry until lightly brown on one side; flip and brown the other side. Remove from the oil and drain on paper towels.

VARIATION

Anise Nutmeg Chin-Chin

Replace the caraway seeds with anise seeds and the cinnamon with grated nutmeg. Coat the fried cakes with confectioner's sugar.

Small Chops

In this region where street foods are a way of life, look for small "chops" or snack cakes everywhere you travel. The cakes' whimsical names make them sound like characters from a kids' TV show. Among others, you'll find puff-puff, a sugar-coated doughnut; chin-chin, a sweetened fried caraway cake; tatali, a fried cornmeal-plantain cake; and yoyo, a fried orange cake dipped in honey syrup.

M'hanncha (Snake Cake)

In Morocco every meal is a special occasion, and almond-paste sweets are always part of the menu. M'hanncha (snake) is made from rolled phyllo pastry coiled to look like a serpent. The orange-flower water and cinnamon flavorings are very North African, revealing the Persian influences in the region.

Orange-Almond Paste
- 3 cups almonds
- ¾ cup confectioners' sugar
- ½ teaspoon ground cinnamon
- ¼ teaspoon ground cardamom
- ¾ cup (1½ sticks) unsalted butter, melted
- 2 egg yolks, beaten
- 1 tablespoon orange-flower water
- 1 tablespoon orange juice
- 1 tablespoon grated orange zest
- 1 teaspoon vanilla extract

Assembly
- 12 (12- by 17-inch) sheets phyllo dough
- ¾ cup (1½ sticks) unsalted butter, melted
- 2 egg yolks, beaten
- 1 tablespoon water
- ½ teaspoon cinnamon

Toppings
- ¼ cup confectioners' sugar
- 4 teaspoons ground cinnamon
- ¼ cup sliced almonds

Makes 1 cake (serves 6 to 8)

TO MAKE THE ORANGE-ALMOND PASTE

Combine the almonds, confectioners' sugar, cinnamon, and cardamom in a food processor or blender and pulse to grind into a coarse meal. Add the butter and egg yolks and pulse until blended. Scrape the paste into a bowl, and stir in the orange-flower water, orange juice, orange zest, and vanilla. Divide the paste into 12 balls, and refrigerate for 30 minutes.

Set the balls on a work surface dusted with confectioners' sugar. Roll each one into a 3½-inch-long log. Refrigerate for 30 minutes.

TO ASSEMBLE THE CAKE

Preheat the oven to 350°F. Butter a large baking sheet. Dust a work surface with confectioners' sugar. Place a sheet of phyllo pastry on the sugared work surface, and fold it in thirds to form a 4- by 17-inch rectangle. Brush the sheet with melted butter. Add another folded phyllo sheet, brush with butter, and repeat, until you have four buttered sheets.

Set four orange-almond paste logs in a row down one long end of the phyllo, and roll the pastry up over them into a cylinder. Fold over the ends and brush on some melted butter to seal the seams. Shape the cylinder into a small, tight coil and place on the baking sheet, seam side down.

Repeat to prepare two more phyllo rolls. Add each to the end of the coil on the baking sheet, forming a large coil.

Combine the egg yolks, water, and cinnamon. Brush the mixture over the top of the cake.

TO BAKE

Bake for 15 to 20 minutes, or until golden. Remove the cake from the oven, and let cool on the baking sheet.

TO SERVE

Stir together the confectioners' sugar and cinnamon. Sprinkle on the cake, and top with sliced almonds.

VARIATIONS

Date-Lime Snake Cake
For the paste, reduce the almonds to 1½ cups, add 1½ cups chopped dates, and replace the orange juice and zest with lime juice and zest.

Individual Snake Cakes
Cut the folded phyllo sheets into 4- by 10-inch pieces, and stack and butter as directed. Place one almond paste log on top of each stack, roll into a cylinder, and shape into a small coil.

Walnut-Lemon Snake Cake
For the paste, replace the almonds with walnuts, replace the orange juice and zest with lemon juice and zest, and add ¼ teaspoon ground cardamom.

Snake Charmers

Moroccan culture has always had a fascination with snakes, and cakes are not the only arena where that interest shows. The practice of snake charming, hypnotizing the snake by playing music and performing, originated in India in ancient times and spread through Southeast Asia and the Middle East. Today snake charmers travel from town to town and perform at festivals throughout Morocco.

Zucchini-Almond Cake with Peach Sauce

The flavors of this tender North African spice cake are distinctively Mediterranean. Moist zucchini, crunchy almonds, and sweet peaches are a fresh and surprising combination. Fresh baby zucchinis with flowers add an elegant touch.

Zucchini-Almond Cake
- 1¼ cups all-purpose flour
- 1 teaspoon baking powder
- 1 teaspoon salt
- ¾ teaspoon baking soda
- ½ teaspoon ground cinnamon
- ½ teaspoon ground cumin
- ¼ teaspoon ground coriander
- 2 eggs
- 1 cup granulated sugar
- ⅔ cup vegetable oil
- 2 cups grated zucchini
- 1 cup chopped almonds
- 1 teaspoon grated lemon zest

Peach Sauce
- 2 cups chopped peaches
- 1 cup granulated sugar
- ¼ cup peach or orange juice
- 1½ teaspoons cornstarch
- 1 teaspoon lemon juice

Toppings
- ¼ cup confectioners' sugar
- 1 whole peach, sliced
- Baby zucchini with flowers

Makes 1 cake (serves 6 to 8)

TO PREPARE
Preheat the oven to 350°F. Butter and flour a 9-inch square cake pan.

TO MAKE THE CAKE
Combine the flour, baking powder, salt, baking soda, cinnamon, cumin, and coriander; set aside. Beat the eggs, sugar, and oil until blended. Add the flour mixture to the egg mixture, stirring until blended. Stir in the zucchini, almonds, and lemon zest.

TO BAKE
Pour the batter into the prepared pan. Bake for 35 to 40 minutes, until a knife inserted in the center comes out clean. Let cool in its pan for 10 minutes, then remove the cake from the pan and set on a rack to finish cooling.

TO MAKE THE PEACH SAUCE
Combine the peaches, sugar, peach juice, cornstarch, and lemon juice in a medium saucepan over low heat. Cook, stirring, until thickened.

TO SERVE
Sprinkle the confectioners' sugar over the cake, and cut into slices. Spoon a bit of peach sauce onto each individual serving plate. Set a slice of cake on the sauce, and top with sliced peaches and zucchinis.

VARIATIONS
Colombian Zucchini-Carrot Cake
In the cake batter, reduce the zucchini to 1 cup, add 1 cup grated carrots, and replace the almonds with pistachios.

Mexican Chocolate-Zucchini Cake
In the cake batter, reduce the flour to 1 cup, and add ½ cup unsweetened cocoa powder, ½ cup chocolate chips, and ½ cup puréed peaches. Top with 4 cups cream cheese frosting (page 316), chocolate shavings, and fresh peach slices.

Tunisian Fusion

The main ingredients in this cake meld to form a uniquely Tunisian fusion dish. Almonds have been a part of the Tunisian diet and industry for centuries, since the Carthaginian era. Zucchini, on the other hand, a new-world native, was brought to Europe by Christopher Columbus, and from there the squash spread to Africa and found a home in Tunisia. The peach was likely introduced to Tunisia from ancient Persia; today it is undergoing a revival in this country, becoming a major export crop.

Upside-Down Pumpkin-Plantain Cake

Pumpkins and plantains are plentiful in Liberian cooking. They're rarely combined in traditional African recipes, but I find that their flavors go together very well, which inspired me to create this upside-down pumpkin cake, with brown-sugared plantains as a topping. Serve with whipped cream if desired.

Caramelized Plantains

- 6 small plantains, peeled
- ½ cup light brown sugar
- ⅓ cup water

Pumpkin Cake

- 2 cups all-purpose flour
- 1 teaspoon ground cinnamon
- ½ teaspoon ground ginger
- ½ teaspoon grated nutmeg
- ½ teaspoon ground cloves
- ½ teaspoon baking powder
- ½ teaspoon salt
- ½ cup (1 stick) unsalted butter, softened
- 1¼ cups granulated sugar
- 1 cup pumpkin purée
- ¾ cup milk
- 2 eggs
- ½ teaspoon baking soda

Makes 1 cake (serves 6 to 8)

TO PREPARE

Preheat the oven to 350°F. Heavily butter a 9-inch round cake pan.

TO CARAMELIZE THE PLANTAINS

Cut 3-inch segments from both ends of the plantains, and cut these segments in half lengthwise. Slice any remaining plantain into rounds. Combine the brown sugar and water in a sauté pan over low heat and cook, stirring, until the sugar has dissolved. Add the plantains and cook until the syrup has thickened, flipping the plantains to coat. Spread the plantain slices on the bottom of the prepared pan, with the long segments radiating from the center and the circles filling the center.

TO MAKE THE CAKE

Combine the flour, cinnamon, ginger, nutmeg, cloves, baking powder, and salt; set aside. In a large bowl, beat together the butter, granulated sugar, pumpkin, milk, eggs, and baking soda. Add the flour mixture to the butter mixture, mixing until well blended.

TO BAKE

Pour the batter over the plantains in the pan and bake for 35 to 45 minutes, until a knife inserted in the center comes out clean. Remove the pan from the oven and let sit for 10 minutes. Then loosen the edges of the cake from the pan with a spatula, and turn the cake upside down onto a serving plate. Replace any plantains that have come loose if needed.

VARIATION
Caribbean Pumpkin-Rum Upside-Down Cake

When caramelizing the plantains, replace the water with rum. Add 2 tablespoons rum and ¾ cup chopped pecans to the cake batter.

Plantains and Pumpkins

Plantains and pumpkins are both imports to Africa, though plantains have been around for a lot longer. They are thought to have originated in Indonesia, but they've been an important crop in Africa since at least 1500. Pumpkins, on the other hand, are native to Central America and have been a staple of Native American diets for thousands of years. The seeds were brought to Europe by early explorers and from there cultivation spread to Africa, the Middle East, and every continent of the world except Antarctica.

Fruit and Vegetable Fritters

Bite-size fritters made from fruits and vegetables are popular everyday snack cakes in West Africa. Typically they're made from tropical fruits such as pineapples, plantains, and bananas, though vegetables such as corn, pumpkins, and sweet potatoes are also used. Traditionally they're eaten plain, but I like them a bit sweeter, topped with confectioners' sugar and honey.

Batter
- 1¾ cups all-purpose flour
- ¾ cup milk
- 2 eggs, beaten
- 3 tablespoons granulated sugar
- 2 tablespoons vegetable oil
- 1 teaspoon baking powder
- Vegetable oil for frying

Fruits and Vegetables
- 1 cup chopped pineapple
- 1 cup sliced banana
- 1 cup sliced plantain
- 1 cup mashed pumpkin
- 1 cup corn kernels
- 1 cup mashed sweet potato

Toppings
- ¼ cup confectioners' sugar
- ¼ cup honey
- 2 tablespoons peanuts

Makes 12 fritters

TO MAKE THE BATTER
Combine the flour, milk, eggs, sugar, vegetable oil, and baking powder in a bowl, and blend well. Add more flour or milk as necessary to reach a pastelike consistency, like that of a thick and sticky pancake batter.

TO FRY
Fill a heavy-bottomed pot with 1½ to 2 inches of oil for frying, and warm over medium heat. Drop ½ teaspoon of batter into the hot oil to test it; when the batter browns quickly, the oil is ready. Line plates with paper towels for draining the fritters.

Place the pineapple, banana, plantain, pumpkin, corn, and sweet potato in separate bowls. Divide the batter evenly among the bowls, and stir to blend. For each fritter, spoon 2 tablespoons of the fruit-batter or vegetable-batter mixture into the hot oil. Fry the fritters until golden brown, flipping to brown each side. Set the fritters on the prepared plates to drain.

TO SERVE
Combine the confectioners' sugar and honey as a dipping sauce. Top the warm fritters with peanuts, and serve immediately, with the dipping sauce.

___

VARIATION
African Peanut Fritters
Add 1 tablespoon peanut butter and ½ cup chopped peanuts to the batter.

THE WORLD TOUR OF
Fried Cakes

AT FESTIVALS, FAIRS, AND CARNIVALS, everyone loves deep-fried fun in the form of funnel cakes and doughnuts — just thinking about them makes me happy. If you think these cakes are all-American, think again. Canadians consume the most doughnuts of any population, and they have the most doughnut stores per capita in the world. Mister Donut is one of the most popular doughnut chains in Japan. In India and Pakistan — and at my favorite local Indian buffet in Los Angeles — fried dough soaked in a generous amount of tasty sweet syrup is a popular dessert. In Germany jam-filled, sugar-coated Berliners (named after the city) are rolled in sugar. These have been adopted by nearby Scandinavia, and in Argentina they have been transformed into facturas, a puff pastry, while in Chile they are filled with manjar, a white dulce de leche.

Fried cakes have been around for thousands of years. Since all that is needed is a flame and a vessel, frying cakes was a primitive form of baking developed about the time pottery was invented to hold the oil or fat, between 5000 and 3000 BCE. Fried cakes can be traced back to ancient China and the Egyptians, and since then, every culture has developed its own version of fried cakes, many of which are still enjoyed today.

Fried dough is made with two types of dough — either a quick-bread-type batter or a yeast dough — although the cooking instructions and intoxicating aroma are basically the same once the dough is ready. (For tips on frying up perfectly hot and crispy dough every time, see page 25.) But fried dough isn't the only kind of fried cake out there. Fritters are also fried cakes, being pieces of fruit or vegetable dipped in batter and deep-fried in oil.

Whether you like your fried cakes filled with jam or glazed with sugar, twisted into knots or flat and crinkly, frittered or fried, yummy treats from around the world await.

AUSTRALIA
In Australia all doughnuts are called "jam doughnuts," even when they have custard inside. The dough is like that of a sweet bun.

AUSTRIA
Krapfen doughnuts are popular during the pre-Lent carnival season. Traditionally they are filled with apricot jam, though the more modern version is filled with vanilla cream.

CAMEROON
Akkra (bean) fritters are common street food.

CANADA
In Canada the beaver tail, also known as an elephant ear, is a large, long, skinny doughnut that is made with lemon and sugar and comes with toppings such as banana and chocolate sauce.

CHILE
Sopaipillas are honey-sweetened fried pastries.

CHINA
Fried doughnut sticks called yóutiáo and yàuhjagwái are served with rice porridge.

CROATIA AND SERBIA
Krafne are cream-filled doughnuts topped with sugar.

FRANCE
Beignets, light, square doughnuts sprinkled with sugar, are popular throughout Europe and the parts of the United States once colonized by the French, especially Louisiana. They are eaten as part of pre-Lent festivities, especially during Mardi Gras.

GERMANY
Fastnachtkuchen, or "fasting cakes," filled with jam are made for Lent.

GREECE
Loukoumathes are simple fried cakes dipped in honey syrup and topped with walnuts. (See variation on page 195.)

INDIA
Vadas are savory fried doughs made with lentils; in north India they are soaked in curd and topped with spices or a sweet or sour chutney. Badushas are fried doughnuts soaked in plain or spiced sugar syrup.

INDONESIA
Donat kentang is a mashed-potato fried cake that is topped with confectioners' sugar or icing.

IRAN
Zooloobiyas are fritters soaked in a sticky sweet rosewater, orange blossom, or citrus syrup.

IRELAND
Oil known as "gravy" is what gives gravy rings, ring-shaped fried cakes from northern Ireland, their name.

ITALY

Fried festival cakes are plentiful in Italy, including bomboloni (filled doughnut holes dusted with sugar), ciambelle (doughnut-shaped cakes made with olive oil instead of butter and using wine for flavoring), crescentine (fried, stuffed dough "pillows"), and zeppole (fried dough; see page 195).

JAPAN

Bean-jam doughnuts are filled with adzuki bean jam.

LITHUANIA

Varškės spurgos are Lithuanian cottage-cheese doughnuts.

MALI

Vegetable fritters (page 214) are the traditional fried cakes.

MEXICO

Donas and churros (page 78) are fried pastries covered with brown sugar, cinnamon, white sugar, or chocolate.

NETHERLANDS

Oliekoecken are ball-shaped fried cakes eaten for Christmas and Lent. Oliebollen, or "Dutch doughnuts," are fritters that contain fruit such as apples and raisins. They are traditionally eaten for New Year's celebrations.

NIGERIA

Chin-chin (page 209) are traditional twisted fried caraway cakes.

PERU

Fried rings of dough called picarones (page 95) are prepared by street vendors for harvest festivals.

LEFT: *zeppole (page 195);* CENTER: *doughnuts (page 44);* RIGHT: *churros (page 78)*

POLAND

Paczki are round, jam-filled doughnuts eaten during carnival, before Lent. You can also find these in any region with large populations of Polish ancestry.

PORTUGAL

The native filhós, which are similar to French beignets, are also popular in the Philippines and Hawaii.

SCOTLAND

Glazed rope-shaped fried cakes are called yum-yums, while ring-shaped fried cakes are known as dough rings.

SOUTH AFRICA

Koeksusters are Dutch-influenced twisted fried cakes soaked in a spiced sugar syrup. Vetkoeks are fried sweet bread served with mince, sugar syrup, honey, or apricot jam.

SOUTH KOREA

Many bakeries offer doughnuts either filled with or made entirely from tteok, the Korean traditional rice dessert. These come in a variety of different colors, though they are normally green, pink, or white. Alternatively, they may be filled with a sweet red bean paste or sesame seeds.

UNITED STATES

Doughnuts, fried cakes in various shapes and with various toppings and fillings, can be found from coast to coast, from fast-food joints to high-end bakeries to home kitchens. Other wonderful fried cakes include the Hawaiian treats known as malasadas, custardy balls of yeast dough deep-fried and coated in sugar. A variation on Portugal's filhós, they were brought to the Hawaiian Islands by Portuguese settlers. And in Pennsylvania, you'll find fasnacht, a potato-starch doughnut prepared to celebrate Fat Tuesday.

FRIED CAKES FAMILY TREE

EASTERN EUROPE
- CROATIA AND SERBIA
- LITHUANIA
- POLAND
- UKRAINE

LATIN AMERICA
- CHILE
- MEXICO
- PERU
- ARGENTINA

MEDITERRANEAN
- ITALY
- GREECE
- PORTUGAL

ASIA
- INDIA
- BENGAL
- BANGLADESH
- CHINA
- JAPAN
- KOREA
- INDONESIA
- THAILAND

NORTH AMERICA
- CANADA
- UNITED STATES
- CARIBBEAN

AUSTRALIA AND NEW ZEALAND

SCANDINAVIA

WESTERN AND CENTRAL EUROPE
- FRANCE
- AUSTRIA
- GERMANY
- NETHERLANDS

AFRICA
- MALI
- NIGERIA
- CAMEROON
- SOUTH AFRICA

MIDDLE EAST
- IRAN
- PALESTINE
- TURKEY

BRITISH ISLES
- IRELAND
- SCOTLAND

Leaf labels:
sopaipillas, manjar doughnuts, pampushky, churros (page 78), syrnik, donas, picarones (page 95), krafne, varškės spurgos, mung-bean fritters, three-chums cake (page 294), paczki, facturas, ciambelle, zeppole (page 195), crescentine, donat kentang, beaver tails, doughnuts (page 44), bombolini, Lady Kenny, bean-jam dougnuts, funnel cakes (page 36), loukou-mathes (page 195), beignets, fastnacht-kuchen, jalebi (page 253), tteok doughnuts, hwäjeon (page 273), Hawaiian malasadas, krapfen, yóutiáo, Berliners, olie-koecken, mango fritters, filhós, yàuhjagwái, strauben, gulab jamun (page 252), bean-jam doughnuts, corn fritters, buñuelos, Finnish tippaleipä, apple fritters, badushas, koeksuster and vetkoek, jam doughnut, gravy rings, oliebollen, vadas, akkra, chin-chin (page 209), fruit and vegetable fritters (page 214), yum-yums, dough rings, fritters (page 214), qatayef (page 237), zooloobiya fritters

Souskluitjie

Don't be tempted to skip this cake because it seems a bit foreign. In this two-hundred-year-old recipe, cinnamon cakes are cooked quickly, like dumplings, in boiling water. Serve these South African mainstays coated with melted butter and cinnamon sugar.

Dumplings

- 2 cups all-purpose flour
- 2 teaspoons baking powder
- ½ teaspoon baking soda
- ¼ teaspoon salt
- 2 tablespoons unsalted butter, cut into pieces
- 2 eggs
- ¾ cup milk
- 1 teaspoon vanilla extract
- ½ cup dried currants
- 1 tablespoon grated orange zest

Toppings

- ¼ cup sugar
- 1 teaspoon ground cinnamon
- ½ cup unsalted butter, melted

Makes 10 dumplings

TO MAKE THE BATTER

Combine the flour, baking powder, baking soda, and salt in a food processor or blender, and pulse a few times to mix. Add the butter and pulse until the mixture holds together. Add the eggs, milk, and vanilla, and beat to a thick batter. Transfer the batter to a bowl and stir in the currants and orange zest.

TO BOIL THE DUMPLINGS

Line a plate with paper towels for draining the dumplings. Fill a large pot with 4 inches of water, and bring to a boil. Reduce the heat to keep the water simmering.

Dip a tablespoon into the boiling water, then use it to scoop a spoonful of batter into the boiling water. Repeat until the pot is full; do not crowd the dumplings. Cover the pot and simmer for 10 minutes. Remove the dumplings from the water with a slotted spoon and set on the prepared plate to drain. Continue cooking until all the batter is used up.

TO SERVE

Mix together the sugar and cinnamon. Dip the dumplings in melted butter and dust with cinnamon sugar.

VARIATION
Rice Dumpling Cakes

Add 2 cups mashed cooked short-grain rice and 2 additional eggs to the batter.

Groundnut (Peanut) Cake

Peanuts, native to South America, were brought by European explorers to Africa in the 1500s. Cultivation of peanuts caught on very quickly in Africa because they were similar to the native groundnut, but peanuts are much easier to grow. They soon replaced the groundnut, even taking on the same name in many recipes.

Peanut Cake

3¾	cups all-purpose flour
1½	teaspoons baking powder
1	teaspoon ground cinnamon
1	teaspoon salt
6	eggs
1½	cups honey
¾	cup granulated sugar
¾	cup light brown sugar
¾	cup vegetable oil
2	teaspoons vanilla extract
1½	cups milk
1½	cups chopped unsalted peanuts, toasted

Toppings

4½	cups peanut frosting (page 316)
1	cup chopped unsalted peanuts

Makes 1 cake (serves 6 to 8)

TO PREPARE

Preheat the oven to 350°F. Butter and flour two 9-inch round cake pans.

TO MAKE THE CAKE

Combine the flour, baking powder, cinnamon, and salt in a medium bowl; set aside. Beat the eggs in a large bowl with a mixer until pale and thick. Add the honey, granulated sugar, brown sugar, oil, and vanilla. Gradually add the flour mixture to the egg mixture, alternating with the milk, and mix until blended. Stir in the peanuts.

TO BAKE

Divide the batter between the prepared pans. Bake for 35 to 40 minutes, until a knife inserted in the center comes out clean. Remove the cakes from the pans and set on a rack to cool.

TO ASSEMBLE

Set one of the cakes on a serving plate. Spread one-quarter of the frosting on it, then top with the second cake. Frost the sides and top of the stacked cakes, and press chopped peanuts into the frosting.

VARIATION

Liberian Peanut-Banana Cake

Mash 2 ripe bananas in a small bowl and add 1 teaspoon vanilla. Spread the mixture between the layers of the cake, on top of the peanut frosting. Serve with 2½ cups banana whipped cream (page 323), and top each serving with 2 tablespoons honey.

Banana Cake with Crunchy N'Dizi

Kenyans snack on bananas covered with roasted peanuts, a treat they call crunchy n'dizi. I added this nutty sweet to my favorite African banana cake and topped it with banana-flavored whipped cream. Crunchy bananas are best when eaten hot right from the oven.

Banana Cake

- 2 cups all-purpose flour
- 1 teaspoon baking powder
- 1 teaspoon baking soda
- ¼ teaspoon salt
- ½ cup (1 stick) unsalted butter, softened
- 1½ cups sugar
- 1 teaspoon grated lemon zest
- 1 teaspoon vanilla extract
- 2 eggs
- 1¼ cups mashed bananas
- ¾ cup yogurt

Crunchy N'dizi

- 6 bananas, peeled and sliced in rounds
- 1 tablespoon water
- 4 tablespoons unsalted butter, melted
- ¾ cup chopped unsalted peanuts

Topping

- 2½ cups banana whipped cream (page 323)

Makes 1 cake (serves 6 to 8)

TO PREPARE

Preheat the oven to 350°F. Butter and flour a 9-inch square baking pan.

TO MAKE THE CAKE

Combine the flour, baking powder, baking soda, and salt in a medium bowl; set aside.

OPPOSITE PAGE: *Banana cake with crunchy n'dizi is the squares on the plates. The groundnut cake is the whole cake with two slices cut out.*

In a large bowl, beat the butter, sugar, lemon zest, and vanilla with a mixer until fluffy. Add the eggs one at a time, mixing well after each addition. Stir in the banana. Stir the flour mixture into the batter, alternating with the yogurt, until blended.

TO BAKE

Pour the batter into the prepared pan and bake for 45 to 50 minutes, until golden and a knife inserted in the center comes out clean. Let the cake cool in its pan for 10 minutes, then remove from the pan and set on a rack to finish cooling.

TO MAKE THE CRUNCHY N'DIZI

Preheat the oven to 400°F. Warm a skillet over medium-high heat. Add the banana rounds and water to the skillet, cover, and let steam for 1 minute. Drain the liquid. Dip the banana rounds in melted butter, then coat with chopped nuts and set on a baking tray. Bake for 4 minutes, then flip the rounds and bake for 4 to 6 minutes, until the peanuts are toasted.

TO SERVE

Top the cake with crunchy n'dizi and banana whipped cream.

VARIATION

American Banana–Chocolate Chip Cake with Peanut Frosting

Add 1 cup chocolate chips to the batter. Top the cake with 4½ cups peanut frosting (page 316). Omit the crunchy n'dizi.

Safari Rally

Banana cake and crunchy n'dizi are just a few of the snacks traditionally sold by vendors to celebrate the annual Safari Rally. This road race takes place on over 2,500 miles of unpaved roads in Kenya during the rainy season, when many roads are more like swamps. Thousands of spectators show up along the route to watch the cars pass. The rally got its start during the coronation celebrations of Queen Elizabeth II in 1953, and it's been going strong ever since.

CHAPTER 10

The Middle East
Ancient Treats and Sacred Sweets

For thousands of years the Middle East was the epicenter of the world: religiously, culturally, and commercially. Today in the Middle East you will find foods rooted
in this ancient history, with culinary traditions and techniques dating back to the Persian and Ottoman empires —
all wrapped up and sold by street vendors in a disarmingly
modern and globally influenced atmosphere.

The cultivation of wheat first took place in the Middle
East, sometime around 8000 BCE. Within the next thousand
years barley too was being cultivated, and at some point
between 5000 and 3000 BCE cake culture developed in the
Middle East, with first flat cakes and then fruitcakes. Flat
cakes are still common street food in the region. In Dubai
and Qatar you may find flat cakes griddled on stones by street
vendors outside a sophisticated French pastry shop. And in
Palestine, street vendors offer qatayef (page 237), a fried
flat cake often filled with cheese, during the sacred month

of Ramadan to break the fast. Contemporary fruitcakes use
many of the same ingredients as ancient versions, including
native figs, dates, cherries, and Persian apples (pears).

In fact, cakes of this region feature some of the world's
most ancient ingredients and spices, including phyllo, rosewater, almonds, pistachios, pomegranates, and honey. They
are most often eaten between meals, as a snack, while fruit is
eaten as dessert. In Saudi Arabia raisin tea is the traditional
accompaniment, while in Turkey a thick coffee with cardamom is served with cakes. You can enjoy this Turkish coffee
with sweets at most Turkish eateries. If you're feeling slug-
gish, this super-strong coffee and a super-sweet cake will put
a jolt in your day!

Perhaps due to the region's unique geographical position
between three continents, Middle Eastern cuisines offer
richness, complexity, and a wide-ranging flavor profile. While
in North America salt and pepper are the only seasonings on

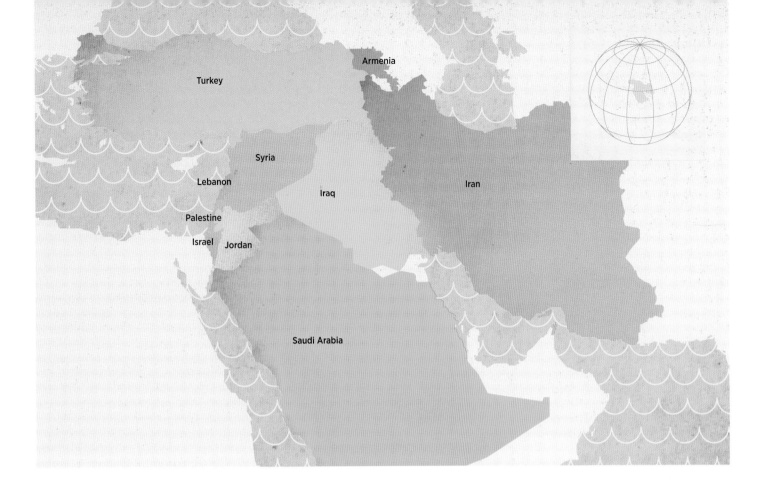

the table, in the Middle East bowls of cloves, cardamom, and mint are also commonly put out as table condiments. The subtle notes of orange-flower water, rosewater, and verbena are traditional flavorings, featured in cakes such as Iranian pistachio-rosewater cake (page 232) and pomegranate cake (page 234).

Early trade routes brought many foreign ingredients and flavors to Middle Eastern cuisine — so early, in fact, that you might think some of these flavors are uniquely Middle Eastern. In the time of the Persian emperor Darius (522–486 BCE), sugar was brought to the region by the Phoenicians, and the Persians developed methods for refining it. Arabs were also responsible for popularizing the burnt-vanilla flavor of caramel — made by heating sugar and removing the water — and this has become an ingredient essential to cake culture the world round. The Spice Islands of Indonesia provided the realm with cloves and nutmeg. Connections to China and the Indian subcontinent brought a cornucopia of fruits, seeds, nuts, and other spices, including apricots, lemons, peaches, cardamom, sesame, ginger, and cinnamon. Such ingredients found their way into now-traditional Middle Eastern cakes such as Israeli honey cake (page 227), Armenian nutmeg cake (page 226), and baklava (page 235).

Religious celebrations generate their own special foods, and since the Middle East is the birthplace of Judaism, Christianity, and Islam, the food traditions here are incredibly rich. And while Christians may love their holiday cakes, food plays a role in Muslim and Jewish cultures more so than for any other religions. In both traditions, religious laws guide when people eat, what they eat, and how they prepare and serve food. During the holy month of Ramadan, for example, Muslims cannot eat or drink from sunup to sundown. When a day's fast is complete, the evening feast is prodigious, and it is topped off with date cake (page 242), semolina sfouf, or other regional specialties. In Jewish tradition, many cakes are steeped with religious symbolism. Cheesecakes for shabbat, seed cakes for Purim (page 230), wine cakes for Passover, and fried cakes for Hanukkah are all symbolically connected to the Old Testament — and delicious even if you aren't aware of the deep symbolism.

Throughout history much of Middle Eastern culture has revolved around food. In fact, French Crusaders developed the word *gourmet* from the Farsi *ghormeh*, a term they learned at decadent Persian banquets. We all have reaped the benefits of this delectable cuisine, and there is more to experience if you are up for a flavor adventure.

Turkish Delight Cake

Chewy Turkish delight is a favorite candy for children around the world, and this cake plays upon its predominant ingredients. It's flavored with almond meal, semolina, pistachios, and rosewater. You can prepare the recipe with just rosewater Turkish delight, or you can make several batches of the candy in different flavors. Add the candy syrup topping for a glimmering presentation.

Turkish Delight Cake

- 1¼ cups all-purpose flour
- ¾ cup Turkish delight
- ¼ cup almond meal
- ½ cup semolina
- 1½ teaspoons baking powder
- ¼ teaspoon salt
- 1 cup (2 sticks) unsalted butter, softened
- 1 cup sugar
- 1 cup Greek-style yogurt
- 1 teaspoon vanilla extract
- 3 eggs
- ½ teaspoon rosewater
- 1 teaspoon lemon juice
- ½ cup chopped pistachios

Toppings

- 2 tablespoons chopped Turkish delight
- 2 tablespoons chopped pistachios
- 1 cup rosewater syrup (page 319)

Makes 1 cake (serves 6 to 8)

TO PREPARE

Preheat the oven to 325°F. Butter and flour an 8-inch square cake pan.

TO MAKE THE CAKE

Pour the flour into a medium bowl. Toss the Turkish delight with the flour, then remove the candy and set it aside. Add the almond meal, semolina, baking powder, and salt to the flour. In a separate bowl, beat the butter, sugar, yogurt, and vanilla until well blended. Add the eggs one at a time, beating well after each addition. Add the flour mixture to the butter mixture, stirring until blended. Stir in the rosewater and lemon juice.

TO BAKE

Pour 1 cup batter evenly over the bottom of the prepared pan. Stir the floured Turkish delight and the chopped pistachios into the remaining batter. Spoon the rest of the batter into the prepared baking pan. Bake for 35 to 40 minutes, until the top is golden and a knife inserted in the center comes out clean. Let cool in its pan for 10 minutes, then remove from the pan and set on a rack to finish cooling.

TO SERVE

Spread the chopped Turkish delight and pistachios on the cake. Pour rosewater syrup over each slice of cake before serving.

VARIATIONS

Lemon Turkish Delight
Replace the rosewater with lemon flavoring.

Lime Turkish Delight
Replace the rosewater with lime flavoring.

Orange Turkish Delight
Replace the rosewater with orange flavoring.

Turkish Delight

Turkish delight is a jellylike candy made from starch and sugar that dates back to the fifteenth century. Traditionally it is flavored with rosewater, lemon, mint, or cinnamon, though it can be found in just about every flavor imaginable. Some versions contain pistachios, hazelnuts, and walnuts. The candy is usually cut into cubes and, because it is very sticky, dusted with confectioners' sugar so that it can be handled more easily. It is commonly eaten at Christmastime.

In centuries past the candy was marketed throughout Europe as an exotic Turkish delicacy. In the nineteenth century, as the cost of sugar decreased, it gained popularity worldwide. North Americans never really caught on to the taste of Turkish delight but instead used it as inspiration for the modern jellybean and other jelly candies. Japanese rice candy is also based on Turkish delight.

You can buy Turkish delight, or you can make your own.

Groundnut (Peanut) Cake

Peanuts, native to South America, were brought by European explorers to Africa in the 1500s. Cultivation of peanuts caught on very quickly in Africa because they were similar to the native groundnut, but peanuts are much easier to grow. They soon replaced the groundnut, even taking on the same name in many recipes.

Peanut Cake

3¾ cups all-purpose flour

1½ teaspoons baking powder

1 teaspoon ground cinnamon

1 teaspoon salt

6 eggs

1½ cups honey

¾ cup granulated sugar

¾ cup light brown sugar

¾ cup vegetable oil

2 teaspoons vanilla extract

1½ cups milk

1½ cups chopped unsalted peanuts, toasted

Toppings

4½ cups peanut frosting (page 316)

1 cup chopped unsalted peanuts

Makes 1 cake (serves 6 to 8)

TO PREPARE

Preheat the oven to 350°F. Butter and flour two 9-inch round cake pans.

TO MAKE THE CAKE

Combine the flour, baking powder, cinnamon, and salt in a medium bowl; set aside. Beat the eggs in a large bowl with a mixer until pale and thick. Add the honey, granulated sugar, brown sugar, oil, and vanilla. Gradually add the flour mixture to the egg mixture, alternating with the milk, and mix until blended. Stir in the peanuts.

TO BAKE

Divide the batter between the prepared pans. Bake for 35 to 40 minutes, until a knife inserted in the center comes out clean. Remove the cakes from the pans and set on a rack to cool.

TO ASSEMBLE

Set one of the cakes on a serving plate. Spread one-quarter of the frosting on it, then top with the second cake. Frost the sides and top of the stacked cakes, and press chopped peanuts into the frosting.

VARIATION

Liberian Peanut-Banana Cake
Mash 2 ripe bananas in a small bowl and add 1 teaspoon vanilla. Spread the mixture between the layers of the cake, on top of the peanut frosting. Serve with 2½ cups banana whipped cream (page 323), and top each serving with 2 tablespoons honey.

Souskluitjie

Don't be tempted to skip this cake because it seems a bit foreign. In this two-hundred-year-old recipe, cinnamon cakes are cooked quickly, like dumplings, in boiling water. Serve these South African mainstays coated with melted butter and cinnamon sugar.

Dumplings

- 2 cups all-purpose flour
- 2 teaspoons baking powder
- ½ teaspoon baking soda
- ¼ teaspoon salt
- 2 tablespoons unsalted butter, cut into pieces
- 2 eggs
- ¾ cup milk
- 1 teaspoon vanilla extract
- ½ cup dried currants
- 1 tablespoon grated orange zest

Toppings

- ¼ cup sugar
- 1 teaspoon ground cinnamon
- ½ cup unsalted butter, melted

Makes 10 dumplings

TO MAKE THE BATTER

Combine the flour, baking powder, baking soda, and salt in a food processor or blender, and pulse a few times to mix. Add the butter and pulse until the mixture holds together. Add the eggs, milk, and vanilla, and beat to a thick batter. Transfer the batter to a bowl and stir in the currants and orange zest.

TO BOIL THE DUMPLINGS

Line a plate with paper towels for draining the dumplings. Fill a large pot with 4 inches of water, and bring to a boil. Reduce the heat to keep the water simmering.

Dip a tablespoon into the boiling water, then use it to scoop a spoonful of batter into the boiling water. Repeat until the pot is full; do not crowd the dumplings. Cover the pot and simmer for 10 minutes. Remove the dumplings from the water with a slotted spoon and set on the prepared plate to drain. Continue cooking until all the batter is used up.

TO SERVE

Mix together the sugar and cinnamon. Dip the dumplings in melted butter and dust with cinnamon sugar.

VARIATION

Rice Dumpling Cakes
Add 2 cups mashed cooked short-grain rice and 2 additional eggs to the batter.

Rosewater Turkish Delight

1¼ cups water
1 cup granulated sugar
1 teaspoon lemon juice
⅓ cup cornstarch
½ teaspoon cream of tartar
½ tablespoon rosewater
3 drops red food coloring
¼ cup confectioners' sugar

Makes about 36 (1-inch) pieces

Line a 6-inch square pan with plastic wrap and oil the plastic wrap.

Bring ½ cup of the water to a boil in a medium saucepan. Add the granulated sugar and lemon juice and stir until the sugar dissolves. Reduce the heat and simmer until the mixture reaches the soft-ball stage (240°F on a candy thermometer). Remove from the heat.

Stir together the cornstarch and the cream of tartar in a saucepan over medium heat. Gradually stir in the remaining ¾ cup water, until smooth. Stirring constantly, cook until the mixture boils and thickens.

Pour the sugar syrup into the cornstarch mixture, stirring until combined. Simmer, stirring occasionally, until the mixture is golden, about 1 hour. Stir in the rosewater and tint with 3 drops red food coloring. Spread the mixture into the prepared pan and cool to room temperature. Let stand overnight to set. When the candy is set, cut it into 1-inch cubes. Coat with confectioners' sugar.

Nutmeg Cake

I live in Glendale, California, home to more Armenians than Armenia itself. This cake is made daily at all of the Armenian bakeries, grocery stores, and coffeehouses in my neighborhood. In most Western recipes, nutmeg is used only in small amounts, but here it is a highlight.

Cake

3	cups all-purpose flour
1½	tablespoons grated nutmeg
2	teaspoons baking powder
1	teaspoon ground cinnamon
¾	teaspoon baking soda
½	teaspoon salt
¾	cup (1½ sticks) unsalted butter, cut into small pieces
2	cups light brown sugar, packed
1½	cups sour cream
1	cup milk
2	eggs, beaten
½	cup chopped walnuts

Topping

¼	cup confectioners' sugar

Makes 1 cake (serves 6 to 8)

TO PREPARE

Preheat the oven to 350°F. Butter and flour a 5- by 12-inch cake pan or a loaf pan.

TO MAKE THE CAKE

Combine the flour, nutmeg, baking powder, cinnamon, baking soda, and salt in a food processor or blender. Add the butter and pulse for about 10 seconds, until the mixture resembles a coarse meal. Mix in the brown sugar, followed by the sour cream, milk, and eggs. Transfer to a bowl and fold in the walnuts.

TO BAKE

Scrape the batter into the prepared pan. Bake for 45 to 50 minutes, until a knife inserted in the center comes out clean. Let cool in the pan.

TO SERVE

Using a stencil, dust the cake with confectioners' sugar, creating a pattern on it.

Armenian Church Festivals

In the year 301, Armenia became the first country to adopt Christianity as its national religion. Most Armenians belong to the national church, the One Holy Universal Apostolic Orthodox Armenian Church, which, being quite a mouthful, is more commonly known as the Armenian Apostolic Church. The "Apostolic" part of the name relates to the fact that the church traces its roots back to the first-century missions of the apostles Bartholomew and Thaddeus.

Immigrant Armenians took their religious dedication with them, and wherever they now can be found in large concentrations, Armenian church festivals are plentiful. I love attending the church festivals in my hometown, where women show off traditional Armenian cakes whose recipes have been passed down for generations. I also collect handwritten and photocopied cookbooks compiled by church members. This recipe is based on one I found in one of these cookbooks.

Mit Lechig (Honey Cake)

Mit lechig is a Yiddish term that translates as "with honey." According to Jewish tradition, honey symbolizes hope and new beginnings, and so honey is a favored food for Rosh Hashanah, the Jewish New Year. Many Jews begin their Rosh Hashanah dinner with an apple dipped in honey and finish with a honey cake. Honey cake is also commonly prepared for a bris (Brit Milah), the Jewish rite of circumcision for a newborn boy.

Honey Cake

- 2 cups all-purpose flour
- 1½ teaspoons baking powder
- ½ teaspoon ground cinnamon
- ½ teaspoon salt
- 1 cup honey
- 3 eggs, separated
- ¼ cup vegetable oil
- 3 tablespoons lemon juice
- 3 tablespoons orange juice
- 1 teaspoon vanilla extract
- ¼ cup packed light brown sugar
- 1 teaspoon grated lemon zest
- ¼ cup raisins
- ¼ cup candied orange peel (page 325)
- ¼ cup chopped dried apricots
- ½ cup slivered almonds

Toppings

- 2 cups honey icing (page 315)
- ¼ cup slivered almonds

Makes 1 cake (serves 6 to 8)

TO PREPARE

Preheat the oven to 375°F. Butter and flour an 8-inch Bundt pan.

TO MAKE THE CAKE

Combine the flour, baking powder, cinnamon, and salt in a medium bowl; set aside. In a separate large bowl, blend the honey, egg yolks, oil, lemon juice, orange juice, vanilla, and brown sugar with a mixer until creamy. Add the lemon zest, raisins, candied orange peel, apricots, and almonds, and stir well. Stir the flour mixture into the batter until blended; set aside. Beat the egg whites in a separate bowl until foamy, then fold them into the batter.

TO BAKE

Pour the batter into the prepared pan and bake for 45 minutes, until a knife inserted in the center comes out clean. Remove from the oven, invert onto a rack, and let cool.

TO SERVE

Top with honey icing and slivered almonds.

Brit Milah

In Jewish tradition, Brit Milah, the rite of circumcision, is done on the eighth day after a boy is born, signifying the covenant between God and the children of Israel. Traditionally the father performs the circumcision, but today most are not trained in this practice and a mohel (circumciser) performs the procedure. The whole extended family attends to witness. A big party follows, and guests indulge in the mit lechig cake.

VARIATIONS

Apricot Honey Cake

Omit the raisins and orange peel and add an additional ½ cup chopped dried apricots. Top with 1¾ cups apricot glaze (page 318) instead of honey icing.

Chocolate Honey Cake

Omit the lemon juice and orange juice. Reduce the flour to 1¾ cups and add ½ cup unsweetened cocoa powder to the batter.

Coffee Honey Cake

Omit the lemon juice and orange juice. Add ½ cup flour and ½ cup double-strength espresso to the batter.

THE WORLD TOUR OF
Baby Cakes

IN MANY CULTURES, cakes are an essential part of rites to welcome a new baby into the family and larger community. In the United States, cakes for the traditional baby shower may be artfully decorated with cutesy themes like baby booties and alphabet blocks. Appreciated for their adorableness, these cakes don't have much meaning beyond that "ah" factor, but many other baby cakes from around the world are steeped in history and tradition. In fact, in most cultures the symbolism and rituals surrounding baby cakes are generations old and are taken very seriously to help ensure the child will have a future as sweet and dear as the cake.

CHINA: ANG KU KUEH (RED TORTOISE CAKES)

The tortoise symbolizes long life in Chinese culture — aptly enough, since tortoises can live more than two hundred years. The color red symbolizes success, courage, fortune, and happiness. To ensure long life and good luck for new babies, red tortoise cakes are served to celebrate births in China, as well as in neighboring Taiwan and Malaysia. They are also often served at parties to celebrate the child's first month and first year. These steamed glutinous rice cakes are customarily made in tortoise-shaped molds and filled with red beans (Taiwanese-style) or mung beans (Malaysian-style), though sometimes corn, coconut, and peanuts are used as fillings. The character for longevity is often part of the mold. Preparing an extra-large red tortoise cake symbolizes the hope that the child will grow up big and healthy.

EUROPE: CHRISTENING CAKES

Christening cake traditions — and superstitions — vary from place to place. In eighteenth- and nineteenth-century England it was believed that harm would come to the newborn child if you put Friday-churned butter or Friday-laid eggs in a christening cake, or if you prepared the cake on a Friday (the thought being that since Jesus was killed on a Friday, food prepared on this day would bring bad luck).

In the late nineteenth century, European christening cakes were multitiered confections as elaborate as today's wedding cakes. In those days, a couple's first baby, and his or her christening ceremony, often occurred within a year or two of the wedding. As wedding cakes became more extravagant, these cakes competed against each other for attention. The wedding cake eventually won the competition, and in the early part of the twentieth century the christening cake was diminished to the top tier of the wedding cake. This small fruitcake (most wedding cakes of that time were fruitcakes) was saved and eaten at the christening. Rarely large enough to feed a big christening crowd, this cake was eaten by the immediate family. Another cake was usually prepared for the guests of the christening party, designed with a religious theme, such as the open pages of a Bible or a cross with the child's Christian name on top.

Later in the twentieth century, as people began to wait longer to have children and the cake was no longer limited to easy-to-preserve fruitcake, it made no sense to hold on to the top tier of the wedding cake until baby number one was born. Over time, it became common

instead for couples to save the top tier of the wedding cake to eat on their first anniversary. (Today there are professional services that freeze the tops of cake to ensure they last until the anniversary — or, if a baby is on the way, the christening.)

In modern times christening cakes have become a tradition for Christians the world over, and they tend to reflect the culture that creates them. French-Canadians, for example, prepare an assortment of petits fours (page 106). They're served alongside Jordan almonds, which symbolize health, wealth, happiness, and fertility. Sicilians make a ring-shaped fruitcake, called a buccellato, which is the traditional gift given to the baby's godparents on the day of the christening. And sheet and layer cakes of all sorts, from austere to decadent, are the norm in the United States.

ISRAEL: MIT LECHIG (HONEY CAKES)

In Jewish tradition, honey symbolizes new beginnings, and so mit lechig, or honey cakes (page 227), are made to celebrate Brit Milah, the rite of circumcision of a newborn boy that takes place on the eighth day after his birth, as a symbol of his covenant with God.

KOREA: HUNDRED-DAY AND FIRST-BIRTHDAY CAKES

In Korea, on the one-hundredth day after a child is born, a celebration is hosted for all the family and friends to celebrate the child's strength and future. Sweet rice cakes and red- and black-bean cakes are traditional. Some are placed in the north, south, east, and west corners of the house in a ritual designed to bring good luck and happiness to the baby. Others are shared among guests. It is said that if the rice cakes are shared with a hundred people, the child will have a long life, so the more the merrier at this party. Rice cakes are also packaged in nice tins and sent to as many friends and relatives as possible. The tins are returned to the family filled with small gifts for the baby.

Rice cakes also feature prominently in tol, a Korean celebration of a child's first birthday. The birthday child is dressed in traditional garb and placed in front of a scattering of objects. The object the child first picks is said to indicate his or her future. A child who picks a cake or other food will be a government official (which makes me wonder why I'm not mayor of my town); picking a book means the child will be a scholar, while a sword foretells a military commander. Departing guests are given rice cakes to take home. This sharing of rice cakes on the first birthday is thought to bring the child long life and happiness.

UNITED STATES: BABY SHOWER CAKES

Parties for an expectant mother's first baby, known as baby showers, are popular throughout the United States. The classic baby shower cake is a golden sheet cake with white buttercream frosting and cute images of storks, baby booties, and rubber ducks adorning the top. I've seen some truly over-the-top baby shower cakes: domed cakes decorated to look like a pregnant belly, a life-size marzipan baby, and even a marzipan mom giving birth with the baby's head popping out of, well, you can guess where! But this is far from standard fare.

Also common at baby showers are multitiered nonedible cakes made out of rolled-up diapers to provide an ample supply for a baby's first months. Diaper cakes may be filled with gifts of baby lotion, shampoo, diaper cream, and other necessities to help the mother care for her baby.

VIETNAM: BANH TET AND BANH CHUNG

On Tet, the Vietnamese New Year, all new babies turn one, regardless of when they were born, and the community celebrates new lives and the New Year all at once. A savory banana-wrapped rice cake filled with green bean paste and fat pork or mung bean is prepared for the celebration. In southern Vietnam the cake is prepared as a log and sliced into rounds, and it's called banh tet. In northern Vietnam the cake is square in shape, and it's known as banh chung.

OPPOSITE, LEFT: *an American baby shower cake in the shape of an alphabet block*
OPPOSITE, RIGHT: *petits fours (page 106)*
RIGHT: *a Chinese baby shares cake with her grandmother*

Seed Cake

Seed cake is a customary treat for the Jewish holiday Purim. Depending on where it's made, the type of seed may vary, with poppyseeds, caraway seeds, sesame seeds, and anise seeds all being popular. This recipe uses a combination of seeds that give it a spicy taste and unique texture.

Seed Cake

- 2 cups all-purpose flour
- 1 teaspoon baking powder
- ½ teaspoon ground allspice
- ½ teaspoon salt
- 1 cup (2 sticks) unsalted butter, softened
- 1 cup sugar
- 5 eggs
- 1 teaspoon vanilla extract
- ¼ cup milk
- 2 tablespoons sesame seeds
- 2 teaspoons anise seeds
- 2 teaspoons poppyseeds
- 1 teaspoon caraway seeds

Toppings

- 2 cups vanilla icing (page 317)
- 2 tablespoons mixed seeds (caraway, sesame, anise, and poppy)

Makes 8 individual-serving cakes

TO PREPARE

Preheat the oven to 375°F. Butter and flour eight 4-inch dome cake pans.

TO MAKE THE CAKE

Combine the flour, baking powder, allspice, and salt in a medium bowl; set aside. In a separate large bowl, cream the butter and sugar with a mixer until light and fluffy. Add the eggs one at a time, beating well after each addition, then stir in the vanilla. Gradually add the flour mixture, alternating with the milk, until well blended. Stir in the sesame seeds, anise seeds, poppyseeds, and caraway seeds.

TO BAKE

Pour the batter into the prepared pans and bake for 20 to 25 minutes, until a knife inserted in the center comes out clean. Let cool in the pans.

TO SERVE

Pour the icing either on the serving plate (setting the cake on top of it) or over the cake. Sprinkle with seeds.

VARIATIONS

American Orange Poppyseed Cake

Replace the vanilla with the juice of one orange. Omit the caraway, anise, and sesame seeds, and increase the poppyseeds to ¼ cup. Omit the allspice. Top with 2 cups orange icing (page 316) instead of vanilla icing.

Cyprus Sunflower Seed Cake

Replace the sesame seeds, anise seeds, caraway seeds, and poppyseeds in the batter with 1 cup sunflower seeds. Sprinkle sunflower seeds on top.

Purim

Purim is a Jewish holiday commemorating the deliverance of Jews in ancient Persia from the massacre planned by Haman, vizier to King Ahasuerus. Ahasuerus was informed of the plot by his wife, Esther, who was a Jew. The story is told in the Old Testament book of Esther.

Purim is celebrated with a carnival-like atmosphere. The Talmud states that everyone should "eat, drink, and be merry," and they do. Celebrations include masquerades, puppet shows, beauty contests, plays, and lots and lots of food. Seeds (mainly poppyseeds) are a traditional ingredient in Purim foods, honoring the sacrifices Queen Esther made to keep kosher when she came to the king's palace as a candidate for his wife: declining to eat the palace's nonkosher meals, she subsisted on poppyseeds, nuts, and legumes.

Purim lays down four mitzvoth, or laws: send gifts to friends, eat a festive meal, give to the poor, and listen to a reading of the book of Esther. So as I see it, this cake can be very handy. You can bake one for a friend, eat one during the meal, give one to the poor, and invite friends over to read the book of Esther and share some cake.

Pistachio-Rosewater Cake

Iranian cakes are influenced by the traditions of India, the Middle East, and Europe. Here, rosewater, cumin, lime, and allspice combine in a marvelous blend. Sweet and nutty pistachios stud the cake, filling, and topping. For a special occasion, top each slice with a candied rose petal. And after you try the main recipe, try the variation with tangy apricots and almonds. Both are excellent with a glass of white wine.

Pistachio Cake
- 1½ cups all-purpose flour
- 1 teaspoon baking powder
- 1 teaspoon salt
- ½ teaspoon ground cumin
- ¼ teaspoon ground allspice
- 1 cup unsalted butter, softened
- 1 cup granulated sugar
- ¼ cup honey
- 1 tablespoon rosewater
- 1 teaspoon lime juice
- 6 eggs, separated
- 1 cup pistachios, toasted and chopped

Candied Rose Petals
- ¼ cup rose petals
- 2 egg whites
- 1 cup coarse sugar

Rosewater Icing
- 2½ cups confectioners' sugar
- 2 tablespoons milk
- 1½ tablespoons rosewater
- 2 teaspoons lime juice

Toppings
- ¼ cup chopped pistachios
- Rose petals

Makes 1 cake (serves 6 to 8)

TO PREPARE
Preheat the oven to 350°F. Butter a 9-inch round cake pan.

TO MAKE THE CAKE
Combine the flour, baking powder, salt, cumin, and allspice in a medium bowl; mix well and set aside. In a separate large bowl, cream the butter and sugar until light and creamy. Add the honey, rosewater, and lime juice, and mix well. Blend in the egg yolks. Gradually mix the flour mixture into the butter mixture, until fully incorporated.

Beat the egg whites until they hold stiff peaks. Fold the whites into the batter, followed by the chopped pistachios.

TO BAKE
Pour the batter into the prepared pan and bake for 35 to 40 minutes, until a knife inserted in the center comes out clean. Remove the cake from the pan and set on a rack to cool.

TO MAKE THE CANDIED ROSE PETALS
Using a small brush, lightly coat both sides of each rose petal with egg whites. Sprinkle each petal with sugar. Set the coated petals on waxed paper or parchment paper and let sit until firm, about 1 hour.

TO MAKE THE ICING
Combine the confectioners' sugar, milk, rosewater, and lime juice, and mix well. Add more milk or sugar as necessary to reach a spreading consistency.

TO SERVE
Spread the rosewater icing over the top and sides of the cake. Create a border around the edges with chopped pistachios and arrange the candied rose petals in the center.

VARIATIONS

Apricot-Almond Cake
Heat ½ cup dried apricots and ½ cup golden raisins in 1 cup white wine and simmer for about 30 minutes, until the wine is absorbed. Add the plumped fruit to the cake batter. Replace the pistachios with almonds.

Cherry-Pistachio Cake
Heat 1 cup dried cherries in ¾ cup cherry juice and simmer for about 30 minutes, until the juice is absorbed. Add the plumped fruit to the cake batter.

Rosewater

Rosewater, made from a solution of rose petals in water, gives Iranian sweets a distinctive floral flavor. Muslims, who abstain from alcohol for religious reasons, often use it as a substitute for wine in cooking. It was common in European and American cooking until the nineteenth century, when vanilla extract became readily available.

Persian Cakes

Since the time of the Persian Empire, Iranians have considered the preparation of food to be an art capable of providing both physical and emotional fulfillment. Food is said to be able to either weaken or strengthen character. Fruits, vegetables, fish, and flower blossoms are said to create powers that make us gentle and noble, while excessive amounts of red meat and fats are said to create evil thoughts and make us selfish. This cake has a bit of both, in my opinion, making those who indulge completely balanced persons.

Pomegranate Cake

Pomegranates are widely used in Iranian cuisine. This cake is my innovation on a Persian butter cake. To boost the flavor and the temptation I have added pomegranate juice and seeds, lime, and a touch of rosewater. The pomegranate sugar syrup that is widely used in Middle Eastern cooking inspired the pomegranate sauce.

Pomegranate Cake

2¾	cups all-purpose flour
½	teaspoon baking soda
¼	teaspoon salt
½	cup granulated sugar
½	cup light brown sugar
½	cup (1 stick) unsalted butter, softened
3	eggs
½	cup milk
½	cup pomegranate juice
	Juice of 1 lime
1	teaspoon grated lime zest
1	teaspoon vanilla extract
¼	teaspoon rosewater
¾	cup pomegranate seeds

Pomegranate Sauce

1	cup pomegranate juice
	Juice of 1 lime
¼	cup granulated sugar
1	teaspoon cornstarch
½	cup pomegranate seeds
¼	teaspoon rosewater

Makes 2 cakes (each serving 4)

TO PREPARE

Preheat the oven to 350°F. Butter and flour two 6-inch round pans with high sides.

TO MAKE THE CAKE

Combine the flour, baking soda, and salt in a medium bowl; set aside. In a separate large bowl, beat the sugars and butter with a mixer until light and fluffy. Add the eggs one at a time, beating well after each addition. Add the flour mixture to the butter mixture, alternating with the milk, and blend well. Stir in the pomegranate juice, lime juice, lime zest, vanilla, and rosewater. Fold in the pomegranate seeds.

TO BAKE

Pour the batter into the prepared pans. Bake for 50 minutes to 1 hour, until a knife inserted in the center comes out clean. Let the cakes cool in their pans for 15 minutes, then remove them from the pans and set on a rack to finish cooling.

TO MAKE THE SAUCE

Combine the pomegranate juice, lime juice, sugar, and cornstarch in a saucepan over medium heat, and stir until the solids are dissolved. Add the pomegranate seeds and cook for 3 to 5 minutes, until the sauce has thickened. Remove the pan from the heat and stir in the rosewater.

TO SERVE

Serve the sauce alongside the cakes; or puddle a spoonful of sauce to one side of each serving plate, slice the cake, and place it on the sauce.

VARIATION

Indian Spice Pomegranate Cake
Omit the rosewater from the cake and sauce. Add ½ teaspoon ground cardamom and ¼ teaspoon ground coriander to the cake batter.

History of the Pomegranate

The tart, fruity taste of pomegranate is relatively new for most of the world, but it has been enjoyed in the Middle East and Asia for thousands of years. There is even a Sanskrit word for pomegranate. Arab caravans, emanating from Baghdad, carried pomegranates with them, and slowly the fruit gained a widening circle of popularity. It arrived in Europe through Sicily, and from there spread to the New World. Appropriately enough, given its great volume of seeds, the pomegranate is a traditional symbol of fertility.

Baklava

Opinions differ on the proper way to make baklava. Some soak this pastry cake with olive oil, while others use butter. Some swear by almonds, while others insist upon pistachios. Some prefer a triangular pastry, some make nests, some make squares or diamonds, and others roll it into a log. I prefer my baklava with butter and a combination of walnuts and pistachios, and I love to make all of the shapes. Unrefrigerated baklava retains its crispy texture, but if you prefer yours chewy, refrigerate it for a few hours before indulging.

Nut Filling

- 4 cups chopped walnuts
- 4 cups chopped pistachios
- ½ cup sugar
- 1 tablespoon ground cinnamon
- 2 teaspoons ground cloves

Assembly

- 1 pound large (14- by 18-inch) phyllo sheets
- 1½ cups (3 sticks) unsalted butter, melted

Topping

- ⅔ cup honey syrup (page 318)

Makes 1 cake (serves 6 to 8)

TO PREPARE

Preheat the oven to 350°F. Butter the bottom and sides of a 14- by 18-inch baking sheet.

TO MAKE THE NUT FILLING

Combine the walnuts, pistachios, sugar, cinnamon, and cloves in a large bowl; mix well.

TO ASSEMBLE

Place a sheet of phyllo on the prepared pan. Brush with melted butter. Repeat with three additional sheets. Spread one-third of the nut filling evenly over the pastry. Repeat these layers until you have stacked three layers of pastry and three layers of the nut filling. Top with a final four sheets of phyllo, brushing each with butter. Brush the remaining butter on top. Use a sharp knife to cut the cake into squares or diamonds, cutting all the way to the bottom.

TO BAKE

Bake for 35 to 40 minutes, until golden. Remove from the oven and let cool on the baking sheet.

TO SERVE

Pour the honey syrup over the cooled baklava. Let sit for 2 to 3 hours before serving.

VARIATIONS

Almond-Pistachio Baklava Nests

Replace the butter with ¾ cup olive oil. Substitute almonds for the walnuts. Shape the phyllo into 2½-inch cups, and top with pistachios. Soak the baked baklava with ⅔ cup lemon syrup (page 318) instead of honey syrup.

Apricot Baklava

Set three sheets of phyllo on the baking sheet, brushing each with butter. Spread ⅓ cup apricot jam over the top phyllo sheet, followed by a layer of nut filling. Roll into a long, skinny log, and brush with butter. Repeat to make four logs. Bake for 20 to 25 minutes. Top with honey syrup.

Walnut Triangle Baklava

Set six sheets of phyllo on the baking sheet, brushing each with butter. Prepare the nut filling as directed, replacing the pistachios with more walnuts, and spread over the phyllo. Roll the phyllo into a wide log, then cut a series of diagonal slits in opposing directions about three-quarters of the way across the top of the log, slashing the top crust into triangle shapes and exposing the filling. Brush the top with butter, bake, and top with honey syrup.

Who Gets Bragging Rights?

Although the Turks claim phyllo pastry as their own, Iranians claim their Persian ancestors saw the potential of this light and layered pastry, adding the syrup and nuts to create baklava, now a staple in Middle Eastern bakeries from Istanbul to Los Angeles. Of course, Armenians and Greeks also love baklava and claim to have invented it too, as do other Middle Eastern and central Asian cultures. When it comes down to it, there's no way to be sure — I'm just glad someone somewhere thought of it!

Kanafeh

Kanafeh is a type of shredded phyllo dough, and the pastry made from that dough carries the same name. You can find the dough in Middle Eastern and Greek markets in different thread sizes; I use the rough variety for this recipe. If you cannot find kanafeh, you can substitute regular phyllo, shredding the sheets into very thin strips with a knife. The most authentic way to prepare kanafeh pastry is with nabulsi, a type of goat cheese with a mild, tangy taste. The goat cheese typically found in the United States is a bit saltier, so I cut it with ricotta to give the kanafeh a sweeter taste. In Jordan sweets like kanafeh are eaten between meals, while fruits are eaten for dessert.

Cheese Filling
1 cup ricotta cheese

¾ cup goat cheese

Assembly
½ pound rough kanafeh

¾ cup (1½ sticks) unsalted butter, melted

Toppings
¾ cup lemon syrup (page 318)

Candied cherries

¼ cup ground pistachios

Makes 1 cake (serves 6 to 8)

TO PREPARE
Preheat the oven to 325°F. Butter and flour a 9-inch square cake pan.

TO MAKE THE FILLING
Combine the ricotta and goat cheese, and mix until smooth.

TO MAKE THE CAKE
Pull apart the kanafeh threads by hand, and set half of them in the prepared pan. Brush on ¼ cup of the melted butter. Spread the cheese filling over the kanafeh. Top with the remaining kanafeh and butter. Bake for 35 to 45 minutes, or until golden brown.

TO SERVE
Allow the cake to cool for 5 minutes, then pour the lemon syrup over it. Serve warm, topping each serving with a candied cherry and ground pistachios.

VARIATIONS

Kanafeh Baklava

Substitute the baklava nut filling (page 235) for the cheese filling.

Kanafeh Nests

Butter and flour two large six-cup muffin pans. Form the kanafeh into a cup inside each muffin cup, leaving a well in the center. Soak the kanafeh with the butter. Fill each kanafeh cup with the 2 tablespoons of the cheese filling and top with

1 teaspoon whole pistachios. Bake for 25 to 30 minutes, until golden brown.

Turkish Kadayif

Add 1 cup chopped walnuts to the cheese mixture and ½ cup chopped pistachios to the syrup. Serve with clotted cream.

LARGE TRAY: *kanafeh baklava (at left), accompanied by baklava variations (page 235);* SMALLER TRAY: *qatayef (page 237);* AT FAR RIGHT AND AT THE BACK: *kanafeh, in squares and nests*

Qatayef

At sunset throughout Palestine during the Muslim holy month of Ramadan you will find vendors with hot plates lining the streets preparing these flat cakes. They are made in many different ways; this version is filled with cheese and nuts and then fried. Instead of the syrup, you can also top the cakes with cinnamon sugar.

Cake
- 1 teaspoon sugar
- ½ teaspoon active dry yeast
- 1¼ cups warm water
- 2½ cups whole-wheat flour
- ½ cup all-purpose flour
- ⅛ teaspoon salt
- Vegetable oil for frying

Walnut-Cheese Filling
- 1 cup chopped walnuts
- 1 cup goat cheese
- 2 tablespoons honey
- 1 tablespoon orange-blossom water

Orange Blossom–Cinnamon Syrup
- 1 cup sugar
- ¼ cup water
- ¾ cup light corn syrup
- ½ teaspoon ground cinnamon
- 2 tablespoons orange-blossom water

Makes 10 to 12 cakes

TO MAKE THE BATTER
Stir the sugar and yeast into the warm water. Let sit for 10 minutes, until foamy. Combine the whole-wheat flour, all-purpose flour, and salt. Add the yeast mixture, mix well, and let sit in a warm place for 30 minutes.

TO MAKE THE FILLING
Combine the walnuts, goat cheese, honey, and orange-blossom water.

TO MAKE THE SYRUP
Combine the sugar and water in a saucepan over medium heat, and heat, stirring, until the sugar is dissolved. Add the corn syrup and cinnamon and continue to cook, stirring, until thickened, 7 to 10 minutes. Remove from the heat and stir in the orange-blossom water.

TO COOK
Butter a large griddle, and set it over low heat. Fill a frying pan with 1 inch of oil, and set it over medium heat. Line plates with paper towels for draining the fried cakes.

Drop a small piece of bread into the oil; when it browns, the oil is ready for frying. Pour the batter onto the buttered griddle in 4- to 5-inch round cakes. When bubbles form in the tops of the cakes, transfer the cakes to a plate (do not flip them). Spread 1½ tablespoons of the walnut-cheese filling on each cake, on the uncooked side. Fold the cake in half and press the edges together to seal.

Drop the cakes into the hot oil in the frying pan. Fry the cakes for 15 to 20 seconds, or until golden on one side, then flip them and cook until the other side is golden. Drain on paper towels.

TO SERVE
Transfer the cakes to serving plates, and serve with the syrup.

VARIATION
Palestinian Coconut Qatayef
Replace the goat cheese with unsweetened shredded coconut and the orange-blossom water with lemon juice.

Ramadan Cakes

Ramadan, the ninth month of the Islamic calendar, is a month of fasting from sunrise to sunset. This is the holiest time of the year for Muslims. At the end of each day, the fast is broken with sweets. In the Middle East they're qatayef, baklava (see page 235), dates, and apricots. In India milk cakes (see page 248) and jalebis (see page 253) are the Ramadan sweets, while in Malaysia sticky rice cakes made with bananas, mangos, durian, and other tropical fruits are traditional.

THE WORLD TOUR OF
Street Cakes

WHEN I TRAVEL, SO DO MY TASTE BUDS. Rather than dining in sit-down restaurants, my taste buds and I prefer to indulge in lunches and snacks sold from stalls, carts, and railroad platforms. Sweet or savory, I love it all, but I have a particular affinity for street cakes and ice cream — the sweets designed to eat on the go. In my journeys, I've discovered that street food is the best way to taste a region's cuisine and trade stories with the locals. I can see what I am ordering even if I can't read the menu. And since snack cakes are often stirred up and fried on the spot, I can pick up preparation techniques simply by watching vendors. It's my favorite kind of performance art.

In Africa, India, Southeast Asia, and Latin America street foods are a way of everyday life, while sit-down meals are for family gatherings and special occasions. In fact, the same may be true for some Manhattanites, who are so proud of the city's pretzels, knishes, and other street-cart fare that they boast that restaurants simply aren't part of their dining repertoire. The same may be said of beach towns, where carts and stands are the very best way to get fed. Wherever your travels take you, city sidewalks, festivals, and open-air markets are all fun places to find great snacks and small meals. Just be sure to learn the local customs. In some cities, like Paris, it is considered rude to eat a brioche while walking (although they make exceptions for festivals and farmers' markets). In Singapore tables are set out to invite street-cart grazers and dim sum lovers to linger awhile, while in Buenos Aires empanadas are A-OK to eat on the move.

Look around and you'll see that many of these ethnic foods have been brought to our urban neighborhoods. In San Francisco you'll see the same street cakes and treats found in Hong Kong. In Santa Fe you'll find stalls selling churros, just like you'd find in Mexico City. A beach vacation to the New Jersey Shore is sure to yield carts of Italian zeppole, just like you'd find in Cinque Terre.

Below are some sweet snacks from distant lands to experience in your travels or without even leaving your kitchen. If you've tasted them before, isn't it high time you indulge again?

ALGERIA
Honey and nut pastries, reminiscent of sweets from the Middle East, are sold by street vendors throughout the country.

BAHAMAS
In the Bahamas, as in most of the Caribbean, you will find many street cakes made with maize or corn flour, such as johnnycakes (page 71).

CAMBODIA
Street vendors sell sweet buns from baskets carried on their heads.

CHILE
Here sopaipillas, puffy pieces of fried dough sweetened with honey, are the street cake of choice.

(continued on page 240)

BOTTOM LEFT: *street vendor selling Christmas cakes and cookies in Germany*
BOTTOM RIGHT: *Chinese street vendor selling potato cakes*
OPPOSITE, TOP LEFT: *street vendor in Ho Chi Minh City, Vietnam*
OPPOSITE, TOP RIGHT: *woman selling cakes in Battambang, Cambodia*
OPPOSITE, BOTTOM: *cakes sold outside a patisserie in Provence-Alpes-Cote d'Azur, France*

CHINA

You can enjoy baozi (page 268), steamed buns filled with various kinds of pastes, sold alongside pastry buns on almost any street.

EGYPT

Basbousa (page 208), a type of semolina cake, is sold from carts in Cairo.

ENGLAND

Buns, buns, buns, that's about it for street food. All types, all the time.

GHANA

The street cakes of choice in Ghana are sweet cassava balls.

GREECE

Tiropitakia is like tiropita (page 205) to go. In this fried pastry the cheese filling is wrapped in phyllo triangles and fried.

HAITI

Coconut cakes (page 68) are sold streetside, along with coconut milk.

INDIA

In the streets of India you'll find fried sweets like gulab jamun (page 252) and milk cakes like malpuas (page 246). Mango fritters are also popular street-cart fare. Places that still bear a Portuguese influence feature rice-flour sweets made with milk, paneer, vermicelli, and almonds.

LEFT, CLOCKWISE FROM TOP: *johnnycakes (page 71), mango cakes (page 70), and coconut cakes (page 68);* CENTER: *malpuas (page 246);* RIGHT: *Mamido burger (page 277)*

INDONESIA

The Indonesian people are passionate about their street foods. Abundant roadside stalls known as warung sell rice cakes and fruits (banana, coconut, durian, pineapple, mangosteen, and more) wrapped in banana leaves.

IRAN

Street vendors will prepare sticky date pastries right before your eyes.

ITALY

Sicilian street vendors sell pastries filled with ricotta, chocolate, and dried fruit, while in Lucca vendors sell savory fried raviolis, and in Venice they hawk sweet semolina fritters with figs.

JAMAICA

Totos are the popular coconut street cake, and bullas are the ginger spice cakes of choice.

JAPAN

Mochi (page 274) can be bought from street stalls in Tokyo, but the food specifically designed for the street is the Mamido burger (page 277). If you are into entertainment, watching dorayaki (page 276), taiyaki, or nangyo-yaki being prepared is a blast.

JORDAN

The common street cake of Jordan is kanafeh (page 236), filled with a mild goat cheese.

KOREA

Sweet rice cakes such as tteok are sold in hundreds of variations from street carts. The playful nut-shaped cakes called hodo kwaja (page 271) are also popular.

MALAYSIA

Sweet cakes can be found everywhere, mainly sticky rice and sticky banana cakes, though steamed sponge cakes such as ma lai gao are also common. Coconut sugar cakes are sold for afternoon tea.

MEXICO

Churros (page 78) and sweet fruit-filled tamales are common street sweets.

NIGERIA

Chin-chin (page 209) can be purchased at most train stations to fortify weary travelers.

PAKISTAN

Indulge in fried jalebi (page 253), mini funnel cakes soaked in rosewater-saffron syrup, and karanji coconut pastries.

PALESTINE

Qatayef flat cakes (page 237) are prepared streetside on hot plates in hundreds of variations.

PERU

Watch the picarone makers spin up their dough into perfect rings and fry it with grace and precision (page 95).

SINGAPORE

Due to government regulations, street food is sold in hawker centers, open-air markets where food carts gather, each vendor offering bites of something different, from Chinese to Malaysian, Indian, or Western food.

THAILAND

If you take a river boat ride anywhere near Bangkok, you can try hot and cold snacks and cakes sold by river dwellers from their homes as you pass by.

UNITED STATES

Carts are the thing in the U.S. Some are as big as a truck, with the vendor riding inside, while others are small handcarts that the vendor pushes. The street food offered at these carts is as varied as the U.S. population. Common street cakes include doughnuts, tamales, hush puppies, and Danishes.

VENEZUELA

You can find fruit-filled empanadas (page 90) at many farmers' markets.

LEFT, CLOCKWISE FROM TOP RIGHT: *bamluchen (German cake popular in Japan), fish cakes, bean curd cake, and chick cakes;* CENTER: *hodo kwaja (page 271);* RIGHT: *empanadas (page 90)*

241

Date Spice Cake

Dates are ubiquitous in Iraqi cuisine. This chewy spice layer cake is packed with a very sweet date filling. For a truly authentic presentation, serve it with fresh figs, dates, mint, and grapes.

Date Spice Cake

- 2 cups all-purpose flour
- 2 teaspoons baking powder
- 2 teaspoons ground cinnamon
- 2 teaspoons ground nutmeg
- ½ teaspoon ground cloves
- 1 cup (2 sticks) unsalted butter, softened
- 1 cup sugar
- 7 eggs
- 2 teaspoons vanilla extract
- 1 cup whole milk
- 1 cup pitted, chopped dates
- ½ cup chopped walnuts

Filling

- 3½ cups date filling (page 321)

Makes 1 cake (serves 6 to 8)

TO PREPARE

Preheat the oven to 350°F. Butter and flour two loaf baking pans, one 8 inches long and one 6 inches long.

TO MAKE THE DATE SPICE CAKE

Combine the flour, baking powder, cinnamon, nutmeg, and cloves in a medium bowl; set aside. In a separate large bowl, cream the butter and sugar until fluffy. Add the eggs one at a time, beating well after each addition. Stir in the vanilla. Stir the dry mixture into the butter mixture, alternating with the milk, and blend well. Stir in the dates and walnuts.

TO BAKE

Fill the larger (8-inch) pan with 1 inch of batter, and fill the smaller (6-inch) pan with 3 inches of batter. Bake the smaller cake for 20 to 25 minutes and the larger one for 45 to 55 minutes, until a knife inserted in the center comes out clean. Let cool in the pans.

TO ASSEMBLE

Stack the small cake on top of the large cake. Use a knife to cut the edges up on an angle, forming a pyramid shape. Remove the small cake, and spread half the date filling over the top of the large cake. Cut the small cake in half crosswise, creating two layers. Set one layer on top of the large cake, and spread three-quarters of the remaining date filling on top of it. Top with the final cake layer, and spread the remaining date filling over it.

The Date Culture

Iraq exports more than 500,000 tons of dates every year and cultivates more than 400 varieties. Long before dates became important for the national economy, though, they were an important part of the local culture. They are believed to be aphrodisiacs, for example, and many Iraqi men eat dozens of them on their wedding day.

Hospitality is a cornerstone of the traditional Iraqi home. Guests are offered many foods, including dates, and are expected to try them all before they can gracefully depart. A guest's refusal to overindulge in such treats would be considered an insult to the host.

CHAPTER 11

The Indian Subcontinent
Milk Sweets, Dumplings, and Candy Confections

IN MANY MELTING-POT CITIES AROUND THE WORLD, from London and Sydney to Buenos Aires and Hong Kong, it's easy to find a little bit of subcontinent cake culture to sample. When I visit the Bengali grocery in my L.A. neighborhood, I may as well be in Bengal, thousands of miles away. A well-stocked Bengali sweets shop is a cultural institution, and my neighborhood store sells more sweets than I can visually process — never mind taste! — in a single visit. Some are fried dumpling-like cakes soaked in sweet syrup for everyday eating. Others are extraordinary sweets glowing with saffron and sparkling with edible vark, a silver metal used on special-occasion cakes. If I venture to Little India, right outside of Los Angeles proper, the all-you-can-eat $6 buffets offer dozens of milk cakes, carrot sweets, and syrupy sweets to choose from.

Sweets have always been a focal point of Indian culture. Since ancient times sugar and honey have been integrated into main dishes, street snacks, and desserts, giving India a reputation for having a sweet cuisine. In Hinduism, the predominant religion of India, sweets have a special significance as foods of the gods, and they are believed to nourish both the mind and the body.

I use the term *sweets* and not *cakes* because that is what they are called throughout the Indian subcontinent. However, these small, super-sweet, milky, cheesy, and fried confections are no less cakes for not being called by that name. Indian sweets are typically dairy based, with milk and cheese as main ingredients. Their spongy texture is similar to that of English puddings or creamy cheesecakes. Milk cooked down to a pastelike consistency, known as

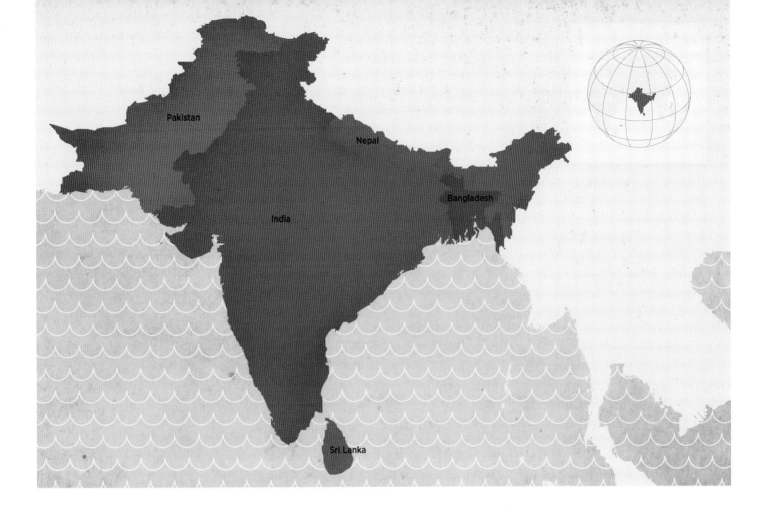

khoya or mawa, is a central ingredient in sweets such as gulab jamun (page 252). Paneer, a soft, crumbly cheese, is another common dairy ingredient; it's used in sweets such as malpuas (page 246).

Soaking sweets in syrup is a common technique. Bangladeshi jalebis (page 253), for example, are soaked in saffron syrup and then dried to a crisp. Other cheese-based dumplings are soaked in rosewater syrup just before being served.

Mango, available in dozens of varieties, is a popular ingredient that contributes both sweetness and flavor. Coconut, dates, cashews, and lemon are other major players in the cakes of the region, and Chinese and Indonesian ginger, cardamom, and cumin make frequent appearances.

Baked cakes as Westerners know them are not a traditional part of Indian culture. However, since Portuguese, Dutch, French, and British traders made their way to India beginning in the sixteenth century, European-style baking has worked its way into the cuisine of the region. Portuguese influences, for example, can be seen in the bebinca of Goa, a custardy, multilayered cake made with coconut milk for Christmastime. And European and American classics such as Black Forest cake, German chocolate cake, and strawberry shortcake have become closely associated with regional celebrations. Bakers usually prepare variations of these Western cakes using local ingredients, such as ghee (clarified butter) as a replacement for sticks of butter, madia flour (a local wheat flour) for cake flour, and barfi (a pistachio paste) for marzipan. As an interesting variation, Nepalese bakers make a chocolate barfi that tastes like the most incredible fudge.

Sri Lanka, an island nation south of India, is famous for its native spices, which include cinnamon, cardamom, and cloves, and they are often used in making sweets. Coconut is another favorite ingredient, and some of the sweets made with paneer cheese in India are made with coconut milk here. In general Sri Lankan sweets capitalize on the nation's tropical fruits, including oranges, bananas, plantains, plums, kiwifruit, and melons. As in India, sweets are given as gifts to the gods. Imagine multitudes of white-clad devotees thronging to temples, cakes in hand, accompanied by a hundred adorned elephants parading through the streets. That's Sri Lanka.

Malpuas

Malpuas are sweet Indian flat cakes. Eaten plain, they are the epitome of ease and simplicity. They are easily dressed up with fruit fillings or saffron-flavored syrup, and for special occasions they may be decorated with chopped almonds, chopped pistachios, and edible silver, known as vark. They can be eaten individually or assembled into a cake, as described in this recipe, with sweet paneer cheese as a filling between the layers. Malpuas are best served hot, with a cup of chamomile tea.

Sweet Paneer Filling
 5 saffron threads
 1 cup milk, warmed
 ¼ cup chopped pistachios
 1 teaspoon ghee or clarified butter
 1½ cups grated paneer or pressed small-curd cottage cheese
 ½ cup sweetened condensed milk
 ¼ teaspoon ground cardamom

Malpuas
 2 teaspoons fennel seeds
 1 cup plain yogurt
 1 cup all-purpose flour
 ½ teaspoon baking powder
 ¼ teaspoon ground cardamon
 ¼ cup ghee or vegetable oil

Toppings
 3 sheets vark, torn into pieces
 1¾ cups lime-saffron syrup (page 318)

Makes 10 malpuas, enough for 2 stacked cakes

TO MAKE THE SWEET PANEER FILLING
Drop the saffron threads into the warm milk and let sit for 1 hour. Combine the pistachios with the ghee in a saucepan over medium heat, and cook for about 3 minutes, until the nuts are toasted. Add the saffron milk, paneer, sweetened condensed milk, and cardamom, and cook over low heat, stirring continuously, for 7 to 8 minutes, until the mixture has thickened.

TO MAKE THE MALPUAS
Toast the fennel seeds in a dry skillet over medium heat until slightly browned, about 5 minutes. Mix the fennel seeds with the yogurt, flour, baking powder, and cardamom.

Warm the ghee in a skillet over medium heat. Pour the batter into the pan in 4-inch rounds. When the cakes are browned on the bottom, flip and cook until browned on the other side and cooked through. Remove the cakes from the pan and blot dry with paper towels. Repeat until you have used up all of the batter, adding more ghee to the pan if necessary.

TO ASSEMBLE
To make one cake, set a malpua on a serving plate, and spread a layer of paneer filling over it. Top with another malpua, spread with another layer of paneer, and repeat until you have stacked four malpuas spread with paneer. Set a final malpua on top, top with vark, and serve with lime-saffron syrup.

VARIATIONS
Pineapple Malpuas
Use 3½ cups pineapple filling (page 322) instead of sweet paneer filling.

Rose Malpuas
Add 1 teaspoon rosewater to the sweet paneer filling. Top each cake with fresh edible rose petals.

Kalakand (Milk Cakes)

In northeast India and Pakistan people enjoy many different types of milk cakes for the festival of Diwali. These cakes are usually made with paneer cheese and nuts, mostly pistachios and cashews. Although they are called milk cakes, Westerners might think of them as candy cheesecakes.

Milk Cake
4 cups milk

2 cups mashed paneer (or ricotta)

1 cup sugar

1 teaspoon ground cardamom

½ cup ground pistachios

Topping
2 mangos, sliced

Makes 1 cake (serves 6 to 8)

TO PREPARE
Butter an 8-inch square pan.

TO MAKE THE CAKE
Bring the milk to a boil in a large saucepan. Add the paneer and cook, stirring, for 4 to 5 minutes, until the mixture has thickened. Add the sugar and cardamom and cook, stirring, for an additional 4 to 5 minutes, until most of the liquid has evaporated and the mixture is very thick.

Spread half the pistachios over the bottom of the prepared pan. Pour the milk mixture over the nuts. Top with the remaining nuts. Let cool in the refrigerator for 3 hours, until the cake becomes dense.

TO SERVE
Cut the cake into cubes. Serve with sliced mangos.

VARIATION
Cashew-Orange Kalakand
Replace the pistachios with cashews. Add 1 teaspoon grated orange zest to the milk mixture.

Diwali
Diwali is a five-day-long festival celebrated by Hindus, Buddhists, Sikhs, and Jains. Many celebrate it as the Hindu New Year. (There are many calendars in Hindu India, with many different New Years.) Diwali is also known as the Festival of Lights, for during its five days celebrants light earthen lamps called diyas as a symbol of the triumph of good over evil. The light is said to represent hope, positive energy, and the renewal of life. The fifth day of the celebration, known as Bhai Dooj, honors the bond between sisters and brothers. Sisters invite their brothers to their homes and show their love by placing a tika (vermilion mark) on their brothers' foreheads. Their brothers, in turn, offer them gifts and sweets, such as milk cakes.

THE WORLD TOUR OF
New Year's Cakes

NEW YEAR'S IS A TIME TO CELEBRATE A FRESH START for yourself and to wish others well in the year ahead. Throughout the world, the new year is a time for cultures to honor gods and ancestors, give thanks for the blessings of the past year, and pray for prosperity and health in the year ahead.

In the twentieth century many countries began celebrating the universal New Year, based on the Gregorian calendar (beginning January 1), along with the New Year of whatever is their traditional calendar. For example, some Eastern Orthodox churches celebrate both the Julian New Year (based on the calendar instituted by Julius Caesar in 47 BCE) and the Gregorian New Year (based on the calendar instituted by Pope Gregory XIII in 1582, which Western culture still follows today). And many Asian cultures celebrate the lunar New Year, based on the lunar calendar.

No matter which calendar they follow, most cultures have cakes as a traditional part of their New Year's Eve and New Year's Day celebrations. Read on for a round-the-globe tour of New Year's cakes.

BRITISH ISLES

Samhain is the traditional Celtic New Year, celebrated on November 1. A pagan holiday, it aligns with the Christian All Saints' Day celebrated in Ireland, Scotland, and parts of England. In Brittany, antler-shaped kornigou cakes are baked to commemorate the god of winter shedding his horns as he returns to his kingdom in the otherworld.

Hogmanay is the Scottish holiday on the last day of the year. It's an all-night party celebrated widely and enthusiastically from New Year's Eve through January 2. While parading around the town, revelers visit friends' homes to pass out black bun cakes, fruitcakes baked in a pastry crust that symbolize a year of plenty.

Monks from Kopan monastery carrying ceremonial cakes in Tibetan New Year (Losar) procession

BULGARIA

The Bulgarian New Year is celebrated with banitsa, a feta pastry cheesecake. Like the Greek vasilopita (page 202), it is a surprise-in-your-breakfast-cake tradition. Lucky charms, coins, a small dogwood branch symbolizing health and longevity, or happy wishes written on paper and wrapped in foil are baked inside the phyllo pastry.

CAMBODIA

The Cambodian New Year, Khmer, is celebrated in mid-April and is a time for people to enjoy the fruits of their harvest and relax before the rainy season begins. Special dishes are prepared for the event, including kralan, a cake made from steamed rice mixed with beans or peas, grated coconut, and coconut milk. The mixture is stuffed inside a bamboo stick and slowly roasted, then the bamboo is peeled back and the cake baked inside it is eaten.

CHINA

Chinese New Year occurs every year on the new moon of the first lunar month. Based on the Chinese calendar, it falls between January 21 and February 21, four to eight weeks before spring. It is considered the most important celebration in Chinese culture. Preparing nian gao (sticky rice cakes; see page 258) for the kitchen god is a very important part of the tradition.

GREECE

Vasilopita (page 202), a breakfast cake similar to a coffee cake, is traditionally served at the first meal of the new year. It is prepared with a hidden coin or trinket; the finder is said to have good luck in the coming year.

INDIA

Diwali is a Hindu and Jainist holiday known as the Festival of Lights. Mango cakes, milk cakes (page 248), fried cakes, and other sweets are eaten and given as gifts during the festival.

IRAN

Nowruz is the Persian New Year, which aligns with the first day of spring. It usually takes place around March 20. Recognized in many countries formerly of Persian rule, it is commonly celebrated in Iran with pistachio-rosewater cake (page 232).

ISRAEL

Rosh Hashanah, the Jewish New Year, takes place in September or October. The most important day in the Jewish calendar, it commemorates the culmination of the seven days of creation, marking God's yearly renewal of the world. Honey is a symbol of new beginnings, so foods with honey, such as mit lechig (honey cake; see page 227), are traditionally eaten.

JAPAN

Japan's Ōmisoka, based on the Gregorian calendar, focuses on housecleaning and other preparations for the new year. Mochi rice cakes (page 274) and kuri kinton (sweet potato and chestnut cakes) are traditional.

KOREA

Seollal, the traditional Korean New Year, is celebrated in late January or early February. It is the most important of the traditional Korean holidays and is celebrated by paying respect to elders and eating rice cakes.

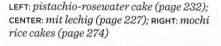

LEFT: *pistachio-rosewater cake (page 232);* CENTER: *mit lechig (page 227);* RIGHT: *mochi rice cakes (page 274)*

MONGOLIA

Tsagaan Sar, the Mongolian New Year, is celebrated with a lavish feast that is prepared for days in advance. Buuz, a savory pastry cake filled with minced lamb, is traditional.

NETHERLANDS

The Dutch like to stretch out the New Year's celebration to a full week filled with dance fairs, theater festivals, and music carnivals. Eating deep-fried oliebollen filled with apples, raisins, and currants is believed to bring good luck in the coming year.

SCANDINAVIA

The kransekake (page 162), a towering marzipan ring cake, is a favored New Year's Eve cake in all of Scandinavia. A bottle of champagne to pop open at the stroke of midnight is often hidden within the rings.

SRI LANKA

Sinhala and Tamil is Sri Lanka's New Year. It occurs in April (the month of Bak) and is determined by astrological signs. The ending of the old year and the beginning of the new year occur several hours apart, and the period in the middle is *nona gathe* (neutral period). Maintaining a happy state of mind at the first family meal is of utmost importance in attaining health for the year. Tea and spice cakes are commonly eaten.

THAILAND

On Songkran, the Thai New Year, Buddhists celebrate for three days, from April 13 to 15. People host open houses and parties, and children play in the streets. Kaungs (small oil cakes) and kokis (crisp and light sweetmeats) are important parts of the celebratory feasts. Modern cakes eaten for Songkran include mango-lychee ice cream cake (page 292) and thong muan, a crisp cookielike pastry rolled like a French pirouette.

VIETNAM

Vietnamese New Year, Tet Nguyen Dan (feast of the first morning), also known as Tet, is celebrated on the same day as Chinese New Year. It is the most important holiday in Vietnam, a time of family gatherings and ancestral worship and house cleaning. Banh bo nuong (cow cake; see page 290) is traditional.

LEFT: *nian gao (page 258);* CENTER: *mango-lychee ice cream cake (page 292);* RIGHT: *banh bo nuong (page 290)*

251

Gulab Jamun

One of my favorite restaurants is a local grocery store with a takeout counter. The owners prepare gulab jamun, little fried dumplings that are soaked in rosewater-saffron syrup. These dumplings are popular at Indian festivals, weddings, and Diwali. Traditionally the milk is cooked to a point that it almost evaporates into a paste, but this recipe uses dry milk as a shortcut. Ghee (clarified butter) is what gives the cakes their authentic taste. The dumplings can be prepared at varying levels of crispness, with color ranging from light brown to black.

2¾ cups rosewater-saffron syrup (page 319)

2 cups dry milk

1½ tablespoons self-rising flour

½ cup milk, warmed

1 pound plus 1 teaspoon ghee

Makes about 12 dumplings

TO PREPARE

Butter a large plate. Line another large plate with paper towels for draining the fried cakes. Pour the rosewater-saffron syrup into a large saucepan.

TO MAKE THE DOUGH

Stir together the powdered milk and flour; set aside. Combine the warm milk and 1 teaspoon of the ghee in a medium bowl. Add the powdered milk mixture and stir to form a dough. Grease your hands, and gather the dough into 1½-inch balls and set them on the buttered plate.

TO FRY

Add 1 pound of ghee to a wok over medium heat, and heat to 215°F. To check the temperature, drop a bit of dough into the hot ghee; if it sizzles and browns quickly, the ghee is ready for frying.

Drop the balls of dough into the heated ghee. Cook, rotating the balls with a wooden spoon, for 15 to 20 minutes. To test doneness, after 15 minutes transfer one ball to the syrup. If it does not collapse within 3 minutes, the dumplings are ready. Remove the dumplings from the hot oil and set them on paper towels to drain. Then drop them into the syrup, and let sit for 2 hours.

To serve, heat over medium heat for 5 to 7 minutes, until warm.

Jalebi

Jalebis are small, bright yellow, web-shaped cakes similar to funnel cakes. They are popular celebration and street cakes in Bangladesh, Nepal, Pakistan, and India. Soaking them in saffron syrup and then drying them gives the cakes a crispy outer shell. They are made with maida flour (a finely milled wheat flour) and Bengal gram flour (a flour milled from chickpeas), both of which can be found at Indian groceries. If you can't find them, use cake or pastry flour. If you can find fresh yeast, use it instead of the dry yeast; that is the traditional method and it adds to the flavor.

1½ teaspoons active dry yeast

1 tablespoon plus ⅔ cup water

1½ cups maida flour

2 teaspoons Bengal gram flour

1½ tablespoons ghee, melted

1½ teaspoons sugar

1 teaspoon lemon juice

4 drops yellow food coloring

2 cups ghee for frying, melted

1¾ cups lime-saffron syrup (page 318)

Makes 8 jalebis

TO MAKE THE BATTER

Dissolve the yeast in 1 tablespoon of the water and let sit for just 10 minutes, and no longer. In a large bowl, combine the maida flour and Bengal gram flour. Add the yeast, melted ghee, sugar, lemon juice, yellow food coloring, and remaining ⅔ cup water and mix until there are no more lumps.

TO FRY THE JALEBIS

Melt enough ghee in a heavy-bottomed pot to fill it 1 inch deep. Line plates with paper towels for draining the fried cakes. Pour the lime-saffron syrup into a saucepan over low heat, to keep it warm. Fit a pastry bag with a small writing tip, and pour the batter into the bag.

Squeeze 2-inch round whorls of batter into the hot ghee, working closely from the center out. Fry until golden brown on the bottom, then flip to fry on the other side until it's golden brown. Remove the jalebis from the oil and set on paper towels to drain. Transfer the hot cakes to the lime-saffron syrup and let soak for a minute or two.

TO SERVE

Serve the jalebis warm in small bowls with syrup. Or you can remove the jalebis from the syrup and set on a rack to dry for 3 to 4 hours, until the syrup has formed a hard shell.

VARIATION

Indian Spice Jalebi

Add ½ teaspoon ground cardamom to the batter and 3 whole cloves to the syrup.

Carrot-Rice Cake with Yogurt Sauce

Carrot halwa is a popular sweet in Nepal and India made from grains, nuts, and sometimes milk. This recipe, made with regional basmati rice, presents the flavors of halwa in a new cakelike way. Serve with the deliciously addictive yogurt sauce and rice fruit salad.

Carrot-Rice Cake
- 2 cups all-purpose flour
- ½ cup rice flour
- 2 teaspoons baking powder
- 1 teaspoon ground cinnamon
- 1 teaspoon freshly grated ginger
- ½ teaspoon baking soda
- ½ teaspoon salt
- ½ teaspoon ground cardamom
- ½ teaspoon ground cumin
- 1 cup cooked basmati white rice
- ½ cup chopped pistachios
- ½ cup golden raisins
- 3 eggs
- 1¼ cups light brown sugar
- ½ cup (1 stick) unsalted butter, melted
- 2 carrots, grated

Yogurt Sauce
- 2½ cups plain yogurt
- ½ cup confectioners' sugar
- 3 tablespoons chopped pistachios

Rice Fruit Salad
- 2 cups cooked basmati rice
- 1 mango, peeled and cubed
- 1 sprig mint, chopped
- 1 orange, peeled, sliced, and chopped
- Juice of 1 lemon

Makes 12 individual-serving cakes

TO PREPARE
Preheat the oven to 350°F. Butter and flour a shortcake pan (a pan that makes a cake with a well in its center) or two cupcake pans.

TO MAKE THE CAKE
Combine the flour, rice flour, baking powder, cinnamon, ginger, baking soda, salt, cardamom, and cumin. Stir in the rice, pistachios, and raisins. In a separate bowl, beat the eggs for 2 minutes, until foamy. Add the brown sugar and beat for an additional 2 minutes. Stir in the melted butter and the grated carrots until blended. Make a well in the center of the flour mixture. Pour the egg mixture into the flour mixture and mix until the batter is just blended.

TO BAKE
Pour the batter into the prepared pan and bake for 25 to 30 minutes, until a knife inserted in the center comes out clean. Let cool in pan.

TO MAKE THE YOGURT SAUCE
Stir together the yogurt, confectioners' sugar, and pistachios.

TO MAKE THE RICE FRUIT SALAD
Combine the rice with the mango, mint, orange, and lemon juice. Toss to mix.

TO SERVE
Spoon some sauce onto the serving plate, and place the cake on it. Spoon the rice salad into the well in the cake.

VARIATION
Carrot-Rice Cake with Saffron Yogurt Sauce

Combine ¼ teaspoon saffron threads with 1 tablespoon warm milk, and let sit for 30 minutes. Add the saffron milk to the yogurt sauce.

Milk Sponge Cake with Avocado Crazy

Milk cakes of the Indian subcontinent can range from the dense candy confection known as kalakand (page 248) to this soft, spongy cake. The key to its great texture is the addition of hot milk and jaggery, a type of brown unrefined palm sugar. It's traditionally served with creamy avocado crazy, another Sri Lankan specialty.

Sponge Cake

- 1 cup all-purpose flour
- 1 teaspoon baking powder
- ¼ teaspoon salt
- ½ teaspoon ground cardamom
- 1 teaspoon jaggery or muscovado sugar
- 2 tablespoons unsalted butter
- ½ cup milk, hot
- 1 cup granulated sugar
- 2 eggs
- 1 teaspoon vanilla extract
- ½ cup ground cashews
- 1 tablespoon sesame seeds

Avocado Crazy

- 3 avocados, pitted and peeled
- 3 tablespoons granulated sugar
- 1 teaspoon lemon juice
- 1 cup heavy cream
- 1 teaspoon rum

Toppings

- 2 avocados, pitted, peeled, and sliced
- 2 tablespoons lemon juice

Makes 1 cake (serves 6 to 8)

TO PREPARE

Preheat the oven to 350°F. Butter and flour an 8-inch round baking pan.

TO MAKE THE CAKE

Combine the flour, baking powder, salt, cardamom, and jaggery; set aside. Combine the butter and hot milk in a large bowl, and stir until the butter is melted. Add the sugar and beat for 3 to 5 minutes, until the mixture has thickened. Beat in the eggs and vanilla. Gradually add the flour mixture, blending well. Fold in the cashews.

TO BAKE

Transfer the batter to the prepared pan and sprinkle with sesame seeds. Bake for 20 to 25 minutes, until a knife inserted in the center comes out clean. Let cool in the pan.

TO MAKE THE AVOCADO CRAZY

Mash together the avocados, sugar, and lemon juice until smooth. Whip the heavy cream until thick but not stiff. Stir the rum into the whipped cream, then fold the whipped cream into the avocado mixture. Cover and refrigerate for at least 1 hour.

TO SERVE

Set the cake on a serving plate, and top with avocado crazy. Top with sliced avocados and lemon juice.

CHAPTER 12

The Far East
Good-for-Your-Soul Sweets

WHY DOES A NICE ITALIAN GIRL FROM STATEN ISLAND spend so much time hanging out at Asian bakeries in Los Angeles? Because I love fried sesame balls, chewy rice cakes, green tea sponge cake, and steamed adzuki-bean buns. I can say without hesitation that the cakes in this chapter are my all-time favorites. Far Eastern cultures often attribute philosophical meanings to foods. Cakes are said to contribute to the balance of mind and body by providing a meaningful life experience. I can testify firsthand that this is true! I am confident that these Asian cakes will bring you deep pleasure and deep thoughts, too.

Cake recipes and traditions from China, Taiwan, Korea, and Japan vary depending on the culture of origin, but there are also many commonalities. Generally I divide the cakes from these regions into two types: traditional Asian cakes and Western-inspired cakes.

Rice flour is the main ingredient in traditional Far Eastern cakes. Depending on the type, rice flour produces a sticky, almost gelatin-like cake or a somewhat chewy cake. Taro and tapioca are also sometimes used as starch bases. These cakes are so different from Western cakes that some critics might not consider them cakes at all. But I love Korean tteok, Taiwanese longevity peach buns, and Japanese mochi precisely because they offer an unfamiliar cake experience. If they are called cakes by the locals, that's good enough for me.

You don't find many sweet pastes in Western cakes, but they're a traditional filling in Asian fare. Many traditional Asian cakes make use of sweet pastes, such as those of lotus seeds, red beans, pineapple, and winter melons. Sweet buns filled with such pastes are often eaten at dim sum, and they're considered fine breakfast or snack cakes much like the pastries, Danishes, or sweet breads in Western cultures.

Western-influenced cakes offer more traditional European and American flavors and presentations, but they often feature a uniquely Asian twist on ingredients or

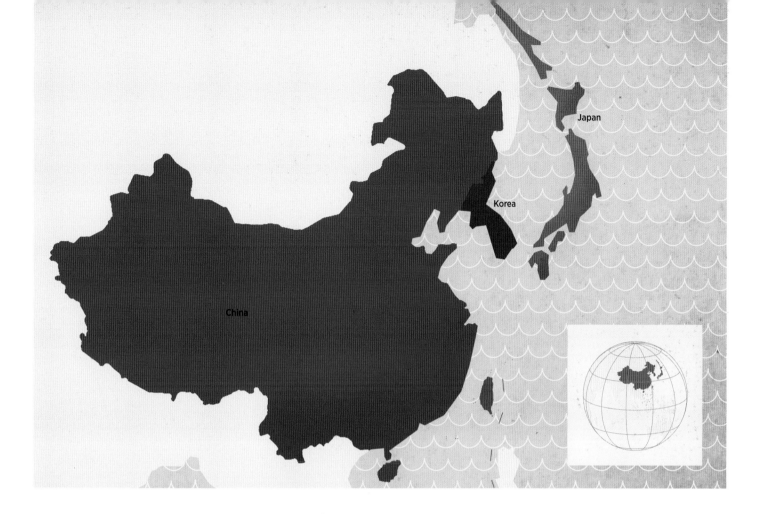

techniques. Asian interpretations of familiar cake recipes can make for some fun surprises. For example, the Japanese add green tea to sponge cakes, and the Chinese steam them in woks. Japanese Swiss rolls feature unique tiger patterns and amazing marbling techniques. In general, these Asian-interpreted cakes tend to be less sweet, minimalist, or prettier versions of the Western originals.

Chinese culture endows an ornate symbolism to its food traditions. Food is seen as a means of nourishing the body, the spirit, and the psyche. Knowing the full attributes of a food creates a more fulfilling eating experience — and life. For cakes, the round shape signifies family union and togetherness. The rich sweetness symbolizes the richness and sweetness of life. The stickiness symbolizes cohesiveness. And the layers signify growth and a long life.

In China and Taiwan dried and candied fruits, seeds, nuts, and ginger are added to cakes whole or as thick pastes. Lotus seed, winter melon, and red bean pastes are popular fillings in everything from traditional mooncakes (page 260) to longevity peach buns (page 268). Fresh-fruit favorites include melons, pineapple, grapes, kumquats, loquats, mangos, apricots, plums, persimmons, oranges, and, most common of all, strawberries, as in steamed almond sponge cake with strawberries (page 264). Cakes are usually white, though to convey joy and luck they may be dyed a bright color like pink or red.

Japanese cakes also make great use of fresh fruits, as well as chestnuts and poppyseeds. Mochi (page 274), a sweet, chewy Japanese cake made with rice flour, can be found in every flavor imaginable. Mochi are used in all religious and agricultural rituals and are an important part of the Japanese New Year's celebration.

In Korea (North and South alike), as in other Far Eastern countries, fruits and nuts are popular in celebration cakes. You'll find pears, sweet potatoes, and chestnuts in Christmas cakes, winter melons in mooncakes for the New Year, and cherries, persimmons, oranges, and grapes in children's cakes. The traditional celebration of a baby's one-hundredth day is a momentous affair employing rice, red bean, and black bean cakes in various rituals. A child's first birthday, or tol, is considered even more important and is celebrated with a great volume of rice cakes. The super-cute Korean saeng cream cakes (page 270) are also traditional birthday offerings.

Nian Gao (Sticky Rice Cake)

Nian gao is molded in banana leaves or pans. Fish-shaped pans are traditional, but any pan will do. The cake is steamed, as are most traditional Chinese cakes. Its main ingredients are glutinous rice flour, peen tong (brown slab candy), dried fruit, and nuts. The peen tong is traditionally scraped down into sugar. It's labor-intensive, so many cooks dissolve the slabs of sugar in water instead — less authentic, but much easier. Glutinous rice flour and peen tong are available in most Asian markets. If you can't find peen tong, brown sugar will also do the trick.

1 tablespoon vegetable oil or nonstick cooking spray

6 banana leaves (optional)

¾ cup chopped dried dates, peaches, prunes, or apricots, or a mixture

⅔ cup chopped peen tong or dark brown sugar

1¾–2 cups water

3¼ cups glutinous rice flour

1 tablespoon milk

¼ cup chopped walnuts

Makes 6 individual-serving cakes

TO PREPARE

Ready a wok or pot for steaming by filling it with 1 inch of water and fitting a rack in it (page 25). Grease a large six-cup muffin tin with vegetable oil or cooking spray. Line each cup with a banana leaf, if using, wrapping the leaf around the edges and over the bottom.

Set the dried fruit in one heat-proof bowl and the peen tong in another. Bring 1 cup of the water to a boil. Pour half over the dried fruit and the rest over the peen tong. Let sit for at least 30 minutes, until the fruit has softened and the peen tong has dissolved. Drain the fruit.

TO MAKE THE DOUGH

Place the rice flour in a large bowl. Make a well in the middle and stir in the sugar mixture. Add the milk and stir to combine. Mix ¾ to 1 cup of water into the dough, 1 tablespoon at a time, until you have smooth dough with a satiny texture. As you are adding the water, add the dried fruits and walnuts as well. When the dough is ready, divide it among the cups of the prepared pan, spreading it out to the edges of each cup.

TO STEAM THE CAKE

Bring the water in the wok or pot to a boil, then reduce the heat to medium. Set the cake pan on the rack, cover, and steam for 45 minutes, or until the edges of the cake pull away from the pan. Remove the cake from the steamer and let cool in the pan.

TO SERVE

Serve the cakes in their banana-leaf cups, and eat with a spoon. If you need to store leftovers, wrap them in plastic and put them in the refrigerator.

VARIATIONS

Nian Gao with Adzuki Beans

Replace ¾ cup dried fruits with ¾ cup adzuki beans (canned, or soaked in water overnight).

Shaped Nian Gao

Prepare the steaming wok or pot by filling it with 1 inch of apple juice instead of water. Omit the banana leaves. Grease a 7-inch fish, ring, or detailed gelatin mold with vegetable oil or nonstick cooking spray. Press the dough into the mold, and steam as directed.

Appeasing the Kitchen God

Nian gao is China's most famous cake. According to custom, this gooey steamed rice cake is prepared for the kitchen god, one of the most important of the Chinese domestic gods, charged with protecting hearth and family. Just before the Chinese New Year, he returns to heaven to give a report to the Jade Emperor (the ruler of heaven) about the family's activities of the past year. Based on the kitchen god's report, the Jade Emperor rewards or punishes the family.

Every year, just before New Year's, Chinese families prepare nian gao for the kitchen god. According to different accounts, the cake is either a bribe, given in exchange for a favorable report, or a means of ensuring that the kitchen god's mouth is too full and sticky from the cake to voice an unfavorable report. In the end, the families who prepare the cakes enjoy them, much like Mom and Dad enjoy cookies left for Santa. Good luck on your character review in the coming year!

Mooncakes

Mooncakes are pastry crusts wrapped around a sweet filling. The crust in this recipe is chewy, in the Guangzhou style. (Suzhou-style mooncakes have a flaky crust, and other mooncakes in China and Taiwan are made with a tender shortcrust pastry.) The cakes are usually shaped and embossed in a mold; if you don't have a mooncake mold, shape them into balls and use red food coloring to emboss them. While the cakes are baking, your house will smell like a delicious Chinese bakery stocking up for the Midautumn Festival.

Filling

2¾	cups lotus seed paste, store-bought or homemade (page 322)
¼	cup chopped walnuts

Pastry Crust

4	cups all-purpose flour
½	cup nonfat dry milk
1	tablespoon baking powder
½	teaspoon salt
3	eggs
1	cup sugar
½	cup shortening, melted and cooled

Egg Wash

2	egg yolks, lightly beaten
1	tablespoon water

Makes 20 mooncakes

TO PREPARE

Preheat the oven to 375°F.

TO MAKE THE FILLING

Combine the lotus seed paste with the walnuts, and mix well.

TO MAKE THE DOUGH

Combine the flour, dry milk, baking powder, and salt. In a separate large bowl, beat the eggs with a mixer until light. Add the sugar and beat for 7 to 10 minutes, until the batter reaches the ribbon stage (it will fall back into the bowl in a ribbon-like line when the beaters are lifted; see page 24). Blend in the shortening, then fold in the flour mixture.

TO SHAPE

Knead the dough on a floured work surface until it is smooth and satiny. Divide the dough in half and roll each half into a log. Cut each log into ten pieces. Roll each piece into a ball, and press it down to make a 4-inch circle about ⅛ inch thick. Spoon 1 tablespoon filling onto the center of each circle. Fold over the dough, pressing the edges to seal.

If you have a mooncake mold, lightly flour its inside. Place a cake, seam side up, in the mold; flatten the dough to conform to the shape of the mold. Remove the cake from the mold and place on an ungreased baking sheet. If you don't have a mooncake mold, shape into a flattened disk. Repeat to shape the remaining cakes.

TO BAKE

Combine the egg yolks with the water. Brush the tops of the cakes with the egg wash. Bake for 25 to 30 minutes, or until golden brown. Transfer to a rack and let cool.

VARIATIONS

Chocolate-Adzuki Mooncake

For the crust, reduce the flour to 3½ cups, and add ½ cup unsweetened cocoa powder. Fill the mooncakes with 2¾ cups store-bought or homemade sweet adzuki bean paste (page 322).

Taiwanese Moonlight Cake

Replace the filling with a blend of 2 cups cooked and mashed sweet potatoes, ¼ cup dark brown sugar, ¼ cup glutinous rice flour, and 1 teaspoon vanilla extract.

The Midautumn Festival

Since ancient times this festival has celebrated the autumn equinox, the full moon of the 15th day of the eighth month in the Chinese calendar (usually falling around late September or early October). Many myths of lunar deities are associated with this holiday, though the most prevalent is the story of Chang'e, the moon goddess, who was in some manner (depending on the storyteller) lifted to the moon. Mooncakes are prepared in celebration of the moon, embossed with an image of a rabbit (where Westerners are said to see a man in the moon, the Chinese see a rabbit) or of Chang'e. Families feast on a meal of roasted pig, fruits, and mooncakes.

Harvest Festival Cakes

ROAD TRIPS TO HARVEST FESTIVALS AND COUNTY FAIRS are one of my favorite pastimes. Many of the cakes you find at these events are regional specialties based on the seasonal local harvest, and since I live in California, the land of nonstop harvest, I can enjoy these festivals year-round. I indulge in the do-it-yourself strawberry shortcake bar at the Strawberry Festival in Ventura. I head out to the desert to the Date Festival in Indio for date cakes and date shakes. I enjoy marzipan and almond cakes at Oakley's Almond Festival. And at the annual Tofu Festival in Los Angeles's Little Tokyo, I gobble up my share of hot bean curd cakes.

Around the world, the harvest season is celebrated through festivals and rituals that express collective gratitude and pride for whatever the harvest brings each year. Humans have been celebrating the harvest since they planted their first seeds and watched them grow. In fact, harvest festivals date back to the ancient Egyptians, who held wheat-harvest celebrations, complete with fruitcakes and honey cakes made from the wheat, fruits, and honey they cultivated.

The ancient Greeks had their own wheat-harvest festival, Thesmosphoria, which celebrated Demeter, the goddess of grain. They made offerings of cakes, seeds, fruits, vegetables, and pigs to Demeter, in the hope that her happiness would ensure a good harvest the next year. Similarly, the ancient Romans celebrated Cerelia, in honor of Ceres, their goddess of grain. Their celebration included a thanksgiving feast with cheesecakes and fruitcakes, plus music, parades, games, and sports — not unlike today's county fairs. Below are some other harvest festivals and traditions from around the world, along with cakes to look out for.

CH'USOK (KOREA)

On Ch'usok, known as the Harvest Moon Festival, Koreans honor their ancestors with offerings made of newly harvested foods. Songp'yon, crescent-shaped rice cakes stuffed with sesame seeds, chestnut paste, or beans, are traditional offerings.

CROP OVER (BARBADOS)

This harvest festival used to be celebrated with a parade of carts, pulled by animals decorated with flowers, carrying sugarcane to plantation owners, who provide a feast for the laborers. Today Crop Over is a holiday of fairs, cane-cutting contests, music, and dancing, complete with rum cakes (page 66).

GAWAI DAYAK (MALAYSIA)

During Gawai Dayak, the Rice Harvest Festival, Malaysian communities gather the stalks together in the rice fields. Traditionally they cut the stalks with a carved knife said to appease *semangat*, the rice spirit. Rice cakes are enjoyed after the harvest.

GREEN CORN FESTIVAL (UNITED STATES)

Many Native Americans celebrate the Green Corn Festival, which coincides with the ripening of corn in late summer. They feast on roasted corn, corn tortillas, corn breads, and corn cakes.

LEFT: *rum cake (page 66);* CENTER: *Welsh cakes (page 148);* RIGHT: *Cherokee wild huckleberry cake (page 42)*

GWL AWST (WALES)

Welsh cakes (page 148), cooked over an open fire, much as ancient Celts would have prepared them, are served with bilberry jam at the Celtic harvest festival Gwl Awst in August. Bara brith, a fruitcake, is also popular.

THE HARVEST FESTIVAL (GREAT BRITAIN)

The Harvest Festival is celebrated by decorating churches with baskets of fruit and food to be distributed to the poor. Brits stuff the baskets with homemade cakes.

KWANZAA (UNITED STATES)

Kwanzaa, whose name means "first fruits" in Swahili, derives from African harvest traditions and falls around Christmastime. Many celebrants prepare cakes including ingredients that traveled with Africans to the Americas, such as yams.

MIDAUTUMN FESTIVAL (CHINA)

The Midautumn Festival, on the full moon of the eighth month of the Chinese lunar calendar, is the big harvest festival of the country. Mooncakes (page 260) are iconic here.

THANKSGIVING (UNITED STATES)

Thanksgiving is a celebration of the harvest of the early Pilgrims in colonial America. It's the biggest harvest festival in the United States, with pumpkin pie being the traditional dessert. Surprisingly, it doesn't have a traditional cake, so I updated a recipe with Cherokee influences (page 42) as an appropriate Thanksgiving cake.

TIONG-CCHIU CHOEH (TAIWAN)

At this traditional Taiwanese harvest festival, celebrants feast on mooncakes filled with sweet potato, pineapple, or pomelos.

TRUNG THU (VIETNAM)

Trung Thu, or the Midautumn Festival, is celebrated in Vietnam with mooncakes filled with coconut or durian. It is the most popular family holiday.

YAM FESTIVAL (GHANA AND NIGERIA)

The Yam Festival celebrates the harvest of this regional staple. Yams are served in plentiful variations, including yam cakes.

BELOW LEFT: *Pingyao-style moon cake for Chinese Midautumn Festival*
BELOW RIGHT: *Midautumn Festival in Vietnam*

Almond Sponge Cake

The Chinese version of sponge cake is steamed, which makes it very moist. Following tradition, this version is flavored with almond extract and topped with a boiled icing, in this case coconut icing. (Nondairy whipped topping is also popular.) For weddings and holidays, Chinese sponge cakes are often topped with chocolate, fresh fruit, and even vegetables. This recipe features a fresh strawberry topping.

Almond Sponge Cake

- 2 cups cake flour
- 2 teaspoons baking powder
- ¼ teaspoon salt
- 10 eggs, separated
- 1 teaspoon cream of tartar
- ¾ cup sugar
- 2 teaspoons almond extract

Toppings

- 4 cups fresh strawberries
- 3¾ cups coconut icing (page 315)
- ¾ cup sliced almonds, toasted
- 2 cups whipped cream (page 323)

Makes 1 cake (serves 6 to 8)

TO PREPARE
Ready a wok or pot for steaming by filling it with 1 inch of water and fitting a rack in it (page 25). Butter and flour two 8-inch square cake pans. Fit a pastry bag with a star tip.

TO MAKE THE BATTER
Stir together the flour, baking powder, and salt; set aside. In a separate large bowl, beat the egg whites until foamy. Add the cream of tartar and beat for 30 seconds. Add ¼ cup of the sugar and beat for another minute, stopping before the egg whites stiffen. Add the egg yolks and the remaining ½ cup sugar, and beat for about 2 minutes more, until the batter is thick and fluffy. Gently stir in the almond extract. Gradually add the flour mixture to the egg mixture, mixing thoroughly, but taking care not to overbeat. Pour the batter into the prepared pans.

TO STEAM THE CAKE
Bring the water in the wok to a boil, then reduce the heat to medium. If both pans fit in the wok or pot, place them on the rack; if only one fits, steam one at a time. Cover and steam for 20 to 25 minutes, until a knife inserted in the center comes out clean. Remove the cakes from the steamer and let cool in the pans.

TO ASSEMBLE
Slice 2 cups strawberries in half, and leave the rest whole. Place one of the cake layers on a serving plate and spread with icing. Top with the halved strawberries. Add the second cake layer, and frost the top and sides with the remaining icing. Press the toasted almonds to the sides. Refrigerate for at least 1 hour, until the icing hardens.

TO SERVE
Pipe whipped cream around the edges of the cake and in the center. Arrange the whole strawberries on top.

VARIATIONS

Tomato-Chocolate Sponge Cake
Add 1½ cups chocolate pieces to the cake batter. Replace the 4 cups strawberries with 2 cups cherry tomatoes.

Tropical Sponge Cake
Replace the strawberries with one whole pineapple and three mangos, cut into thin wedges.

Cake Symbolism

The Chinese seem to have special cakes rich with symbolism for every life-cycle celebration, holiday, and event. There are tortoise cakes for baby celebrations, eight treasure and double happiness cakes for weddings, and pink steamed buns for funerals. Longevity peach buns (page 268) and strawberry cream cakes are served at birthday celebrations. There are even special cakes to send along with wedding announcements. Household gods enjoy cakes, too, so during parties and celebrations, cakes are placed around the house or offered on altars.

Persimmon Festival Cakes

The Taiwanese city of Hsin-chu is famous for its dried-persimmon cake, and this recipe takes that cake as its inspiration. There are two types of persimmons: puckery (crispy) persimmons and sweet (soft) persimmons. I like the soft ones, but both work in this recipe. I have topped these individual-size cakes with dried persimmon chips. Drying intensifies the sweetness of the fruits and gives them a chewy texture.

Persimmon Cake

- 3 cups all-purpose flour
- 1 teaspoon baking soda
- 1 teaspoon ground cinnamon
- ½ teaspoon salt
- 1 cup (2 sticks) unsalted butter, softened
- 1½ cups sugar
- 1 tablespoon lemon juice
- 2 teaspoons vanilla extract
- 3 eggs
- 2¼ cups peeled and chopped persimmons

Persimmon Chips

- 3 persimmons, sliced thin

Makes 12 individual-serving cakes

TO PREPARE

Preheat the oven to 325°F. Butter and flour two large six-cup muffin pans.

TO MAKE THE CAKE

Stir together the flour, baking soda, cinnamon, and salt in a medium bowl; set aside. Beat the butter, sugar, lemon juice, and vanilla with a mixer until creamy. Add the eggs one at a time, beating well after each addition. Gradually add the flour mixture to the butter mixture, stirring until blended. Stir in the chopped persimmons by hand.

TO BAKE

Pour the batter into the prepared pans. Bake for 25 to 30 minutes, until a knife inserted in the center comes out clean. Run a knife around the edges of the cakes to loosen them, and let them cool in the pans.

TO MAKE THE PERSIMMON CHIPS

Preheat the oven to 200°F. Lay the persimmon slices on a baking sheet without overlapping. Bake for 2 to 3 hours, flipping once, until the edges curl and the persimmons are dry. Use as a garnish on the cakes.

VARIATION

Turkish Persimmon-Walnut Cake
Prepare the cake with the soft persimmons. Add ½ teaspoon grated nutmeg, ¼ teaspoon ground cloves, 1 teaspoon orange zest, and ½ cup chopped walnuts to the batter. Top with 1½ cups orange icing (page 316).

Persimmons and the Monsoon

Taiwan has a very long history of cultivating persimmons. The fruits are often dehydrated to crystallize the sugars and sold dry. Sometime between September and December, the northeastern winds come. These winds show up for ten days to a month straight and have the perfect drying effect for the persimmons. The whole or sliced persimmons are placed in bamboo baskets and left in the sun for three or four days. They are then pressed flat and dried under the sun for a few more days.

Feng Li Su (Pineapple Cake)

Pineapple cakes are a type of mooncake with a buttery sweet shortbread crust and pineapple filling. Western pastries influenced the shortbread crust, and Eastern mooncakes influenced the filling. Pineapple paste, made from winter melon and a little pineapple, is the traditional filling for these cakes, but it can be difficult to find pineapple paste in markets, so I have created this version with a homemade pineapple filling. If you like thick crusts, use less pineapple filling; if you like thin crusts, use more filling.

Shortbread Crust

- 2½ cups all-purpose flour
- 1 teaspoon baking powder
- 1½ cups (3 sticks) unsalted butter, chilled and cubed
- ¾ cup sugar
- 2 medium eggs
- 1 teaspoon vanilla extract
- 3 tablespoons milk

Filling

- 3½ cups pineapple filling (page 322)

To Serve

Origami paper

Makes 12 cakes

TO PREPARE

Preheat the oven to 350°F. Butter two baking sheets.

TO MAKE THE CRUST

Combine the flour and baking powder; set aside. In a separate large bowl, blend the butter and sugar with a mixer until combined. Add the eggs, vanilla, and milk, and beat until combined. Blend the flour mixture into the butter mixture. Gather the dough into two balls, wrap each in plastic wrap, and chill for 30 minutes, until firm.

TO SHAPE

Unwrap the chilled dough, pinch off about 2½ tablespoons, and shape into a ball. Press a groove into the center of the ball with your finger. Fill the groove with pineapple filling. Pinch off another teaspoon of dough, press it down over the filling to encapsulate it, and smooth the seams. Shape the package into a square by pressing it into a square mold or the corners of a square pan. Set on a prepared baking sheet. Repeat until you have used up all the dough.

TO BAKE

Bake the cakes for 15 to 20 minutes, until golden brown. Transfer the cakes to a rack and let cool.

TO SERVE

Wrap each cake individually in origami paper.

VARIATIONS

Green Tea Pineapple Cakes

Add 2 teaspoons green tea powder to the dough.

Lan Mei Su (Blueberry Cakes)

Replace the pineapple filling with 3½ cups blueberry filling (page 321).

Yu Tou Su (Taro Cakes)

Replace the pineapple filling with taro paste (available at Asian grocery stores).

The Taiwan Tourist Cake

Pineapple cakes are a true Taiwanese specialty. The pineapple is considered a lucky fruit that brings love, success, and prosperity. Though the pineapple filling is traditional, today you can find these cakes in many flavors, including blueberry, green tea, and taro.

As a nation, Taiwan has selected pineapple cake to be its official "tourist gift," and it's well represented in the island's airports. These square pastries are wrapped in easily identifiable colorful packaging. Snack-cake versions are wrapped in hard-to-throw-away origami paper packaging. Gift-cake versions are wrapped in boxes. The next time you're passing through, be sure to grab some for yourself and others for gifts.

Sou Tao (Longevity Peach Buns)

The peach is a powerful symbol of longevity in Chinese culture. These sweets, which are shaped like peaches, are traditionally eaten for birthday celebrations, symbolizing hope for a long life for the celebrant. This recipe calls for lotus seed paste, which you can make yourself or purchase at most Asian markets. If you're making the paste yourself, you might notice that there are two types of lotus seeds: brown and white. Both taste great, so choose either.

3¼ cups all-purpose flour

2½ tablespoons instant yeast

1 cup milk

2 tablespoons sugar

2 tablespoons vegetable oil

½ teaspoon salt

2 eggs, separated

2¾ cups lotus seed paste, store bought or homemade (page 322)

Bright pink food coloring, if desired

Makes 8 buns

TO MAKE THE DOUGH

Stir together 1½ cups of the flour and the yeast in a large mixing bowl; set aside. Heat the milk, sugar, 1 tablespoon of the oil, and the salt in a medium saucepan just until warm. Add the warm milk to the flour mixture.

In a separate bowl, beat the egg whites with a mixer at low speed for 30 seconds. Then beat at high speed for 3 minutes, until foamy. Combine the egg whites with the flour-milk mixture. Stir in the egg yolks, and gradually add the remaining 1¾ cups flour, until the mixture has the consistency of bread dough.

Knead the dough on a floured work surface until it is elastic, 8 to 10 minutes. Form into a ball. Butter a bowl with the remaining 1 tablespoon oil, and set the dough in the bowl, turning it to grease it on all sides. Cover and set in a warm location to rise for 1 to 2 hours, until it has doubled in size.

TO SHAPE

When the dough has risen, turn it out onto a floured work surface and knead for 10 to 15 seconds, until smooth. Divide the dough into eight pieces and form each into a ball. Place the balls in a deep baking pan, cover, and let sit in a warm location for 20 to 25 minutes, until the dough begins to rise again.

On a floured work surface, flatten each ball into a 3- to 4-inch round. Spoon about 1 heaping tablespoon of lotus seed paste onto the center of each round. Stretch the edges of the dough over the filling and pinch to seal. Gently shape into a ball. Set the balls back in the baking dish and let rise for 20 to 30 minutes, until they have expanded by about one-third in volume.

Draw the back of a butter knife around the middle of each ball to create an impression resembling a peach seam. Pinch a small peak on that line, as the bottom of the peach, and on the opposite side press in with a finger to make an indentation, as the top of the peach.

TO STEAM

Ready a wok or pot for steaming by filling it with 1 inch of water and fitting a rack in it (page 25). Bring the water to a boil, then reduce the heat to medium. Fill the rack with buns, seam side down, not letting them touch one another. Cover the remaining buns and store in the refrigerator. Cover the steamer and let steam for 15 to 20 minutes, until the buns spring back when touched. Remove the buns from the steamer and set on a rack to cool. Repeat to steam the remaining buns.

TO COLOR THE BUNS TO LOOK LIKE PEACHES

Dilute the food coloring by half (1 part food coloring to 1 part water). Spray or brush the food coloring on half of each bun.

VARIATIONS

Chocolate Baozi

Fill the buns with chocolate pudding instead of lotus seed paste.

Longevity Buns with Red Bean Paste

Substitute sweet adzuki bean paste, store bought or homemade (page 322), for the filling.

Yam Baozi

Replace the lotus seed paste with yam paste: Boil 3 cups of chopped yams for 20 minutes. Drain, mash, and mix in ½ cup dark brown sugar. Let cool.

Saeng Cream Cake

Saeng is the Korean version of sponge cake, most commonly prepared for birthdays and Christmas. It's traditionally made with rice flour. You can substitute cake or all-purpose flour, but rice flour will give you a more authentic flavor. The golden sponge cake is coated with buttercream (or nondairy whipped topping) and topped with fresh and canned fruits. For Christmas it's decorated with super-cutesy Santas, elves, and Christmas trees.

Génoise Sponge Cake

- 1⅓ cups cake flour
- 1 cup cornstarch
- 12 eggs
- 1½ cups superfine sugar
- ⅔ cup unsalted butter, melted and cooled
- 2 teaspoons vanilla extract

Toppings

- 4 cups nondairy whipped topping or whipped cream (page 323)
  Fruits, whole, sliced, or chopped
  Candies, for decoration (optional)
- 2 cups fondant (page 324), for building decorative sculptures (optional)

Makes 1 cake (serves 6 to 8)

TO PREPARE

Prepare the sponge cakes as directed on page 108, baking them in two 8-inch round pans for 30 to 40 minutes, until the cakes are golden brown and shrink away from the sides of the pans. Fit a pastry bag with a large writing tip.

TO ASSEMBLE

Set one cake on a serving plate. Spread whipped topping over it, followed by a layer of fruit. Set the second cake on top. To prevent crumbs from ruining the final frosting, coat the entire cake with a thin layer of whipped topping, and refrigerate for about 30 minutes, until set. Then frost the cake with a final layer of whipped topping.

TO DECORATE

Fill the pastry bag with whipped topping, and use it to pipe a decorative border around the top of the cake. Arrange fruit, candies, fondant sculptures, or other decorative items as desired.

VARIATIONS

Chinese Christmas Cake

Set mandarin orange segments in a border around the bottom of the cake. Add tomatoes, chocolate chunks, and orange slices to the selection of fresh fruit.

Japanese Christmas Cake

Dust the sides of the cake with unsweetened cocoa powder, and add marzipan sculptures and chocolate to the decorations.

Hwan-Gap

In Korea, the 60th birthday, known as hwan-gap, is a special event. Though it may not seem like a big deal today, in the past living to the age of 60 was a great accomplishment. Today the holiday is a good excuse to honor parents. Children organize a large feast with traditional foods, and a saeng cream cake is often served. The guest of honor dresses in traditional Korean garb.

Hodo Kwaja (Walnut Cakes)

These snack cakes are popular street food in Korea. They are made in walnut-shaped waffle irons and served hot. They come with a variety of fillings including adzuki bean, walnut, chestnut, and sweet potato. It is hard to get the walnut shape without a special griddle, but the cakes taste just as good as round balls.

Dough

2½ tablespoons active dry yeast

1 tablespoon granulated sugar

3 tablespoons warm water

2½ cups all-purpose flour

⅛ teaspoon salt

⅓ cup milk

1 tablespoon maple syrup

Adzuki-Walnut Filling

2 tablespoons sesame oil

1⅓ cups sweet adzuki bean paste (page 322)

¾ cup chopped walnuts

1 cup light brown sugar

1 teaspoon ground cinnamon

Makes 20 cakes

TO PREPARE

Preheat the oven to 350°F. Grease two 12-cup muffin tins with vegetable oil.

TO MAKE THE DOUGH

Mix the yeast with the sugar and water in a small bowl; set aside for about 10 minutes, until foamy.

Combine the flour, salt, milk, and maple syrup in a medium bowl. Add the yeast mixture and mix well. Cover and let stand for 3 to 4 hours, until doubled in size.

TO MAKE THE FILLING

Coat a wok with the oil. Add the adzuki bean paste, walnuts, brown sugar, and cinnamon and stir-fry for 3 to 5 minutes, until dry. Refrigerate for at least 1 hour.

TO SHAPE

Divide the dough into 20 balls, and flatten them into 2½- to 3-inch rounds. Set 1 teaspoon of filling in the center of each cake, and pull up the edges to seal the dough. Form into balls. Score a series of parallel indented lines into the balls with the back of a butter knife to mimic the look of a walnut shell. Place the balls in the compartments of the prepared pans.

TO BAKE

Bake for 14 to 18 minutes, until golden. Remove from the oven and serve warm.

VARIATIONS

Armenian Walnut Cakes

Add ¼ cup ground walnuts to the dough. Fill the balls with walnut butter.

Chestnut Hodo Kwaja

Replace the walnuts with chestnuts. Replace 1 cup of the all-purpose flour with chestnut flour.

Peanut Hodo Kwaja

Fill the balls with peanut butter.

Sweet Potato Hodo Kwaja

Replace the adzuki bean paste in the filling with mashed sweet potatoes.

Chrysanthemum Steamed Lemon Cake

This recipe combines two Korean traditions, steaming cakes and topping cakes with flowers. Here I steamed my favorite lemon cake, added chrysanthemum petals to the batter, and topped it with fresh and sugared chrysanthemums. For an extra zesty tang, I gave it a citrus rice wine sauce. For more flavor, you could replace the water for steaming with wine.

The cakes with purple flowers are chrysanthemum steamed lemon cakes; the cakes with pink flowers are sugared-flower hwajeon.

Sugared Chrysanthemums

12 chrysanthemums

1 egg white, beaten

¼ cup superfine sugar

Chrysanthemum Cake

1½ cups all-purpose flour

2 teaspoons baking powder

¼ teaspoon salt

3 eggs

1 cup granulated sugar

Grated zest of 2 lemons

1 teaspoon vanilla extract

1 cup heavy cream

½ cup chrysanthemum petals

Three-Citrus Rice Wine Sauce

½ cup orange juice

1 tablespoon lemon juice

1 tablespoon lime juice

½ cup granulated sugar

2 cloves

1 teaspoon cornstarch

½ cup rice wine

Makes 1 cake (serves 6 to 8)

TO MAKE THE SUGARED CHRYSANTHEMUMS

Remove all of the leaves and stems from the flowers. Wash the blossoms in cold water, and pat dry with a paper towel. Brush a light coat of egg white on the top and bottom of each flower. Sprinkle both sides with sugar. Dry on waxed paper for 1 hour, or until firm.

TO MAKE THE CAKE

Butter a 9-inch round springform pan. Cover the outside of the pan with foil to seal the edges.

Combine the flour, baking powder, and salt in a medium bowl; set aside. Beat the eggs until they are thick and pale. Add the sugar, lemon zest, and vanilla and beat until smooth. Gradually add the flour mixture to the egg mixture, alternating with the cream, until well blended. Fold in the chrysanthemum petals. Pour the batter into the prepared pan.

TO STEAM

Prepare a wok or pot for steaming by filling it with 1 inch of water and fitting a rack in it (page 25). Bring to a boil, then reduce the heat to medium. Place the cake on the rack, and cover the steamer. Steam for 45 to 50 minutes, until a knife inserted in the center comes out clean. Remove the cake from the wok and let cool in the pan.

TO MAKE THE SAUCE

Combine the orange juice, lemon juice, lime juice, sugar, and cloves in a saucepan and simmer for 5 minutes. Remove the cloves. Dissolve the cornstarch in the rice wine and stir into the sauce. Simmer for 5 minutes, stirring, until thickened.

TO SERVE

Remove the cake from the pan. Top with sugared chrysanthemums and serve with citrus sauce.

Sugared-Flower Hwajeon

Hwajeon are small, flat rice cakes that are topped with sugared edible flowers. There are many different types made throughout the year. These, made with fresh-picked spring flowers, are prepared in spring for Samjinnal. If you prefer a more modern recipe, try the steamed lemon cakes with chrysanthemums (page 272).

Sugared Flowers

- 18 edible flower blossoms
- 2 egg whites, beaten
- ½ cup superfine sugar

Hwajeon

- 1½ cups water
- 1⅓ cups rice flour
- 1 teaspoon salt
- ¼ cup vegetable oil

Makes 10 hwajeon

TO SUGAR THE FLOWERS

Wash the blossoms in cold water and pat dry with a paper towel. Brush a light coat of egg white on the top and bottom of each flower. Sprinkle both sides with sugar. Let dry on waxed paper for about 1 hour, until firm.

TO MAKE THE HWAJEON

Bring the water to a boil. Pour over the rice flour and salt in a medium bowl, and mix well to create a dough. If the dough is too sticky, add a bit more flour; if it's dry, add a bit more water.

Transfer the dough to a floured work surface and roll out to ½-inch thickness. Cut into 2½-inch rounds with a cookie cutter.

TO FRY

Heat the oil in a large skillet over medium heat. Line a plate with paper towels for draining the fried cakes.

Place several hwajeon rounds in the skillet and fry for 2 to 3 minutes, until the bottom side is golden brown. Flip and cook on the other side for 1 to 2 minutes, until the other side is golden brown. Drain on paper towels.

TO SERVE

Place the rice cakes on a serving plate and top with sugared flowers.

VARIATIONS

Beotkkot Hwajeon
Top the cakes with sugared cherry blossoms and cherries.

Hwajeon with Chrysanthemums
Top with sugared chrysanthemums (page 272).

Ihwajeon
Top the cakes with sugared Korean pear flowers and slices of Korean pears.

Jangmi Hwajeon
Top the cakes with sugared roses or rose petals and honey.

Maendrami Hwajeon
Top the cakes with sugared cockscomb and sesame seeds.

Hwajeon Nori

Samjinnal is a traditional Korean celebration of the arrival of spring. It falls on the third day of the third lunar month. (The number 3 has yang positive forces in Korean culture, and so the third day of the third month is an especially lucky one.) On Samjinnal, tradition calls for hwajeon nori, "flower cake play," a custom dating back to the Goryeo Dynasty (918–1392). Women carry rice flour and a frying pan to a picnic and prepare rice cakes over an open fire, using fresh-picked spring flowers. They also use the flowers to make a honeyed punch called hwachae. In the fall, people make a similar hwajeon with fall chrysanthemums, which is eaten with rice wine.

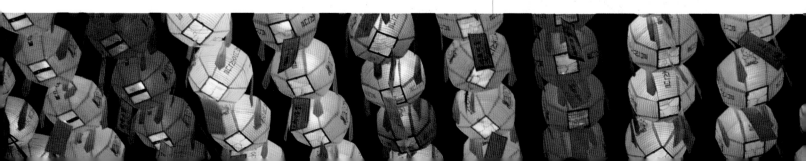

Apricot Mochi Rice Cakes

When I lived near Los Angeles's Little Tokyo, I used to frequent a mochi shop with so many different kinds of these chewy, moist rice cakes that I always had a hard time choosing. Chocolate, orange, green tea, mango, mugwort — you name it, there's a mochi for it, and it can come uncooked, baked, or fried. This is a basic uncooked recipe, filled with fresh apricots and with a wrapper flavored with apricot nectar.

Apricot Filling

2 cups chopped apricots

½ cup light brown sugar

1 teaspoon vanilla extract

Wrapper

½ cup granulated sugar

1 cup boiling water

1 cup apricot nectar

2 cups glutinous rice flour

Potato starch

Makes 6 to 8 cakes

Popular Mochi Wagashi

DAIFUKU: Mochi stuffed with anko

DANGO: A sweet, sticky mochi skewered on a stick

HANABIRAMOCHI: A red-and-white mochi wrapped around anko and a strip of candied burdock

KUSAMOCHI (GRASS MOCHI): A sweet mochi with mugwort and anko

MATSUNOYUKI (SNOW ON THE PINE): A sweetened mochi in the shape of a pine tree sprinkled with ground sugar

TO MAKE THE FILLING

Mix together the apricot, sugar, and vanilla; set aside.

TO MAKE THE WRAPPER

Dissolve the sugar in the pan of boiling water. Stir in the nectar. Add the rice flour to the syrup and stir until blended. Remove from the heat and let cool for 5 minutes.

TO ASSEMBLE

Sprinkle potato starch on a work surface, and transfer the wrapper dough to it. Pinch off 1½-inch balls, and flatten each to a 3½-inch disk. Set 1 tablespoon of the apricot filling in the middle of each disk. Gather the edges together, shape the package into a rectangle, and pinch the seams to close. Arrange the mochi on a plate, seam side down.

VARIATIONS

Adzuki Mochi

Replace the apricot filling with sweet adzuki bean paste, store-bought or homemade (page 322).

Ice Cream Mochi

Replace the apricot filling with green tea or adzuki bean ice cream. Freeze for 3 hours before serving.

Mango Mochi

Replace the fresh apricot and nectar with fresh mango and mango nectar.

Papaya Mochi

Replace the fresh apricot and nectar with fresh papaya and papaya nectar.

Ube Mochi

Replace the apricot filling with ube jam (page 322).

Wagashi

Wagashi are traditional Japanese sweets that are often served with tea. They are traditionally based on ingredients from nature. In fact, they began as simple fruits, berries, and nuts. Over the years, wagashi making has evolved to include mochi, molded sugars, jellies, and other sweets.

The term *wagashi* was coined in the early twentieth century to differentiate traditional Japanese sweets from those being imported from abroad. There are many different types of wagashi, and they are generally classified by their water content. Namagashi contain 30 percent or more moisture, han namagashi contain 10 to 30 percent moisture, and higashi contain 10 percent or less moisture. Most mochi qualify as han namagashi or namagashi. Today mochi are still integrated into the tea ceremony, but their most ceremonial use is as the Japanese New Year's cake. Eating mochi at the first meal of the year is meant to bring good luck in the coming year.

Dorayaki

Dorayaki are such popular snack cakes in Japan and Korea that they are eaten by anime characters. They are sandwich cakes: two fluffy honey-vanilla pancakes filled with sweet adzuki bean paste. Dorayaki are easy to make at home. If you're going to make the adzuki bean paste yourself, make it a day ahead of time. If you are short on time you can also purchase the paste at an Asian market.

Pancakes

3	eggs
½	cup sugar
½	teaspoon baking soda
3	tablespoons milk, warmed
1	cup all-purpose flour
1	teaspoon vanilla extract
2	tablespoons vegetable oil

Assembly

¼	cup honey
2¾	cups sweet adzuki bean paste (page 322)

Makes 8 individual-serving cakes or 16 mini cakes

TO MAKE THE PANCAKES

Beat the eggs and sugar with a mixer in a medium bowl. Dissolve the baking soda in the milk, and add the milk to the egg mixture. Slowly blend the flour into the egg mixture. Stir in the vanilla.

TO FRY

Warm the oil in a large skillet over medium heat. Pour the batter into the skillet in 2-inch or 4-inch rounds. When bubbles appear on the top surface of the cakes, flip them, and cook until they are golden brown on both sides. Repeat with the remaining batter. Let cool.

TO ASSEMBLE

Spread the honey on half the cakes. Spread the sweet adzuki bean paste on the remaining cakes. Sandwich the honey and adzuki cakes together.

VARIATION
Taiyaki

Prepare the batter and cook in a shaped waffle iron. Sandwich the adzuki bean paste or soybean jam between two waffles.

Taiyaki and Ningyo-yaki

Taiyaki, another popular snack cake similar to dorayaki, are prepared in a waffle iron — the more unique the waffle iron, the better. They are filled with red or white soybean jam. Street vendors mold taiyaki in fish-shaped grills that seal the jam in the center. In Japan, the fish shape is a symbol of good luck.

Ningyo-yaki is yet another version of molded snack cake. Its name translates as "fried dolls," and indeed, the cakes are molded into many different doll-like shapes, from Bunraku puppets to gods and pop culture characters including Hello Kitty. They are sold in beautiful packages and often are given as gifts.

Hamburger and Fries

In Japan, many businessmen love cake but find it a bit too feminine to sit down to a slice of cake in public. That's where Mamido's burger shop comes in. Located in one of the hippest neighborhoods of Tokyo, this shop aims to disguise cakes as fast food. The outside of the place looks like a takeout restaurant. The cakes look like hamburgers and french fries. Here's a recipe to try at home, where nobody but your family will catch you eating them.

Devil's Food

- 1 cup water
- 4 ounces semisweet chocolate, cut into chunks
- 2¼ cups cake flour
- 1½ teaspoons baking powder
- 1 teaspoon baking soda
- ¼ teaspoon salt
- 1 cup (2 sticks) unsalted butter, softened
- 1½ cups dark brown sugar
- 1 cup granulated sugar
- 3 eggs
- 2 teaspoons vanilla extract
- ½ cup buttermilk

Génoise Sponge Cake

- 1⅓ cups cake flour
- 1 cup cornstarch
- 12 eggs
- 1½ cups superfine sugar
- ⅔ cup unsalted butter, melted and cooled
- 2 teaspoons vanilla extract
- ½ teaspoon sesame seeds

Assembly

- 2 batches marzipan (page 324)
  Red and green food coloring
- ¼ batch vanilla buttercream (page 317)

Makes 12 burgers

TO PREPARE

Preheat the oven to 350°F. Butter and flour four large six-cup muffin pans and an 8-inch square cake pan.

FOR THE BURGERS

Prepare the devil's food batter as instructed on page 52. Pour into the cups of two of the muffin pans, filling each one-third full. Bake for 15 to 20 minutes, until a knife inserted in the center comes out clean. Let the cakes cool in the pans.

FOR THE BUNS

Prepare the génoise sponge cake batter as instructed on page 108. Pour into the cups of the remaining two muffin pans, filling each cup half full. Reserve ¼ teaspoon of the sesame seeds, and use the rest to top the batter in the cups. Pour the remaining batter into the square cake pan. Bake for 20 to 25 minutes, until a knife inserted in the center comes out clean. Let the cakes cool in the pans.

TO SHAPE THE MARZIPAN

Divide the marzipan into two equal parts. Use food coloring to color half green for the lettuce and half red for the tomatoes. Shape the green marzipan to look like 12 lettuce leaves. Use a real lettuce leaf as a model for trimming each leaf, and press each marzipan leaf into the real leaf to emboss a leafy texture. Brush with additional green food coloring to create color variation.

Shape the red marzipan to look like tomato slices. Use a real tomato slice as a model. Press your fingers into the slices to to create the indented "soft" parts of the tomatoes. Brush additional red food coloring into the soft parts to create color variation, and sprinkle with reserved sesame seeds.

TO COLOR THE BUTTERCREAM

Use food coloring to dye the buttercream the red of ketchup.

TO ASSEMBLE

Slice the sponge cake disks in half crosswise, making two layers. Spread red buttercream over the bottom half of each. Top with a devil's food disk and a marzipan lettuce leaf and tomato slice. Set the top layer of sponge cake on top. Slice the square cake into strips to look like french fries. Serve with additional red buttercream on the side, as ketchup, if desired.

Baked Cheesecake with Coffee Jelly

Like many Japanese cakes, the Japanese cheesecake is a bit less sweet than its Western cousins, and it's also lighter and a bit softer. For a unique combination I like to serve this baked cheesecake with coffee jelly and whipped cream.

Cheesecake
- 8 ounces cream cheese, softened and cut into pieces
- ½ cup (1 stick) unsalted butter, softened
- ½ cup confectioners' sugar
- 2 eggs, separated
- 1 tablespoon lemon juice
- 1 teaspoon grated lemon zest
- 2 tablespoons milk
- ½ cup cake flour
- 1 teaspoon baking powder
- ¼ teaspoon salt
- ¼ teaspoon cream of tartar

Coffee Jelly
- ½ cup granulated sugar
- Two 2¼-ounce envelopes unflavored gelatin powder
- 2 cups hot coffee, double strength
- 1 cup water
- 1 tablespoon lemon juice
- ¼ cup milk

Toppings
- 1½ cups whipped cream (page 323)
- ½ teaspoon unsweetened cocoa powder

Makes 1 cake (serves 6 to 8)

TO PREPARE
Preheat the oven to 400°F. Line a 9-inch oval loaf pan (or a 9-inch round springform pan) with parchment paper. Butter the paper. Prepare a water bath: Set the cake pan in another pan that is at least 2 inches larger all around. Pour water into the larger pan until it is half full. Then remove the cake pan and set the larger pan in the oven to preheat.

TO MAKE THE CHEESECAKE
Beat the cream cheese, butter, and ¼ cup of the confectioners' sugar with a mixer until smooth. Add the egg yolks, lemon juice, lemon zest, and milk, and mix well. Mix in the flour, baking powder, and salt; set aside. Beat the egg whites until foamy. Add the cream of tartar, and gradually add the remaining ¼ cup confectioners' sugar, beating until soft peaks form. Fold the egg whites into the cream cheese mixture just until blended; do not overmix.

TO BAKE
Pour the batter into the prepared cake pan, and set the pan in the preheated water bath. Bake for 30 to 40 minutes, or until set. Remove from the oven and raise the heat to a broil. Set the cake back in the oven and broil for 30 seconds to 1 minute to brown the top. Keep a careful eye on it. Then turn off the oven heat and let the cake cool in the oven, with the oven door ajar, for about 1 hour. When it's cool, remove the cake from the pan and peel off the parchment paper. Return the cake to the pan and refrigerate until you are ready to serve it.

TO MAKE THE COFFEE JELLY
Combine the sugar and gelatin with the coffee, water, and lemon juice in a saucepan over medium heat, stirring until the solids are dissolved. Divide the mixture in half, and add the milk to one batch. Divide the mixtures among various small molds, and refrigerate for 3 hours, or until set.

TO SERVE
Spoon whipped cream on top of the cake, and dust with cocoa powder. Add the coffee jelly on the side or on top.

VARIATIONS

Chocolate Cheesecake
Reduce the flour to ⅓ cup and add ¼ cup unsweetened cocoa powder to the batter. Top the cake with chocolate shavings.

Marble Matcha Cheesecake
Prepare a graham cracker crust (page 38) in a springform pan. Prepare the batter and divide into two equal batches. Stir 2 tablespoons matcha powder into one batch. Pour the batters over the crust, and swirl a knife through them to marble. Bake as directed.

Strawberry Mirror Cheesecake
Replace the coffee jelly with strawberry gelatin: Heat 1 cup chopped strawberries, 2 tablespoons sugar, 1 (2¼-ounce) package gelatin, and 1 tablespoon water in a saucepan until the solids are dissolved. Let cool for 30 minutes. Spread whipped cream over the cake, and pour the strawberry mixture over the top. Refrigerate to set.

Japanese Cheesecakes

Once the Japanese discovered cheesecake, they ran with it, creating many amazing variations. There are three different types of Japanese cheesecakes: baked, rare (unbaked), and soufflé. Rich baked cheesecakes are made with cream cheese, eggs, and sugar. Soft, unbaked rare cheesecakes are made with gelatin and served with fresh fruit or fruit sauces. Light and puffy soufflé cheesecakes are made with beaten egg whites. If you like cheesecake, you will love them all.

Kasutera Cake (Castella Cake)

Namban-gashi is the Japanese term describing cakes of Spanish or Portuguese origin. The golden kasutera cake is the most popular namban-gashi. The cake is very moist, and the top and bottom are brown and sugary. It is most often flavored with honey, although many variations exist, making use of everything from simple syrup to green tea, chocolate, and peaches. Although simple, this cake requires sensitivity to the ingredients, as is the case for most sponge cakes. It's all about getting the eggs beaten just right. Perhaps this is the reason home bakers are so proud to show off their kasutera cakes online. (And boy are they!) Traditionally the cake is baked in a folded origami-like newspaper mold, but you can also use an 8-inch cake pan lined with parchment paper.

2   cups plus 2 teaspoons sugar

3   tablespoons milk

¼   cup honey

8   eggs

2   cups cake flour, sifted

Makes 1 cake (serves 6 to 8)

TO PREPARE

Set one oven rack in the top third of the oven, and set another rack in the lower third. Preheat the oven to 350°F. Butter an 8-inch square cake pan. Line the pan with parchment paper, allowing the paper to hang over the edges. Butter the paper, and sprinkle with 2 teaspoons of the sugar.

TO MAKE THE CAKE

Combine the milk and honey in a saucepan over low heat. Cook, stirring constantly, until the mixture is just ready to boil. Remove from the heat and set aside.

Beat the eggs with an electric mixer for 1 minute. Then beat in the remaining 2 cups sugar on high speed, until the mixture thickens and turns pale yellow. Add the milk and honey mixture and beat for 2 to 3 minutes, until creamy. Gradually add the flour and beat on medium speed for 2 to 3 minutes, until the mixture becomes a thick batter.

TO BAKE

Pour the batter into the prepared pan. Bake for 8 to 10 minutes on the upper rack of the oven. Then move the cake to the lower rack, lower the temperature to 325°F, and bake for 1 hour, until a knife inserted in the center comes out clean. Leave the cake in the oven for 10 minutes, with the door slightly ajar. Then remove the cake from the oven and remove from the pan. Peel off the parchment paper.

TO FINISH

Trim off the sides of the cake to expose the golden edges. Serve while warm. If storing, cover with plastic wrap and seal tightly to preserve moisture buildup.

VARIATIONS

Chocolate Castella

Add 3 ounces melted and cooled semi-sweet chocolate to the batter.

Fa-Gao (Taiwanese Brown Sugar Castella)

Substitute 1½ cups light brown sugar for the granulated sugar.

Green Tea Castella

Add 2 tablespoons matcha powder to the batter.

Honey-Glazed Castella

Thin 2 tablespoons honey with 1 tablespoon warm water. Brush on top of the cake before serving.

Misuzu Castella

Pour the cake batter into mini cupcake pans. Bake for 20 to 25 minutes, until a knife inserted in the center comes out clean.

History of Castella Cake

It's amazing what you can learn by doing a search of your name online. Yes, I am guilty of this self-indulgent activity. A few years ago, when I searched for "castella" and "cake" online, to my surprise I found many people posting photos of their prized homemade creations, the castella cake. I soon found out that this cake is wildly popular in Japan and has been for over four hundred years. I don't know how a cake lover like me could not know there's a cake out there carrying my name, but you can imagine how excited I was to find out more.

What I learned was this sweet sponge cake was brought to Nagasaki by Portuguese seamen in the sixteenth century. It was known as the "bread of Castile" (hence the name *castella cake*), after the Spanish kingdom that prospered in the Middle Ages. Eventually the Portuguese were kicked out of Japan (for being too religious), but the cake stayed and over time has evolved into a new type of sponge cake to suit the less-sweet Japanese palate. It is now a popular festival cake and street food and is often accompanied by green tea. Castella cake is made commercially and sold in Japanese markets worldwide, usually in long boxes. Misuzu castella cakes, bite-size versions, are often seen being eaten by anime characters.

Friendship Cherry Blossom Cake

According to Japanese tradition, cherry blossom flowers represent friendship. Sometimes cherry fruit flavor, cherry blossoms, and friendship kanji are used together to emphasize the point, as in this cake. This is a great recipe for a friendship celebration or for a good friend as a thank-you. The cherry cake is topped with cherry icing, with the kanji symbol of friendship piped on top in buttercream. Fondant cherry blossoms decorate the sides and top.

Cherry Cake

- 3 cups all-purpose flour
- 1 tablespoon baking powder
- ¼ teaspoon salt
- 1 cup (2 sticks) unsalted butter, melted and cooled
- 3 eggs
- 1 cup sugar
- ⅔ cup milk
- 1 teaspoon vanilla extract
  Juice of 1 lemon
- 2½ cups fresh cherries (about 60), pitted and chopped

Toppings

- 4 cups cherry icing (page 315)
- 2 cups vanilla buttercream (page 317)
  Black and pink food coloring
- 2 cups fondant (page 324)
  White and pink candy balls (optional)

Makes 1 cake (serves 6 to 8)

TO PREPARE

Preheat the oven to 375°F. Butter and flour two 9-inch round cake pans.

TO MAKE THE CAKE

Combine the flour, baking powder, and salt in a medium bowl; set aside. Cream the butter, eggs, and sugar until fluffy. Beat in the milk, vanilla, and lemon juice. Add the flour mixture and stir just until moistened. Fold in the cherries.

TO BAKE

Divide the batter between the prepared pans. Bake for 30 to 35 minutes, until a knife inserted in the center comes out clean. Remove from the oven and let cool in the pans.

TO ASSEMBLE

Stack the two cake layers, using the cherry icing as a filling between them. Spread more icing over the top and sides of the cake.

Dye half of the buttercream black; leave the rest white. Scoop the black buttercream into a pastry bag fitted with a medium writing tip, and use it to create kanji characters on the cake.

Scoop the white buttercream into a pastry bag fitted with a medium tip. Use it to create decorative borders around the top and bottom of the cake. Chill in the refrigerator to set, until the fondant flowers are ready to be applied.

Dye half of the fondant pink; leave the rest white. Roll out both colors on a floured work surface to ⅛-inch thickness. Cut the pink fondant into cherry blossom shapes. Curve the flower petals upward into a cup, and attach a candy ball in the center of each using buttercream as glue. Set the flowers on an upward-curving surface to harden (the inside of a small rounded bowl works well). Press the flowers into the icing on the cake.

Cherry Blossom Traditions

Japan is home to more than four hundred different kinds of cherry trees, and the cherry blossom (sakura) is the country's national flower. The cherry blossom is considered to be an omen for friendship, good luck, love, and affection. In fact, Japan has given the United States many cherry trees over the years as a symbol of friendship. Cherry blossom festivals are held throughout the country from January through June, depending on when the trees are blooming, with tea ceremonies, performances, and traditional foods.

VARIATION

President Washington Cherry Almond Cake

Add ¼ cup ground almonds, 1 tablespoon amaretto, and 1 tablespoon kirsch to the batter. Arrange sliced almonds as a border on the cake.

Kanji

Kanji are the characters used for modern Japanese writing, adapted from Chinese script. This cake calls for the symbols for friendship, but you might also want the symbol for love for a wedding or romantic event, or the symbols for success, peace, or happiness for good wishes.

友情
friendship

愛
love

成功
success

平和
peace

幸福
happiness

CHAPTER 13

Southeast Asia
Welcome to the Spice Islands

SOUTHEAST ASIA IS A SPRAWLING REGION of active volcanoes, jungle-clad mountains, coastal lowlands, and tropical islands. Culturally it is diverse, encompassing Hindu, Muslim, Buddhist, and Christian peoples. I may sound like a tourist brochure when I say that the people are united in their hospitality, but it's true. To say hello in Southeast Asia, people ask, "Have you eaten?" This says a lot about local priorities. There is no such thing as an invitation: everyone is welcome all of the time. Households keep sweet treats on hand for guests who drop by. Creamy sweet iced tea and iced coffee are abundant and ready for visitors, along with coconut sticky rice cakes, mango ice cream cakes, and pandan layer cakes. (Pandan is a local seasoning.) When offered refreshments, guests must accept; to decline would be considered an insult to their host.

Southeast Asian cakes share many similarities from country to country. The major differences are the spices. Nutmeg, pepper, ginger, cloves, lemongrass, and other spices are all native and have been harvested by local peoples since at least 300 BCE. Trade in these spices inspired not only the heyday of the Byzantine culture but also the very concepts of globalization and worldwide commerce. Spices from the region became the root of food creativity in Asian, Arab, and eventually European and American cuisines.

Because of its rich natural resources (spices included), this region became an important stop on early European trade routes, and it was heavily colonized. You can taste the European influences in cakes developed over the past few hundred years everywhere. In the Philippines you can find Spanish-influenced custard cakes, while the steamed bean-flour buns of Singapore were inspired by traditional

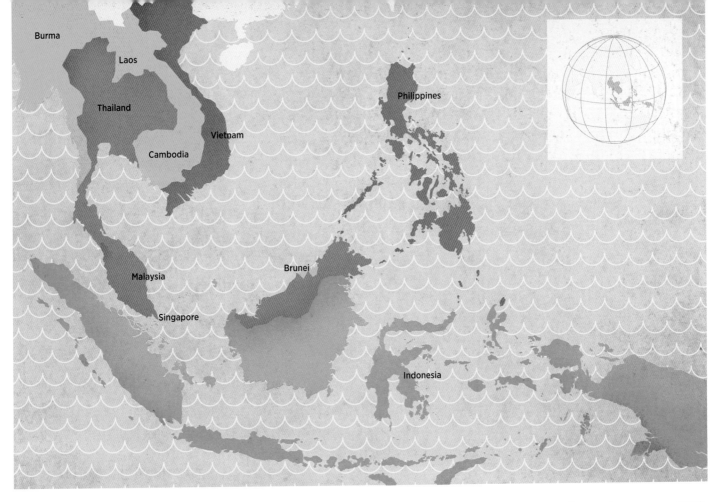

British bun cakes and the butter-rich Indonesian spice cake known as lapis surabaya combines Dutch baking practices and local spices. Throughout the region agar-agar, a sweetened seaweed-based gelatin, is used between layers of cakes in the same way Westerners might use buttercream frosting or fruit preserves.

Modern bakeries in Thailand have developed European-style cakes with a focus on presentation, inspired by the local tradition of carving garnishes into incredible shapes. Here you'll find cakes adorned with beautifully carved coconuts, pumpkins, mangos, and lychees. Ice cream cakes made with peanut crusts or fruity sauces, such as mango-lychee ice cream cakes (page 292), are also popular.

In Vietnam, French, Chinese, and Spanish influences permeate local cooking traditions and ingredients, with wonderful results. A delightful Vietnamese twist on a génoise sponge cake (page 108) is to add some mint, basil, or lemongrass to the batter and to top the cake with caramelized tropical fruit. As in China, mooncakes, also known as midautumn cakes, are popular, though here they contain mung beans, coconut, and durian (a gigantic, odorous fruit). Tet, the New Year, is an important Vietnamese holiday, a combination harvest festival and birthday celebration for every baby who was born during the past year. The traditional New Year's celebration cake is banh bo nuong (cow cake; see page 290), a very spongy sweet cake soaked in coconut sauce.

Malaysian and Indonesian cuisine reflects Chinese, Japanese, Indian, Arabic, Dutch, and Spanish influences. Cakes make great use of local ingredients, such as sweet potato, maize, taro, and tapioca as the starchy base. Coconut milk often replaces dairy milk, and palm sugar replaces granulated sugar. Fruits are popular additions, including pineapple, coconut, star fruit, jackfruit, papaya, banana, rambutan, mangosteen, tamarind, lime, and durian. Popular local spices include turmeric, candlenut, and lemongrass. And sweet peanut sauce, like the kind eaten with satay, is sometimes used as a cake topping.

Filipino cakes display mostly Spanish influences, with some Chinese and French flourishes mixed in. The local purple yam, known as ube, is often used in cake batter, as in traditional ube cake (page 289); the bright purple color it yields is a surefire indicator of a Filipino cake. Sweet rice and cassava cakes are also popular. All kinds of citrus fruits, including pomelo, mandarin oranges, and calamansi (which has a sweet and sour taste), are used as flavorings, much like Westerners might use orange zest or lemon juice. In addition, the Philippines is one of the largest producers of coconut oil, and its people put it to good use in their cakes.

Tapioca Pearl Raisin Cake

It seems like everyone in Malaysia has a secret family recipe for tapioca cake. Some insist that tapioca pearl is better, others say tapioca root is better. The pearls give the cake the texture of a pudding cake. The tapioca root (yuca), when grated, gives the cake the texture of a carrot cake or mashed potato cake. A good accompaniment for the cake is fruit salad made with Malaysian fruits: star fruit, mangosteen, durian, pineapple, rambutan, and papaya.

Tapioca Cake

¾	cup small tapioca pearls, uncooked
⅔	cup raisins
¼	cup milk, warmed
1	cup yuca flour or all-purpose flour
1	teaspoon baking powder
1	teaspoon powdered lemongrass
1	cup (2 sticks) unsalted butter, softened
¾	cup sugar
6	eggs, separated
2	teaspoons lime juice
½	teaspoon grated fresh ginger

Topping

1¼	cups rum syrup (page 319)

Makes 1 cake (serves 6 to 8)

TO PREPARE

Preheat the oven to 350°F. Butter and flour an 8-inch ring or square cake pan.

TO MAKE THE CAKE

Cook the tapioca as directed on the package. Combine the raisins with the milk and set aside to soak for 15 minutes.

Combine the yuca flour, baking powder, and lemongrass; set aside. Cream the butter and sugar in a large bowl until fluffy. Beat in the egg yolks, lime juice, and ginger. Stir in the tapioca and the raisins-milk mixture. In a separate bowl, beat the egg whites until stiff peaks form. Fold the egg whites into the batter.

TO BAKE

Pour the batter into the prepared pan and bake for 30 to 35 minutes, until a knife inserted in the center comes out clean. Remove the cake from the oven and let cool in the pan.

TO GLAZE

Brush rum syrup over the cake several times, allowing it to soak in.

VARIATION
Tapioca Root Raisin Cake
Replace the tapioca pearls with grated tapioca root.

FRONT: *tapioca pearl raisin cake;* CENTER: *Malaysian banana cakes (page 181);* REAR, ON RIGHT: *pandan puto (page 277), ube puto (page 289), and sweet potato puto (page 289)*

Pineapple Huat Kueh

Although I wrote a whole book on cupcakes, I had never steamed a cupcake until I started experimenting for this book. These pineapple cupcakes have a texture halfway between a cake and a bun. If you are lucky, the cake will "explode" during the steaming — the tops of the cakes will split and form flowerlike shapes. This beautiful effect is caused by the wheat starch, a gluten-free thickening powder used in many Asian foods.

⅔ cup wheat starch

¾ cup water

1¾ cups cake flour

1½ tablespoons baking powder

¾ cup sugar

¾ cup pineapple juice

¼ cup coconut oil

1 egg white

1 cup pineapple chunks

Makes 8 individual-serving cakes

TO PREPARE

Ready a wok or pot for steaming by filling it with 1 inch of water and fitting a rack in it (page 25). Line a large pan or steamer with muffin-size paper liners, spacing them ½ inch apart.

TO MAKE THE CUPCAKES

Whisk together the wheat starch and water in a small bowl. In a separate bowl, combine the flour and baking powder. In another separate large bowl, mix the sugar, pineapple juice, coconut oil, and egg white with a mixer for 1 minute. Blend the flour mixture into the sugar mixture, and then add the wheat starch mixture, stirring until the batter is smooth. Fold in the pineapple chunks. (If the pineapple chunks are juicy and thin the batter, add a pinch more cake flour; in my experience, the thicker the batter, the better the explosion.)

TO STEAM

Pour the batter into the liners, filling each two-thirds full. (You may have to steam in more than one batch.) Bring the water in the wok or pot to a boil, then reduce the heat to medium. Set the cupcake pan on the rack, cover, and steam for 15 to 20 minutes, until the cakes explode. Remove from the steamer and let cool.

VARIATIONS

Chocolate Huat Kueh

Add ⅓ cup unsweetened cocoa powder and ¾ cup mini semisweet chocolate chips to the batter.

Strawberry Huat Kueh

Add 2 tablespoons strawberry jam to the batter.

Pandan Cake

Pandan leaf juice is common in Southeast Asian baking. It has a nutty, botanical flavor and a vibrant green color. (If you can't find it, vanilla extract is an acceptable substitute.) This light, fluffy pandan cake is gussied up with white buttercream and reveals a colorful surprise when cut.

Pandan Cake

- 2¼ cups all-purpose flour
- 1½ cups sugar
- 1 tablespoon baking powder
- ¼ teaspoon salt
- 1½ cups plain yogurt
- ¾ cup vegetable oil
- 1½ teaspoons pandan extract
- 4 eggs
- 3 drops green food coloring

Topping

- 4½ cups vanilla buttercream (page 317)

Makes 1 cake (serves 6 to 8)

TO PREPARE

Preheat the oven to 350°F. Butter and flour two 8-inch round cake pans.

TO MAKE THE PANDAN CAKE

Combine the flour, sugar, baking powder, and salt in a medium bowl. Add the yogurt, oil, and pandan extract, and stir until well blended. Beat the eggs in a small bowl until fluffy. Fold the eggs into the batter, then stir in the food coloring to brighten.

TO BAKE

Pour the batter into the prepared pans and bake for 35 to 40 minutes, until a knife inserted in the center comes out clean. Let the cakes cool in the pans.

TO SERVE

Stack the cakes on a serving plate, using the buttercream as a filling between them. Frost the outside of the cake with the rest of the buttercream.

VARIATIONS

Filipino Pandan Ube Cake

This colorful cake is made with alternating green and purple layers (see facing page). Prepare half recipes of pandan cake and ube cake (page 289) batter. Bake each cake in an 8-inch round cake pan as directed. Once cooled, cut the cakes in half crosswise, so that you have four layers. Assemble by alternating the cake layers, using 3¾ cups ube jam (page 322) as a filling. Frost the cake with buttercream.

Pandan Puto

Replace the all-purpose flour with rice flour. Pour the batter into mini cupcake pans, and steam the cupcakes for 20 to 25 minutes instead of baking them. Top with desiccated sweetened coconut. (For a photo of this cake, see page 286.)

Indonesian Independence Day

Indonesia was a Dutch colony for 300 years before becoming an independent nation in the midtwentieth century. This cake is influenced by European baking practices, but the pandan and yogurt give it a Southeast Asian flavor. It is the perfect cake to celebrate Indonesia's Independence Day on August 17.

Ube Cake

This stunning bright violet cake is made from ube, the purple yam of the Philippines. The ube is one ingredient that sets Filipino baking apart from that of other Southeast Asian cultures; where other bakers might use cassava, potato, or orange yam in their cakes, Filipinos use ube. To accentuate the purple color, ube coloring and flavoring are often added. Halayang (ube jam) is the filling for this cake. It can also be eaten on its own or on toast.

Ube Cake
1½ cups peeled and diced ube
1 cup milk
1 teaspoon ube flavoring
1 teaspoon ube coloring
3½ cups cake flour
1¼ cups sugar
1½ teaspoons baking powder
½ teaspoon salt
8 eggs, separated
¾ cup vegetable oil
1 teaspoon cream of tartar

Fillings and Toppings
3¾ cups ube jam (page 322)
1½ cups vanilla buttercream (page 317)

Makes 1 cake (serves 6 to 8)

TO PREPARE
Preheat the oven to 350°F. Butter and flour two 8-inch round cake pans.

TO PREPARE THE UBE
Cover the ube with water in a saucepan. Bring to a boil, then reduce the heat and simmer until the ube is softened. Drain. Combine the cooked ube with ½ cup of the milk and the ube flavoring and ube coloring; whip with a mixer.

TO MAKE THE CAKE
Mix the flour, ¾ cup of the sugar, the baking powder, and the salt in a medium bowl. Create a well in the center, and add the egg yolks, oil, and remaining ½ cup milk to the well. Mix well. Stir in the ube mixture and blend well.

In a separate bowl, whip the egg whites with the cream of tartar and remaining ½ cup sugar with a mixer until they form stiff peaks. Gently fold the egg mixture into the batter.

TO BAKE
Pour the batter into the prepared pans. Bake for 35 to 40 minutes, until a knife inserted in the center comes out clean. Remove from the oven and let the cakes cool in their pans.

TO ASSEMBLE
Set one cake on a serving plate. Spread with the ube jam. Set the other cake on top. Frost the outside of the cake with buttercream.

VARIATIONS
Ube Puto
Replace the all-purpose flour with rice flour. Pour the batter into mini cupcake pans, and steam the cupcakes for 20 to 25 minutes instead of baking them. Top with desiccated sweetened coconut. (For a photo of this cake, see page 286.)

Sweet Potato Puto
Replace the ube with sweet potato and the all-purpose flour with rice flour. Pour the batter into mini cupcake pans, and steam the cupcakes for 20 to 25 minutes instead of baking them. Top with desiccated sweetened coconut. (For a photo of this cake, see page 286.)

Banh Bo Nuong (Cow Cake)

Banh bo nuong is a kind of spongy candy cake. It is most flavorful when prepared with coconut sauce. Sometimes food coloring is added to give the cake a bright color.

Cow Cake
- ¾ cup rice flour
- 1 tablespoon baking powder
- ¾ cup coconut milk
- 1 cup sugar
- 1½ teaspoons vanilla extract

Toppings
- 1½ cups coconut-peanut sauce (page 320)
- 2 tablespoons sesame seeds

Makes 1 cake (serves 6 to 8)

TO PREPARE
Preheat the oven to 350°F. Line the bottom of an 8-inch round baking pan with parchment paper, and butter the paper.

TO MAKE THE CAKE
Combine the rice flour and 1½ teaspoons of the baking powder; set aside. Combine the coconut milk and sugar in a saucepan over medium-high heat and simmer, stirring, until the sugar is dissolved. Remove from the heat and let cool. Stir in the remaining 1½ teaspoons baking powder and the vanilla. Then add the flour mixture, and mix well. Let the batter sit for 30 minutes to generate air pockets.

TO BAKE
Pour the batter into the pan from high above, in ripples, to create bubbles in the batter. Bake for 10 minutes, then lower the heat to 300°F and bake for an additional 20 to 25 minutes, until a knife inserted in the center comes out clean. Cover the cake with plastic wrap and let cool in its pan for 1 hour.

TO ASSEMBLE
Remove the cake from the pan and peel off the parchment paper. Cut into small triangular slices. Top each slice with coconut-peanut sauce and a sprinkling of sesame seeds.

VARIATION
Pandan Banh Bo Nuong
Add 1 teaspoon pandan extract to the cake and ½ teaspoon pandan extract to the sauce.

Bak Tong Goh

Banh bo nuong is prepared each year for Tet, the Vietnamese New Year. It is inspired by the popular Chinese cake known as bak tong goh (white sugar cake). Both cakes have a chewy texture and air pockets throughout. The Chinese version is bright white with a slightly sour taste that comes from the cake's fermenting. The Vietnamese version can be white, but it may also be yellow, pink, green, or purple. Unlike the Chinese version, it is not sour, having a sweet coconut taste instead. It is usually served with a sauce made with coconut, peanuts, and sesame seeds.

Why Cow Cake?
A folk tale relates how a poor Vietnamese man who could not feed his family had a cow appear to him. The cow taught him how to make this cake to nourish his family. In thanks, the man named the cake after the friendly cow. He also became very wealthy selling cow cakes.

Mango-Lychee Ice Cream Cake

If you're a fan of Thai flavors, here is a perfect summertime dessert: a tropical ice cream cake. The crunchy peanut crust is infused with the flavors of coconut and lemongrass. The ice cream, made with coconut milk, combines the most popular tropical fruits of Southeast Asia: mango, lychee, and banana.

Crust

- ½ cup ground peanuts
- ½ cup shredded coconut
- 2 tablespoons sugar
- ½ teaspoon powdered lemongrass
- 3 tablespoons unsalted butter, melted
- 1 tablespoon lime juice

Ice Cream

- 4 eggs
- 1 cup sugar
- 2 cups heavy cream
- 2 cups coconut milk
- 1 teaspoon vanilla extract
- 1 mango, cubed
- 1 banana, mashed
- ¼ cup chopped lychees

Toppings

- ¾ cup chopped peanuts (optional)
- 1 mango, peeled and diced
- 6 lychees, pitted
- ¼ cup peanut halves
  Flaked unsweetened coconut

Makes 1 cake (serves 6 to 8)

TO PREPARE

Line a loaf pan approximately 8 inches long by 4 inches wide by 3½ inches deep with two layers of plastic wrap, leaving a 4-inch overhang on the long sides.

TO MAKE THE CRUST

Combine the peanuts, coconut, sugar, and lemongrass in a food processor or blender. Add the butter and lime juice and mix until combined. Press the mixture into the prepared pan to cover the bottom.

TO MAKE THE ICE CREAM

Mix the eggs and sugar in a double boiler over low heat until blended. Raise the heat and cook for 8 to 10 minutes, until the mixture is thick and creamy. Remove from the heat and refrigerate for 30 minutes.

Beat the cream in a medium bowl until thick and whipped. Gently stir in the coconut milk, vanilla, cooled egg mixture, mango, banana, and chopped lychees.

Pour the ice cream mixture over the crust and loosely cover with waxed paper. Freeze for 8 to 10 hours.

TO SERVE

When the ice cream is fully frozen, remove the cake from the freezer and let thaw for 5 minutes. Lift the cake out of the pan, using the plastic wrap as a sling, and transfer to a serving plate. If you like, slice the cake in half lengthwise, sprinkle the chopped peanuts in the middle, and then replace the top half. Top with mango, lychees, peanuts, and flaked coconut.

Funeral Cookbooks

The Thai people have an amazing funeral tradition that I'd love to see catch on around the globe. Before their death, individuals prepare small, beautifully designed cookbooks with their favorite recipes and food anecdotes. At their funeral, the books are distributed to mourners so that the deceased can be remembered for their taste in foods and celebrations with family.

Kanom Sam Kloe
(Three Chums Cake)

Here is a Southeast Asian take on a wedding cake. These fritters are based on na kachik, a coconut–sesame seed filling used in many Thai desserts. Balls of na kachik are stuck together in groups of three, dipped in a thick batter, and fried in oil.

Na Kachik
½ cup mung beans, toasted
¾ cup glutinous rice flour
⅓ cup water
2 cups shredded sweetened coconut
1 cup sesame seeds, toasted
½ cup palm sugar

Coating
1½ cups rice flour
½ teaspoon salt
½ cup light coconut milk
2 eggs, beaten

Deep-Frying
Vegetable oil, for frying

Makes 15 balls (5 groups of 3)

TO MAKE THE NA KACHIK
Grind the mung beans in a food processor or blender. Mix the ground mung beans with the glutinous rice flour and the water in a large saucepan over medium heat and cook, stirring, for 3 to 5 minutes, until the mixture forms a paste. Remove from the heat and stir in the shredded coconut, sesame seeds, and sugar. The mixture should be sticky; if it is not, add a bit more water.

TO SHAPE
Roll the na kachik into balls about ½ inch in diameter, and press them together in groups of three.

TO MAKE THE COATING
Combine the rice flour and the salt in a medium bowl. Stir in the coconut milk and eggs.

TO FRY
Fill a wok or heavy-bottomed pot with 1½ inches of vegetable oil, and warm over medium heat. Line plates with paper towels for draining the fried cakes.

Drop one of the na kachik balls into the hot oil; if it browns readily, the oil is ready for frying. Dip the balls into the batter and fry, turning regularly, for 3 to 5 minutes, until golden on all sides. Do not crowd the cakes; you will have to fry them in batches. Set on paper towels to drain excess oil. Serve in sets of three.

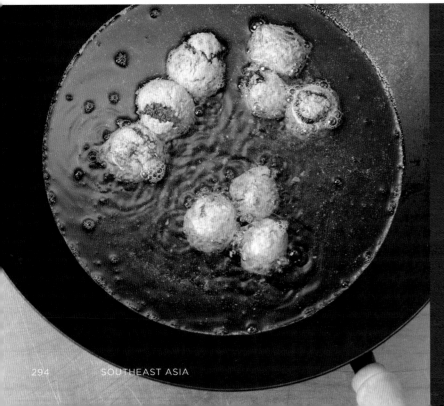

Three Chums Predictions

Three chums cakes are traditionally served at Thai weddings and are said to predict the couple's future. If the three balls stick together while being fried, the marriage will be a happy one. If one ball separates, the couple will be childless. If all the balls separate, the couple is doomed. Getting the balls to stick together is hard, so many people stick them together with toothpicks for cooking, to ensure good luck, and then remove the toothpicks before serving the cakes.

wedding headdress being prepared in northern Thailand

THE WORLD TOUR OF
Wedding Cakes

COUPLES AROUND THE WORLD imbue their wedding cakes with great significance. But what that meaning is, and how it shapes the choice of cake, is inextricably linked to a couple's cultural heritage. In fact, you might say that the cake most grounded in tradition and driven by trend is the wedding cake.

Being the earliest cakes in existence, honey cakes, fruitcakes, and sweet breads were probably the earliest wedding cakes. Wedding cakes gained popularity in medieval Europe, when cakes and puddings with dried fruits were served at weddings as symbols of fertility and prosperity. Seventeenth- and eighteenth-century bride cakes were more contemporary fruitcakes but carried the same symbolism.

The multitiered form of the modern Western wedding cake was inspired by the bell tower of St. Bride's Church in London in the late seventeenth century. The tower has four tiers, each slightly smaller than the one below it. Bakers were inspired by the form and modeled their cakes after this fanciful tower. In some traditions the bottom tier represents the foundation of both families, the top tier represents the couple, and the layers in between signify the number of children the couple will have.

Though the classic presentation of the multitiered wedding cake is an enduring tradition, a growing trend is the presentation of multiple cakes carefully stacked to represent the tiers of the more traditional cakes. Sometimes these are individual cakes or cupcakes, so that each guest can enjoy his or her own private treat. In other cases they are larger cakes in artful arrangements; in contemporary Chinese and Greek weddings, for example, the cake has become a massive installation with sometimes more than a dozen individual cakes stacked on pillars, with staircases leading up to the topper.

Some wedding-cake rituals are common across cultures, such as the traditional cake-cutting ceremony, in which the bride and groom cut and feed each other a bite of cake as a symbol of sharing and respect for each other. Sharing the cake with the wedding guests is meant to bring the couple luck in their future together. Sometimes a small cake is mailed to each of the invitees who could not attend so they can participate in this tradition.

Other wedding-cake rituals are unique to a particular culture, such as the entertaining performance that surrounds the so-called imposter cake popular at contemporary Japanese weddings. This cake is a fake cake made of Styrofoam and rubber. It explodes with puffs of smoke when the couple cuts into it. At each and every wedding the guests are so amazed they scream and laugh as if they were seeing this spoof for the first time.

Wedding cakes are big business. In fact, there's an entire industry devoted to forecasting cake trends and an entirely separate industry devoted to making them. Because wedding cakes cost an average of US $500, some people choose to rent elaborately decorated Styrofoam cakes. A real but simple sheet cake is cut and served from behind the scenes, and the caterers who offer this service claim the guests will never know the difference. Although this practice may seem tacky, it is not new: elegant faux cakes were also displayed at some Renaissance weddings. For those who prefer to skip the cake expense, a wonderful tradition is to ask friends to each bring one of their own favorite cakes, to create a cake buffet for guests. And certainly there are many to choose from.

AUSTRALIA
Fruitcakes decorated with small flowers made of icing are the traditional wedding cake in Australia. Today American mud cakes and cupcakes are also in vogue.

AUSTRIA AND GERMANY
The wedding cake is often a chocolate sponge cake soaked with cognac and filled with cream, chocolate, nougat, jam, and marzipan. It is iced with royal icing, ganache, or marzipan and decorated with molded or piped chocolate artwork and sugar flowers.

BERMUDA
In Bermuda traditionally two cakes are made. The bride's cake is a three-tiered fruitcake called the silver wedding cake because it is covered in silver leaf, which symbolizes prosperity. The groom's cake

Indian women carrying sweets to a wedding in colorful saris

Las Vegas wedding chapel

is a pound cake that is covered in edible gold leaf, symbolizing the authority of the head of the family. It is topped with ivy, rosebuds, and a real cedar sapling, symbolizing the couple's growing love. After the wedding ceremony the couple plants this sapling and treats it with great care throughout their lives.

BRITAIN
A highly decorated fruitcake is traditional for a British wedding. Dates, prunes, raisins, and orange peel are soaked in liqueur (usually cognac) and baked into a very boozy, moist cake. It is often topped with marzipan, but brandy butter and fondant are also used.

CHINA
Happiness cakes, also known as dragon and phoenix cakes, are traditional Chinese wedding cakes. They are filled with lotus-seed, red-bean, or green-bean paste and are embossed with an image of a dragon and phoenix. Customarily the groom's family gifts these cakes to the bride's family as part of the engagement celebration. The bride's family offers some of the cakes to their deceased ancestors and sends the rest to the living ancestors, along with the wedding invitation.

Another traditional Chinese wedding cake is the lapis surabaya, a gigantic multilayered cake in which each layer represents a layer of success for the couple. This cake usually is taken to the extreme, with bridges, columns, and walkways connecting the layers. At the cake-cutting ceremony the bride and groom cut the cake from the bottom up. They serve the first pieces to the grandparents and parents, in honor of their role as the foundation of the family.

CROATIA
Licitar, an ornmental cake from Croatia, has traditionally been given as gifts at weddings. Though still popular as wedding favors, licitar has become such a symbol of cultural heritage that it is now widely sold in the region as tourist souvenirs.

FRANCE
Croquembouche wedding cakes (page 99) are formed by stacking profiteroles in a cone shape and binding them with caramel. They are often decorated with spun sugar, candied almonds, chocolate flowers, or ribbon.

(continued on next page)

GREECE

Greeks don't just make a single cake, they make a cake installation at least eight tiers high. These massive displays are adorned with golden figurines of horses and carriages, angels and doves, bridges, towers, and domes, and sometimes, for the pinnacle of romance, real flowing waterfalls. The traditional Greek wedding cake is a honey cake filled with sesame seeds and quince; these ingredients symbolize the couple's enduring commitment to each other. Today a flourless almond cake, filled with vanilla custard and fruit and covered in sliced almonds, is more common.

INDONESIA

Indonesian wedding cakes are Western in style, but the height of the cake is important. The higher the cake, it's said, the more prosperous the marriage will be. Six tiers is the minimum for the construction, and the tiers may be held up by light-up columns or tree branches.

IRELAND AND SCOTLAND

Layered fruitcakes are popular in Ireland and Scotland. Bourbon, brandy, or whiskey are the liquors of choice, and almond paste is the traditional filling. The bride and groom usually lean together for a kiss over the cake.

ITALY

Italians have many beloved wedding cakes. One is the millefoglie, a light pastry filled with chocolate and vanilla cream and topped with strawberries. Another is the everyday trifle, which for a wedding may be elaborately constructed, filled with chocolate, vanilla, and rum cream, spiked with pieces of fresh fruit, and covered with detailed flowers made from royal icing. Still another Italian favorite is dolce, a liquor-soaked cake sure to lighten the guests' moods.

KOREA

Traditionally Koreans serve rice cakes covered in red bean powder at weddings. A more modern favorite is a sponge cake filled and topped with nondairy whipped cream and fresh fruit.

LUXEMBOURG

The shortcake-like rings of the traditional wedding cake are formed around and cooked on a rotating rod. The rings are then glazed, stacked, and topped with a crown of almonds and sugar.

MACEDONIA

Macedonian tradition calls for the bride's family to spend the four days prior to the wedding baking the wedding cake. A young boy in the family stands in as the groom and protector and watches over the baking. A young girl puts a ring representing the wedding ring into the batter while nobody is looking. The person who receives the piece of cake containing the ring is said to be the next to marry.

MEXICO

Mexican wedding cakes are decorated with a pictorial narrative that tells the story of the couple's courtship. Edible dolls are positioned in scenes around the cake.

PHILIPPINES

Whether it's a traditional sponge cake or a purple ube cake (page 289), a Filipino wedding cake will be adorned with hundreds of fresh flowers. Expect it to be accompanied by a whole roasted pig.

BELOW, LEFT TO RIGHT: *croquembouche (page 99) of France; kransekake (page 162) of Scandinavia; licitar of Croatia.*

Decorative wedding bread for sale in Greece

SCANDINAVIA

The traditional wedding cake in Norway as well as most other Scandinavian countries is the kransekake (page 162), a cake of concentric rings stacked to form a tower 18 tiers high. The cake has a unique texture that is a cross between an almond cake and marzipan. The internal void is filled with small sweets such as cookies and chocolate, fresh fruit, sorbet, or the traditional bottle of wine or champagne. Marzipan portraits of the bride and groom are sometimes attached to the outside of the cake. It is common for couples to purchase a do-it-yourself kit from a baker to assemble and customize their own kransekake.

Brudlaupskling, a wedding sweet bread topped with cheese, cream, and syrup, is also served at weddings in Norway.

SLOVENIA

In Slovenia as well as Poland, Croatia, and several other eastern European countries, potica (a nut roll; see page 182) is served at weddings. Dozens of rolls are prepared for guests to enjoy, usually alongside a large, more modern multitiered wedding cake.

THAILAND

Three chums cake (page 294), a fried cake made with three balls of dough, is the traditional wedding cake in Thailand.

UKRAINE

The korovai, a sweet bread, is considered a sacred part of the wedding feast in Ukraine. It is decorated with patterns that represent the joining of the two families for eternity.

UNITED STATES

A dense, spicy fruitcake was the common wedding cake in colonial America and on through Victorian times. Since that time, light sponge cakes with buttercream frosting have become the norm. The bride and groom wedding cake topper became a popular icon in America in the 1950s and is still popular today.

The apple stack (page 40), the wedding cake of the Appalachians, is a uniquely American tradition. The bride's family brings the frosting and the groom's brings the filling, and each guest is responsible for a layer. The wedding party assembles and decorates the cake as part of the celebration, and all share in the enjoyment.

The Cajun tradition is for the bride's family to start baking cakes weeks before the wedding. The cake room at the reception is filled with dozens of cakes in all shapes, sizes, and flavors.

WEST INDIES

In the West Indies, a fruitcake filled with tropical fruits, rum, sherry, and wine is the traditional wedding cake. It may be hidden under a fine white fabric until the cake-cutting ceremony. Guests pay the couple a gifting fee to get a lucky peek at the cake.

Australia and New Zealand
Cakes with Character

SMALLEST OF THE CONTINENTS, Australia is the lowest, flattest, and, apart from Antarctica, driest continent. Cross the Tasmanian Sea and you'll reach New Zealand, its relatively cool, wet, and mountainous cousin. The native peoples and the first wave of convicts transported from Europe were not much of a baking bunch. But in the early 1800s Australia and New Zealand saw their first settlers from Great Britain, Scotland, and Ireland, and home baking has been part of this region's heritage ever since.

In the Victorian era Australian bakers were way ahead of the times, producing more cookbooks focusing on cakes than any other region of the world. Each week Australian housewives would set Saturday aside for baking "afters" (dessert) for the week's indulgences and breakfast cakes, too. Because Australia and New Zealand were British colonies at that time, many of the favorites were British inspired, such as the Lamington (page 304), said to be a variation of the Victoria sponge cake (page 136). Of course, British cuisine of the time was itself being influenced by Mediterrean flavors and techniques, thanks to the nobility's Spanish and Italian

servants, and so sponge cakes and trifles also made their way to Australia and New Zealand. Later, as Chinese, Indonesian, Malaysian, Japanese, and other Asian immigrants arrived in the region, cakes began to include macadamia nuts, berries, pistachios, kiwifruit, ginger, and other common ingredients from the Pacific Rim.

Although Australia and New Zealand share a historical brilliance for baking, they can be territorial about their traditional cakes. The famous light-as-a-feather meringue Pavlova (page 302) is equally at home in Australia or in New Zealand. Yet both countries boast that they created it, along with several other regional specialties. The Australian Lamington, named after a Lord Lamington, is called a Lemmington in New Zealand, after a town. The New Zealand custard square is the Australian vanilla slice.

Can you tell an Aussie cake from one that comes from even further Down Under? There are a few subtle differences. Cakes of New Zealand tend to be sweeter than Australian cakes due to the influence of a large number of Scottish settlers (Scots are known for having a sweet tooth). The no-bake

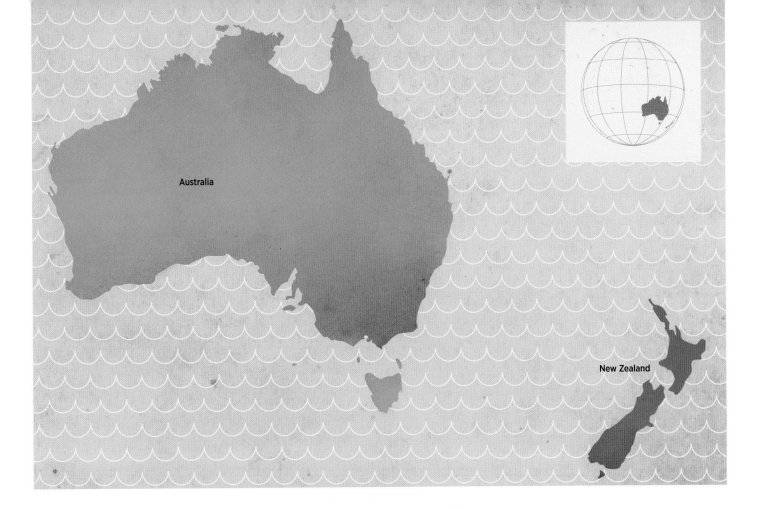

lolly log (page 307) made of fruit puffs (similar to marshmallows) is the sweetest, most candylike cake in this book. Also, New Zealand's more temperate climate led to a stronger agricultural base, which in turn led to a greater emphasis on freshness in dairy products and fruit in the country's cakes. While early New Zealand immigrant farmers grew Mediterranean crops, the native Maoris of the time cultivated taro, sweet potatoes, and bottle gourds. These root vegetables are still grown today and are sometimes featured in the country's cakes, such as taro cheesecake (page 308), which is also popular in China and Hawaii.

In contrast to New Zealand's agricultural base, Australia is urban and multicultural; nearly all its almost 20 million people live along the east and southeast coasts, and of these about 40 percent live in the cities of Sydney and Melbourne. Australian cities are filled with immigrants from all over the world; at this time one in four people living there was not born there. The result? Fusion cuisine. Just try to imagine British, German, Chinese, Italian, and Greek foods combined all at the same meal.

Modern Australian cakes are decidedly Western in style, but where Americans would use a strawberry, Australians will use a kiwifruit. Where Americans would use walnuts,

Australians will use macadamia nuts. And they are absolutely nuts about cake decoration.

Food festivals and cake competitions in Australia feature the work of everyone from overachieving homemakers to celebrity chefs. Cake decoration is so popular here that the term "Australian method" designates a particular challenging aesthetic technique mastered by only the most serious of sugar craft artists involving very detailed royal icing piping into string work over rolled fondant.

On the other end of the decorating spectrum are the easy-to-make character cakes called frog cakes (page 310). Also popular are white individual-size cakes with a single dainty piped flower on top. The occasional spring rains in the outback can yield spectacular wildflowers, and you can find almost every one of those flowers represented here. These cakes featuring local flora and fauna are a great hit with tourists.

Vintage cake books from Down Under are the best. That's where I first discovered the region's wonderful character cakes, mostly of uniquely Australian animals like the wombat, koala, platypus, kangaroo, and echidna. Whenever I find one of these old cookbooks at a flea market or library sale I know it will reveal remarkable decorating details or novelty cakes imbued with a lively sense of humor.

Pavlova

The modern Pavlova is a light, crisp meringue cake with a marshmallow-like center topped with whipped cream and fruits. It's much larger than its European ancestors tended to be, which allows for extended appreciation of the soft center. Traditionally the cake is topped with whatever regional fruits are in season, from strawberries and kiwifruits to bananas, cherries, grapes, passion fruit, and peaches. Modern-style Pavlovas may also be topped with caramel, nuts, chocolate, nougat, and candies.

Meringue

1	teaspoon white vinegar
1	teaspoon vanilla extract
2	teaspoons cornstarch
	Pinch of salt
4	egg whites
1¼	cups superfine sugar

Toppings

2½	cups fresh fruit
	Juice of 1 lemon
2	cups whipped cream (page 323)
1	cup whole macadamia nuts

Makes 1 cake (serves 6 to 8)

TO PREPARE

Preheat the oven to 250°F. Line a cookie sheet with parchment paper, and draw a 7-inch circle on the paper with nontoxic marker.

TO MAKE THE MERINGUE

Combine the vinegar, vanilla, cornstarch, and salt in a small bowl, and stir until the cornstarch has dissolved. In a separate bowl, beat the egg whites with an electric mixer at high speed until soft peaks form. Then beat in the sugar, 1 teaspoon at a time, until it is completely dissolved, the whites are no longer gritty, and stiff peaks form. Gently fold the vinegar mixture into the egg-white mixture.

TO BAKE

Use a spatula to scrape the meringue onto the prepared parchment paper, shaping it inside the circle you drew and making the edges higher than the center. Bake the meringue until the outside is crisp, dry, and cream colored, about 1 hour and 10 minutes. Cracks may form in the top of the center; this is normal. Turn off the oven and let the meringue cool in the oven, with the door slightly open, which will prevent droplets from forming on the meringue.

TO ASSEMBLE THE CAKE

Chop the fruit toppings as desired, and toss with the lemon juice. Place the meringue on a serving plate. Place half of the fruit in the well of the meringue. Use a spatula or pastry bag to sculpt the whipped cream over the fruit. Top with the remaining fruit and macadamia nuts.

VARIATIONS

Australian Pavlova

Instead of mixed fruits, top the meringue with 2½ cups passion fruit.

Canadian Pavlova

Replace the mixed fruit topping with sautéed pears and apples: Slice one or two apples and/or pears, and cook over low heat in ¾ cup apple juice and ¼ cup light brown sugar, until the fruits have softened and absorbed the juice. Top the meringue with the pear and apple mixture, plus fresh blueberries.

Anna Pavlova

The Pavlova is named in honor of the Russian prima ballerina Anna Matveyevna Pavlova, who visited Australia and New Zealand in the 1920s. Born in St. Petersburg, Russia, she joined the Imperial Ballet in 1899 and became a prima ballerina in 1906. After 1913, she danced with her own independent company all over the world. The chef who invented this meringue cake presented it to her, claiming it was "light as Pavlova," referring to her proficiency as a dancer.

VARIATIONS, CONTINUED

Caramel-Almond Pavlova

Instead of mixed fruit, top the meringue with toasted almonds and 1 cup dulce de leche (page 321).

Chocolate-Nougat Pavlova

Instead of mixed fruit, top the meringue with chopped nougat and 1 cup chocolate sauce (page 320).

English Pavlova

Instead of mixed fruits, top the meringue with 1 cup fresh raspberries and 1 cup raspberry sauce (page 320).

New Zealand Pavlova

Instead of mixed fruits, top the meringue with 2½ cups chopped kiwifruit.

Supermarket Pavlova

Supermarkets in Australia and New Zealand sell a Pavlova made with fresh fruit and gummy candy. To make, add 1½ cups gummy candy to any traditional Pavlova.

Australia or New Zealand?

Both Australia and New Zealand claim the Pavlova as their own invention, and over the years there has been much debate on the subject. The Pavlova is recognized as Australia's national dessert, but the first records of it place its invention in New Zealand. The main difference between the Pavlovas of each country is the topping. In Australia it is commonly topped with passion fruit, while in New Zealand you will find it topped with kiwifruit.

Lamingtons (Lemmingtons)

These small, square, bite-size cakes — known as Lamingtons in Australia and Lemmingtons in New Zealand — are eaten as an accompaniment to afternoon tea. The cakes are dipped in chocolate icing, fruit jam, or both and covered in desiccated coconut. The thin icing or jam soaks into the cakes, making them moist and flavorful. In Australia they're often prepared for Australia Day, the national holiday commemorating the establishment of the first British settlement on the continent, and they are tremendously popular as fund-raiser cakes.

Lamington Cake

- 2 cups all-purpose flour
- 2 teaspoons baking powder
- ¼ teaspoon salt
- ½ cup (1 stick) unsalted butter, softened
- ¾ cup sugar
- 2 eggs
- ½ cup milk
- 1 teaspoon vanilla extract

Toppings

- 2¼ cups unsweetened desiccated coconut, finely chopped
- 4 cups cocoa icing (page 315)

Makes 32 to 36 bite-size cakes

TO PREPARE

Preheat the oven to 350°F. Lightly butter and flour two 8-inch square cake pans.

TO MAKE THE CAKE

Combine the flour, baking powder, and salt in a small bowl; set aside. Cream the butter and sugar with a mixer until light and fluffy. Add the eggs one at a time, beating well after each addition. Stir in the milk and vanilla. Gradually add the flour mixture to the butter mixture.

TO BAKE

Spread the batter in the prepared pans. Bake for 25 to 35 minutes, until the cake tops are slightly golden and a knife inserted in the center comes out clean. Remove the cakes from the oven and allow to cool in the pans. When they have cooled, remove the cakes from the pans, wrap them in plastic wrap, and refrigerate for at least 2 hours.

TO ASSEMBLE

Remove the plastic wrap from the cakes. Measure the height of each cake. With a knife, lightly score a grid of squares that are as long and wide as the height of the cake. Cut the cake along those lines, producing evenly sized cubes. The larger the squares, the less likely they are to fall apart; the smaller the squares, the more impressive.

Spread the coconut on a large plate. Warm the cocoa icing, if necessary, in the top of a double boiler, adding a little more milk if it is thick. Spear the cake pieces one at a time with a fork or bamboo skewer. Dip into the cocoa icing to cover completely, then roll in the coconut until completely covered. Set on a serving plate to dry. Continue until all the pieces are coated.

If you intend to transport the cake cubes, spread coconut on the base of the carrying container to prevent the cakes from sticking to it.

VARIATIONS

Cream-Filled Lamingtons

Cut each cake square in half, spread the bottom half with a pastry cream (page 323), then press on the top half. Proceed as directed.

Jam-Filled Lamingtons

Cut each cake square in half, spread the bottom half with jam, then press on the top half. Proceed as directed.

Super-Speedy Lamingtons

Purchase a pound or sponge cake. Cut into squares and proceed as directed.

Victoria Lamingtons

Replace the cocoa icing with a fruity one: Spread 1½ cups superfine sugar in a warm baking dish and bake at 250°F for 15 minutes. Mash 1½ cups strawberries, raspberries, or plums in 1 cup of water and slowly bring to a boil. Gradually add the sugar, stirring until it is dissolved.

Lamington Drives

Lamington drives, named after Lamington cakes, of course, are a favorite of many Aussies and New Zealanders. While American bake sales rely on every member of the organization to bring a baked treat from home to the sale, for Lamington drives cake orders are taken. When all the orders are in, the members of the organization gather to prepare the Lamingtons together. Sometimes the group bakes the cakes from scratch. In other cases they order sponge or pound cakes from a bakery and then cut, dip, roll, and plate the cake cubes. The Lamington cakes are then nicely packaged and delivered to the donors.

Kiwifruit-Macadamia Nut Cake

If you've never combined kiwifruit, macadamia nuts, and white chocolate, you're in for a treat. These are authentic tastes of New Zealand, and you must try them.

Kiwifruit-Macadamia Nut Cake

1½ cups all-purpose flour

1 teaspoon baking powder

½ teaspoon salt

½ cup (1 stick) unsalted butter, softened

1 cup granulated sugar

2 teaspoons lemon juice

2 eggs

⅓ cup milk

1 cup puréed kiwifruit

1½ cups chopped macadamia nuts, toasted

White Chocolate Buttercream

1¼ cups chopped white chocolate

3 tablespoons unsalted butter, softened

3 tablespoons milk

1 teaspoon vanilla extract

3 cups confectioners' sugar

Filling and Topping

2 cups sliced kiwifruit

Makes 1 cake (serves 6 to 8)

TO PREPARE

Preheat the oven to 350°F. Butter and flour two 8-inch round cake pans.

TO MAKE THE CAKE

Combine the flour, baking powder, and salt in a small bowl; set aside. In a separate large bowl, cream the butter and granulated sugar until fluffy. Stir in the lemon juice. Add the eggs one at a time, beating well after each addition. Add the flour mixture, alternating with the milk, beating until well blended. Fold in the puréed kiwifruit and the macadamia nuts.

TO BAKE

Transfer the batter to the prepared pans and bake for 25 to 30 minutes, until a knife inserted in the center comes out clean. Let cool in the pans for 10 minutes, then remove the cakes from the pans and set on a rack to finish cooling.

TO MAKE THE WHITE CHOCOLATE BUTTERCREAM

Combine the white chocolate, butter, and milk in a saucepan over medium heat, stirring until the chocolate and butter are melted. Remove from the heat. Stir in the vanilla. Gradually add the confectioners' sugar, stirring constantly, until combined. Add more milk or sugar to reach a spreadable consistency.

TO ASSEMBLE

Set one cake on a serving plate, and spread the white chocolate buttercream over it. Top with one-third of the sliced kiwifruit. Set the second cake on top. Frost the entire cake with the remaining buttercream, and top with the remaining kiwifruit.

VARIATIONS

Chinese Kiwifruit-Strawberry Cake

Omit the nuts from the batter. Instead of 1 cup puréed kiwifruit, prepare ¾ cup puréed kiwifruit and ¾ cup puréed strawberries. Before adding the purées, divide the batter in half, and add the kiwifruit purée to one batch and the strawberry purée to the other. Bake in separate pans. To assemble, add ½ cup puréed strawberries to the white chocolate buttercream, and replace the sliced kiwifruit with a mixture of sliced kiwifruit and strawberries.

Indian Cashew Cake

Omit the kiwifruit topping and filling. Replace the macadamia nuts with cashews. Add ¼ teaspoon cardamom and ¼ cup fresh minced coriander to the cake batter. Top with mango slices.

Indonesian Candlenut Cake

Omit the kiwifruit topping and filling. Replace the macadamia nuts with roasted candlenuts. Top with chopped candlenuts.

Kiwifruit

Though named for New Zealand's flightless bird, kiwifruits are native to southern China, and they're popular in the cakes of both countries. They're grown on vines with vigorous pruning, like grapes. The plants are dioecious, meaning their flowers are either male or female, and pollen from male flowers must come into contact with the female flowers in order to fertilize them. They are difficult to pollinate, however, because bees, the primary pollinators, aren't crazy about them. To force pollination, farmers saturate their orchards with beehives, raising such intense competition for pollen that bees are forced to visit the kiwifruit flowers.

Lolly Log Cake

The lolly log cake is a fun no-bake cake that is unique to New Zealand. It's made of lollies, or fruit puff candies — it's a super sugar overload. If you can't find lollies, just about any type of candy and marshmallows will do, so pick your favorites and go for it. The other main ingredient is malt biscuit, a cookie that tastes like malt. Look for malt biscuits at an international grocery store; if you can't find them, use graham crackers instead.

No-Bake Cake

- 4 cups crushed malt biscuits
- ¼ teaspoon ground cinnamon
- 1 cup (2 sticks) unsalted butter
- 1 (14-ounce) can sweetened condensed milk
- 2 cups chopped fruit puffs, marshmallows, or gummy candies
- 1½ cups shredded sweetened coconut

Toppings

- 1 cup colored sugar and nonpareils
  Vanilla buttercream (page 317)
- 1 cup fruit puffs, marshmallows, or gummy candies
- ½ cup shredded unsweetened coconut

Makes 1 cake (serves 8 to 12)

TO MAKE THE CAKE

Crush the biscuits in a food processor or blender by pulsing 4 or 5 times. You want crumbs here, not a fine dust. Stir in the cinnamon and set aside.

Combine the butter and condensed milk in a medium bowl and microwave on high for 20 seconds, then beat with a mixer until creamy. Add the fruit puffs, coconut, and biscuit crumbs, and mix well. The mixture should stick together. If it doesn't, add more condensed milk until it does. Roll the mixture into a log.

TO DECORATE

Mix together the colored sugar and nonpareils, and spread the mix over a work surface. Spread a thin coat of buttercream over the log. Roll the log in the sugar mixture, pressing a coating into the surface.

Spoon the remaining buttercream into a pastry bag fitted with a large writing tip. Pipe the buttercream in a thick strip down the top of the log. Press fruit puffs into the buttercream, and coat with shredded coconut. Cover and refrigerate for 2 to 3 hours, until the toppings are set.

VARIATIONS

Caramel Lolly Log

Replace the fruit puffs with caramel candies.

Peanut-Chocolate Lolly Log

Replace the fruit puffs with peanuts and chocolate chips.

Lolly Log Fund-Raiser

Like the Lamington (page 304), the lolly log is a popular fund-raising cake. Schoolchildren around New Zealand prepare giant lolly logs to sell cut in thick slabs at bake sales. I have seen one prepared over 40 feet long.

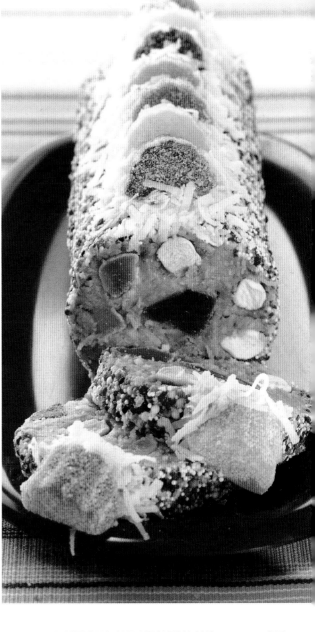

Taro Cheesecake

Taro, a staple of the Maori diet, is a root vegetable with a light, bright flavor. Here it is integrated with a three-citrus cheesecake to give the cake a creamy texture and nice purple color. The crust is made with the local favorite, Anzac biscuits.

Crust

- 1½ cups crushed Anzac biscuits
- 2 tablespoons raw sugar
- 2 tablespoons unsalted cashew pieces
- ⅛ teaspoon salt
- 4 tablespoons (½ stick) unsalted butter, melted

Taro Filling

- 1¼ cups peeled and cubed taro
- 2 tablespoons water
- 24 ounces cream cheese, softened
- 1 cup granulated sugar
- ⅓ cup light brown sugar
- 2 eggs
- 2 egg yolks
- ½ cup sour cream
- 1 teaspoon vanilla extract
- ¼ cup all-purpose flour
- ½ cup heavy cream
- ½ teaspoon salt
- ½ teaspoon grated orange zest
- ½ teaspoon grated lemon zest
- ½ teapoon grated lime zest

Topping

- 2 tablespoons confectioners' sugar

Makes 4 cakes (each serving 2)

TO PREPARE

Preheat the oven to 325°F. Butter and flour four 3½- to 4-inch springform pans, and line their outer seams with aluminum foil to prevent leaks. Prepare a water bath: set the springform pans in one or more larger pans, fill the larger pan(s) half full of water, then remove the springform pans and set the larger pans in the oven to preheat.

TO MAKE THE CRUSTS

Combine the biscuits, raw sugar, cashews, and salt in a food processor or blender, and pulse to mix. Stir in the butter. Press the mixture into the prepared pans and bake for 10 to 12 minutes.

TO MAKE THE FILLING

Set the taro in a saucepan with an inch of water. Bring to a boil, then reduce the heat and simmer, covered, for 30 minutes, until soft. Drain and let cool.

Purée the taro and the water in a food processor or blender until smooth; add more water if necessary to make the mixture slightly sticky. Beat the cream cheese, granulated sugar, and brown sugar until fluffy. Beat in the eggs, yolks, sour cream, and vanilla. Add the flour, cream, salt, citrus zests, and taro purée and stir until smooth.

TO BAKE

Divide the filling among the prepared springform pans. Set the pans in the water bath and bake for 40 to 50 minutes, until the tops of the cheesecakes jiggle but are not cracked. Turn off the heat, set the oven door slightly ajar, and let cool for 1 hour. Then remove the cheesecakes from the oven and refrigerate for at least 2 hours.

TO SERVE

Cover part of the top of each cheesecake with confectioners' sugar.

VARIATIONS

Dominican Sweet Potato Cheesecake

Add ½ teaspoon ground ginger to the filling, and replace the taro with sweet potato. For the crust, replace the Anzac biscuits with gingersnaps and replace the cashews with pecans.

Hawaiian Pineapple-Taro Cheesecake

Prepare the crust with graham crackers instead of Anzac biscuits. Top the cheesecake with pineapple wedges.

Large Taro Cheesecake

Prepare the cake in a single 9-inch round springform pan, baking for 1 hour 15 minutes to 1 hour 25 minutes.

Marbled Taro–Sweet Potato Cheesecake

Prepare the crust in a single 9-inch round springform pan. Replace the 1¼ cups taro with ⅔ cup taro and ⅔ cup sweet potato, and steam and purée separately. Once you've combined all the filling ingredients except the puréed vegetable, divide the filling into two batches, and add the taro purée to one and the sweet potato purée to the other. Pour one batch into the prepared pan, followed by the second batch, and marble by swirling the end of a knife through the two batches. Bake for 1 hour 15 minutes to 1 hour 25 minutes.

Anzac Biscuits

The name Anzac stands for Australian and New Zealand Army Corps. The exact origin of the recipe is unknown, but when the army corps became involved in World War I, women began baking these biscuits and sending them off to their soldiers far from home. The recipe calls for no milk or eggs, meaning that the biscuits are relatively nonperishable, and they are relatively inexpensive to make. They may be derived from the Scottish oatcake. They are sweet, cookielike biscuits made with rolled oats and coconut. (And if you can't find Anzac biscuits, oatmeal cookies make an acceptable substitute.)

BOTTOM: *taro cheesecake;* TOP: *Dominican sweet potato variation*

Frog Cakes

A traditional frog cake looks like a frog with its mouth open, exposing the cream inside. Beneath the dome-shaped head is a square sponge cake filled with raspberry glaze. Frog cakes are customarily covered with a thin layer of green fondant, though for ease of prepartion I use vanilla icing instead. You could also use pourable fondant, which is available in cake decorating supply stores. The secret to making a stiff dome for these cakes is to use very thick and dense buttercream, or to use ice cream. For a clean seam, cut the mouth open with a hot knife.

Génoise Sponge Cake

- 1⅓ cups cake flour
- 1 cup cornstarch
- 12 eggs
- 1½ cups superfine sugar
- ⅔ cup unsalted butter, melted and cooled
- 2 teaspoons vanilla extract

Assembly

- 1¾ cups raspberry glaze (page 319)
- 2 cups vanilla icing (page 317)
- Green and pink food coloring
- 4½ cups vanilla buttercream (page 317)
- 2 tablespoons black icing or small round black candies

Makes 20 cakes

TO MAKE THE CAKE

Prepare the génoise sponge cake batter as directed on page 108. Bake in a 10-inch square pan for 35 to 45 minutes, until the cake is golden brown and shrinks away from the sides of the pan. Let cool in its pan.

TO FORM THE BASES

Remove the cake from its pan. Cut the cake in half crosswise, forming two layers. Spread the raspberry glaze on the bottom layer. Place the two halves back together. Cut the cake into 2-inch squares.

TO ASSEMBLE

Divide the vanilla icing in half. Add green food coloring to one batch and pink to the other, dyeing each a pastel. The icing should be thin so that it can be poured; use warm water to thin it if necessary.

Set the cakes on two wire racks, with an equal number on each rack. Set rimmed baking trays below each rack. Use a small ice cream scoop to top each cake with a dollop of buttercream in a dome shape. Pour the icing over the cakes to coat them entirely, using the pink icing for one set of cakes and the green icing for the other set. The icing will drip through the rack into the baking trays below. Collect the dripped icing, set in containers (keeping the colors separate), and cover. Let the cakes set for 30 minutes, then pour a second coat and let set another 30 minutes.

Heat a knife by dipping it in boiling water, and use it to slice through the icing to shape the mouth. Press the knife slightly up and down to open the mouth, revealing the buttercream. Add tiny dots of black icing or the black candies for the eyes.

VARIATION

Ice Cream Frog Cakes with Rolled Fondant

Replace the buttercream with ice cream. Instead of icing, top the cakes with a single layer of rolled fondant (page 324): Dye it green, roll it out to ¼-inch thickness, cut into 6-inch rounds, press the rounds over the cakes, and clean up the edges with a knife. Cut the mouth and add the eyes. Freeze for 30 minutes before serving.

Frog Cake History

Frog cakes dominate the special occasions of South Australia. They are always called frog cakes, even when they're shaped like Father Christmas, chicks, snowmen, pumpkins, or anything else. The frog cake was first introduced in 1922 at Balfours Bakery in Adelaide. John Balfour, co-owner of the bakery, found inspiration for it in his travels in Scandinavia, where he saw the bakelser cake, a variation of the prinsesstårta (page 160). Today frog cakes are symbolic of the region and are given at social and political occasions to promote the state. In 2001, to honor its cultural significance, the frog cake was listed as a South Australian Heritage Icon by the National Trust of Southern Australia.

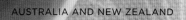

THE WORLD TOUR OF
Character Cakes

HOW MANY KIDS DO YOU ENCOUNTER who request a fruitcake or Black Forest cake for their birthdays? Not many. Since the dawn of the twentieth century, every generation in every culture has developed its own beloved pop culture, and each kid a favorite television, movie, or book character that they yearn to see featured on their birthday cake. Flavor is secondary (though a desire for lots of sugary frosting seems to be almost universal). A little girl from Queensland may yearn for a cuddly koala cake, while her counterpart from Queens, New York, may want Dora the Explorer; either way, the prominent placement of the loveable character on the cake makes it a mascot — or perhaps an alter ego — on her special day.

When it comes to pop culture, for better or worse, the United States has often led the charge, and the popularizing of character cakes is no exception. The earliest character cakes celebrated children's book characters popular in the United States in the early 1900s, including Beatrice Potter's Peter Rabbit, Raggedy Ann and Andy, and Teddy Roosevelt's Teddy Bears (the product of a cartoon poking fun at a presidential hunting expedition).

In the 1920s many homemakers took an interest in cake decorating and began producing their own character cakes. The manufacture and sale of specialty cake pans, tools, and toppings to create these cakes exploded internationally. In the 1960s and '70s Disney's Winnie the Pooh and Jim Henson's Kermit the Frog, Big Bird, and Cookie Monster topped the list. Amazingly these are still the most requested character cakes even today. Through the years they've been joined by everything from Barbie and Strawberry Shortcake to Smurfs, Star Wars, SpongeBob, and Harry Potter. And since characters are exported globally, you may very well find that a little Japanese boy is just as likely to have Superman on his cake as a kid from Ohio is likely to have the Japanese anime Astro Boy cake.

Although the characters are different, the format for these cakes is the same everywhere and falls in two genres. The first is sheet cakes with images drawn on top or with three-dimensional narratives made from cake toppers. The second is characters molded from cakes baked in shaped pans, then decorated in appropriate colors. Some of these cake pans are flat and the character is molded in one piece. Others have multiple pieces that fit together to build a three-dimensional shaped cake. Here are some tips for the perfect character cake in either genre.

TO MAKE A MOLDED CHARACTER CAKE

1. Purchase a character cake pan and food coloring in appropriate colors for the frosting. Prepare and bake your favorite cake in the pan. Let cool, then brush off any crumbs.
2. Prepare enough white frosting to frost and decorate your cake. You will need at least double the standard frosting recipe. (Make sure to choose a frosting recipe, not an icing recipe, because icing is too transparent.) Reserve half of the white frosting. Transfer the remaining frosting into small bowls to color.
3. Crumb-coat the cake by covering it entirely with a thin layer of white frosting, and let dry for 1 hour.
4. Using a pastry bag or icing spatula, outline each shape created by the pan with the appropriate color frosting. Fill in the rest of the cake with appropriate colors. For a simple graphic look simply spread the colors on the cake. For a textured look use a star tip.

TO MAKE A SHEET CHARACTER CAKE

1. To prepare the image, enlarge or reduce it to actual size on a photocopy machine or print it out from the computer.
2. Prepare a sheet cake in a square or rectangular pan.
3. Prepare a white frosting in generous amounts depending on the size of your cake. Again, make sure to choose a frosting recipe, not an icing recipe. Reserve half of the white frosting. Transfer the remaining frosting into small bowls to color.
4. Cover the cake with the white frosting, spreading it out until smooth. Let dry for 1 hour.
5. Transfer the image using one of the following methods:

- *Using an image of the character as a guide, draw the image with a toothpick on the cake. Fill in with appropriate colors with a piping bag or piping gel.*

- *Cut the image into stencil pieces to create large blocks of shape. Outline each shape with a toothpick to create the character in the frosting. Outline the shapes with colored frosting, then fill in with remaining frosting.*

- *Purchase or have an edible transfer made of the character to put on the cake. Edible transfers are very detailed and can be purchased premade or custom made.*

6. Add additional themed cake toppers that will help set the scene, like cars, rocket ships, or train tracks. Also candies can be used to draw or build an environment.

OPPOSITE PAGE: *"doll princess cake," based on the prinsessatårta (page 160)*

Toppings and Fillings from Around the World
Frostings, Icings, and Buttercreams

THE TERMS *FROSTING* AND *ICING* ARE OFTEN USED interchangeably. In general, frostings are assumed to be thick, while icings are generally thin. They are made primarily with confectioners' sugar, some sort of liquid, and flavorings.

Boiled icing, the original cake icing, is fluffy and sticky, with the consistency of melted marshmallows. It is made by beating hot sugar syrup into stiffly beaten egg whites, like making an Italian meringue.

Sinfully rich and fluffy, buttercream at its most basic is made by creaming butter and sugar to a spreadable consistency, but variations abound. Some buttercreams are cooked, while others aren't. Some may be flavored with simple extracts, while others may be blended with melted chocolate or syrups, and still others may have zests or fruits folded into them.

The recipes yield a varying amount of frosting, depending on the viscosity of the finished mixture. The thinner the frosting, the less you need to coat and/or fill a cake. For a two-layer 9-inch round cake, you might need 1 to 1½ cups as a filling and 1½ to 2½ cups as a topping. For a thicker frosting, you'd need 1½ to 2 cups as a filling and 3 to 4 cups as a topping. In general, each frosting recipe yields enough for a single cake recipe.

Almond Icing

¼ cup water
1½ teaspoons almond extract
1½ teaspoons vanilla extract
⅛ teaspoon salt
2½ cups confectioners' sugar

Makes about 2 cups

Combine the water, almond extract, vanilla, and salt. Mix in the confectioners' sugar gradually, until the icing reaches the desired consistency.

VARIATION

Honey Icing

Reduce the water to 2 tablespoons. Replace the almond extract with 1½ tablespoons honey.

Bittersweet Chocolate Buttercream

8 ounces bittersweet chocolate, chopped (about 1⅓ cups chocolate chips)
2½ cups (5 sticks) unsalted butter, softened
¾ cup confectioners' sugar
3 tablespoons unsweetened cocoa powder
1½ teaspoons vanilla extract

Makes about 4 cups

Melt the chocolate in a microwave or double boiler; let it cool but not harden. Beat the butter until creamy. Add the confectioners' sugar, cocoa, vanilla, and melted chocolate. Mix until smooth.

VARIATION

Dark Chocolate Buttercream

Replace the bittersweet chocolate with 12 ounces dark chocolate (at least 60% cacao). Increase the confectioners' sugar to 1½ cups.

Cherry Icing

4 cups confectioners' sugar
½ cup (1 stick) unsalted butter, softened
½ cup cherry juice
6 maraschino cherries, finely chopped (optional)

Makes about 4¼ cups

Cream 2 cups of the sugar and the butter until smooth. Stir in the cherry juice. Mix in the remaining confectioners' sugar gradually, until the icing reaches the desired consistency. Stir in the chopped cherries, if using.

VARIATION

Cranberry Icing

Replace the cherry juice with cranberry juice. Omit the chopped cherries.

Chocolate Ganache

2½ tablespoons unsalted butter
8 ounces semisweet chocolate, chopped (about 1⅓ cups chocolate chips)
2 tablespoons light corn syrup
1 teaspoon vanilla extract

Makes about 1½ cups

Melt the butter in a double boiler over medium-high heat. Add the chocolate and corn syrup and cook, stirring constantly, until the chocolate is melted. Remove from the heat, stir in the vanilla, and let cool.

Cocoa Icing

3 tablespoons unsalted butter
⅔ cup Dutch-processed cocoa powder
3½ cups confectioners' sugar, sifted
¾ cup milk
1 teaspoon vanilla extract

Makes about 4 cups

Melt the butter in a double boiler over medium-high heat. Add the cocoa powder and stir until combined. Mix in the confectioners' sugar, alternating with the milk, until combined. Remove from the heat and stir in the vanilla. Add more milk or sugar as necessary to achieve a thin but spreadable consistency.

Coconut Icing

2 cups coconut milk
2 cups sugar
½ cup all-purpose flour
4 eggs, lightly beaten
1 teaspoon almond extract
1 teaspoon vanilla extract

Makes about 3¾ cups

Combine the coconut milk, sugar, flour, and eggs in a saucepan over medium heat and cook, whisking constantly, for 5 to 7 minutes, until thickened. Remove from the heat, stir in the almond extract and vanilla, and let cool.

Chocolate Toppings

Often one type of topping can be easily substituted for another. For the chocolate lovers out there, here's a list of the chocolate toppings, in case you prefer, for example, bittersweet over semisweet, or mocha over dark chocolate.

- Bittersweet chocolate buttercream (page 315)
- Chocolate ganache (page 315)
- Chocolate glaze (page 318)
- Cocoa icing (page 315)
- Dark chocolate buttercream (page 315)
- Mocha buttercream (page 316)
- Semisweet chocolate buttercream (page 317)
- Semisweet chocolate icing (page 317)

Coffee Buttercream

⅔ cup sugar
½ cup double-strength espresso
6 egg yolks
1½ cups (3 sticks) unsalted butter, softened

Makes about 3 cups

Bring the sugar and espresso to a boil in a small saucepan, stirring until the sugar is dissolved. Continue to boil until the syrup registers 238°F on an instant-read thermometer (the soft-ball stage). Beat the egg yolks with a mixer until fluffy. While continuing to beat, add the hot syrup to the yolks in a slow stream. Let cool completely. Beat in the butter a little at a time, until thickened and smooth.

VARIATION

Mocha Buttercream

Add 3 tablespoons unsweetened cocoa powder to the sugar and espresso before bringing the mixture to a boil.

Cream Cheese Frosting

1 (8-ounce) package cream cheese, softened
6 tablespoons (¾ stick) unsalted butter, softened
3 cups confectioners' sugar
1 teaspoon vanilla extract

Makes about 4 cups

Cream the cream cheese and butter until smooth. Slowly sift in the confectioners' sugar, and continue beating until all the lumps are gone. Add the vanilla and mix until fully blended and smooth.

VARIATION

Lemon Cream Cheese Frosting

Replace the vanilla with 2 tablespoons lemon juice and 1 teaspoon grated lemon zest.

Lemon Icing

4 cups confectioners' sugar
½ cup (1 stick) unsalted butter, softened
½ cup lemon juice
1½ teaspoons grated lemon zest
Yellow food coloring (optional)

Makes about 3½ cups

Cream the sugar and butter until smooth. Mix in the lemon juice, lemon zest, and a drop of yellow food coloring, if using.

VARIATIONS

Lime Icing

Replace the lemon juice with lime juice and the lemon zest with lime zest.

Orange Icing

Replace the lemon juice with orange juice and the lemon zest with orange zest.

Mango Buttercream

2 medium mangos, mashed
¾ cup water
1½ cups sugar
½ teaspoon cream of tartar
3 eggs
3 egg yolks
¾ cup (1½ sticks) unsalted butter, softened

Makes about 4¼ cups

Combine the mashed mangos with ¼ cup of the water and ¼ cup of the sugar in a saucepan over medium heat, and cook until thickened. Remove from the heat. Strain the thick pulp from the mixture with a small sieve.

Combine the remaining ½ cup water, the remaining 1¼ cups sugar, and the cream of tartar in a saucepan over medium-high heat, and cook until the mixture reaches the soft-ball stage (242°F). Remove from the heat.

Beat the eggs and the egg yolks until the mixture is pale and holds a ribbon (page 24), about 5 minutes. Add the sugar syrup to the eggs and beat for 5 to 8 minutes, until slightly thickened. Let cool, then add the butter a little at a time, beating until fluffy. Stir in the mango purée and blend well.

Meringue Frosting

1½ cups superfine sugar
½ cup water
3 tablespoons light corn syrup
6 egg whites, at room temperature
⅛ teaspoon salt
¼ teaspoon cream of tartar

Makes about 2½ cups

Combine the sugar, water, and corn syrup in a medium saucepan over medium heat, and cook, stirring, until the sugar dissolves. Stop stirring, and continue to heat until the mixture is clear and reaches 248°F on a candy thermometer. Remove from the heat.

Beat the egg whites with a mixer on medium speed until foamy. Add the salt and cream of tartar, and continue to beat until soft peaks form. Reduce the speed to low, and while still beating, slowly add the hot syrup to the whites by pouring it against the side of the bowl. Increase the mixer speed to medium and beat for 2½ to 3 minutes, until the mixture stops steaming. Use immediately.

Peanut Frosting

1¼ cups (2½ sticks) unsalted butter, softened
⅓ cup peanut butter
1 tablespoon honey
½ teaspoon salt
4½ cups confectioners' sugar
¼ cup milk

Makes about 4½ cups

Combine the butter, peanut butter, honey, and salt and beat until smooth. Beat in the confectioners' sugar gradually, alternating with the milk, until the mixture reaches a spreadable consistency.

Royal Icing

Royal icing is designed specifically for decorating. It is usually piped, and it hardens as it dries.

- 3 cups confectioners' sugar, sifted
- 2 egg whites
- 2 teaspoons vinegar

Makes about 2½ cups

Combine the confectioners' sugar, egg whites, and vinegar, and mix well.

Semisweet Chocolate Buttercream

- 9 ounces semisweet chocolate, chopped (about 1½ cups chocolate chips)
- ½ cup (1 stick) unsalted butter
- 3 tablespoons milk
- 1 teaspoon vanilla extract
- 4½ cups confectioners' sugar

Makes about 4½ cups

Combine the chocolate and butter with the milk in a saucepan over medium heat, and warm, stirring, until the chocolate is melted. Remove from the heat and stir in the vanilla. Mix in the confectioners' sugar gradually, until combined. Add more milk or sugar as needed to make the mixture spreadable.

Semisweet Chocolate Icing

- 8 ounces semisweet chocolate, chopped (about 1⅓ cups chocolate chips)
- ½ cup water
- ¼ cup milk
- ¼ cup (½ stick) unsalted butter, cut into small pieces
- ¼ cup confectioners' sugar

Makes about 2½ cups

Combine the chocolate, water, and milk in a double boiler over medium-high heat. Heat, stirring, until the chocolate is melted. Remove from the heat and add the butter and confectioners' sugar, stirring until the mixture is smooth.

Vanilla Buttercream

- 2 cups (4 sticks) unsalted butter softened
- 1 pound confectioners' sugar, sifted
- 1 teaspoon vanilla extract
- ⅛ teaspoon salt

Makes about 4½ cups

Combine the butter, sugar, vanilla, and salt. Beat with a mixer at high speed for 2 to 3 minutes, until smooth.

Vanilla Icing

- 4 tablespoons unsalted butter, softened
- 2 cups confectioners' sugar
- 3 tablespoons milk
- 2 teaspoons vanilla extract

Makes about 2 cups

Cream the butter and sugar until smooth. Mix in the milk and vanilla. Add more sugar or milk as needed to reach the desired consistency.

Glazes and Syrups

Glazes are thin toppings that are brushed, poured, drizzled, or dripped over cakes. They may give the cake a shiny finish or a hardened shell, or they may soak into the cake for additional flavor. Like frostings, they come in multitudes of variations, from simply sugary to fruity or chocolaty.

Apple Glaze

- 2 cups apple cider
- ¾ cup sugar
- 1½ teaspoons cornstarch
- ½ teaspoon ground cinnamon

Makes about 2 cups

Combine the cider, sugar, cornstarch, and cinnamon in a medium saucepan over high heat. Bring to a boil, then reduce the heat and simmer, stirring occasionally, for 5 to 8 minutes, until thickened. Remove from the heat and let cool.

Apricot Glaze

- ¾ cup sugar
- ½ cup water
- 3 cups chopped fresh apricots
- 2 tablespoons lemon juice

Makes about 3½ cups

Combine the sugar and water in a medium saucepan over high heat. Bring to a boil, then reduce the heat and simmer, stirring, for about 5 minutes, until the sugar has dissolved and the syrup is clear. Add the apricots and simmer for 25 to 30 minutes, stirring occasionally, until the fruit has broken down and the mixture is thick and smooth. Stir in the lemon juice and cook for 5 minutes longer. Then remove from the heat and let cool.

VARIATION

Dried Apricot Glaze

If you can't find fresh apricots, use dried: Replace the fresh apricots with 2 cups dried apricots, and increase the water to 1 cup.

Chocolate Glaze

- 6 ounces semisweet chocolate, chopped (about 1 cup chocolate chips)
- 4 tablespoons unsalted butter

Makes about 1 cup

Melt the chocolate and the butter in a double boiler over medium-high heat. Remove from the heat and let cool a few minutes, until just warm, before using.

Honey Syrup

- ¼ cup honey
- 5 tablespoons water

Makes about ⅓ cup

Combine the honey and water in a small saucepan over medium heat, and cook, stirring, until the mixture is smooth. Remove from the heat and let cool a few minutes, until just warm, before using.

Lemon Syrup

- 1 cup water
- 1 cup sugar
- 1½ tablespoons honey
  Juice of 1 lemon

Makes about 1¾ cups

Bring the water to a boil in a small saucepan. Add the sugar and honey and stir to dissolve. Remove from the heat and add the lemon juice. Let cool.

VARIATION

Orange Syrup

Replace the lemon juice with orange juice and ½ teaspoon grated orange zest.

Lime Glaze

- ⅓ cup lime juice
- ¾ cup sugar

Makes about ¾ cup

Combine the juice with the sugar in a saucepan over high heat. Bring to a boil, then reduce the heat and simmer, stirring occasionally, for 7 to 8 minutes, until thickened. Remove from the heat and let cool.

VARIATION

Lemon Glaze

Replace the lime juice with lemon juice.

Lime-Saffron Syrup

- ¾ cup water
- ¼ cup lime juice
- 1 cup sugar
- 1 teaspoon grated lime zest
- 5 saffron threads
- 5 cardamom pods, crushed

Makes about 1¾ cups

Combine the water, lime juice, sugar, lime zest, saffron threads, and cardamom pods in a medium saucepan over high heat. Bring to a boil, then reduce the heat and simmer for 7 minutes, which is just long enough for the flavors to fuse. Remove from the heat and let cool.

Maple Glaze

¾ cup warm water
¼ cup maple syrup
2 teaspoons honey
3 cups confectioners' sugar

Makes about 3¼ cups

Combine the water, maple syrup, and honey in a medium bowl, and mix well. Gradually stir in the confectioners' sugar, until the glaze reaches a dribbling consistency.

Orange Glaze

1¼ cups confectioners' sugar
3 tablespoons orange juice
½ teaspoon lemon juice

Makes about 1¼ cups

Combine the confectioners' sugar with the juices, and mix until blended.

Raspberry Glaze

¼ cup lemon juice
3 tablepoons water
⅓ cup light brown sugar
1 tablespoon cornstarch
1½ cups fresh or frozen raspberries, mashed

Makes about 1¾ cups

Combine the lemon juice, water, brown sugar, and cornstarch in a small saucepan over low heat, and cook, stirring, until the sugar and cornstarch are dissolved. Add the raspberries and continue to cook, stirring frequently, for 7 to 10 minutes, until the mixture has thickened and has a smooth consistency. Remove from the heat and let cool.

Rosewater Syrup

¾ cup water
¾ cup superfine sugar
¼ cup honey
3 tablespoons lemon juice
1 teaspoon rosewater
¼ teaspoon ground cardamom

Makes about 1¾ cups

Combine the water, sugar, honey, lemon juice, rosewater, and cardamom in a medium saucepan over low heat, and cook, stirring, until the sugar is dissolved. Remove from the heat and let cool.

Rosewater-Saffron Syrup

1½ cups sugar
1½ cups water
2 teaspoons rosewater
½ teaspoon ground cardamom
½ teaspoon powdered saffron

Makes about 2¾ cups

Combine the sugar and water in a medium saucepan over high heat. Bring to a boil, stirring to dissolve the sugar. Remove from the heat, stir in the rosewater, cardamom, and saffron, and let cool.

Rum Syrup

½ cup sugar
¼ cup water
¾ cup dark rum

Makes about 1¼ cups

Combine the sugar and water in a saucepan over medium-high heat and cook, stirring, until the sugar is dissolved. Remove the syrup from the heat and let cool for about 5 minutes. Stir in the rum and use immediately, while still warm.

Sauces

Sauces are thick liquid accompaniments to cakes. Some, like chocolate and vanilla sauces, are smooth and creamy. Others are more chunky and fruity. They can be poured on top of cakes or dolloped onto the serving plate in a decorative puddle.

Blueberry Sauce

- ¾ cup water
- ¼ cup orange juice
- ¼ cup granulated sugar
- ¼ cup light brown sugar
- ⅛ teaspoon salt
- 4 teaspoons cornstarch
- ½ teaspoon grated orange zest
- ¼ teaspoon grated nutmeg
- 2 cups chopped fresh or frozen blueberries
- ½ cup whole fresh or frozen blueberries

Makes about 3 cups

Combine the water, orange juice, granulated sugar, brown sugar, and salt in a medium saucepan over low heat, and cook, stirring, until the sugars are dissolved. Stir in the cornstarch, orange zest, and nutmeg, followed by the chopped blueberries, and cook for 3 to 5 minutes, until the mixture thickens. Stir in the remaining blueberries, remove from the heat, and let cool for about 5 minutes. Serve warm.

Chocolate Sauce

- ½ cup (1 stick) unsalted butter
- 1 cup unsweetened cocoa powder
- 6 ounces semisweet chocolate, chopped (about 1 cup chocolate chips)
- ⅔ cup dark brown sugar
- ½ cup granulated sugar
- ⅛ teaspoon salt
- 1 cup heavy cream

Makes about 3¾ cups

Melt the butter in a double boiler over medium heat. Add the cocoa powder, chocolate, brown sugar, granulated sugar, and salt, and cook, stirring, until the chocolate is melted and the mixture is smooth. Slowly add the cream, and cook, stirring, for 3 to 5 minutes, until the mixture thickens. Remove from the heat and let cool for a few minutes, until just warm, before using.

Coconut-Peanut Sauce

- 1 cup coconut milk
- ½ cup sugar
- ½ teaspoon salt
- ¼ cup peanuts, chopped and toasted

Makes about 1½ cups

Combine the coconut milk, sugar, and salt in a saucepan over medium heat and cook, stirring, until the sugar is dissolved. Remove from the heat and stir in the peanuts. Let cool.

Cranberry Sauce

- 1 cup water
- 1 cup sugar
- 1 (12-ounce) package fresh cranberries

Makes about 3½ cups

Combine the water and sugar in a saucepan over medium heat and cook, stirring, until the sugar is dissolved. Stir in the cranberries and cook for 7 to 10 minutes, until about half of the cranberries have popped. Remove from the heat and let cool; the sauce will thicken.

Raspberry Sauce

- 4½ cups fresh or frozen raspberries
- ⅓ cup sugar
- ¼ cup water
- 1 tablespoon lemon juice

Makes about 3¾ cups

Combine the raspberries, sugar, water, and lemon juice in a saucepan over medium heat and cook, stirring, for 8 to 10 minutes, until the raspberries have broken down and the mixture has thickened. Remove from the heat and let cool for about 5 minutes. If you like, strain the mixture through a fine-mesh sieve to eliminate the seeds. Serve warm.

Vanilla Sauce

- 3 egg yolks
- ¼ cup sugar
- 1 cup milk
- 1 tablespoon vanilla extract

Makes about 1¼ cups

Beat the egg yolks and sugar with a mixer until the yolks reach the ribbon stage (the batter is stiff enough that it falls back into the bowl in a ribbonlike line when the beaters are lifted). Heat the milk to a simmer in a saucepan over medium heat. Beat in the egg yolk mixture, and stir until thickened. Remove from the heat and stir in the vanilla. Serve warm.

Fillings, Pastes, and Jams

Fillings, pastes, and jams are most often hidden surprises used between cake layers to highlight and contrast flavors. Thinner fillings and jams are designed to soak into the cake layers, while thicker ones and pastes are themselves flavor features.

Blueberry Filling

- ¼ cup sugar
- ⅛ teaspoon salt
- ½ cup water
- 2 tablespoons cornstarch
- 3 cups chopped fresh or frozen blueberries

Makes about 3½ cups

Combine the sugar, salt, and water in a saucepan over low heat and cook, stirring, until the sugar and salt are dissolved. Add the cornstarch and blueberries and cook, stirring, for 5 to 8 minutes longer, until the mixture has thickened. Remove from the heat and let cool; the filling will thicken further as it cools.

VARIATION

Cherry Filling
Replace the blueberries with fresh or canned cherries.

Cream Cheese Filling

- 1 (8-ounce) package cream cheese, softened
- ¼ cup sugar
- 3 tablespoons all-purpose flour
- 1 egg yolk
- 1 teaspoon lemon juice
- 1 teaspoon vanilla extract

Makes about 1½ cups

Combine the cream cheese, sugar, flour, egg yolk, lemon juice, and vanilla in a bowl, and blend until smooth.

VARIATION

Green Tea Filling
Add 2 tablespoons matcha powder to the mixture, omit the lemon juice, and increase the vanilla to 2 teaspoons.

Date Filling

- 1 pound pitted dates, chopped
- 1 cup sugar
- 1 cup water
- ½ cup fresh lemon juice

Makes about 3½ cups

Combine the dates, sugar, and water in a saucepan over medium heat. Bring to a boil, stirring continually, and let boil for 4 to 5 minutes, until the mixture has thickened and the sugar is dissolved. Remove from the heat, stir in the lemon juice, and let cool.

Dulce de Leche

- 2¼ cups sugar
- 8 cups milk
- 1 teaspoon salt (preferably sea salt)

Makes 2 to 3 cups

Combine the sugar, milk, and salt in the saucepan over medium heat. Whisking continually, bring the mixture to a boil. Then reduce the heat and let simmer, stirring occasionally, for 3 to 3½ hours, until the mixture is reduced to 2 to 3 cups and resembles caramel. Remove from the heat and let cool.

Lemon Curd

- ⅓ cup unsalted butter
- 1½ cups sugar
- ¾ cup freshly squeezed lemon juice (from about 3 lemons)
- 1 tablespoon grated lemon zest
- 4 eggs, lightly beaten
- 1 tablespoon cornstarch

Makes about 2¼ cups

Combine the butter, sugar, lemon juice, and lemon zest in a medium saucepan over low heat and cook, stirring, for about 5 minutes. Add the eggs and cornstarch and continue cooking, stirring continually, for 5 to 7 minutes, until the mixture thickens. Remove from the heat and cool in the refrigerator for at least 1 hour.

VARIATION

Orange Curd
Substitute orange juice and orange zest for the lemon juice and lemon zest. Before setting the mixture in the refrigerator to cool, stir in 2 tablespoons orange curaçao.

Lotus Seed Paste

- 1¼ cup lotus seeds (brown or white), soaked overnight and drained
- 1 teaspoon baking soda
- ¼ teaspoon salt
- 1¼ cups sugar
- ⅓ cup peanut oil
- 1 teaspoon vanilla extract

Makes about 2¾ cups

Cover the lotus seeds with water in a large saucepan. Bring to a boil, then reduce the heat and simmer for 15 minutes. Drain the murky water, then return the seeds to the pot, add enough fresh water to cover, and stir in the baking soda. Bring to a boil, then reduce the heat and simmer for 1½ to 2 hours, until the seeds have softened and absorbed most of the water. Drain.

Combine the seeds and the salt in a food processor or blender, add ¼ cup fresh water, and purée. Combine the purée with the sugar, oil, and vanilla in a saucepan (the one you used for cooking the seeds is fine). Cook over low heat, stirring, for 4 to 5 minutes, until thick. Remove from the heat and let cool.

Pineapple Filling

- 2 tablespoons cornstarch
- 1¼ cups water
- 2 cups sugar
- 3 cups pineapple chunks

Makes about 3½ cups

Dissolve the cornstarch in ¼ cup of the water; set aside. Combine the remaining 1 cup water with the sugar in a large saucepan over medium heat, and cook, stirring, until the sugar dissolves. Add the pineapple and cook for 4 to 5 minutes, until softened. Raise the heat to high, mix in the cornstarch, and cook, stirring, for 3 to 4 minutes, until the filling is thick and much of the liquid has evaporated. Remove from the heat and let cool.

VARIATION

Canned-Pineapple Filling

If you can't find fresh pineapple, you can use canned: Measure out 2 cups crushed pineapple with juice. Drain the juice into a saucepan, reserving the pineapple. Add ½ cup sugar and 1½ teaspoons cornstarch to the juice. Set over medium heat and cook, stirring, until the sugar and cornstarch are dissolved. Add the reserved pineapple and continue cooking, stirring, for 7 to 10 minutes until the mixture has thickened.

Poppyseed Filling

- ¾ cup sugar
- 2 teaspoons cornstarch
- 1¼ cups poppyseeds
- ¼ cup blanched almonds
- ¾ cup milk
- ½ teaspoon almond extract

Makes about 2¾ cups

Combine the sugar and cornstarch in a small bowl; set aside. Combine the poppyseeds, almonds, and milk in a food processor or blender and grind. Place the mixture in a saucepan. Bring to a boil, then reduce the heat, add the sugar mixture, and simmer, stirring, for 7 to 10 minutes, until thick. Remove from the heat, stir in the almond extract, and let cool.

Raspberry Filling

- 2¼ cups fresh raspberries
- ¼ cup sugar
- 1¼ teaspoons cornstarch
- ¼ cup water
- 2 tablespoons lemon juice

Makes about 2 cups

Combine the raspberries, sugar, cornstarch, water, and lemon juice in a saucepan over medium heat and cook, stirring, for 8 to 10 minutes, until thickened. Remove from the heat and let cool.

VARIATION

Strawberry Filling

Replace the raspberries with sliced strawberries.

Sweet Adzuki Bean Paste

- 1⅓ cups adzuki beans, soaked overnight and drained
- 2 cups sugar
- 1 teaspoon salt

Makes about 2¾ cups

Cover the beans with water in a large pot. Bring to a boil, then reduce the heat and simmer for 15 minutes. Drain the murky water, then return the beans to the pot and cover with fresh water. Bring to a boil, then reduce the heat and simmer for 1½ to 2 hours, until the beans are soft. Drain.

Return the beans to the pot with the sugar and salt and cook over low heat, stirring, until the mixture is thick and chunky. Remove from the heat and cool.

Ube Jam

- 1½ cups water
- 2 pounds ube, peeled and diced
- 4 tablespoons unsalted butter
- ¾ cup sweetened condensed milk
- ½ teaspoon vanilla extract
- ¾ cup evaporated milk

Makes about 3¾ cups

Bring the water to a boil in a medium saucepan, add the ube, and cook for 30 minutes, until soft. Drain the ube and let cool. Pulverize the ube in a food processor or blender.

Melt the butter in a medium saucepan over low heat. Stir in the condensed milk, vanilla, and ube purée. Cook, stirring occasionally, for 20 to 25 minutes, until the mixture is sticky. Add the evaporated milk and continue to cook, stirring, for 10 to 15 minutes longer, until the liquid is mostly absorbed. Remove from the heat and let cool.

Pastry Creams and Whipped Creams

Whipped cream is a light, airy confection made with cream and sugar. It may be flavored or not. It's usually used as a topping, though for some delicate pastries it may be used as a filling. In Asian countries, where lactose intolerance is prevalent, nondairy whipped topping is common. Made from coconut or palm oil, it is sweeter than whipped cream.

Pastry cream, in contrast, is a rich, delicate custard made with milk, eggs, sugar, flour, and flavorings. It's used to fill cakes, doughnuts, pastries, and many other desserts.

Banana Whipped Cream

- 1 cup heavy cream
- 1 teaspoon vanilla extract
- 2 tablespoons confectioners' sugar
- 1 banana, mashed

Makes about 2½ cups

Beat the cream, vanilla, and confectioners' sugar until stiff peaks form. Fold in the mashed banana.

Chocolate Pastry Cream

- 1½ cups unsweetened cocoa powder
- 1 cup sugar
- Pinch of salt
- 4 cups milk
- 2 vanilla beans, split lengthwise
- 8 egg yolks
- ⅔ cup all-purpose flour

Makes about 3½ cups

Combine the cocoa powder, ½ cup of the sugar, and the salt with the milk in a medium saucepan. Slowly bring to a boil, then remove from the heat. Add the vanilla beans and let steep for 10 minutes. Scrape the seeds from the bean shells, and discard the shells. Stir the seeds into the mixture and set aside.

Using a mixer, beat the egg yolks with the remaining ½ cup sugar in a large bowl until pale. Stir in the flour. Reheat the milk mixture over low heat and gradually whisk in the egg yolk mixture. Increase the heat to medium-high and continue heating, whisking continually, until the mixture begins to bubble. Lower the heat to medium and continue to whisk until smooth. Remove from the heat and let cool for a few minutes. Then cover the pastry cream with plastic wrap, pressing the plastic against the mixture. Set in the refrigerator to chill for at least 2 hours.

VARIATIONS

Banana Pastry Cream
Omit the cocoa powder. Mash 2 medium-ripe bananas until smooth. Fold into the pastry cream before refrigerating.

Mocha Pastry Cream
Reduce the milk to 3½ cups. Stir ½ cup espresso into the pastry cream before refrigerating.

Strawberry Pastry Cream
Omit the cocoa powder. Fold 2 cups chopped fresh strawberries into the pastry cream before refrigerating.

Vanilla Pastry Cream
Omit the cocoa powder, and increase the flour to 1¼ cups.

Whipped Cream

- 1 cup heavy whipping cream
- 1 teaspoon vanilla extract
- 1½ tablespoons sugar

Makes about 2 cups

Combine the cream, vanilla, and sugar and beat with a mixer until soft peaks form. Refrigerate until ready to serve.

VARIATIONS

Almond Whipped Cream
Replace the vanilla with 1 teaspoon almond extract or amaretto liqueur. Fold ¼ cup chopped almonds into the whipped cream.

Brandy Whipped Cream
Replace the vanilla with 1 teaspoon brandy.

Chocolate Whipped Cream
Add ⅓ cup unsweetened cocoa powder to the mixture.

Rum Whipped Cream
Replace the vanilla with 1 teaspoon rum.

Fondant and Marzipan Sugar Pastes

Fondant is a candy sugar paste that is pliable and moldable. It can be rolled out into sheets to top or fill cakes, or it can be sculpted into pieces to decorate cakes. Classic fondant requires some skill to make — the sugar mixture must be heated and cooled in a precise way so crystals don't form. Store-bought fondant is the simplest alternative, but for those who'd like to give making their own a try, I offer an alternative recipe that doesn't require any heating.

Marzipan is an almond paste that can, like fondant, be rolled out in sheets or sculpted into decorative three-dimensional pieces. You can buy prepared marzipan at most grocery stores, but it's also easy to make at home.

Fondant

This recipe makes enough for decorating a cake with fondant sculptures, such as for the Japanese friendship cherry blossom cake (page 282).

- 1 egg white
- 1 tablespoon liquid glucose
- 3 cups confectioners' sugar, plus more for dusting
  Food coloring (optional)

Makes about 2 cups

TO MAKE FONDANT

Combine the egg white and glucose in a bowl, and stir together with a wooden spoon. Add the confectioners' sugar and mix with a rubber spatula, using a chopping motion, until the icing binds together. If it seems sticky, add more confectioners' sugar. Knead the mixture with your fingers until it forms a ball. Fondant dries out quickly, so keep it covered with plastic wrap when you're not working with it.

TO DYE FONDANT

Add food coloring to the fondant a little at a time, kneading it into the fondant to distribute the color evenly, until you've achieved the desired color.

TO SHAPE FONDANT

Dust a work surface and rolling pin with confectioners' sugar. Flatten the fondant into a disk, then roll it out on the sugared work surface to the desired thickness. Cut with a utility knife, cookie cutter, or fondant cutter, and shape as desired.

Work with only a small batch of fondant at a time, and keep the rest covered with plastic wrap so it doesn't dry out.

Marzipan

This recipe makes enough for covering a cake with marzipan, such as for the English Battenberg cake (page 142). If you want only enough marzipan for decorative elements, halve the recipe.

- 3 cups ground almonds
- 2 eggs, at room temperature
- 2 teaspoons lemon juice
- ½ teaspoon almond extract
- 4½ cups confectioners' sugar
  Food coloring (optional)

Makes about 5½ cups

TO MAKE MARZIPAN

Combine the almonds, eggs, lemon juice, and almond extract in a medium bowl, and stir until blended. Add the confectioners' sugar a bit at at time, mixing well after each addition, until thick. Dust a work surface with confectioners' sugar, and knead the marzipan on it for 4 to 6 minutes, until it's smooth, adding a bit more lemon juice if needed to achieve a stiff paste. Marzipan dries out quickly, so keep it covered with plastic wrap when you're not working with it.

TO DYE MARZIPAN

Add food coloring to the marzipan a little at a time, kneading it into the marzipan to distribute the color evenly, until you've achieved the desired color.

TO SHAPE MARZIPAN

Dust a work surface and rolling pin with confectioners' sugar. Flatten the marzipan into a disk, then roll it out on the sugared work surface to the desired thickness. Cut with a utility knife, cookie cutter, or fondant cutter, and shape as desired. Work with only a small batch of marzipan at a time, and keep the rest covered with plastic wrap so it doesn't dry out.

Raw Eggs

Fondant and marzipan cream contain raw eggs. You can substitute liquid pasteurized egg whites in the fondant or pasteurized eggs in the marzipan. If you opt not to, do not serve this recipe to those for whom the consumption of raw eggs poses a serious health risk, including children under the age of four, the elderly, pregnant women, and anyone with a compromised immune system.

Dust a work surface, a baking sheet, and a rolling pin with confectioners' sugar. Roll out the marzipan on the sugared work surface to ⅛- to ¼-inch thickness. Transfer the marzipan sheet to the sugared baking sheet. Cover with plastic wrap and refrigerate for 15 minutes.

Coat the cake with a glaze or syrup to create a sticky surface. Remove the marzipan from the refrigerator. Center the marzipan over the cake. Press it onto the cake, and then smooth out any wrinkles with your fingers, working first across the top of the cake and then down its sides. Trim the edges of the marzipan at the bottom of the cake. If you're not serving right away, cover the cake to prevent the marzipan from drying out.

Candied Citrus Peel

Though you can buy prepared candied citrus peel, it's quite easy to make your own, and by making your own you can be sure that it's fresh. If you can, purchase organic fruits, to avoid the possibility of pesticide residue.

Candied Citrus Peel

- 1 cup sugar
- ½ cup water
- 2 tablespoons corn syrup
  Rinds of 2 oranges, cut into very thin strips
  Rinds of 2 lemons, cut into very thin strips
  Rinds of 2 limes, cut into very thin strips

Makes about 1½ cups

Combine the sugar, water, and corn syrup in a saucepan over medium-high heat. Bring to a boil, add the rinds, and simmer for 20 minutes, stirring occasionally.

Remove the peels from the hot liquid and set on a rack to cool and dry. Let dry overnight.

VARIATION
Candied Orange Peel
Replace the lemon and lime rinds with additional orange rinds.

METRIC CONVERSIONS

Unless you have finely calibrated measuring equipment, conversions between U.S. and metric measurements will be somewhat inexact. It's important to convert the measurements for all of the ingredients in a recipe to maintain the same proportions as the original.

General Formula for Metric Conversion

Ounces to grams	multiply ounces by 28.35
Grams to ounces	multiply grams by 0.035
Pounds to grams	multiply pounds by 453.5
Pounds to kilograms	multiply pounds by 0.45
Cups to liters	multiply cups by 0.24
Fahrenheit to Celsius	subtract 32 from Fahrenheit temperature, multiply by 5, then divide by 9
Celsius to Fahrenheit	multiply Celsius temperature by 9, divide by 5, then add 32

Approximate Equivalents by Volume

U.S.	Metric
1 teaspoon	5 milliliters
1 tablespoon	15 milliliters
¼ cup	60 milliliters
½ cup	120 milliliters
1 cup	230 milliliters
1¼ cups	300 milliliters
1½ cups	360 milliliters
2 cups	460 milliliters
2½ cups	600 milliliters
3 cups	700 milliliters
4 cups (1 quart)	0.95 liter
1.06 quarts	1 liter
4 quarts (1 gallon)	3.8 liters

Approximate Equivalents by Weight

U.S.	Metric	U.S.	Metric
¼ ounce	7 grams	0.035 ounce	1 gram
½ ounce	14 grams	1.75 ounces	50 grams
1 ounce	28 grams	3.5 ounces	100 grams
1¼ ounces	35 grams	8.75 ounces	250 grams
1½ ounces	40 grams	1.1 pounds	500 grams
2½ ounces	70 grams	2.2 pounds	1 kilogram
4 ounces	112 grams		
5 ounces	140 grams		
8 ounces	228 grams		
10 ounces	280 grams		
15 ounces	425 grams		
16 ounces (1 pound)	454 grams		

INDEX

Page numbers in *italics* indicate photos.

A

adzuki beans. *See also* sweet adzuki
    bean paste
    Nian Gao with Adzuki Beans, 258
Africa, 20, *20,* 206–7
    African Peanut Fritters, 214
    African Pumpkin-Mango Cake, 64
Algeria, street cakes of, 238
almond extract
    Almond Icing, 315
    Almond Sponge Cake, 264
    Almond Whipped Cream, 323
almonds
    Almond-Peach Potica, 182, *183*
    Almond-Pistachio Baklava Nests, 235
    Almond Sponge Cake, 264
    Apricot-Almond Cake, 232
    Barrigas de Freira (Nuns' Bellies), 200
    Basbousa, 208
    Candied Sicilian Rice Cake, 194
    Caramel-Almond Pavlova, 303
    Chinese Egg Roll Cake, 118
    Chocolate-Almond Cake, 79
    Chocolate-Almond Prinsesstårta, 160
    Crostata di Ricotta (Roman Ricotta
        Cheesecake), 190, *190*
    Dundee Cake, 146
    Egyptian Basbousa with Fig Balls, 208
    Kransekake (Wreath Cake), 162, *163*
    Mazurek, 180, *180*
    Mexican Almond Roll with Cajeta, 92
    M'hanncha (Snake Cake), 210, *211*
    Mit Lechig (Honey Cake), 227, *227*
    Muscat Italian Rice Cake, 194
    Opera Gateau, 104, *105*
    Orange-Almond Angel Food Cake, 34
    Orange-Almond Cake, 79
    Orange-Almond Panforte, 186
    Panettone, 188, *189*

Petit Fours Glacés, 106, *107*
President Washington Cherry
    Almond Cake, 282
Queen of Sheba Cake, 101
Rehruecken, 124, *125*
Runeberg Cakes, 164, *165*
Simnel, 150, *151*
Stollen, 122
Sweet Scottish Scones, 147, *147*
Tarta de Santiago
    (St. James' Cake), 199, *199*
Torta del Cielo, 79
Vasilopita, 202, *203*
Zabaglione Cream-Berry Trifle,
    140, *141*
Zucchini-Almond Cake with Peach
    Sauce, 212, *212*
amaretto
    Chocolate-Amaretto Fondue, 114
American cakes, 20, *20. See also* North
    American cakes
    American Banana-Chocolate Chip
        Cake with Peanut Frosting, 221
    American Blueberry Scones, 147
    American Coffee Potica, 182
    American Corn and Cranberry
        Trifle, 140
    American Layered Carrot Coconut
        Cake, 137
    American Orange Poppyseed Cake, 230
    Angel Food Cake, 34, *34*
    Apple Stack Cake, 40, *41*
    Cherokee Wild Huckleberry
        Cake, 42, *43*
    Cinnamon Buttermilk Doughnuts,
        44, *45*
    Devil's Food Cupcakes, 52, *53*
    in early America, 8–9
    Funnel Cakes, 36, *37*
    German Chocolate Cake, 48–49
    German Chocolate Cupcakes, 49

King Cake, 50–51, *51*
New York Cheesecake, 38, *39*
President Washington Cherry
    Almond Cake, 282
Red Velvet Cake, 46–47, *47*
regional cakes, 60, 157, 166, 167, 192,
    217, 229, 241, 262, 263, 299
Strawberry Shortcake, 35
Amish cakes, 36
Angel Food Cake, 34, *34*
animal cakes, 208
anise seed, *231*
    Anise Nutmeg Chin-Chin, 209
    Hazelnut-Anise-Chocolate Chip
        Vasilopita, 202
    Seed Cake, 230
    Vasilopita, 202, *203*
Anzac biscuits, 309
    Taro Cheesecake, 308, *309*
Appalachia
    Apple Stack Cake, 40, *41*
    Appalachian wedding cake, 41
apple cider
    Apple Glaze, 318
apples
    Apple Fries (Mexican Funnel
        Cakes), 36
    Apple King Cake, 51
    Apple-Lemon Charlotte Russe, 112
    Apple Pound Cake, 54
    Apple Stack Cake, 40, *41*
    Apple Strudel, 123, *123*
    Canadian Pavlova, 302
    Dorset Apple Cake, 144, *145*
    Dutch Apple Fritters, 195
    Jewish Apple Cake, 144
    Rolled-Oat Parkin with Tart Apple
        Glaze, 132
    of southern England, 145
apricots/apricot glaze
    Apricot-Almond Cake, 232

Photo Contributors

© ANDERS BLOMQVIST/LONELY PLANET IMAGES: 297 left

© ANTONY GIBLIN/LONELY PLANET IMAGES: 295 bottom

© BILL WASSMAN/LONELY PLANET IMAGES: 239 bottom

© BRIAN BOYL: v (#11), 37, 51, 59 top right, 64, 68 right, 70 right, 124, 184, 187, 197 bottom, 214 top, 252 center & right, 253 right, 259, 261 top right, bottom left and right, 264, 265 left, 269 top, bottom left, 275 middle, 286 top, 292

© BRIAN CRUICKSHANK/LONELY PLANET IMAGES: 209

© BRUCE BI/LONELY PLANET IMAGES: 263 left

© COREY WISE/LONELY PLANET IMAGES: 39 left, 233 bottom

© DANITA DELIMONT/ALAMY: 304

© DAVID MONNIAUX/WIKIMEDIA COMMONS: 3 right

© DAVID TOMLINSON/LONELY PLANET IMAGES: 96 bottom left

© DIAN MAYFIELD/LONELY PLANET IMAGES: 299

© EMILY BROOKE SANDOR: 16 middle right, 17 top & bottom right, 18 bottom left, 45, 54, 57, 59 bottom left, 60, 78, 91, 107, 111 left, 113, 123, 136, 159, 166 right, 167 left, 176, 180, 189, 213, 217 center, right, 228 right, 233 top, 241 center, right, 250 left, 271, 276, 283 bottom left, 289, 303, 314

© FREDERICK MAGNUSSON/WIKIMEDIA COMMONS: 158

© GRANT ROONEY/ALAMY: 132

© GREG ELMS/LONELY PLANET IMAGES: 244

© HOLGER LEUE/LONELY PLANET IMAGES: 237

© IMAGE SOURCE/ALAMY: 71 left

© ISTOCKPHOTO.COM/ALEX JEFFRIES: 248 right, BASHKAR A.V.: 247 top, CARLA LISINSKI: 217 left, CHRIS 102: 273, CODE6D: 130, DARREN BRODE: 10 left, DAVID KERKHOFF: 222, DMITRY BODROV: 170, FLOORTJE: 96, FOTOGRAFIABASICA: 177, FRANK SEBASTIAN HANSEN: 297 right, GEORGII DOLGYKH: 306, ISAAC KOVAL: 283 top, JENS CARSTEN ROSEMANN: 121 bottom, JEREMY EDWARDS: 96 top left, JOEL SHAWN: 101, KE YU: 229, LILLISPHOTOGRAPHY: 178, MAL-ERAPASO: 10 right, MARCIO SILVA: 8 right, MATT OLSON: 200, MERRY-MOONMARY: 75 bottom, MICHAEL UTECH: 152, MIKEUK: 119, PAUL BUTCHARD: 146, PHILIPPA BANKS: 242, RADU RAZVAN: 275 top, ROMAN MILLERT: 183, S. GREG PANOSIAN: 108, SRDAN: 149 top left, STUART PITKIN: 7 right, SUMNERGRAPHICSINC: 300, SYAGCI: 284, TERRY WILSON: 9, TJASA MATICIC: 281 bottom, VLADIMIRS GUCULAKS: 279 left

© JAKE LYELL/ALAMY: 71

© JANE SWEENEY/LONELY PLANET IMAGES: 211 bottom

© JEAN-BERNARD CARRILET/LONELY PLANET IMAGES: 105 bottom

JIALING GAO/WIKIMEDIA COMMONS: 3 left

© JOHN BORTHWICK/LONELY PLANET IMAGES: 295 top

© JOHN LANDER/ALAMY: 263 right

© JULIET COOMBE/LONELY PLANET IMAGES: 238 right

© JUSTIN BASTIEN: 68 left, 206, 305 left

© KRYSTINA CASTELLA: 67

© LOUISE BATALLA DURAN/ALAMY: 75 bottom left

© LUCINO CANDISANI/MINDEN PICTURES/ NATIONAL GEOGRAPHIC STOCK: 88

© MAGICAL ANDES PHOTOGRAPHY/ALAMY: 75 bottom right

© MARGIE POLITZER/LONELY PLANET IMAGES: 90

MARS VILAUBI: 274, 275 bottom, 298 right

© MARTIN MOOS/LONELY PLANET IMAGES: 145 bottom

© MICAH WRIGHT/LONELY PLANET IMAGES: 149 bottom

MILA ZINCOVA/WIKIMEDIA COMMONS: 8 center

© ONASIA IMAGES PTE, LTD/ALBERTO BUZZOLA: 266, CHAU DOAN: 239 top left, 290, FRANK BIENEWALD: 77 top, JEAN CHUNG: 11, JONAS GATZER: 239 top right

© PAT VINING: 219 left, 221, 225 top left

© PAUL BEISSEN/LONELY PLANET IMAGES: 247 bottom left

PHOTO8/WIKIMEDIA COMMONS: 8 left

© RICHARD I'ANSON/LONELY PLANET IMAGES: 41 top, 247 bottom right, 249, 308

© ROBERT M. BOYL: 238 left, 288

© SCOTT ZETLAN/ALAMY: 75 top left

© 2003–2010 SHUTTERSTOCK IMAGES LLC/ ALBERT CAMPBELL: 32, NEWPHOTO-SERVICE: 204 top, STEPHANIE FREY: 36, TESSARTHETEGU: 211 right

© STREETFLY STOCK/ALAMY: 228 right

© THOR VAZ DE LEON/LONELY PLANET IMAGES: 214 bottom

TOMTCHIK/WIKIMEDIA COMMONS: 6 left,

© TORTUGA RUM COMPANY, LTD.: 66, 262 left

© VIVIANE PONTI/LONELY PLANET IMAGES: 72

W. A. DJATMIKO/WIKIMEDIA COMMONS: 70 left

WIKIMEDIA COMMONS: 4, 5, 6 right, 7 left, 138, 302

OTHER STOREY TITLES
YOU WILL ENJOY

250 Treasured Country Desserts, by Andrea Chesman & Fran Raboff.
A nostalgic collection of more than 250 recipes for home bakers to rely on for all occasions.
416 pages. Paper. ISBN 978-1-60342-152-2.

Apple Cookbook, by Olwen Woodier.
More than 140 recipes to put everyone's favorite fruit into tasty new combinations.
192 pages. Paper. ISBN 978-1-58017-389-6.

The Baking Answer Book, by Lauren Chattman.
Answers every question about common and specialty ingredients, the best equipment,
and the science behind the magic of baking.
384 pages. Flexibind. ISBN 978-1-60342-439-4.

Cookie Craft, by Valerie Peterson & Janice Fryer.
Clear instruction, practical methods, and all the tips and tricks for beautifully decorated
special occasion cookies.
168 pages. Hardcover. ISBN 978-1-58017-694-1.

Cookie Craft Christmas, by Valerie Peterson & Janice Fryer.
Fresh inspiration and fabulous decorating from authors of *Cookie Craft,* with more than
60 new designs for Christmas cookies.
176 pages. Hardcover with jacket. ISBN 978-1-60342-440-0.

The Donut Book, by Sally Levitt Steinberg.
A deliciously engaging book that explores the nostalgia and history of the donut.
192 pages. Paper. ISBN 978-1-58017-548-7.

These and other books from Storey Publishing are available
wherever quality books are sold or by calling 1-800-441-5700.
Visit us at *www.storey.com.*